CONCEPTS AND METHODS FOR POLITICAL ANALYSIS

MARY GRISEZ KWEIT
ROBERT W. KWEIT
University of North Dakota

Prentice-Hall Inc., Englewood Cliffs, New Jersey 07632

Library of Congress Cataloging in Publication Data

KWEIT, MARY GRISEZ.
  Concepts and methods for political analysis.

  Bibliography: p.
  Includes index.
  1. Political science research. I. Kweit, Robert W.,
  joint author. II. Title.
JA86.K83   320'.072   80-23971
ISBN 0-13-166520-0

TO OUR PARENTS
AND CATHY

©1981 by Prentice-Hall, Inc., Englewood Cliffs, N.J. 07632

*All rights reserved. No part of this book
may be reproduced in any form or
by any means without permission in writing
from the publisher.*

Printed in the United States of America

10 9 8 7 6 5 4 3 2 1

Editorial/production supervision
   and interior design by Virginia Cavanagh Neri
Cover design by Mario Piazza
Manufacturing buyer: Edmund W. Leone

Prentice-Hall International, Inc., *London*
Prentice-Hall of Australia Pty. Limited, *Sydney*
Prentice Hall of Canada, Ltd., *Toronto*
Prentice-Hall of India Private Limited, *New Delhi*
Prentice-Hall of Japan, Inc., *Tokyo*
Prentice-Hall of Southeast Asia Pte. Ltd., *Singapore*
Whitehall Books Limited, *Wellington, New Zealand*

Contents

Preface vii

PART ONE
PHILOSOPHY OF POLITICAL SCIENCE 1

one   Introduction   5
What is Political Science? 8   Summary 15
Study Questions 15

two   Science and Political Research   16
The Scientific Method 17
Evaluation of the Standard View 29
The Traditionalist-Behavioralist Debate 34
Defense of "Scientific" Political Science 37
Summary 39   Study Questions 40

three   Ethical Issues in Political Analysis   42
Ethics and Political Research 42
Relationship with Subjects 44
Relationship with the Scientific Community 49
Relationship with Society 51
Summary 54   Study Questions 55

PART TWO
CONCEPTUAL ANALYSIS 57

four The Setting of Politics 61

Political Socialization 63 Political Culture 76
Summary—Political Socialization 83
Summary—Political Culture 84 Study Questions 85

five Political Interactions 86

Power 88 Group 93 Conflict 100 System 106
Communications 114 Summary—Power 117
Summary—Group 118 Summary—Conflict 119
Summary—Systems 119
Summary—Communications 120 Study Questions 121

six The Products of Politics 122

Decision-Making 123 Policy 137
Summary—Decision-Making 145 Summary—Policy 146
Study Questions 147

PART THREE
POLITICAL RESEARCH 149

seven Planning Research 153

Selecting the Topic 154
Background Library Research 156
Formulating the Question 158 Research Design 163
Concepts and Operationalization 164
Building Generalizations 174 Building Theories 176
Study Questions 177

eight Gathering Information 178

Deciding What Data to Collect 178 Choosing a Research
Strategy 186 Primary Data Gathering 194
Secondary Data Gathering 208 Study Questions 210

Contents v

nine   **Storing Data**   **211**

Coding 213   Codebook 216
Introduction to Computers 217   Summary 226
Study Questions 227

PART FOUR
STATISTICAL ANALYSIS 229

ten   **Describing the Data**   **233**

Measures of Central Tendency 237
Measures of Variation 239
Frequency Distributions: Nominal and Ordinal Data 242
Frequency Distribution: Interval Data 245
Constructing Cross-Tabulation or Contingency Tables 248
Summary—Measures of Central Tendency 253
Summary—Measures of Variation 254
Study Questions 254

eleven   **Testing Hypotheses**   **255**

Eliminating Alternative Explanations 257
The Effects of Chance 260
The Normal Curve Sampling Distribution 264
The t Sampling Distribution 272
The Chi Square Sampling Distribution 274
Summary—Tests of Significance 278   Study Questions 278

twelve   **Measuring Association: Nominal and Ordinal**   **280**

Nominal Level Measures of Association 281   Measures of
Association for Ordinal Level Data 286
Summary—Measures of Association 296
Study Questions 297

thirteen   **Measuring Association: Interval Data**   **299**

Regression Analysis 300
Pearson's Correlation Coefficient 312
Multivariate Measures 315   Tests of Significance 321
Summary—Measures of Association and Tests of Significance 324
Study Questions 325

PART FIVE
EPILOGUE 327

fourteen   Doing Political Analysis   329
The Research Report 331   Conclusion 338

Appendix   339
Suggested Readings 340   Glossary 348
Statistical Tables 360

Index   369

Preface

With politics becoming an increasingly dominant part of our lives, it is probably safe to say that all of us, at one time or another, perform a little political analysis. But all too often our attempts to analyze what is happening in the political world are far from rigorous. We judge; we blame; we criticize. We do not usually have the resources necessary to think in depth about what is happening.

It should be clear that understanding how to analyze politics would be a valuable skill. We believe that to be able to analyze the political world, it is necessary to understand the process of research. The way the question is phrased, the kind of evidence which is gathered to answer the question, the way the evidence is manipulated for interpretation, and the way the answer to the research question is integrated with and related to other information will all affect whether or not we feel we can rely upon the information.

For example, anyone who is interested in politics knows that it is frequently the case that the President says one thing, the Congress says another thing, and the media has a third point of view. While it may not be easy to reconcile these various viewpoints, knowing research techniques may help us decide which viewpoint is most correct. We would want to consider sources of bias in each point of view. We would want to review the information used to reach the conclusions. We would want to know if the conclusions follow from the information available, and so forth. By asking these questions, we are performing political analysis.

Learning about political research techniques is a topic which is usually approached with a great deal of reluctance, and at times, fear. After all, we want to know about politics—not about a philosophy of knowledge or about statistical manipulations of data. And so we focus, both in and out of the classroom, on the substance of politics rather than on the method of gathering information. We read reports of various claims and counterclaims and fail to ask the crucial questions: "How do you know?" and "So what?"

The problem is, we feel, that people do not see the connection between *what* we know about politics—the substance which interests them—and *how* we know what we know—the methods which bore them or frighten them. This is unfortunate. By not seeing this connection, people cannot really evaluate information about the substance of politics.

We believe that it is important to integrate the scope and methods of political science with the facts that make politics interesting. Therefore, in this book on research methodology, we have tried to integrate substance and method. In Part One, we discuss the standards which we use to organize information about politics. First we consider what delineates the subject matter of political science. Next we consider the basic assumptions which provide the foundation of scientific research. Finally we argue that research does not occur in a vacuum and we must consider the ethical implications of our research. This section, then, is devoted to the philosophy which underlies the process of empirical research.

In Part Two, we consider how far political scientists have progressed toward a political theory. To do this we examine the literature which has been developed using nine different conceptual approaches to analyze politics. We discuss this literature in terms of the obstacles which must yet be overcome to attain the goal of producing theory and suggest directions for future research. This section, then, is concerned with the substance of politics and its connection with the research process.

In Part Three, we consider the processes of planning and conducting an empirical research project. We discuss finding a topic, reviewing the literature, phrasing the hypothesis, choosing between primary and secondary data, sampling, controlling variance, gathering data, and storing data. In Part Four, we explain ways of using statistics to summarize and analyze information in these data. Finally, in the Epilogue we discuss the circular nature of research to emphasize the connection between substance and method. Research moves from questioning, to gathering evidence to answer the questions, and back to considering what the answer means. That is, research involves moving constantly between substance and methods.

Learning how to perform research may sound boring to some. But we do not feel it should be either boring or irrelevant. What could be more exciting than learning how to discover political relationships on your own? What could be more important than developing the ability to understand the impact of events in the real world? We hope that this book will convince you that understanding research is important and interesting.

ACKNOWLEDGMENTS

Any list of acknowledgments will undoubtedly exclude more of those people to whom we are indebted than it can include. We hope those who are excluded will understand. We owe a debt to Henry Teune, Charles Elder, and Wayne Francis for our intellectual foundations in methodology as well as for the belief that it was both useful and interesting. Much of our academic philosophy can be attributed to Oliver Williams and Henry Abraham. We wish to thank all our many colleagues, but especially those who interacted with us in methodology—Jeff Ross, Richard Suttmeier, Ronald Pynn, Donald Poochigian, and Theodore Pedeliski. We also wish to thank Laurence O'Toole for his encouragement and support.

We would also be remiss if we did not thank our students who suffered through earlier drafts of this manuscript and constantly reminded us to simplify.

We wish to thank the folks at Prentice-Hall, especially Stan Wakefield, Audrey Marshall, and Ginny Neri, who provided constant assistance, support, and patience throughout our efforts to transform our ideas into a book. A debt of gratitude is also owed to Tom Rundle.

Last, but certainly not least, we would like to thank our Student Assistant, Sid Bender, and LuAnn Griggs, Cheryl Johnson, Kristie Wagner, and Cheryl Momerak, the work-study students who typed the drafts. Special accolades are due our department secretary, Irene Wagner, who is much more than a transcriber of words and who typed the final draft of the manuscript during her vacation; and Ethel Fontaine, who did the mopping up.

One further word is in order. It is customary to thank one's spouse for being good-natured despite the fact that you were toiling on your manuscript. When working together, it is even more important—and harder—to be patient. Nonetheless, patience prevailed.

M.G.K.
R.W.K.

Philosophy of Political Science

Part One

This is a book about doing research in political science. There are three points we want to make right at the beginning. The first point is that, contrary to what you might believe, the topic of how to do research is not separate from the rest of the discipline of political science. Too many students see a course on research as a bitter pill to be swallowed. It is an uncomfortable experience to be survived—and then promptly forgotten. We will try to show you that research is part and parcel of the rest of political science.

The second point is that understanding the standards and procedures of research is something that could be very useful to you. We all consume the products of research constantly. Our knowledge is the result of more or less systematic research. If we are to go beyond simply swallowing all information hook, line, and sinker, and if we are to be able to evaluate that information on our own, we must understand the processes by which information is gathered and verified. Understanding these processes can make you a much more intelligent consumer of all information, whether it appears in a scholarly journal or in your daily newspaper. It will also enable you to gather and evaluate your own information to answer questions that interest you.

The final point is that research involves much more than simply the memorization of certain techniques. There are techniques of research which you should learn. More important than memorization of technique, though, is a thorough understanding of the whole process of doing research. There are two ways we will try to give you an understanding of research. In the first place, we will examine the fundamental assumptions on which research is based. There are various ways to research political phenomena. We will be discussing one of these: research on empirical phenomena based on the dictates of science. This is not the only way of studying political phenomena. There are many paths by which "truth" is sought. We believe that the scientific approach is one of the most fruitful. We will discuss this further in the first section.

Any research must begin with specifying answers to certain fundamental questions. For example, researchers must know what kind of information they wish to gather. They must have standards to use to verify the accuracy of the information they gather. They must know the purpose of the research. What we are saying is that research is based on a philosophy of what is knowledge, how we confirm or verify knowledge, and how knowledge is to be used. We will consider the scientist's answers to these questions because we think you must understand the answers before the research process can really make sense to you.

A second way we will try to help you understand research is by explaining why things are done as they are and by pointing out the problems and dilemmas of research. Too often, people learn about research by what is called the "cookbook" approach. The book says "do this," and the student does it. By just following directions, you will never really understand why things are done as they are. And, as anyone who has ever done research knows, in real life the easy directions can almost never be followed precisely. All sorts of decisions have to be made constantly. These decisions, which usually involve compromises with the ideal model of research, will require individual judgment. Only by understanding the total process of research—its goals and standards as well as its procedures—can such decisions be made wisely by the researcher.

In this first part of the book we will focus on the assumptions which are the foundation of scientific research. We will discuss the assumptions and consider some of the advantages and disadvantages of using the scientific method to do research on politics. Finally, we will discuss ethical questions which political scientists must resolve before doing research.

Introduction

Chapter One

This is a book about the scope and methods of political science. In our examination of scope and methods, we will focus on the process of doing political research. We will discuss both the concepts which are the foundations of research and the techniques which are employed.

It is a good bet that regardless of how interested you are in politics or how many courses you have had in political science, you approach a book which deals with the scope and methods of political science with something less than enthusiasm. It is likely that it was your interest in understanding "real life" politics which enticed you into studying political science. And you may feel now that learning about such abstract topics as building theories and doing research is a waste of time because these things have nothing to do with the real world. Nothing, we will argue, could be further from the truth. It is the basic contention of this book that an understanding of the processes of building theory and doing research is a necessary part of understanding both what political science is and what real life politics is all about.

Understanding the way information about politics is gathered should be fundamentally important to you for two reasons. In the first place, only by knowing the techniques of research can you ever be competent to evaluate the accuracy and utility of information produced by other researchers. If you do not understand the standards of research, there is no way you can determine if a given piece of political research—whether it be a newspaper story or a scholarly article—has produced information on which you would be willing to rely. The second reason why understanding the processes of political research is important to you is that such knowledge frees you from relying on others to produce information. If you know how to do research, you can gather on your own whatever information you may desire, within certain practical limits, of course. In both these cases we are arguing that understanding the process of doing political research will free you from reliance on others to evaluate or to produce the information you desire. Understanding research makes you a coequal partner in the process of creating and evaluating knowledge about the political world in which you are interested, instead of simply a passive receiver of that knowledge.

We are also arguing here that there is no clear division between the scope of political science—information concerning the political world in which you are interested—and the methods by which this information was discovered. In fact, scope and methods are but opposite sides of the coin. What we know about politics (scope) has been produced by political research. How much we know and how accurate the information is depends on the quality of past research. What we do not yet know will be the subject for the research of the future. Both scope and methods are pieces of the same puzzle. The ultimate aim of the puzzle is to sort out and explain the political world which surrounds us. The discussion throughout the rest of this book will focus on this theme: There is an intimate and necessary interrelation between the scope and methods of political science.

There is no doubt that learning about the scope and methods of political science can be dull, but there is no reason why this is necessarily so. In many ways the processes of political research are analogous to the techniques of investigating mysteries. Political scientists try to be very systematic about the procedures they use. If you think about it, however, the most effective detectives also seem to be those who are the most organized. For instance, Sherlock Holmes is always gathering evidence which others overlook and using his clues to determine the identity of the culprit. While it may not be as dramatic, this is basically the process the political scientist uses to understand the political world. And regardless of how organized and systematic they are, both detectives and political scientists benefit from serendipity—an accidental and fortunate discovery. This transforms the process of research from the mundane application of technique to the fascinating process of discovery. This book will help you become a capable political detective.

To become a good political researcher, we think you should keep in mind two very simple but very important guidelines.

The first guideline is that the most important part of any research project is to *think* thoroughly and precisely about the question you will be investigating. Research is simply the process we use to gather evidence to answer questions which interest us. Research is not, therefore, our end goal, but the means we use to reach the goal of increased knowledge and understanding of the world around us.

Too often, researchers tend to reverse the goals. They get so fascinated with the techniques of research that the techniques themselves become the end. Remember that all of the sophisticated techniques of gathering and analyzing data will be of no use if the researcher does not understand exactly what purpose those data are supposed to serve.

We hope that the first two parts of this book will help you think clearly about research questions. The first part of the book examines the way in which scientists organize data to develop theories which explain the empirical world. The second part discusses several conceptual approaches which political scientists often use as a starting point for their efforts to create political theories.

A second guideline to keep in mind is that the knowledge and understanding which researchers claim to give us must be supported by evidence. Research is the process by which this evidence is gathered. This means that it is not acceptable for researchers simply to "spout off" about what they believe to be the truth or what seems to be the case. For instance, if someone claimed all wealthy people are Republicans, we should always ask how he or she knew that. In scientific research, which is the kind of research examined in this book, two kinds of evidence must be cited to verify knowledge and understanding. First, researchers should demonstrate to us that the findings "make sense." That is, there should be some logical way of understanding what the researcher claims. It is to help us make sense out of the findings that researchers try to develop theories to explain those findings. For instance, a researcher may attempt to link wealth with the desire to preserve the status quo and therefore with conservative political attitudes, attitudes which tend to be espoused by the Republican party. In this way a logical linkage can be made between wealth and voting Republican.

The other kind of evidence is empirical. Researchers must demonstrate that which they claim can actually be observed. For instance, a researcher could survey a number of people of varying incomes and examine what proportion of wealthy people are Republican compared to the proportion of poor people. This empirical evidence ideally should be more general than one instance or one case. Saying that Aunt Hattie is both wealthy and Republican is simply not satisfactory evidence to establish the claims that *all* wealthy people are Republican. Aunt Hattie, however, is one piece of evidence which, when joined with other information, may provide adequate support for the claim. The last two parts of this book will investigate ways of gathering evidence and using it to answer our research questions.

Determining what "makes sense" or what is "adequate" evidence is, of course, somewhat subjective. Each of us must decide if we or others have built up satisfactory cases to answer the questions being investigated. The purpose of this book is to give you standards to use to help you determine if the evidence is adequate.

WHAT IS POLITICAL SCIENCE?

Before beginning to examine the process of research, however, we feel we should spend some time giving you an overview of this thing called political science. Political science courses are infrequently taught at the high school level. Therefore, few students who enroll in political science courses in college know what to expect or what is expected of them. Even after taking several courses, it is possible for students to lack a very clear conception of what political science is all about. Perhaps the most frequent misconception held by students is that political scientists are "inside dopesters." In this conception, the role of a political scientist is to carry around a vast number of bits of information dealing with such things as the number of people in Congress, the structure of the Libyan government, the difference between unitary and federal systems of government, and so on.

The student will probably come to realize eventually that the average political scientist carries around with him only a finite amount of such information. This is not because political scientists believe that such information is unimportant. Rather, it is simply the case that political scientists are human. The range of political phenomena is virtually limitless. There is so much political information that it is impossible for anyone, including a political scientist, to have all of it committed to memory. In addition, the determination of what is relevant is constantly changing.

What then does distinguish a political scientist? What distinguishes political scientists from both the layman and from people in other disciplines is the way they organize the information with which they deal. Different people can look at the same phenomenon and give entirely different interpretations of its meaning. For example, we could describe a picture of a father reading Longfellow's "A Midnight Ride of Paul Revere" to a child in bed. A political scientist would probably consider what kind of political learning is occurring in this process. That is, the child is probably learning of the noble origins of our country and of the heroic men who fought for the country's independence. Learning these things should teach the child patriotism. A psychologist, on the other hand, may think of how important it is for the child's emotional stability to have close and warm relationships with the parents. A layman may simply think of what a good idea it is to bore the child with the poem to make sure he or she goes to sleep.

What this example illustrates is that a single phenomenon can be viewed from a variety of perspectives. What distinguishes one discipline from another is the particular perspective—or slant—which each discipline uses to interpret the world. Thus, to understand what political science is, you must first understand the ways political scientists organize and process the information with which they deal. Organizing and processing information are the fundamental steps of research. Therefore, we hope that by focusing on the research process in this book we will give you a better idea of what the discipline of political science is all about. We also hope, as we have said before, that by introducing you to how political scientists think we will provide you with the ability to gather political information and to analyze that information on your own. Let us try to distinguish what information is most relevant to political scientists.

There is no easy answer to what exactly constitutes politics. Philosophers since the time of Aristotle, who is sometimes referred to as the first political scientist, have labored long and hard to define politics, but no one has produced a definition on which there is a consensus. We will not try to resolve the dispute over what constitutes an adequate definition of politics. Instead we will try to give you an idea of what politics is by examining the kinds of topics which have been the focus of research by people in the discipline. In Part Two of this book we will discuss the current state of the art in political science in terms of what we know and what we still need to know.

The predominant issues and topics, which constitute the *scope* of the discipline, have changed over time. For the most part, new topics did not supersede the old, but rather were added to them. This means that the discipline now is a composite of the dominant concerns of various periods in the past. Therefore, to give you an overview of the scope of political science we will examine what have been the major concerns of the discipline at various periods of its development.

For centuries there was no recognized discipline called political science.[1] But that did not mean that people were not thinking and writing about things they considered politics. For the most part these people could be considered moral philosophers. The kinds of political topics they examined demonstrated this moral philosophical background. They searched for the essence of ideas such as justice and good. They considered such questions as what is good government; what is sovereignty; and what should be the obligation of citizens to the state and, conversely, of the state to the citizens. The vast bulk of the literature was both *normative* and *deductive*. Normative analysis is concerned with assumptions that certain characteristics are good or desirable, and with the prescription of ways to attain those characteristics. Deductive analysis is based on reasoning from a general premise to a specific conclusion. The early literature in political science is deductive because it begins from basic premises concerning the nature of man. It is normative because the conclusions prescribed how governments should be established and conducted. Examples of this literature would be Plato's model of the ideal Republic, or the examination by either Locke or Hobbes of the nature of social contract.

---

1. The following discussion of the history of political science relies heavily on Albert Somit and Joseph Tanenhaus, *The Development of Political Science: From Burgess to Behavioralism* (Boston: Allyn and Bacon, 1967).

INTRODUCTION

In the latter part of the nineteenth century, the first attempts were made to define a separate field of study known as political science and to distinguish it from other disciplines. As Somit and Tanenhaus argue in their history of the development of the discipline, these founding fathers of modern political science were less than successful in defining exactly what the scope of study should be.[2] Most, they argue, were content with Bluntchli's description of the discipline as the "science of the state."[3] The literature produced during this period gives us some indications of what they considered to be the proper scope. This literature still was concerned with deducing laws concerning the development of government from a priori principles. In addition, some of these first political scientists argued that it was the responsibility of the discipline to be concerned with practical politics and to specify what the modern state should do. This added to the scope of political science a concern for dealing with current issues and for encouraging the development of good government and good citizenship. Finally, some of these researchers were beginning to produce studies comparing governments by analyzing historical documents at the start of the twentieth century.

In the early years of the twentieth century the discipline was given greater legitimacy by the formation of the American Political Science Association and by the eventual publication by that association of the *Review*. Despite this, there was little concern for delineating what should be the scope of the discipline or for distinguishing political science from other disciplines.[4] Again, examination of the literature at the period indicates what seemed to be the major concerns of political scientists. Most studies examined the formal, legal structures and processes of governments in great depth. The source of data for these studies were such written records as statutes, constitutions, and so forth. With some notable exceptions, the scholars never bothered to ask if the government actually was structured and did function as the written documents indicated it should. There was little concern for theory, deductive, normative, or otherwise. As Somit and Tanenhaus conclude: "With a few exceptions the political science of this period tended to be legalistic, descriptive, formalistic, conceptually barren. . . ."[5]

During the period between the two world wars there began some reaction to this essentially sterile focus on the legal aspects of government.[6] There were several intellectual forces which tended to push political science

---

2. Ibid., pp. 24–27.
3. Ibid., p. 24.
4. Ibid., p. 65.
5. Ibid., p. 69.
6. For a discussion of the forces leading to behavioralism, see Barbara Leigh Smith, and others, *Political Research Methods: Foundations and Techniques* (Boston: Houghton Mifflin, 1976), pp. 7–12.

away from the purely legalistic, descriptive studies of the early twentieth century as well as from purely normative, deductive theory which was the focus of the discipline in the nineteenth century. These forces were a changed conception of human nature, pragmatism, and pluralism. In the first place, there was a growing recognition that human nature was varied and complex. This recognition had three implications. First, it meant that laws of what constitutes good government, which were based on assumptions about an unvarying human nature, were called into question. Secondly, it meant than since humans vary, not all humans will behave identically within a given institution. Therefore, the focus on the legal and structural aspects of institutions became of limited utility. Thirdly, it meant that the study of human nature itself became a legitimate field of research.

The second force which affected political science was pragmatism. Pragmatism emphasized that ideas and actions can only be evaluated by their results, not by their logic, consistency, etc. Pragmatists, such as John Dewey, criticized the political science of that time for focusing on deductions concerning how the state arose rather than on what were the consequences or effects of the state now. Significantly, when political scientists switched their attention to the consequences of the state, they found that many were profoundly dissatisfied with the effects of those very institutions that the discipline had been describing in such laborious detail. Practicing politicians of the day were organizing new political movements, such as the Populist Party and the Progressive Party, to protest and to attempt to reform the institutions of American government. And scholars, such as Robert Michels, were pointing out that the institutions of democracy do not function as the statutes or Constitution say they do. Michels argued that the supposedly democratic institutions inevitably become ruled by an oligarchy.[7]

The third intellectual force which had an effect on political science was pluralism. It was argued that power in politics is shared among various groups and parties in addition to the institutions of government. Once again, this obviously meant that a focus solely on the legal structure of government was inadequate. The pluralists directed the attention of political researchers to the parties, groups, and individuals in the society who share political power with the institutions of government.

What in essence was happening during this period was, in the words of Thomas Kuhn, a scientific revolution. Kuhn argues that during periods of "normal science," a discipline is bound together by agreement on the basic questions, concepts, and methods to be used as a foundation for research.[8] Kuhn called this foundation for research a *paradigm.* Kuhn believes that periodically a crisis will arise in a discipline because the current paradigm is

---

7. Roberto Michels, *Political Parties* (New York: Macmillan, 1962).
8. Thomas S. Kuhn, *The Structure of Scientific Revolutions,* 2nd ed. (Chicago: The University of Chicago Press, 1970).

not capable of handling various anomalies or violations of what would be expected given the current paradigm. The problems raised for political science by the new conception of human nature of the pragmatists and of the pluralists can be seen as anomalies for the existing paradigm, as much as one existed. The result of such a crisis caused by the recognition of anomalies is a scientific revolution in which a new paradigm is created.

If what did happen in political science was not a total revolution, it was certainly a very large uprising. In the period following the second world war a new movement arose in the discipline—behavioralism. That single term actually masked a significant amount of disagreement among its advocates. Behavioralism was not a single idea but rather a combination of components, and different people tended to emphasize different combinations of those components.

The essence of behavioralism was the belief that political science should move toward becoming a real science. This emphasis on becoming more scientific meant a change not only in the scope of the discipline but also in its methods and goals. We will discuss the changes in the methods and goals in the next chapter which examines the nature of scientific inquiry. Here we will discuss three basic changes in the scope of the discipline brought about by the emphasis on science.

One change in the scope of political science was a new focus on individual and group behavior.[9] It was from this emphasis on behavior that the movement got its name. This focus on behavior obviously is the result both of the awareness that human nature is complex, as well as dissatisfaction with the focus on institutions. A second change in the scope was a new interest in coordinating political research with research in other social sciences. This belief in the importance of coordination stems largely from the emphasis on behavior. A institution like Congress may be purely political but individual behavior can never be segmented into purely political or social or economic. While researchers may divide their labors by focusing on one or the other aspects of human behavior, the reality is that individuals are whole and not just political or economic beings. Therefore, complete understanding of human behavior can only be produced by coordinating the findings of all those who research aspects of human behavior.

A third change in the scope was the attempt to separate questions of fact and questions of value. A *fact* is something which can be substantiated by experience or observation while a *value* refers to something which has subjective rather than an objective meaning. The origin of the belief that fact and value are separate is usually attributed to Hume who argued that value statements cannot be logically derived from fact statements.[10] For example,

---

9. For a listing of the characteristics of behavioralism, see Robert A. Dahl, "The Behavioral Approach in Political Science: Epitaph for a Monument to a Successful Protest," *American Political Science Review*, 55 (December, 1961), 763-72.
10. David Hume, *Treatise on Human Nature*, Book III, Part 1, Section i.

it may be possible to observe whether or not a given individual voted in an election. The empirical process of watching the individual vote would establish the voting as a fact. On the other hand, watching the individual vote in no way substantiates whether voting is valuable. While some attacks have been made on Hume's argument it is generally accepted that fact and value are distinct.[11] Many behavioralists believed that not only should fact and value be separate, but that values should have no place in political analyses. They wanted research to be totally objective and devoted solely to discovering what *is*. This belief was a reaction to the normative, deductive philosophy which had formed such a large part of early political science.

This did not mean that behavioralists wanted to do nothing but gather facts. As we will discuss in greater depth in the next chapter, behavioralists argued that political science research should be directed toward the creation of theory. The theory the behavioralists desired was not the theory of the early political scientists which prescribed what was good, but a theory which could *explain* the human behavior which the researchers observed. This meant that theory was not to be simply the logical product of someone's mind but must be relevant to things observed empirically. Theory should be a way of ordering and making sense out of the empirical observations.

An enormous debate arose among political scientists concerning the value of behavioralism. Those who opposed behavioralism were lumped together under the term *traditionalist*. As with the behavioralists, traditionalists were by no means a single, unified, homogeneous group of people. The essence of traditionalist arguments was that politics cannot be studied scientifically. Since most of their arguments involve questions concerning the appropriateness of the scientific method, they will be examined in the next chapter.

The traditionalist—behavioralist debate at times became quite vehement. It often consisted of one side or the other setting up extreme statements of the other's positions and then attacking and annihilating these "straw men." To a certain extent this debate has waned because of a greater willingness to recognize middle positions on which agreement can be achieved.[12]

One example of such a middle position would be that espoused by a new movement, the postbehavioralists. The postbehavioralists, in essence, argue that while the scientific research of the behavioralists has produced some valuable research, it has also had the negative effect of focusing research on trivial topics. Voting behavior is studied because it is easily observed and quantified while other, perhaps more significant, topics are ignored. Harold Lasswell, who was a pioneer of the behavioralist revolution, was also an early

---

11. John Searle, "How to Derive 'Ought' from 'Is'," in *The Is–Ought Question*, ed., W.D. Hudson (New York: St. Martin's Press, 1969), pp. 120-34.
12. Malcolm B. Parsons, "Perspectives on the Study of Politics: An Introduction," in *Perspectives on the Study of Politics*, ed. Malcolm B. Parsons (Chicago: Rand McNally, 1968), pp. 17–18.

advocate of what came to be the postbehavioral movement. In 1951 Lasswell argued that since it had been established that the scientific method was appropriate and desirable for studying politics (in his mind, at least) the time had come for political scientists to direct their research to "the choice of significant problems on which to apply and evolve method."[13] In other words, Lasswell was arguing that the techniques of the scientific method should be followed, but rejected the argument that research must focus only on fact to the exclusion of values.

Lasswell's plea was not generally heeded until late in the 1960s. The sixties, of course, was a decade of considerable social and political unrest. Many political scientists noted with dismay that their discipline not only failed to anticipate the unrest but could provide society little guidance or direction in the midst of the crisis. In Kuhn's terms, here was another anomaly which precipitated another revolution in the discipline. In 1971, David Easton echoed Lasswell in arguing the scope of the discipline must include topics which are relevant to the current problems facing society.[14] In addition, Easton believed that political scientists should include in their analyses recognition and consideration of values. The postbehavioralists thus represent a repeat of the earlier concerns of the discipline with current events and values. But the postbehavioralists do not represent a complete negation of the behavioralist movement since they argue that the method of science should be the basis of political research, where possible. They simply argue that the techniques of the scientific method can be most useful as a means to attain knowledge necessary to create a better world.

We have given you this brief overview of the development of political science in an attempt to demonstrate the kinds of subjects which become the focus of research in the discipline. Although the emphasis of the discipline has changed over time, the scope of the discipline now includes aspects of each of the various periods. The course offerings of many political science departments illustrate this point. There are usually courses, often called political theory courses, which examine and analyze the normative, deductive theory of both ancient and modern political philosophers. Comparative politics courses continue the interest in comparing the structure, functioning, and relations of various countries. International relations focuses on traditional concerns about the way in which states interact. It examines such things as war and peace, the international system, interdependencies, and foreign policy. Constitutional law courses maintain the interest in the legal foundations of government. Courses such as legislative or executive process are the descendant of the early concern for investigating in depth the structure and functioning of particular institutions of government while

---

13. Harold D. Lasswell, "The Policy Orientation," in *The Policy Sciences: Recent Developments in Scope and Method,* ed. D. Lerner and H. D. Lasswell (Stanford: Stanford University Press, 1951).
14. David Easton, *The Political System: An Inquiry Into the State of Political Science,* 2nd ed. (New York: Alfred A. Knopf, 1971), pp. 323–27.

usually adding a behavioral dimension. Courses on political behavior of various kinds are remnants of the behavioral movement. And, finally, courses dealing with policy analysis express the interest of the post-behavioralists in current and relevant issues.

Obviously, each school organizes its course offerings in political science differently. The fields listed above may or may not all be covered at your school. And, in addition, your political science department may include many other fields. We hope, though, the listing has served the purpose of giving you a better idea of the kinds of things in which political scientists are now interested. These different subfields serve to organize the data which political scientists study. Different political scientists specialize in different kinds of political data. Yet despite this diversity, to a large extent, political scientists will be asking similar kinds of questions in their analyses of these different data bases. This is so because political scientists often rely upon the same concepts to structure and organize data regardless of the area or subfield in which they specialize. Another way of looking at the scope of political science is to examine the concepts which political scientists use to organized data, as we will do in Part Two of this book. These concepts tie the discipline together despite the wide diversity in the kinds of data.

SUMMARY

In this chapter we have attempted to introduce you to the kinds of subjects which have been the focus of research by political scientists. There have been disagreements among political scientists for some time concerning the scope of the discipline. There have also been disagreements concerning what methods should be used to study politics. This debate has focused primarily on the question of whether the method of science could or should be used. In the next chapter we will examine what the scientific method is and discuss the opposing points of view on its utility and desirability as a basic research method for political science.

STUDY QUESTIONS

1. In what fundamental ways did the behavioralist movement differ from earlier political science?
2. In what ways did the postbehavioralist movement provide a melding of early concerns of political science with the concerns of the behavioralists?
3. What distinguishes a political scientist from a layman or a journalist?
4. In what ways is the job of a detective similar to the job of the political scientist?
5. In what ways has the development of political science as a discipline reflected the development of society in general and government in particular?

Science and Political Research

Chapter Two

In the last chapter we mentioned that a major part of the behavioral "revolution" was a call for the use of the scientific method to analyze politics. Actually, as Somit and Tanenhaus point out in their history of the discipline, political scientists have always been concerned about whether or not they deserve the title of scientist.[1]

The initial proponents of a separate discipline concerned with politics argued that the new discipline could and should be scientific. By the beginning of the twentieth century, however, there was a decline in the belief that science was a useful way of analyzing politics. This was a period in which political scientists were conducting detailed descriptions of governmental structures and processes. In 1921, Charles E. Merriam, a major political scientist of that time, launched a campaign to make the discipline more scientific.[2] He was not successful in his campaign, but as we noted, other pressures in the period between the two world wars resulted in the behavioral movement. In this chapter we will examine the nature of scientific

---

1. Albert Somit and Joseph Tanenhaus, *The Development of Political Science: From Burgess to Behavioralism* (Boston: Allyn and Bacon, 1967).
2. Charles E. Merriam, "The Present State of the Study of Politics," in *American Political Science Review,* 15 (1921), 173-85.

methodology and the arguments for and against the use of that methodology in political science.

THE SCIENTIFIC METHOD

We should make clear that philosophers of science do not agree totally on what constitutes scientific methodology. Nevertheless, there is one conception which has been so widely accepted that it has been called "the standard view."[3] It is this standard view on which we will focus. According to it, the goal of science is to develop explanations of the empirical world, or the world which is knowable by experience or observation. As we discussed in the last chapter, David Hume argued that empirical observations cannot substantiate values.[4] Because of this distinction, science, which is concerned with the empirical world, is not concerned with values. This is not to say that empirical research is totally value free. Values play an important role in determining what a researcher will study, how it will be studied, and how the research will be used. This emphasis on empiricism does not mean that science does nothing but accumulate stores of facts. As we said, the goal of science is *to explain* the empirical world. To do this, scientists direct their research toward the development and verification of theories. The basis for the construction of these theories is the attempt to observe and to substantiate commonalities and patterns in the facts observed. Scientists thus assume that there are causes for the phenomena they are studying and direct their research toward discovering those causes. This assumption that everything has a cause is known as *determinism*. In other words, scientists assume events do not happen randomly, but follow set patterns which are discoverable. A phenomenon can be explained by saying it is one instance of such a general causal pattern or relationship.

In brief, what scientists do is conduct research to gather information, or facts, about the empirical world. On the basis of this research, they posit the existence of commonalities among phenomena. These commonalities are summarized by a word which is known as a *concept*. Scientists also attempt to establish the existence of relationships among these concepts. Such statements of relationship are known as *generalizations*. To explain those relationships, scientists move to statements of greater abstraction and generality than the generalization developed from observation. These more general and abstract statements, when interrelated, compose a *theory*. The generalizations and the theory must, in turn, be verified by continued research aimed at discovering if observations conform with what would be expected if the generalizations and theory are true. There are thus three basic steps in

---

3. Israel Scheffler, *Science and Subjectivity* (New York: Bobbs-Merrill, 1967), pp. 7-15.
4. David Hume, *Treatise on Human Nature,* Book III, Part 1, Section i.

this process: (1) creating concepts to express commonalities among phenomena, (2) creating generalizations to express relationships among those concepts, and (3) creating theories to explain the relationships observed. At each of these stages, the scientist must gather observations to be sure those observations conform to his formulations. Let us now look at each of these stages in greater depth.

Concept Formation

Language is the means we use to communicate with others. This language is composed of many different kinds of words. Concepts may be defined as universal, descriptive words.[5] To help you understand what this definition means, we must examine the terms descriptive and universal. A descriptive word is one which refers to something. Such descriptive words may be contrasted to logical words which simply provide structure to the language. Examples of logical words include and, or, both, none, etc. Logical words do not refer to anything. That is, there is no such thing as an "and." On the other hand, the word chair is an example of a descriptive word since it refers to a particular set of objects on which you can sit. Chair is also a universal descriptive word since it refers to a general set of objects rather than to a specific, unique object. Our gray rocking chair is not a universal descriptive word since it only refers to one unique chair rather than to the whole class of objects which are chairs. Such universal descriptive words thus refer to a whole class of objects which have certain similarities. Notice that this does not mean that the objects are all identical. Chairs come in a vast array of different sizes, shapes, colors, etc. But we feel that there is enough similarity within this diversity that it makes sense to refer to them all with a single term.

Concepts make communication more efficient by making it possible to speak in generalities rather than having to refer to each phenomenon as unique. Of course, by focusing on general similarities among things we of necessity lose much detail. For example, by referring to an object simply as a chair we do not have a very clear picture of what the chair actually looks like. There is a very definite trade-off between looking at similarities among phenomena and focusing in depth on the unique properties of particular phenomena. Much information is lost by generalizing. This is a trade-off which will have to be faced all through the theory-building process. There is

---

5. For other discussions of concepts on an introductory level, see the following: Alan C. Isaak, *Scope and Methods of Political Science* (Homewood, Illinois: The Dorsey Press, 1975), Chap. 5; David H. Everson and Joann Poparad Paine, *An Introduction to Systematic Political Science* (Homewood, Illinois: The Dorsey Press, 1973), Chap. 3; and Dickinson McGaw and George Watson, *Political and Social Inquiry* (New York: John Wiley, 1976), Chap. 5. For more advanced discussions, see Carl G. Hempel, *Fundamentals of Concept Formation in Empirical Science* (Chicago: University of Chicago Press, 1952).

no universal or automatic solution to this dilemma. Rather, this is a question which researchers must face at various stages throughout any research project.

Therefore, concepts serve the purpose of expressing commonalities among various phenomena. The next question is how do we develop concepts. A variety of objects characterized by vastly different sizes, shapes, and colors can be used to support an individual in a sitting position. What leads us to the conclusion that we may define them all with the single term, chair? A philosopher would say that out of all this diversity there is an underlying essence which the concept chair connotes. Philosophers since the time of Plato have attempted to discover the true essence of such concepts as truth, beauty, good. Political philosophers are concerned with essential definitions of such concepts as justice, law, government, and so forth.

Scientists, on the other hand, are not concerned with the search for such *essential definitions.* This is due both to their emphasis on empiricism and to a certain pragmatism in their approach. The work of philosophers to refine and clarify concepts is obviously potentially of great value to scientists who will do research based on those concepts. But scientists do not feel that it is necessary to wait until such time that the concepts are defined in essential terms before beginning empirical research. What the scientist tries to do is to define concepts in terms of characteristics which are relevant to his research. His main concern is not that these definitions are the "true" essential definitions. Instead he is trying to convey to others exactly what he means when he uses a concept such as chair. Such a definition, which is called a *nominal definition,* may be judged good or bad because of its clarity or usefulness. However, since it makes no claims of describing the true essence, it may not be judged true or false. Traditionalists claim that by using nominal definitions, the behavioralists have nothing to say about the real world which is ultimately concerned with essences. The behavioralists, on the other hand, argue that we cannot communicate if people use their own terms to define what they feel is the essence of a phenomenon.

Now let us examine how a political scientist may actually go about constructing a concept. Let us give an example from our own research. We were investigating patterns of citizen participation. Among other things we were interested in discovering what kinds of people participate in various political institutions and structures in two southern cities. What we found was that the same people tend to participate in all, or a large number of, institutions and structures. These people organize and are active in neighborhood organizations. In addition they are likely to take the initiative in writing or personally contacting government officials. Because of the visibility of these citizens, officials tend to think of them first when appointing citizens to various advisory groups. We felt we had found a commonality and we wanted to summarize it by developing a single term so that we could easily communicate that commonality to others. We decided to call these citizens who participated constantly "professional participators." In the process of forming this concept we observed several instances of units which we felt shared some characteristic or property. We then developed a term to express what we believed to be that common property. The term, professional participator, is the concept. The property it refers to, that is, a tendency to participate in many political activities and to be recognized by government officials as a citizen representative, is the nominal definition of the concept.

Unlike the philosophers' search for essential definitions, the scientists' reliance on nominal definitions is a very pragmatic approach. We have developed our own concept and definition. Other researchers looking at the same data may see somewhat different patterns in what they observe. They may then want to develop their own concepts to describe precisely what they see and want to communicate. The same desire for precise communication may lead a scientist to avoid using words which are in common usage in society because such words often come to have multiple meanings. For instance, democracy has been used so many ways that it is hard to know precisely what people mean when they refer to a country as democratic. Political scientists may want to develop new concepts to express precisely what they mean when they speak of democracy rather than trying to use the more common terms.

This reliance on nominal definitions may result in two problems. In the first place, a discipline may begin to resemble the Biblical Tower of Babel, with each scientist speaking a different language. Secondly, a discipline may become very jargonized because of the creation of new and specialized terms. In both cases the concepts developed are by no means universal, contrary to the fact that we defined concepts as universal words.

What then is the advantage of the use of nominal definitions? The basic advantage can be summarized in a single term: precision. Scientists, remember, want to explain the empirical world. As a basis for doing that they must establish agreement on what they observe empirically. They therefore want to develop terms which express what each observes as precisely as possible. This enables other researchers to observe the same or similar data and decide if they too agree with the observations of other scientists. This makes it possible to accumulate evidence and knowledge. This ability to replicate studies and to compare observations, which is known as *intersubjectivity*, is perhaps the most important way that scientists try to exert a control in the event that bias has affected interpretations and conclusions in research.

Developing precise concepts and defining those concepts in such a way that others know exactly what is meant is thus extremely important in science. In some cases, this precision presents no major problem. For example, with concepts such as chair or professional participator, there is no problem fulfilling the requirement of empiricism since those concepts refer to things which can be observed. With a concept such as political trust there would be more trouble. A concept like trust, which refers to something which cannot be directly observed, is known as a *construct*. To make sure that scientists can agree that they are observing something called trust, the construct must not only be defined precisely but some guide must be given so that all scientists can use the same standards. In scientific research it is insufficient to define a concept as Justice Potter Stewart defined pornography, "I know it when I see it."[6] It would be necessary to specify operations which, when performed, would lead researchers to some empirical indicator of the existence of trust. The operation may be simply asking individuals if they believe the government always does the right thing. The answers to this question then are empirical indicators of how trusting the individuals are of their government. This process of specifying operations which will produce empirical indicators of concepts is known as *operationalization*. We will talk about this process of operationalization in greater depth in Part Three when we discuss measurement. For now, just remember operationalization is important to science because it makes it possible for scientists to agree on what they observe and therefore accumulate knowledge about the empirical world.

We have briefly discussed how to develop and to define concepts; let us now consider how we can evaluate concepts.

It is important for you to understand how to evaluate concepts, even if you never do any empirical research yourself. The quality of concepts will determine the quality of theory. We think you should keep these criteria in mind whenever you read anything—whether it be an academic article or a newspaper story. Many a seemingly good argument crumbles when the concepts which are its base are examined closely. The first thing which you should ask about a concept is whether it is clearly and precisely defined. You should know exactly what is being described. Secondly, you should consider whether or not the concept has empirical import. A concept, remember, is a descriptive word, and, therefore, it must refer to something. If the concept refers to something which is not directly observable, there should be an operationalization. This is especially so if the concept is used in a scholarly article. But even in magazine and newspaper articles, operationalization would increase precision and therefore be helpful. Wouldn't you like to know exactly what people mean when they call someone a conservative, or a radical, or a communist? If in fact the concept is operationalized, you should be sure that the operationalization is consistent with the definition.

Finally, you should determine if you believe the concept has some potential use. Remember, we construct concepts to aid in the attempt to build theories. To construct a theory, concepts must be related together in generalizations. Therefore, a good concept is one which can be shown to

---

6. *Jacobellis* v. *Ohio*, 378 U.S. 184 (1964), 197.

have some kind of relationship with other concepts. This is sometimes called systematic import.[7] This systematic import is much harder to determine than most of the other criteria we listed. Often, of course, the systematic import cannot be determined without further research. However, some consideration on the part of researchers for the general usefulness of concepts, both to other researchers and to society as a whole, may be a useful counterbalance to the tendency we mentioned earlier of constantly creating new terms to fit one's own individual purposes at the moment. These, then, are the questions you should ask concerning at least the major concepts in anything you read.

Developing concepts, while fundamental to the process of building theory, is really only the first step in that process. Concepts are important because they compose the content which is the focus of the theory. But while concepts categorize what is being discussed, they really do not help us to explain, which is the aim of theory, as long as they stand in "splendid isolation." Concepts, as we indicated above, are most useful when they can be related to each other in generalizations. Hence, we are now going to turn our attention to the process of building generalizations.

Formulating Generalizations

A generalization is a statement which relates two or more concepts. Building generalizations is very important in the understanding of political events.[8] Although every political event is in some ways unique, the scientist focuses primarily on the commonalities among events. Scientists also assume events are not random. Their goal is, then, to identify underlying patterns, expressed in terms of generalizations. Let us consider how this is done and some pitfalls which you should try to avoid.

Let us assume that a researcher has some information on a group of people. She examines the information and happens to notice that all people with a yearly income in excess of $50,000 vote Republican and all those with incomes below $50,000 vote Democrat. In this particular set of data, she has observed a relationship between two concepts—income and party identification. Now the dilemma facing the researcher is whether it is possible to conclude on the basis of this observation that these two concepts are related throughout the entire population. That is, does this generalization refer only to an accidental relationship which has occurred by chance in her data or one which is true generally?

---

7. Hempel, *Fundamentals of Concept Formation in Empirical Science*, pp. 45–49.
8. For other discussions of generalizations on an introductory level, see the following: Alan Isaak, *Scope and Methods of Political Science*, Chap. 6; Lawrence C. Mayer, *Comparative Political Inquiry* (Homewood, Illinois: The Dorsey Press, 1972), Chap. 3. For more advanced discussion see Eugene J. Meehan, *The Theory and Method of Political Analysis* (Homewood, Illinois: The Dorsey Press, 1965), Chap. 4.

To make a general statement that the concepts are related in the population as a whole based on the evidence of individual cases is the process of *induction.* Induction involves an inferential leap which is really a leap of faith. This is so for several reasons. In the first place, the researcher in this example quite obviously does not have information on all the units in a population but only on a subset or sample of the population. To conclude from that data that the greater people's wealth, the more likely they are to vote Republican than Democratic is to assume that the sample accurately represents characteristics of all other people who were not questioned. There are techniques of sampling, which we will discuss later, which improve the probability that those sampled are representative of the rest. But it is still impossible to be absolutely sure your sample is completely representative of the population. There would even be a problem making the inductive leap if the data are comprehensive. Although a researcher may contact all people who are now wealthy, there is no way to contact all those who have been wealthy or who will become wealthy in the future. Therefore, there is no way of knowing if those people have voted or will vote Republican, although the generalization constructed by the researcher would imply that that would be the case.

What is the justification for making such an inductive leap? The goal of scientific research is not to develop an understanding of one sample or one point in time. The goal is to understand general patterns in the empirical world. The only way we can develop such a general understanding is to gather evidence, one piece at a time. There is no other way for us to learn about the empirical world around us than by observation, and we can never observe everything simultaneously.

Since we are limited to observing only parts of the empirical world, how can we be sure our inductive leap is justified? The answer is that we can never be *sure,* but there are ways we can try to build up a good "case" to support our generalization. When we make observations and discover what we believe to be a relationship, that generalization is known as a *hypothesis.* A hypothesis is a generalization which has been tentatively proposed. That is, the statement that two concepts are related is considered at the moment to be an educated hunch, or guess. What researchers must then do is to try to build up a good enough case for the hypothesis so that it may be accepted as a *law.* A law is a generalization which has been generally accepted as true.

In science, there are two steps in building a good case to support a hypothesis. The first step is empirical. The researcher observes one set of data and discovers a pattern. To establish that the pattern is not just accidental, a fluke in that set of data, that researcher and others must continue to observe other data, in other situations, and over time. This constant verification is fundamental to the scientific process. Because of the importance of constant verification, the generalization must be testable. This means that the concepts which compose the generalization must be defined precisely and operationalized. This is necessary because many researchers will be searching data to see if they, too, observe a given relationship, and they must be given guidance to be sure they are looking at the same things the initial researcher did.

The generalization must also be disconfirmable. That is, it should not be a statement which is necessarily true, such as two plus two equals four. Such a statement is purely logical, based on the assumptions of a mathematical system. Scientific generalizations are supposed to deal with empirical reality rather than with the world of pure, analytical logic.

The second step in building a good case for a hypothesis is an acceptable answer to the question, "Does it make sense?" The answer is sought by trying to establish that there is some logical reason why we might expect the two concepts to be related.

This search for a logical reason raises a very fundamental issue. When we talk about a relationship, we are not talking solely about the fact that two things tend to occur together. For instance, we might find that in European cities the number of storks seems to vary directly with the birth rate. That is, as the number of storks increases, so does the birth rate, and vice versa. Regardless of that empirical evidence, it is very unlikely anyone would hypothesize that storks are related to births. Why do we not make such a hypothesis when the empirical evidence seems to point to it? We do not make such a hypothesis because the relationship is obviously not one involving causation—at least not if what the doctors tell us is true. The point is, the kind of relationship between concepts in which scientists are interested is one in which one factor is believed to be a cause of the other.

Scientists make this focus on causation explicit by the terms they use to identify the components of generalizations. Rather than referring to concepts, scientists will usually refer to *variables*. A variable is a concept which can take various values. It is by observing how the values of two variables change together in a patterned way that scientists try to establish there is some empirical relationship between the two variables. One of the variables is designated an *independent variable*. This variable is believed to produce or to *cause* something. That effect which is caused by the independent variable is referred to as *dependent variable*. Its value depends upon the value of the first variable. We use the independent variable to explain the dependent variable.

In some instances, which variable is independent and which is dependent is quite obvious. Consider, for instance, the following generalization: The older a person, the more conservative he is. It would be nonsensical to try to claim that a person's age could be dependent on, or caused by, his conservatism. On the other hand, in other instances, determining which is the independent and which is the dependent variable is not quite so easy. Consider our first example. We saw income as the independent variable because we assumed it is a factor which precedes and does not depend on party identification. An argument could also be made that party identification may precede income. In this case the choice of which is the independent variable and which is the dependent must depend basically on what makes the most sense to the researcher or on what the researcher wants to explain. You should also realize that an independent variable in one study may be a dependent variable in another. We may consider income as independent here, but at another time we may want to examine it as a dependent variable and consider on which factors income may depend.

Having pointed out that scientists are interested in relationships which are causal, let us consider what is involved in establishing causation. We must immediately point out that the philosopher David Hume argued that no empirical evidence could *prove* that one thing causes another.[9] He believed that the statement that things are causally related can be based on nothing more substantial than inference. Others, however, have pointed to conditions which can provide support for such an inference of causation, even if these empirical conditions do not prove causation.

Ernest Nagel has established a fairly rigorous set of criteria which, if met, he claims would imply that a relationship is causal. The standards established by Nagel could rarely be met by social scientists.[10] Hans Zetterberg, therefore, has established a set of conditions less rigorous than Nagel's which are more applicable for social science data.[11]

Zetterberg argues that we can infer causation if the relationship meets four requirements. First, in order to infer a relationship is causal, one event must either follow the other in time or the two must be shown to occur together at one point in time. If you are following an event over time you can notice if the appearance of one variable occurs before a reaction in another variable. When you are looking at a set of data collected at one point in time (as is the case with much social science data), it is impossible to establish empirically which occurred first. It is possible to observe, however, that in these data there seems to be some pattern in the values of variables. For example we may notice that wealthy people vote Republican. Zetterberg argues that even though we cannot tell which variable preceded the other, the pattern in the values can be used to infer that there is a causal relationship. Determining which is cause and which is effect will have to be based on theoretical reasoning.

Second, Zetterberg argues that causal relationships may be either irreversible, that is, A⟶B, or reversible, that is, A⟶B or B⟶A. Getting older may lead to more conservative political attitudes, but conservative

---

9. David Hume, *The Treasise of Human Nature,* Book 1, Part 3, Section 3.
10. Ernest Nagel, *The Structure of Science* (New York: Harcourt Brace Jovanovich, 1961), pp. 73ff.
11. Hans L. Zetterberg, *On Theory and Verification in Sociology,* 3rd ed. (Totowa, New Jersey: The Bedminister Press, 1966), pp. 59-72.

attitudes don't make one get older. This is an example of an irreversible relation. In political science, though, we often encounter reversible relationships. For instance, increasing communication between two nations may result in increased trade. It is equally plausible that increased trade will result in increased communication.

Third, Zetterberg argues that causal relationships may be universalistic (always hold) or probabilistic (occur with a certain probability). Of course you could make a strong case for a causal relationship if every rich person in the United States voted Republican. Since it is unlikely we will ever have such universalistic relationships in social science, we must be satisfied with being able to say that wealth has caused people to vote Republican in some known percentage of cases.

Finally, Zetterberg argues that causal relationships can (1) be sufficient or contingent, and (2) necessary and substitutable. The strongest causal argument could be made in cases where the relationships specified were both necessary and sufficient. In a necessary relationship, the cause *must* be present for a given effect to occur. In a sufficient relationship, that cause alone is adequate to produce a given effect. A necessary and sufficient relationship is one in which one cause alone will always produce a given effect. In the physical sciences, there are examples of necessary and sufficient conditions. To boil water it is necessary to apply heat, and the application of heat is sufficient to cause the water to boil.

Rarely, if ever, are there necessary and sufficient conditions in political science. Given the complexity of human behavior, it is rare that any single variable is sufficient to cause a reaction in another variable. Instead, we usually have contingent relationships in which one variable has a given effect if other specified conditions are met. For instance, income may affect voting preference if some other factor, such as political interest, is present. We are also unlikely to find many necessary relationships. High occupational status may cause one to vote Republican, but high income may produce the same effect. Income and occupation are, therefore, substitutable.

To summarize, Zetterberg states that we may infer causal relationships under the following conditions, if these relationships are consistent with the structure of an argument:

1. Relationship may or may not have a temporal sequence
2. Relationship may be irreversible or reversible
3. Relationship may be universalistic or probabilistic
4. Relationship may be
   a). necessary or substitutable and
   b). sufficient or contingent

Let us now examine one final point about generalizations: the function of generalizations in the process of scientific explanation. To a scientist, to explain something is to show that it follows from a basic premise. Thus, in order to explain something it is necessary to know two things. In the first place it is necessary to know the existing characteristics of the thing to be explained. These characteristics are called *initial conditions*. An example of a relevant initial condition is the following: This man is wealthy. Wealthy is a characteristic of this particular man. But you should realize that wealthy is also a concept which refers to an entire group of people. The second thing necessary for explanation is a universal generalization which states a relationship between that concept and some other characteristic. Such a universal generalization indicates that all people who belong to the group characterized as wealthy would also possess some other specified characteristic. For instance, we might have the following generalization: The greater people's wealth, the more likely they are to vote Republician. As noted before, we believe there is a logical linkage between wealth and voting since wealthy people may want to preserve the status quo. Now, by knowing that this particular man is wealthy and by knowing that all wealthy people vote Republican, we can now understand why it is he votes Republican. When a universal generalization is used to explain a particular phenomenon, it is called a *covering statement*.

Perhaps we can give you a better grasp of the process of explanation by looking at it in terms of symbols:

Covering statement:	A → B	(Wealthy people vote Republican)
Initial Condition:	A	(This man is wealthy)
	∴ B	(Therefore, this man votes Republican)

The process of logically deriving a conclusion from a premise is called deduction. The process of explanation based on deduction is known as the *nomological model*.

Generalizations are used to explain individual phenomena. But what if we want to explain a generalization? What if, for instance, we want to know why wealthy people vote Republican? To explain generalizations, scientists construct theories. Let us now look at this final goal in the research process.

Building Theory

The term theory is often misunderstood by people. Let us try to eliminate some misconceptions people have about theory. When we talk about theory, we are not referring to the product of a fuzzy-headed dreamer or a pointy-headed intellectual sitting in an ivory tower. Theory is something which is very useful because it helps us understand the empirical world around us. To say it works in theory but not in reality is to say there is a disparity between the two. But a good theory is one whose conclusions fit with empirical data. This means that if we had a good theory there would be no difference between theory and practice.

We define theory as a series of logically related, lawlike generalizations. Theory is developed when researchers begin to see some order and patterning among the generalizations they are constructing and verifying. Theory thus provides an order or structure into which generalizations can be fitted. For example, let us tentatively propose the following generalizations, recognizing that they have not actually been recognized as lawlike by social scientists: High social status leads to desire to protect the status quo; desire to protect the status quo leads to support for political movements espousing traditional values.

There are several things which you should notice about these generalizations. In the first place, there is a logical relationship between them. They fit together into a logical structure. The second thing you should notice is that, because of the logical relation between the generalizations, it is possible to derive from these statements a third generalization: People of high social status support political movements which espouse traditional values. A good theory is one which can produce new hypotheses. The process we used to produce the new hypothesis should look familiar to you. In the last section of this chapter we discussed how individual phenonomena are explained when they can be derived from a basic premise. Here we have derived a generalization from two premises which are logically related. This means that the logical structure, or theory, has explained the generalization.

There is a third thing you should notice about this theoretical structure. The concepts being related are relatively abstract. It would be impossible to observe directly such concepts as social status or support for status quo. Theories will often involve such abstract terms because such terms increase the scope of the theory. For example, previously we created a generalization based on observations of data: Wealthy people vote Republican. Such a generalization has a broader scope than any individual fact, such as wealthy Aunt Hattie votes Republican. But its scope still is more limited than the generalization we derived from the theory: High social status leads to support for political movements espousing traditional values.

As we move from facts which can be observed directly to generalization to theory, we move to increasing levels of abstraction and increasing scope. And yet facts, generalizations, and theory are all related. From an observation of facts we inductively create generalizations, and then constant observation of other facts is used to verify the generalization and give it the status of law. In an attempt to explain these generalizations we build theories. Since theories are composed of generalizations including abstract terms, they can never be directly observed. Yet theories must be tested to see if they conform to the empirical world, since, as we said before, the fundamental purpose of theories is to help us understand the world around us. Theories are tested by logically deriving generalizations which can be compared to our observations of facts. If the facts observed are congruent with the generalization, not only is the generalization itself given confirmation but so is the theoretical structure which produced the generalization. Science, in this standard view, involves a constant movement from fact to higher levels of abstraction and back to facts to verify the abstraction.

You should be warned that the scientific method is not a formula for doing quality research. The principles we have discussed are a general outline of scientific research. Working scientists rarely follow the outline in lock step fashion, but constantly move back and forth between ideas and data.

Let us now briefly examine criticisms of this standard view. There are two types of criticisms which we will consider. In the first place we will discuss criticisms which philosophers of science have raised about this standard view of science and the rebuttal to those criticisms. Secondly, we will consider the traditionalists' criticism of the use of the scientific method to study politics and the behavioralists' rebuttal.

EVALUATION OF THE STANDARD VIEW

Some philosophers of science have identified three basic problems with this standard view of the scientific method. The problems have to do with (1) the distinction between observational and theoretical statements; (2) the distinction between facts and values; and (3) the structure of explanation. Let us look at each of these in turn.

The observational–theoretical distinction: The standard view of science involves an assumption that there is a distinction between observational and theoretical statements. An observational statement is presumably directly verifiable because it can be compared to the empirical world. For instance, the statement "All wealthy people vote Republican" can be verified by asking all wealthy people for what party they vote. Theoretical statements, on the other hand, are not directly verifiable but are constructed on a foundation of the observational statements and serve to explain them.

Kuhn, among others, has argued that the distinction between observational and theoretical statements is not as clear as it may first appear.[12] He points out that observation is affected by a variety of factors.

> . . . much neural processing takes place between the receipt of a stimulus and the awareness of a sensation. Among the few things that we know about it with assurance are: that very different stimuli can produce the same sensations; that the same stimulus can produce very different sensations; and, finally, that the route from stimulus to sensation is in part conditioned by education. Individuals raised in different societies behave on some occasions as though they saw different things.[13]

---

12. Thomas S. Kuhn, *The Structure of Scientific Revolutions,* 2nd ed. (Chicago: University of Chicago Press, 1970).
13. *Ibid.,* p. 193.

Kuhn is arguing, then, that what we observe is affected by the set of characteristics and expectations we bring to the situation. Our example in the last chapter of the father reading "The Midnight Ride of Paul Revere" to his child illustrates this same point. A psychologist would observe one thing in this situation and a political scientist would see something entirely different. This illustrates that the set of "beliefs, values, and techniques" of a discipline, or "paradigm" in Kuhn's terms, can significantly determine what observations a researcher makes and how he interprets them.[14] The use of observation to verify our theories thus becomes suspect since those observations are affected by the theory we are testing.

A second distinction which has been called into question is that between fact and value. Hume argued that values could not be logically derived from fact statements.[15] Yet philosophers have attacked that claim. John Searle has argued that there are two kinds of facts: physicalist and institutional. Physicalist facts are such things as "John has short hair." There is no way such brute facts can be used to establish values. Searle argues that institutional facts, on the other hand, can be used to derive value statements.[16] Institutional facts refer to "any state of affairs which entails some institution in order to be what it is."[17] Let us look at Searle's example of how such institutional facts can be used to derive value judgments. He starts with a fact statement: Jones says he owes Smith $5.00. There is no doubt that that statement is a fact, verifiable by empirical observation. Searle argues that fact can lead to the derivation of the conclusion that Jones *should* pay Smith the money. To Searle this conclusion is dependent on the institution of promise-keeping.[18]

Charles Taylor has also attacked the distinction between fact and value.[19] He based his attack on the following claims: First, in logic similar to Kuhn's, he argues that explanation constrains evaluation. This is so because explanations specify what is to be explained (observed) and how it is to be explained. Taylor argues that observations beyond the range of the explanation will not be taken seriously. Secondly, Taylor argues that a statement to the effect that something is good cannot stand unsupported. Unless such a statement is to be nothing more than emotional (I like X), it must be supported by rational, empirical reasons. Finally, Taylor argues that something which "fulfills human wants, needs, or purposes always constitutes a

---

14. *Ibid.*, p. 175.
15. Hume, *Treatise on Human Nature*, Book 3, Part I, Section i.
16. John Searle, "How To Derive 'Ought' from 'Is'," in *The Is-Ought Question*, ed., W.D. Hudson (New York: St. Martin's Press, 1969), pp. 120-34.
17. Fred M. Frohock, *Normative Political Theory* (Englewood Cliffs, N.J.: Prentice-Hall, 1974), p. 26.
18. *Ibid.*, p. 27.
19. Charles Taylor, "Neutrality in Political Science," in *Politics, Philosophy and Society*, third series, ed. P. Lasslett and W. Runciman (Oxford: Basil Blackwell, 1967).

reason for calling that something good." To say that something fulfills human wants is a fact statement. To say something is good is a value statement. Thus, Taylor is arguing that there is a connection between fact and value.

The final attack on the standard view of science focuses on the nature of scientific explanation. Opponents have argued that the nomological model is simply not an accurate description of explanations in science.[20] They argue that in many cases explanations which fit the model are not very satisfactory because the causal laws are too vague and general to give us much understanding. For example, to say that we can explain why John Doe votes for candidate X because of the causal law that voters pick candidates whom they think are best, does not really tell us anything very new or interesting. Secondly, opponents argue that scientists are at times satisfied with explanations which do not include such causal laws. For example, political scientists feel they can do a relatively good job of explaining voting behavior by pointing to a combination of the effects of various factors rather than using causal laws. For instance, voting choice is related to religion, race, income, and so forth. A third attack on the nomological model is made by those who point out that many relationships are probabilistic rather than universalistic.

Let us now give time for a rebuttal of the criticisms of the standard view. Perhaps the primary point which can be made in defense of the standard view is that the criticisms in no way undermine the utility of the scientific method. It is good to point out that science is not a purely mechanical and technical process leading to automatic and infallible truth. It is unfortunate that at times the standard description of science seems to give the impression of a sterile and somewhat inhuman activity. But scientists are human. This means that they, too, like the rest of us, tend to see what they want to see. Because of this, as Kuhn and Taylor agreed, scientists' observations may be affected by their expectations.

This does not mean, however, that we should give up the attempt to be scientific. The very strength of the scientific method is its realization that scientists are human and may be consciously or unconsciously biased in their observations. The ultimate goal of science is to minimize that bias. It is that goal which is the foundation of the standard view. There are several aspects of the standard view which are aimed at minimizing bias. First, of course, is the emphasis on the role of direct observation in developing theory. Secondly, the observation by a single scientist of a single set of data is not accepted as verification for a scientific law. Constant observation by many scientists is required. Thirdly, to facilitate the accurate sharing of observational experiences among a community of scientists, researchers are ex-

---

20. Barbara Leigh Smith, and others, *Political Research Methods: Foundations and Techniques* (Boston: Houghton Mifflin, 1976), pp. 53–54.

pected to specify clearly what operations they performed in their research. This clear specification makes it possible for other scientists to replicate the study and compare findings. It is of course possible, even probable, that scientists trained in the same way may tend to see the same things. But, as Kuhn himself points out, scientific revolutions do occur when observations present scientists with a series of anomalies which can not be explained by given theories and can no longer be tolerated.[21]

The argument that fact and value are not totally distinct also does not undermine the standard view of science. Both Searle and Taylor point out that facts, in some cases, can be used to derive values. However, it is still crucial that the initial facts be established and verified. Once again we can say that the scientific method is the most rigorous process men have yet devised to establish and verify facts. This is so because it rests on constant observation of different data over time by different researchers and the sharing and comparing of those observations to build a cumulative basis of support for a law.

Finally, there is no doubt that the nomological model does not always accurately describe explanations offered and accepted. Actually, the nomological model has always been recognized by scientists as an ideal, which means its requirements may not always be achieved. Yet, since that is the ideal, it is the goal toward which scientific research is aimed. Therefore, to understand what scientists do it is necessary to understand the model of explanation which guides their research efforts. This does not mean, of course, that other explanations are not useful.

A more difficult issue concerns the use of probabilistic generalizations. Such generalizations are those in which the cause results in a given effect in a certain percentage of cases. You should realize such generalizations present scientists with a serious obstacle in their attempt to derive conclusions. Let us see why this is so. Let us assume that scientists over time have established not that all wealthy people vote Republican, but that 78% of all wealthy vote Republican. And let's assume we have a statement of initial condition: This man is wealthy. What conclusion can the scientist logically derive in this case? Obviously, the scientist can make no logical statement about how *this* man will vote since there is no way of knowing if this man is one of the 78% who vote Republican or one of the 22% who do not vote or vote for other parties.

There is disagreement among philosophers of science on the status of such probabilistic generalizations.[22] Some philosophers argue that probabilistic generalizations, while they may help us understand certain phenomena, are not really deductive explanations, but rather are explanation sketches which need to be filled in with other information or inductive

---

21. Kuhn, *The Structure of Scientific Revolutions,* Chap. 6.
22. Nagel, *The Structure of Science,* pp. 73ff.; Zetterberg, *On Theory and Verification in Sociology,* pp. 59–72.

knowledge. Others argue that such generalizations are deductive explanations but can simply not be used to derive conclusions about *individual* behavior.[23]

We cannot presume to resolve this debate. But we do feel it is important to make two points about probabilistic generalizations. First, we feel it is important to emphasize that such probabilistic generalizations cannot be used to explain *individual* behavior. If we know that 78% of wealthy people vote Republican, we still cannot conclude Aunt Hattie will vote Republican because she is wealthy.

Second, we feel that even if such generalizations cannot explain individual behavior, they are still useful. Students often will argue that although the professor says that wealthy people vote Republican, the generalization is obviously incorrect since Aunt Hattie is wealthy and she votes for Democrats. When the professor points out we can never explain every individual case, such as Aunt Hattie, many students will protest that such general statements are not very useful if there are exceptions. Basically this comes down to a question of whether you see the glass as half empty or half full. We may discover that 80% of people of higher socioeconomic status in the United States vote. That means 20% of such people don't vote and we may not know precisely who they are or why they do not vote. But by knowing that 80% vote, we know more than we did before and we can henceforth direct our research to finding out what we can about the 20%. One reason we are unable to understand all situations is that few phenomena are affected by only one variable. Consideration of multiple variables may give us a fuller picture of reality. The price of this is to make our study more complex. For instance, by considering another variable, such as race, we may be better able to explain which of the high socioeconomic status (SES) group will not vote. To say our knowledge is incomplete is not the same as saying it is totally useless. Obviously, if there are many exceptions, it means that a great deal of research and analysis has to be done before we have a good understanding of the general patterns in which we are interested. We must proceed one step at a time.

Another aspect of this argument deals with the question of whether it is possible to have theories if generalizations are probabilistic. Those who believe a theory must permit deduction would also believe that probabilistic generalizations cannot be used to build theories. Such deductive theories would require universal generalizations, and, as we pointed out before, there are none in the social sciences. But there is no reason to throw in the towel. Others believe it is still possible to have theory without universal generalizations. Abraham Kaplan has argued that a theory exists if general statements can be related to each other by their common focus on a particular phenomenon. For instance, several generalizations have been produced

---

23. Nagel, *The Structure of Science*, p. 22.

in the literature on American voting behavior. We know of a number of factors, such as income, education, age, and so forth, which have been used to explain the same phenomenon: a person's tendency to vote. Kaplan would argue that such a collection of generalizations related by a common focus is a *concatenated theory*.[24] While such concatenated theories may not be as powerful an explanatory tool as a deductive theory, they may still fulfill some of the goals of theories. They can organize information, suggest new hypotheses, and are empirical. There seems, therefore, to be no good reason for us to turn up our noses at such concatenated theories simply because they may not be as powerful as deductive theories.

Basically, we have argued here that the scientific method, though perhaps not perfect, is the most rigorous and precise means we have to gather knowledge and understanding of the empirical world around us. We don't feel that the criticisms of the standard view have actually undermined the basic utility of science. But we must deal with one last set of criticisms. These do not deal with the nature of science itself, but with an estimation of the scientific method as a useful way to study politics. Let us now turn to the traditionalists' attack on the use of science in politics and the behavioralists' rebuttal.

THE TRADITIONALIST-BEHAVIORALIST DEBATE

The traditionalists have raised four basic criticisms of the use of science to study politics.[25] First they argue that the subject matter of politics is too complex to permit construction of scientific generalizations identifying causes and effects. Secondly, they argue that humans act on the basis of free will, and, therefore, it is impossible to identify causes for that behavior. Thirdly, they point to the fact that humans behave differently when they know they are the focus of study, and, therefore, what the scientists observe is not really an accurate reflection of human behavior. Finally, they point to a problem we discussed before: the intrusion of values in the scientists' analysis. Let us look at each of these arguments and then consider a defense of the use of science to study politics.

Complexity of Human Behavior

One way in which human behavior is complex is that it is affected by many factors, and these factors are constantly changing. For example, how do we expect to be able to explain a man's decision how to vote when that decision is affected by a huge conglomeration of factors, some conscious and

---

24. Abraham Kaplan, *The Conduct of Inquiry* (San Francisco: Harper & Row, 1964), pp. 298 ff.
25. For critiques of behavioralism, see James C. Charlesworth, ed., *The Limits of Behavioralism in Political Science* (Philadelphia: American Academy of Political and Social Sciences, 1962); Herbert Storing, ed., *Essays on the Scientific Study of Politics* (New York: Holt, Rinehart & Winston, 1962).

some unconscious, which may change in importance from one day to the next? One response to this criticism is simply that physics and chemistry deal with subject matters which are complex, too. But physicists and chemists have an important advantage over social scientists because they can establish experiments. Experiments are the best way to eliminate the effect of possible alternative causes. The basic idea of an experiment is the establishment of a controlled environment in which *only* the experimental variable is allowed to vary. For many reasons, experiments are often difficult and sometimes impossible to use in studying humans.

There are three main problems in using experiments to study human behavior. First, many feel it is unethical and immoral to play with people's lives. If we feel that people with lower educational levels are less likely to vote, we would not want to deprive some people of an education just to test this. (We will discuss the question of ethics in research in greater depth in the next chapter.)

Secondly, political scientists in most instances don't have the power to establish experimental settings. For example, a political scientist may suspect that the form of government is related to the levels of citizen trust, but he can't order a country, or state, or even a city to change its form of government so that he can observe changes in the levels of trust. Even if he could order such a change, it would be impossible for him to control all other changes in the environment to ensure that it was actually the change in government which was changing the level of trust. The final problem of using experiments to study humans is related to human nature. Unlike the subject matter of natural sciences, humans are intelligent, thinking beings. If we become aware that we are part of an experiment, that awareness itself may well become another factor causing our behavior. (See Chapter Eight for a fuller discussion of experiments.)

For these three reasons, experiments cannot often be used to study politics, and this means it is often difficult to unravel the effects of the multiple factors which cause political behavior.

In addition to being the result of many factors, another way in which human behavior is complex is the fact that much of it is unique and will not recur. For instance, the 1976 election in the United States was obviously a one-time-only event. Since science develops knowledge by constant replication of observations over time, some traditionalists would argue that the method of science cannot be used to develop knowledge about such unique events.

Free Will

Other traditionalists argue that the search for scientific generalizations concerning human behavior is not just difficult, it is meaningless because regularities of behavior do not exist. Science rests on a fundamental assumption of determinism. Determinism refers to a belief that everything has a cause. The fundamental goal of the scientific method is to identify patterns of cause and effect. Some traditionalists would argue that human behavior is not governed by such patterns of cause and effect. Rather, they argue, humans have a free will and that freedom of choice means that human behavior cannot be classified.

Human Reaction

Other traditionalists point to another problem associated with human nature. Numerous studies have demonstrated that when people become the focus of study, they behave differently. This is the case with experiments, as noted above, but it also applies to any means of data gathering. This means that the existence of the study becomes another of those multiple variables which affect human behavior, and one which cannot be controlled. It also means that observations, which lie at the base of the scientific method, will be useless since what is observed will not reflect normal patterns of human behavior.

Fact–Value Distinction

As we said before, science has traditionally been based on the belief that there is a logical distinction between fact statements and value statements. Critiques of that distinction have been made by philosophers who argue that fact and value are not as separate as Hume argued they were. Traditionalists have argued that it is especially impossible to keep facts and values separate when studying politics. They feel it is misleading to claim to be value-free when there are value premises underlying analyses of politics. To prove their claim, traditionalists have pointed to many studies which have claimed to be free of values but which have really been based on value premises, such as democracy is good, or countries should follow the western model of development.[26] Traditionalists would argue that to claim such studies are value free is to be guilty of false advertising.

Not all traditionalists agree among themselves on all of these criticisms of the use of science, nor do they agree about the role of science in studying politics any more than do the behavioralists concerning the uses of science. There are some traditionalists who argue that science has no relevance at all to politics, as there are some behavioralists who believe the method of science can be used without limit to study politics. But there are many political scientists who take positions between these polar extremes

---

26. Christian Bay, "Politics and Pseudopolitics: A Critical Evaluation of Some Behavioral Literature," *The American Political Science Review,* 59 (1965).

and who cannot be easily classified as either traditionalist or behavioralist. Many feel the method of science can be used to study politics, but only in a modified and limited way. Others feel science can and should be used, but only to study certain aspects of political phenomena rather than all of politics. Many traditionalists argue that the scientific method is only applicable for trivial questions. Others claim the method of science is not applicable to politics, but politics can be studied by methods which, though different, are just as scientific as the standard scientific method. For example, they often urge that rather than trying to understand political behavior by observation, political scientists should try essentially to "get inside the head" of others and understand behavior "from the actor's own frame of reference."[27]

These, in brief, are some of the various positions on the extent to which science can, and should be, used to study politics. We will now conclude this chapter by rebutting some of the traditionalists' criticisms of the use of science and by attempting to justify our focus in this book on the use of scientific methods to study politics.

DEFENSE OF "SCIENTIFIC" POLITICAL SCIENCE

Let us begin this defense with a discussion of one criticism which we cannot logically rebut: the argument that human behavior is the result of free will rather than of patterned cause–effect relationships. This argument rests on an *assumption* of free will, as the philosophy of science rests on the assumption of determinism. These assumptions cannot be proven, or disproven, empirically. As Hume pointed out, there is no way to prove causation empirically. Therefore, it is impossible to prove causation exists in human behavior. It is also impossible to prove the *absence* of those causes since our lack of knowledge of them does not prove they do not exist.

We feel, however, that there is good reason for accepting the assumption of science that there are causes for our behavior. To show you why we feel that way let us first consider in slightly greater depth the concept of free will. Free will basically refers to the ability of humans to be free in choosing their actions. There is no reason, however, to believe that because we are free to choose, we exercise that choice randomly. If you think about it, we think you will realize that we actually live our lives in accordance with the scientific assumption of determinism. For example, you are not required by law to attend college. You have in a sense made a free choice to extend your education. Presumably, although that was a free choice, it was not random. You probably thought that going to college would bring about, or cause,

---

27. Robert Bogdan and Steven J. Taylor, *Introduction to Qualitative Research Methods* (New York: John Wiley, 1975), p. 2.

some desired effect, such as increasing your chances to get a good job, increasing your enjoyment of life, or increasing your parents' satisfaction with you and getting them off your back.

If only because we do try to order our lives, it can be shown empirically that there are patterns and regularities in human behavior. We may not be able to prove those patterns involve causation, but we can further our understanding of human behavior by searching for and verifying the existence of those patterns. Any study of human behavior which did not assume such patterning could never go beyond the stage of recording every action as a separate and unique event, an exercise which we feel would not be particularly useful.

The charge that science is not useful as a method because of human free will is a criticism unique to the social sciences. The other criticisms by the traditionalists deal with problems which face all scientists. Human behavior is undoubtedly complex but, as we argued before, the subject matter of other disciplines is also complex. We would not doubt it is possible to study chemistry scientifically, despite the fact that there is much that is still not known about chemistry, and the subject matter is extremely complex. Chemistry, as a discipline, has been in existence for a much longer time than has the scientific study of politics. Much of what is now known about chemistry would have been considered impossible by alchemists, the early ancestors of modern chemists, who labored unsuccessfully to turn iron into gold. No discipline can expect total understanding instantly. The point is, the unknown always seems impossible, but there is no logical reason for concluding that because something is difficult to unravel, it is therefore impossible.

Political scientists are also not alone in having to deal with events which do not recur. For example, geologists who study earthquakes face the same problem. Although any individual event, such as the San Francisco earthquake, may not recur, earthquakes are relatively common. Geologists can increase their understanding of unique occurrences of earthquakes by observing other earthquakes. Similarly, political scientists can increase their understanding of the 1976 election by gathering data on other elections as they occur.

Political scientists, of course, are more limited than are chemists in their ability to set up experiments to control other factors besides those on which they are focusing. This simply means that political scientists must be more creative in developing other techniques to examine the effect of multiple variables. We will discuss some of those techniques in Part Four.

The problem of the effect of the study on what is being studied is obviously more serious when dealing with humans than when dealing with atoms or gases. Yet other scientists also have to be concerned about the effect of measurements they take in the process of their research. For example, measuring the temperature of matter can affect the temperature, however slightly. And Pavlov noted that the reactions of the dogs which were the subject of his research on stimulus–response were affected by such things as blinking or movement of the eyes of the researchers.[28] Again, it may be difficult to overcome the reactions of humans to the process of being studied, but that does not mean it is useless to try. In the chapter on gathering data we will point out ways of designing surveys and conducting observations to try to minimize the effect of the study itself on those being studied (see Chapter Eight).

Finally, let us once again consider the role of values. Humans have values, be they scientists or not, and those values will affect their observations of the world around them. As we pointed out before, all scientists must be aware of this. However, this is not an impossible barrier to science. The scientific method has actually been designated as an attempt to minimize the extent to which the values of scientists result in bias in their interpretation of the world around them. Constant observation over time of different sets of data by different scientists is necessary before a generalization is accepted by a scientific community as law. That comparison of observation and accumulation of experience is designated to control the effect of each individual's values.

To study politics scientifically does not mean that political scientists must never evaluate or prescribe. As the postbehavioralists argue, it is possible to combine the scientific study of politics with a concern for questions of value. Fundamental to prescription and evaluation is an accurate understanding of what patterns and regularities exist. Before prescribing how society should change it is necessary to know what society is like at the moment and what changes (causes) will produce the desired results (effects). Science, in this view, is not opposed to values but is a fundamental prerequisite to any evaluation or prescription based on values.

SUMMARY

In summary, we feel the traditionalists are perfectly correct in arguing that studying politics scientifically is difficult. Yet we do not feel that this means studying politics scientifically is impossible. Actually we feel that in many ways we all use a very simple form of the scientific method to gain an understanding of the world around us. To gain that understanding we observe our world and try to construct in our minds some vision of order and pattern. We do not act as though we believe life is random. Once we have some image of what we believe to be the pattern in the world, we try to check, or verify, that image by comparing it to continued observations.

In these ways our relations with our world do not differ from those of a scientist. The major difference between the methods which we normally use

---

28. Ivan Petrovich Pavlov, *Essential Works of Pavlov*, ed. by Michael Kaplan (New York: Bantam Book, 1966), pp. 108–9.

to try to understand and cope with the empirical world and the methods scientists use is the standards scientists establish for themselves to determine when something can be accepted as truth. To a scientist, truth can only be established by a slow and tortuous process of accumulating evidence. Laymen may observe, conclude, check once, and settle for life on certain conclusions. Scientists on the other hand are bound to the process of constant testing and checking of their initial conclusions.

In addition, scientists recognize that any individual's observations, numerous though they may be, are not sufficiently adequate to verify a scientific law. They are very aware of the fact that the empirical world is complex, that individual values can affect observations. Therefore, science also demands that knowledge can only be verified by agreement among a community of scholars. This means that scientists are bound to communicate clearly and precisely how they conducted their observations of the world around them.

Therefore, they must define and operationalize their concepts, specify how they gathered their data, and make clear what standards they used to determine if the data supported their hypothesis. Such clear, precise communication makes it possible for others to conduct their own observations and to see if they agree about the truth of the hypothesis. It is by such methods that science attempts to move beyond the way each of us individually tries to understand the world around us. The goal of science is to build a precise network of communication which makes it possible to compare experiences and to accumulate evidence to support, or to refute, hypotheses about the patterns in the empirical world. As we have said before, the scientific method, while not perfect, is the most rigorous way yet devised to develop knowledge and understanding of the empirical world.

In the first chapter we briefly considered the sort of topics which have been the focus of research by political scientists. In this chapter we have considered the fundamental debate concerning what methods should be used to study politics. There is still one more fundamental issue about political research which must be raised. That issue, which is the subject of Chapter Three, concerns the ethics of research on politics.

STUDY QUESTIONS

1. Describe the standard view of the scientific method.
2. Provide and define a list of concepts which would help you organize information about elections.
3. List five generalizations about the U.S. Government. Are any of these laws? Hypotheses?
4. To say political scientists are engaged in building theories sounds as though they are only involved in academic or "ivory tower" concerns. Can you imagine ways in which political theory, as we have defined it, could be useful in the "real world"? Give examples.

5. Can political scientists produce deductive theories? Why or why not? Are there other opinions?
6. The following ideas lie at the heart of the controversy concerning the ability to be scientific in political science. Discuss the debates involved in the following ideas:
   a. causation/free will
   b. fact–value dichotomy
   c. complexity
   d. observer interference
7. In light of the various critiques of the standard view of the scientific method, what are the strengths and weaknesses of this approach? On balance, do *you* think we can or should try to be scientific?
8. Eugene Meehan argues that you should not throw out politics in the search for science. What does he mean by this? In other words, what are the pitfalls of trying to be too scientific?

Ethical Issues in Political Analysis

Chapter Three

Research on politics, like any research which affects human beings, raises questions concerning ethics. There is no easy answer to the question of what is ethical and what is unethical in research. In this chapter, we will not be able to give you any final answers or absolute standards. What we will attempt to do is to make you aware of, and sensitive to, some of the major ethical problems which must be considered in performing research. Before we can discuss the problems of being ethical we should attempt to define ethics and to consider in what areas political scientists must be concerned about ethical questions.

ETHICS AND POLITICAL RESEARCH

In general, to be ethical means that one conforms to moral standards of conduct. However, this does not get us very far in understanding precisely what is ethical conduct. The problem is that there is no single, universal moral standard of conduct to which all humans adhere. What is moral is determined by agreement, and the agreement differs in different places and at different times. For example, different cultures have different accepted standards of conduct. In Eskimo society it would be considered unethical for a husband not to offer his wife to a male guest. In our society, this would certainly be considered a violation of moral standards of conduct. Another example of varying ethics would be the treatment of criminals. The standard punishment for robbery under Islamic law is to have one's hand cut off. In our legal system, such mutilation would be considered unethical.

You are all probably aware of such differences in ethical standards in different cultures. However, you should also be aware that the boundaries of ethical behavior are not always clear, even within a single culture. For example, people in the United States disagree on the ethics of cheating on income taxes or of taking a long lunch hour. The basic point is that what is ethical is relative. There are no absolute standards. It is this relativity of ethics which complicates attempts by humans to behave ethically and also plagues the attempt by researchers to be sure their behavior (conducting research) is ethical.

Let us consider the three general areas in which ethical issues arise in political science research. First, there are questions concerning the relationship between the researcher and the people who are participants in the study. Some people may feel that any attempt to study humans scientifically is unethical. Scientists would discount such complaints. The ultimate goal of the discipline of political science is to develop knowledge about politics. The scientific method is a powerful tool for developing knowledge, and there is no reason why political scientists should not avail themselves of it. However, if the scientific method is to be used, it is vitally important that researchers take great care in assuring that the procedures used be ethical. We should point out that concern about the relationship between the researcher and the subject of research is not a unique problem of political scientists. Consider the problems which medical researchers face in determining the effects of various drugs on humans.

A second area in which ethical issues arise is the relationship between researchers and the scientific community of which they are a part. Research is supposed to be directed toward accumulating evidence concerning the accuracy of hypothesized relationships in an attempt to build and test theory. Researchers, although they may work individually, are, therefore, only a part of a broader communal effort. Researchers must realize this and be concerned about maintaining ethical relationships with the community of scientists.

Finally, researchers must be concerned about ethical issues concerning the impact of their research on society as a whole. Political research must affect humans not only because it uses them as subjects, but also because the findings of research will certainly have implications for future human behavior. The topics of political research include such fundamentally important issues as war or peace and freedom or tyranny. The question of whether the research findings are used for constructive or destructive purposes is, thus, not an insignificant concern, but a question which involves the welfare of us all. Now let us examine some of the ethical issues which arise in each of the three areas we listed.

RELATIONSHIP WITH SUBJECTS

There are two ethical guidelines which are supposed to govern the relationship between the researcher and the individuals who are the subjects of the research. The first guideline specifies that the participation in research should be voluntary. The second specifies that no harm should be caused to the subjects as a result of participation in the research. Most people, we presume, would tend to feel these are reasonable guidelines. But even if it were possible to get universal agreement on these principles, the dilemmas of the researcher would not be automatically resolved since there are always "gray" areas. Let us look at some of the issues which may arise under each of these guidelines.

Presumably, we would all agree that obvious use of force to assure participation in a research project would be wrong. On the other hand, you should realize that this goal of allowing subjects to determine if they will participate conflicts with a basic goal of science—to develop general knowledge about the empirical world. Because it is not possible to observe all of that world at one time, we must instead be content to examine subsets, or *samples*. Since we want to use these samples to be as representative as possible of the whole population you should realize that the ethical goal of making participation in research voluntary conflicts with the goal of science to include as many subjects as possible and to assure there is no systematic bias in the kinds of people who are included.

Because of this conflict, scientists may at times consider using information on people or gathering that information without the knowledge or consent of those involved. Before researchers make their decision they should consider two questions: (1) How does the value of the research compare to the rights of the individuals being used? This is an obvious example of trying to compare apples and oranges, but it is a question which should be considered; (2) What is the possibility that the research could in some way harm the individuals? Obviously, voluntary participation is more crucial in research where harm could come to the participants.

If the researcher plans to gather information directly from the subjects, the people have the option of refusing to cooperate, unless, of course, the researcher plans to beat the subjects into submission. There are some instances, though, where the use of force is more subtle and may potentially result in involuntary participation. Consider, for example, the case of professors using the students in their classes as subjects. No matter how careful a professor might be about emphasizing that participation is voluntary, there would always be the possibility that some students would feel that refusal to participate would somehow affect their grades. The same sense of subtle pressure may arise with the use of any "captive audience," especially if the researcher has any form of authority over that audience. We should remember that whether or not consent is obtained we should be sensitive to the participant's right of privacy. Where one is an unknowing participant the issue may be quite serious, as discussed in the Humphrey study below. Even when informed consent is given, we should realize that we ask individuals in the name of science to share aspects of their lives which are sometimes quite embarrassing and intimate. Therefore, we must try to minimize any potential discomfort to the participant.

There are other instances where a researcher could focus on people without their knowledge or consent. One way that a researcher could use people in research without their knowledge is to use existing data. For example, in this age of computerized data storage, there are voluminous files available on most of us. The political researcher must consider if it is ethical to make use of those files without the knowledge and consent of the individuals. To use the files without contacting those people would obviously mean their "participation" would be involuntary. On the other hand, there would probably be a real temptation to use that data without contacting the individuals. For one thing, consider the practical, logistical problems of tracking down these people to secure their permission. The other reason why researchers might be tempted to use the data, as we indicated before, is to avoid the possibility that there might be some systematic pattern to the refusals and acceptances. This pattern might result in creating a bias in the results of the study.

Another source of existing data may be various written records or documents. In many cases, researchers are only interested in such records if they were produced by public figures. Such people presumably would be aware of the potential examination of such records by researchers, and, therefore, the release of the information may be considered equivalent to agreeing to participate in research. Yet it is still possible that public figures would not have been willing to release such documents if they knew exactly what use would be made of them by researchers. In this case, the right of the individual to privacy must be weighed against social value of the research.

Another way to gather data on people without their being aware they are the subject of research is by observation. Researchers must decide if they will tell the people involved that they are the focus of a research project. There is no doubt that if they are not told they are part of a research project their participation in that project is termed involuntary. Yet there are several problems which may arise if the people are consulted. First there is the perennial problem that there might be some pattern in the kinds of people who would agree to take part.

Also, there are some kinds of activity which could very probably not be observed if people were asked to volunteer. An example of research which very probably would not have been conducted if the norm of voluntary participation had been followed is Laud Humphreys' study of homosexual conduct.[1] Humphreys frequented public restrooms and offered to be a lookout while others engaged in homosexual activity. He would then track down these individuals and, in disguise, interview them in their homes to gather background information. This study resulted in an ethical furor. Critics argued that he had been guilty of deceit and invasion of privacy. Others, however, saw the research as a creative way of providing information which probably could not be gathered in any other way. Again, the value of the research must be weighed against the ethics of the way the information was gathered.

Another problem which must be considered in deciding whether to inform people they are being observed as a part of a research project is that those who know they are being observed tend to behave differently than they normally would. This tendency is known as the "Hawthorne effect" since it was first documented in studies done at General Electric's Hawthorne plant.[2] The focus of the research was the effect of lighting on the efficiency of workers. Researchers found that an increase in light increased the workers' efficiency. The researchers continued to increase the light with resulting increases in efficiency. Then they *decreased* the light and once again the efficiency increased. The point is that the workers, aware they were being observed, altered their behavior.

All this means that trying to adhere to the ethical principle of voluntary participation in research to be conducted by observation may result in biased research findings, or no research findings at all. This is so because there may be some pattern in the kinds of people who agree to participate; those who participate may behave differently because they know they are part of a research project, and probably few, if any, people would agree to permit some kinds of behavior to be observed.

There is a final issue we want to raise concerning the responsibility of a researcher to use voluntary participants. This issue concerns the responsibility of a researcher to be completely honest and thorough in explaining the purpose of the research before requesting subjects' participation. Telling people exactly what the purpose of the research is may either make them unwilling to participate or may affect how they behave if they do participate. Yet not telling them is actually securing their agreement under false pretenses.

An example of the use of such false pretenses and of the problems which can arise was research which was performed by Stanley Milgram.[3] Partici-

---

1. Laud Humphreys, *Tearoom Trade: Impersonal Sex in Public Places* (Chicago: Aldine, 1970).
2. F. J. Roethlisberger and William J. Dickson, *Management and the Worker* (Cambridge, Mass: Harvard University Press, 1939).
3. Stanley Milgram, "Behavioral Study of Obedience," *Journal of Abnormal and Social Psychology*, 67 (1963), 371–8; and Stanley Milgram, "Some Conditions of Obedience and Disobedience to Authority," *Human Relations,* 18 (1965), 57–76.

pants in Milgram's experiments were told that they would be taking part in a learning experiment and agreed on that basis. In actuality they were participating in an experiment investigating humans' obedience to authority. Under such circumstances it is questionable how truly voluntary their participation was.

The Milgram experiments also raised issues concerning the second ethical guideline we proposed: that no harm should come to the participants. Let us briefly consider the issue of harm and then examine in what ways the Milgram experiments raised ethical issues concerning the harm caused to participants. The issue of harm must be considered very broadly. It is obvious that the researcher should not inflict serious physical pain. What is serious, however, becomes a subjective question. We would probably all agree that breaking a person's arm would be considered to be in poor taste! But is it also unethical to administer a tiny electric shock? Researchers should also be aware of the possibility that research could cause participants psychological harm. By placing people in stressful situations researchers could conceivably cause permanent psychological damage.

One way that harm may be mitigated or minimized is by debriefing the participant. Here you should make clear why any questionable practices (if any) were introduced, how their participation was essential, and what good you expect to result from the study. Let us look at some ways in which research may result in harm to the participants.

First we will return to a discussion of the Milgram experiments.[4] The participants in the Milgram study were placed at a console which they were told would allow them to administer electric shocks to individuals in another room. They were instructed to administer a shock every time the individual in the next room gave an incorrect response to a question. The incorrect answers would be indicated by a light on the control panel since the volunteer could not see the individual in the next room. The volunteer was told to increase the voltage of the shock into a range which was clearly specified to be dangerous. Despite screaming, kicking, begging, and so forth from the other room, a majority of the participants continued to administer the shocks. In case you hadn't guessed, the "shocks" were not real and the sound effects were a part of the experiment.

As we said above, the real purpose of the experiment was to examine human obedience to authority and the results of the experiment showed that people will do just about anything if an authority figure issues a command. But the participants did not obey eagerly. Most asked to be allowed to stop. Many exhibited symptoms of considerable psychological trauma during what was obviously an ordeal to them. Was this research ethical? Hitler's Germany and some American incidents in Vietnam indicate the serious consequences of blind obedience. The question of human obedience is,

---

4. Ibid.

therefore, certainly a significant issue for study. Yet each of us should consider for ourselves if the value of such research outweighs any possible psychological harm which might have been done to the participants.

Ethical questions often arise in attempts such as Milgram's to study human behavior by experimentation. For example, if we wanted to determine if good nutrition resulted in improved learning skills, we would have to deprive (or at least not provide) some people of a nutritious diet to see if there is a difference in learning between those with good and those with bad nutrition. Is it ethical to be sure that some remain undernourished so this test can be performed? Our example of nutrition may be extreme, but in general, experiments will involve choosing some people to be used as guinea pigs. This will mean doing something to them which may be potentially harmful or depriving them of something which may be potentially beneficial. Ethical issues will constantly arise in such activity.

Partially because of such ethical dilemmas, experiments are not frequently used to study politics. However, questions of possible harm also arise in other forms of data gathering. For example, the use of questionnaires may potentially cause some psychological damage to those who have participated and later read reports of the study. Even if they are not named they may find that those who responded as they did were classified as bigoted or ignorant, or whatever. This may affect their self-esteem. The possibility of harm may also arise in studies based on observation, especially if the observer is participating in the activity. The observer's actions may affect the behavior of the others. At times, this may be equivalent to manipulation by the observer which, if discovered by the others, may be seen as a threat to their human freedom and dignity.

A major source of potential harm to the participants in research is the possibility that what they do or say may become public or cause repercussions. For example, if you were doing a study of marijuana usage (an illegal act) and you reported the names of those who smoked pot you would be placing them in a position which could result in legal harm. The point is that the findings of research should be reported in a way to preserve the anonymity of your subjects. Oftentimes a study will not use names to help protect the privacy of the participants. Even here you must be very careful. A thinly disguised identity can become quite clear to many, with all the potential for embarrassment or harm. Of course it would not be unethical to report the names of participants if they have initially been warned that "anything they say may be held against them." Yet under such circumstances participants are likely to be less than candid and the results of the study may therefore be invalid.

Respondents are likely to be most candid when no one, not even the researcher, knows how they responded. This is of course impossible in any kind of research where the researcher and the participant have a personal contact. It may, however, be possible if a survey is mailed to respondents. It is possible to set up a mailed survey so the returned questionnaires can in no way be traced to the individual respondents. This provides maximum anonymity to the participants.

This anonymity, however, makes it impossible for the researcher to follow-up if information is missing or to relate the information on the questionnaire to other data on the individuals. One major eastern university tried "to have its cake and eat it too" by both assuring complete anonymity and also using a code to identify the respondent. In a study of cheating, the school mailed out a questionnaire which the students were to fill out and then return in a self-addressed, stamped envelope. It turned out that under the stamp was a code used to identify the respondent. Such a procedure obviously involves questionable ethics.

In this section we have considered some ethical issues which arise in the relationship between researchers and the people who are the focus of research. What we have considered is the responsibility the researcher has to those research participants. In an attempt to ensure this responsibility, many universities have established committees to screen experiments which might produce harmful effects on the participants. It is also the case that researchers have a responsibility to the community of scholars of which they are a part. Let us consider some of the ethical issues concerning the relationship of researchers with the scientific community.

RELATIONSHIP WITH THE SCIENTIFIC COMMUNITY

The major guideline concerning the relationship of researchers with the scientific community is that of *objectivity*. Research should be presented and received in an unbiased manner. As we noted before, one of the tenets of scientific research is that the scientist should be a neutral observer and interpreter of the world around him. We have also pointed out that others have questioned the ability of man to be totally objective. Even the decision to use science as a methodology entails a set of assumptions which affect perceptions. Perceptions, therefore, are influenced by the values of science. Yet science is directed toward the goal of minimizing the extent to which values can result in bias in research findings which will lead to inaccurate understanding of the empirical world.

There are two aspects of researchers' responsibility in achieving objectivity. First researchers must report their research completely and accurately. This helps to maximize objectivity by permitting other researchers to evaluate the techniques and conclusions and possibly even to replicate the study to determine if the values of the initial researcher biased the conclusions. A second aspect of the responsibility of scientists to be objective is that they must constantly evaluate new evidence and new theories in a fair, unbiased manner. Let us consider both of these aspects in greater depth.

The first aspect of objectivity refers to the fact that all stages in the research process should be clearly specified. This way others will be able to determine if they think the researcher's values in any way affected choices made in selecting samples, techniques, etc. The research should be specified so clearly that other researchers could replicate the research. Such replication by other researchers is the most effective way science tries to guard against the bias of individual researchers. If different researchers perform the same research and reach the same conclusions then confidence in the findings is increased.

Also, all research findings should be reported, even negative findings which do not support the research hypothesis. The purpose of the research is to gather evidence to determine if a hypothesized relationship accurately reflects the patterns found in the real world. Evidence that such a relationship does not exist is as important to the scientific process of accumulating information as is evidence that it does exist.

It should be obvious that it is considered highly unethical to tamper with the research findings. There really are ways to "lie with statistics." We hope that by the time you finish Part Four of this book you will be better equipped to avoid such attempts. Yet the point is that there still are ways to present arguments and data to give a false impression to the reader. Such deceit only impedes progress toward the ultimate goal of furthering our understanding of the empirical world. Unfortunately the urge to do whatever is necessary to report positive findings is often encouraged by the tendency of journals to only publish such reports and to likewise exclude reports of research which do not indicate positive support for the hypothesis being tested.

A second aspect of researchers' responsibility to the scientific community is the willingness of all researchers to give fair consideration to all new research findings. Too often a given theory is given a status virtually equivalent to God-given law. Scientists may begin to believe it is unquestionable. This, of course, is totally contrary to the basic belief of science that relationships must be constantly verified. When some theory or law becomes so inviolate, contrary evidence is likely to be ignored. It is this tendency to ignore certain findings which forms the basis of Kuhn's critique of the standard view of science.[5]

There are, unfortunately, many examples of new findings being ignored by the community of scientists because the findings conflicted with the established view of reality. For example, Copernicus was labeled as a heretic in the 16th century because he went against accepted theories of astronomy. He argued that the earth revolved around the sun and not vice versa. It took many years and much scientific and personal abuse before his ideas were accepted by the "objective" scientific establishment. Times have not changed

---

5. Thomas S. Kuhn, *The Structure of Scientific Revolutions,* 2nd ed. (Chicago: University of Chicago Press, 1970).

all that much for those who have attacked accepted scientific dogma, as the example of Dr. Immanuel Velikovsky illustrates. Dr. Velikovsky was a respected scientist in 1950 when he published a book called *Worlds in Collision*. In this book he challenged existing theories of astronomy, geology, and biology. His theories challenged Newton and Darwin among others. The reaction in the scientific community was far from an objective evaluation. His research was denounced by many who admitted they had never read his work, and he and his few followers were shunned by their colleagues. His work was classified by many as science fiction. This image was buttressed by the fact that much of his work was published in popular, rather than scholarly, journals.

Of course, it is conceivable that his articles were rejected solely on their scientific merits. This seems unlikely, though, since Velikovsky's publisher was at one point threatened with a boycott by the scientific community.[6] Regardless of the merits of his work, it seems that his thesis was not met with dispassionate skepticism. This reaction hardly seems ethical and is a severe threat to objective reporting of research findings. If incidents like this become more widespread people may be unwilling to report findings which would move the discipline forward by challenging the status quo.

Another threat to objectivity in reporting findings is the necessity to obtain funding. Few significant research efforts can be mounted and pursued by individuals alone. Social scientists rely heavily on government and private foundations for grants to do research. It is hard to be objective if you know your findings may alienate a source of funding. Being ethical is often hard, but if ideas are not pursued and findings not accurately reported we cannot advance our knowledge, and we may, in fact, move in the wrong direction.

This last point concerning the relationship between research findings and the values of funding agencies is related to a final area where ethical issues of research become relevant: the question of how research findings are used—or abused—in society. Let us now consider this final area of ethical issues.

RELATIONSHIP WITH SOCIETY

There are three ethical issues which arise in the relationship between scientists and the larger society of which they are a part. First, there is the concern that since science studies what *is*, not what *ought to be*, scientific research, therefore, implicitly supports the status quo. Secondly, there is the fear that knowledge of human behavior produced by scientific research would give

---

6. Alfred de Grazia, and others, *The Velikovsky Affair* (New Hyde Park, N.Y.: University Books, 1966), pp. 1-2.

some people the means of controlling and manipulating others. Finally, the most fundamental question concerns what use will be made of the research findings and whether scientists have any responsibility concerning what use is made of the research. Let us consider each of these concerns in turn.

First, does science provide support for the status quo? To answer this, it is important to realize that the knowledge produced by scientific research is neutral. The knowledge does describe and explain the status quo, yet that knowledge may include information about trends in society. There will certainly be information about patterns and relationships. By understanding these things in the present world, we should surely be in a better position to predict what the future will be and to prescribe ways to alter that future. The knowledge which science produces about the present, then, can be used to affect the future if society should so desire.

This last point raises the second concern about the use of scientific research. Is it possible that scientific research opens the way for a controlled society? It is important to realize that it is the knowledge of human behavior that creates the potential of control. If one were to subscribe to this fear, the logical response should be to dismantle all social studies since their goal is to develop knowledge about human behavior, and all such knowledge may be used for control. Knowledge of political behavior could be used to end war as well as it could be used to create a repressive totalitarian political system.

The point again is that knowledge about causes and effects of human behavior is neutral. The fundamental ethical question facing scientists, then, is what is their responsibility concerning the utilization of the information. In that sense, then, the question of the use of knowledge either to support the status quo or to manipulate people becomes a special aspect of the third concern of the researchers' relationship with society: the possibility that the knowledge produced will be used in ways contrary to the desires of the scientist who performed the research. What is the responsibility to society of scientists who conduct research which produces unpopular findings or findings which could potentially be used by those whose values are contrary to those of the scientists? Scientists' responsibility to the community of scholars would dictate the quest for knowledge and the complete reporting of all research findings. On the other hand, the responsibility of scientists to the larger society may seem to dictate just the opposite: suppression of the research. Let us look at an actual example of such an ethical dilemma.

James Coleman conducted a study to investigate the relationship between educational opportunity and race. What he found was that there was little difference in the performance of blacks in integrated as opposed to segregated schools. He also found that higher expenditures on schools seemed to have little impact on improving the performance of children. It should be quite clear that such research could be used to oppose both efforts to increase racial integration in the schools and to increase government expenditure on schools. Coleman also found that the most important determinant of school success was the level of motivation which was affected by the family and the composition of the student body.[7]

The first question raised by Coleman's study is whether or not these findings should be reported when they may obviously be used in ways to oppose the goal of racial equality in the schools. This dilemma is by no means unique to social scientists. A similar problem faced nuclear scientists whose research findings led to the development of the most destructive weapon yet known to man—the atomic bomb. In fact, American scientists worked eagerly on the development of the bomb to assure what they saw as an unquestionably desirable goal: American victory in the Second World War. Therefore, they never questioned releasing the information to the government. Only when the bomb was used on the cities of Hiroshima and Nagasaki did some of the researchers become concerned about the ethical implications of what they had done. This research illustrates again the problem of establishing absolute ethical standards for research.

A second question which is raised by Coleman's study is whether the researcher has a responsibility to interpret the findings and to prescribe policy. Because of the finding that the motivation and capability of a child's peers was an important determinant of school success, and despite the fact that black children did only slightly better in integrated schools, Coleman recommended busing to achieve school integration. He later admitted this advice was bad because, in part, of the unexpected political and social furor. Perhaps the most abject example of the excesses of scientists prescribing for society is that of William Shockley. Shockley, a Nobel Laureate in physics, studied racial genetics and concluded blacks were inferior to whites. On the basis of this finding, by no means accepted by other scientists, Shockley recommended sterilization of those with low I.Q.'s, primarily blacks.[8]

The postbehavioralists in political science would argue that it is the responsibility of scientists to prescribe for society because of their superior knowledge in their specific area of expertise. For example, they may provide information concerning which policy alternatives will be most likely to achieve a certain goal. While not refuting that argument, we feel both the Coleman and the Shockley examples indicate some of the problems that arise in trying to prescribe. Scientists should ask themselves if they are sure they know enough to prescribe action which will vitally affect the lives of others. The fact that scientific findings never "prove" anything and most social science laws are at best probabilistic underscores this dilemma.

We have considered if scientists should report findings which may be used in ways contrary to their own values or contrary to the values of the

---

7. James S. Coleman, and others, *Equality of Educational Opportunity* (Washington, D.C.: U.S. Government Printing Office, 1966).
8. Berkeley Rice, "The High Cost of Thinking the Unthinkable," *Psychology Today,* 6 (December, 1973), 89–93.

dominant society and if the scientist should interpret the findings and prescribe for society. Let us now consider if scientists should even conduct research if the results may be used in an undesirable way.

During the 1960s the Department of Defense awarded a contract to American University to study the causes of, and the means to, deter revolutions. This study was known as Project Camelot. On its face this sounds like a highly significant and ethical project designed to prevent war. However, at the time the project gained attention, charges were made that findings would be used by the government for counterinsurgency in Latin America. A major controversy ensued and the project was disbanded.[9] Is it ethical to disband such potentially useful research just because of the fear that the results may be misused?

SUMMARY

As you can see, there are some serious and complex dilemmas regarding the relationship between scientists and society. There are no easy or absolute answers to the question of what is the responsibility of scientists for the use made of research findings just as there are no easy and absolute answers to any of the ethical dilemmas we raised in this chapter. We hope, however, we have made you more aware of the ethical concerns which are inevitably part of any scientific research, and that you will, therefore, be more sensitive to such issues in your own research.

Devising ethical standards for research often comes down to a balance between the value of the research and the possible negative consequences of the research in terms of its harm to the participants and its potential for misuse. Research is valuable if it facilitates our understanding of human behavior, makes a positive contribution toward solving societal problems, or aids the research participant.[10] This is to be balanced against physical and psychological harm as well as the invasion of privacy of participants. In addition, the researcher must consider possible negative consequences for the society. These ethical issues are not major problems in all research. In most cases, negative effects will be slight. Only by being sensitive to those negative aspects, though, can we make certain that what we wish to do is basically ethical and that we have minimized any negative consequences.

With this in mind we can proceed to Part Two which will discuss the state of the art of political science or how far our scientific research has taken us. Parts Three and Four will deal with the techniques needed to further our knowledge—in an ethical manner, we hope.

---

9. Irving Louis Horowitz, *The Rise and Fall of Project Camelot* (Cambridge, Mass.: M.I.T. Press, 1967).
10. Stuart W. Cook, "Ethical Issues in the Conduct of Research in Social Relations," in *Research Methods in Social Relations*, 3rd ed., ed. Claire Selltiz, and others (New York: Holt, Rinehard & Winston, 1976), p. 235.

STUDY QUESTIONS

1. Why is it not always possible to get informed consent of research subjects, and what ethical dilemmas does that create?
2. In what ways might research create psychological harm for participants and how might it be minimized?
3. Were the studies by Humphreys and Milgram ethically justifiable? Defend your position.
4. Discuss the problems of objectivity in doing and evaluating research.
5. What is the scientist's responsibility to society in considering the implications of his study?
6. Under what conditions is it ethical for political scientists to use their research to make policy prescriptions?
7. Develop a "code of ethics" for the political researcher.

Conceptual Analysis

Part Two

Political scientists, like other scientists, can't just sit down on a nice summer's day and produce theories. They, like the rest of us, can produce fine schemes and logical patterns in their minds. But science is empirical, and scientific theories must explain the real world which often does not appear to be very logical. So all scientists, including political scientists, must plod along slowly toward the goal of understanding.

Science produces few instant discoveries. More likely the "instant" discovery is the process of finally being able to fit together the apparently random pieces of prior discoveries as one would fit together pieces of a large and very complex jigsaw puzzle in new and more meaningful ways. Science, thus, is cumulative. Each discovery builds on prior knowledge and becomes the basis for more advancement in the future. To many, therefore, scientific discovery is often exciting only in looking back, not at the stage of plodding, seemingly randomly, toward some insight or discovery. To those with patience and some foresight, this plodding is a bearable cost because the potential benefits are great. Keep this in mind as you read through the next chapters which examine research by political scientists aimed at theory building.

There is a parable which states that the longest journey begins with a single step, and so it is with research. In scientific theory building, that first step is in many ways the biggest one. We should not begin by impetuously collecting data right and left, but rather we should consider the problem to be investigated in depth. Good research, as we argued, is not just application of a particular technique but is derived from the process of building theory. So, to commence a research project, you should begin by examining what you believe to be regularities among various phenomena. This examination should be guided from the start by concepts which will focus your attention to a particular aspect of the problem. Concepts structure one's thoughts and form the foundation for the research to come. It is around this first step in theory building, which is also the first step in research, that this section of the book is organized.

There are, of course, a multitude of concepts which may facilitate an understanding of political phenomena. We have used two criteria in the selection of concepts to be included. In the first place we have attempted to select concepts which are used most frequently by political scientists. Secondly, we have chosen concepts which we feel are useful in trying to answer the three basic questions vital to the understanding of political phenomena. The first question is, "What is the setting for politics?" or "What are the attitudes and values of the general public, how are these learned, and what are the consequences?" The second question is, "What is the nature of political interactions?" In other words, we want to know what is the process of politics. Lastly, we wish to know, "What are the results of political activity?"

In order to understand a political event it is necessary to seek answers to all three questions, not just one, although any one question can provide a focal point for political research. We should proceed by investigating a political situation from as many angles as possible in order to get a complete picture. Political phenomena are very complex. To attempt to understand such complex events by looking at only one aspect, or one concept, would be as hopeless as a blind man attempting to describe an elephant after touching only one part of its body. If he were to touch the elephant's trunk, he would have a far different picture than if he had touched the ears. Only by feeling the entire elephant can he begin to get an accurate picture.

By examining various concepts often used by political scientists we hope to be able to show you some of the perspectives from which a given political phenomenon can be viewed.

It should be stated that the number of concepts used in political science is endless. No book could hope to do justice to all the concepts, or even all the major concepts in political science. Therefore, we have had to be selective—we have tried to choose concepts which are broad enough to be used to analyze many different kinds of political phenomena. These are concepts which you are very likely to encounter in your political readings. You may already be familiar with some of them.

Because of their general applicability and the frequency with which they are used, these concepts are sometimes referred to as *approaches* to political analysis. That is, each of these concepts provides the foundation for an entire framework that guides political analysis. The existence of such a framework means that attempts have been made to link the concept together with other concepts and to create a structure to order and interrelate research findings. Such steps, of course, are the beginnings of theory building.

It should also be noted that the discussion of each concept is also abridged. For reasons of time and space, we have limited the discussion of each concept to what we believe to be the major insights gained through each. This is not meant to be a thorough review of the literature, or a critique of the use of the concept. Rather, the discussion is meant to be suggestive of how the concept can be used in research. It is concerned with what questions each conceptual approach suggests and what problems of research must be raised and resolved—or at least recognized.

Looking at things from various angles should give you new insight and should suggest new questions which can form the basis for further research. The discussion of each concept will follow the same general outline. First we will define the concept. In every case, we unfortunately will find that there is not universal agreement on the exact definition, but there is enough of a consensus to point to an accepted meaning. After defining the concept, we will consider how the concept has been used in research. This will involve discussing the operationalization of the concept as well as some of the major problems with the research. Finally, we will consider some of the major research findings produced by research using the concept. In this discussion we will point to some of the major generalizations produced by the research and, if relevant, consider how these generalizations have been interrelated into rudimentary or concatenated theories.

The Setting of Politics

Chapter Four

At its base, politics obviously has to do with people. It is the interaction of people with each other which makes up the process of politics. But people do not enter into these political interactions as "blank slates." They carry with them orientations to politics which are composed of their knowledge, attitudes, values, and expectations. It is these political orientations which form the setting in which political interactions take place since they affect political behavior.

There are two points we should make about these orientations. In the first place, we are not only talking about the orientations of political leaders. Obviously, it is important to know the orientations of those who will be making decisions. A government with Adolph Hitler at its head would be significantly different from one with Abraham Lincoln in charge. But it is also important to know about the orientations of all the people.

This point may be obvious if we are talking about countries which have democratic governments. In a democracy, the citizens are supposed to participate in their government, even if only by choosing the government officials in elections. The political orientations of the people will determine whether they participate, how they participate, and what goals they seek to achieve in that participation—important determinants of the policy and stability of a government.

Let us look at such an example. In the United States, people from the middle and upper classes are more likely to participate than are those from the lower class. This participation may mean that the views of the middle and upper classes are more likely to be heard and responded to by political leaders than are the views of the lower class. This in turn may lead to unrest among the poor that may threaten the stability of the government. Why is it that the lower class does not participate? One answer, perhaps, is that they do not develop orientations which normally lead to participation. Examples of such orientations are interest in politics and belief that their participation will influence decision makers.[1]

Citizen orientations are also important to governments that are not democratic. If such governments do not have at least the grudging acceptance of their citizens, they must allocate large amounts of resources to maintain their control. The level of trust citizens have of their government, the kind of government they have come to expect, and so forth, are factors which affect the satisfaction of citizens with their government.

Obviously, when we talk about the importance of citizen orientations, we are not usually talking about what each separate individual feels and thinks, unless, of course, the individual has a tremendous amount of power. Rather, we are talking about what large groups or classes of people think and feel. The basic point, however, is that citizen orientations have important effects on the political process, whether or not the governmental structure is democratic.

The second point we wish to make about these orientations is that, in this chapter, we are primarily interested in purely political orientations. Examples of such political orientations are party identification, or political ideology, and trust of the government. But there are also other orientations which may be important to the political process. Some orientations may seem to be only private matters but may in some circumstances become important to the process of politics. For instance, racial, religious, or other kinds of prejudice may seem to be purely individual matters. But when these prejudices are shared by large numbers of people and when they lead to widespread discrimination or violence, then governments must often intervene. Trying to give a comprehensive list of other such orientations would be as difficult as trying to define precisely the scope of politics.

Since citizen orientations of various kinds are important to governments, they are also important to those who study governments. Political scientists have, therefore, developed a variety of conceptual approaches to study these orientations. Some of the approaches focus on this individual level and examine individual attitudes, values, or personality. Two other approaches attempt to bridge the gap between the individual and the gov-

---

1. For thorough examination of these points see Sidney Verba and Norman Nie, *Participation in America* (New York: Harper & Row, 1972).

ernment by focusing on general patterns of orientations in a society. These two approaches, political socialization and political culture, are what we will be discussing in this chapter.

Political socialization focuses attention on the process by which we learn our orientations. The argument is that the way we learn and what we learn will be important factors in any attempt to build generalizations about those orientations and their relationship to political behavior. Political culture is closely related to political socialization. It refers to the distribution of political ideas and values within a particular population. The assumption is that these ideas and values have been learned in the socialization process. Let us now examine each of these concepts in depth and consider the different sorts of research questions each would suggest.

POLITICAL SOCIALIZATION

Long before you ever took political science courses, it is likely you knew a surprising amount about politics. You knew you were a member of a particular nation-state. You knew the symbols of that state. You probably had at least a general idea of the basic structure of government and the nature of political parties. And you undoubtedly had definite feelings, evaluations, and opinions about these political institutions. All of these bits of information, feelings, and so forth are political orientations that you possessed long before you started studying political science. This list of orientations could almost certainly be extended. Obviously, you were not born with these orientations; these things are not transferred in the genes. The question is, then, how do you learn about politics. This is the fundamental question addressed in research on *political socialization*. Let us define socialization and then turn to an examination of questions suggested by the concept of socialization.

What is Political Socialization?

It is very easy to give a general definition of political socialization. It is simply the process by which individuals learn about politics. As we have indicated, other kinds of information besides factual information is learned through socialization. We also learn such things as values (democracy is good), emotions (I love my country), and behaviors (voting, petitioning). One aspect of what is learned is the *political culture,* which will be discussed later in this chapter.

Of course, as with all the concepts mentioned in this section, there is not a total consensus on the definition of political socialization. Some political scientists would add a qualification to the definition we gave above. We defined political socialization as the process of learning all political attitudes, values, behaviors, and so forth. Some researchers, though, see socialization as the process of learning only those things which will lead to a stable political system.[2] These researchers, then, would only be interested in studying how we learn those things which are believed to maintain the current status quo. For instance, they would be interested in discovering how we develop feelings of patriotism. Or they would like to know how we learn respect for our leaders, or how we learn the importance of using peaceful, rather than revolutionary, means to replace those leaders. The basic focus of people who define socialization in this way is on the question of how political processes persist over time.

We will be using the more general definition of political socialization in this chapter, primarily because we feel this will give you a more comprehensive overview of the use of the concept in political science. Of course, either definition is equally valid. You should, however, be aware of these two definitions because which definition is used will obviously affect how you would conduct research on socialization. Different questions would have to be asked if you were interested in all political learning rather than just that political learning which will lead to persistence of the status quo. You should also be aware of which definition is used when you are reading socialization literature. Seemingly contradictory findings may result from researchers using different definitions, or from the use of different operationalizations of the definition.

Having considered what we mean by political socialization, let us now turn to examining the kinds of research questions suggested by the concept. Those who study political socialization assume that the political attitudes and behaviors of the citizens of a government are an important determinant of the functioning of that government. Socialization researchers also believe, therefore, that it is important to know how people learn these attitudes and behaviors. There is a fundamental question which is suggested by the concept of political socialization: What is the impact on the political system of what we learn about politics? Jack Dennis calls this establishing the "system relevance" of socialization.[3] There are many other important research questions beyond this fundamental one. For instance, we are interested in the process of learning about politics. Are there stages of development? To what extent are childhood experiences manifested in adulthood? Who teaches us? We are also interested in what things are most likely to be learned in socialization. Are different things learned by different groups, in different areas of the country, or in different countries? Why are there such differences, and what relationship is there between these differences and the way the government functions? Having considered what we would like to learn

---

2. Roberta Sigel, "Assumptions About the Learning of Political Values," *The Annals*, 361 (1965). 1.
3. Jack Dennis, "Major Problems of Political Socialization Research," in *Socialization to Politics*, ed. Jack Dennis (New York: John Wiley, 1973), pp. 5–7.

about socialization, let us now consider how the concept of political socialization has been used in research and what information has been produced from that research.

How Has Political Socialization Been Studied?

Most political scientists who have studied political socialization have used survey research. The respondents are usually asked to fill out a questionnaire designed to discover their attitudes toward, and/or knowledge about, political phenomena. For example, in one study children were asked to indicate their attitude toward the President, among other things. They were asked to respond to the following: "Think of the President as he really is":

1. Would always want to help me if I needed it
2. Would most always want to help me if I needed it
3. Would usually want to help me if I needed it
4. Would sometimes want to help me if I needed it
5. Would seldom want to help me if I needed it
6. Would not usually want to help me if I needed it.[4]

This example of a question used in a socialization study should give you a general idea of one way that the concept has been operationalized. A question like that above gets at what someone knows or feels about political phenomena. In other words, political socialization has often been operationalized in terms of what has been the content of socialization—of what knowledge, emotions, or evaluations have been learned.

Just looking at the content of socialization, of course, ignores the other way in which socialization may have an effect, that is, through the process by which the content is learned. But some attention has also been paid to the process of socialization which has usually been operationalized by comparing the attitudes, knowledge, and so forth of the respondents with those of people with whom the respondent has interacted, family, teachers, peers, and others.[5] For example, if a congruence in party identification is discovered between children and their parents, it is concluded that interaction with one's family is the process by which party identification is learned. It should be obvious that it is much easier to find out what people know or feel (although that is far from simple) than it is to discover how they have learned those things. Consequently, we know much more at this time about the

---

4. Robert D. Hess and Judith V. Torney, *The Development of Political Attitudes in Children* (Garden City, New York: Anchor Books, 1968), p. 268.
5. For overviews of the process of socialization, see the following: Hess and Torney, *The Development of Political Attitudes in Children*, chaps. 5 and 6; Robert Weissberg, *Political Learning, Political Choice, and Democratic Citizenship* (Englewood Cliffs, N.J.: Prentice-Hall, 1974), chap. 8.

content, rather than the process, of socialization. This is, in fact, one of the criticisms of the socialization literature.

The group which has frequently been the focus of survey research studies has been school children. A sample is drawn from children in particular grades, for example, two through eight. Research of this kind, which concentrates on young children, creates special problems for the researchers. The children may have a very limited vocabulary or they may be incapable of dealing with the complex abstracts in which the researchers are interested. (How do you get children to tell you their attitude toward government if they don't understand what government means?) Many researchers have been very creative in dealing with such problems with the use of resources such as visual aids and careful wording of questions.[6]

There is, however, one problem of such research which has yet to be resolved. Research on the political attitudes and knowledge of young children is based on a very important assumption. These studies assume that what a person learns in childhood is important in determining how one thinks and behaves as an adult. As we noted above, this is the all-important question in any research on political socialization. If this assumption is not valid, then studies of children in grades two through eight are not very significant, since children have little impact on the functioning of politics. To determine if, in fact, the attitudes and knowledge of children persist into adulthood, a researcher would have to keep track of the children whom he questioned and do a follow-up study when the children have grown up. So far, no researcher has taken the time or effort to do this.

We might expect that early learning would be less likely to persist into adulthood when discontinuities exist in the socialization process. A *discontinuity* indicates there has been an abrupt change in the values, expectations, etc., which are being taught. Such discontinuities often occur in developing countries. For example, a formerly authoritarian government may suddenly attempt to become a democracy. The citizens were formerly expected to be obedient and passive. In a democracy they are expected to be active and vote. Such a situation could obviously create confusion for the individual.

Discontinuities also can occur in countries which we consider developed. For instance, a black child in an urban ghetto may learn one thing about the policeman on the corner in his preschool years and be told something entirely different when he goes to school. Another example of discontinuity affected the United States as a whole. Traditionally, Americans have viewed their Presidents as beyond reproach. Yet the Watergate incident severely shook our trust in the presidency. Some research immediately following Watergate indicated that the level of trust of school children had

---

6. For examples of such techniques, see the following: Hess and Torney, *The Development of Political Attitudes in Children*, Jack Dennis, Future Work on Political Socialization," p. 497, in *Socialization to Politics*, ed. Dennis, pp. 266–270. Edwin D. Larsen, "The Development of Patriotism in Children: A Second Look," *Journal of Psychology*, 55 (1963), 279–86.

significantly decreased. Whether this change was permanent or temporary is not yet known.

In all cases of discontinuity, there is an obvious need for more research. These cases present perfect opportunities to investigate such questions as how persistent early learning is and which agent of socialization is most influential. But again, to examine changes in socialization, it is necessary to have data over time, or what is called *longitudinal data.*

One way of attempting to deal with questions which require longitudinal data is to focus on people of high school or post– high school age, and ask those being interviewed to recall their early learning about politics. The flaw in this scheme, of course, is that people may not remember accurately experiences from ten or fifteen years ago. Unfortunately, the question of whether or not what is learned about politics persists into adulthood is still unresolved and is a problem with the socialization literature. Much more research on this fundamental question needs to be done. Some circumstantial evidence has, however, been found to indicate there is at least some persistence of early learning. We will talk about that evidence when we discuss what is learned in socialization.

There are two more general problems of research which have been discussed in political socialization. These problems could more easily be resolved than the problem we discussed above. The first problem is the fact that much research has only looked at the socialization of Americans. There is no doubt that understanding how Americans learn about politics is important. But as we indicated above, one of the things we hope to gain by studying socialization is an understanding of why different people think and behave differently. The only way to achieve this is by examining those with different patterns of attitudes and behaviors and by trying to discover a relationship between those differences and the process of socialization. An example of research which did find a relationship between political patterns and the socialization process was that of Converse and Dupeux.[7] They attempted to discover why the French tended to change party identification more frequently than did Americans. The usual explanation given was that the French were more intensely ideological than were Americans and could not tolerate membership in a party whose platform differed from their own beliefs. On the contrary, what Converse and Dupeux found was that French children are not taught a party identification at an early age, as are American children. They concluded that fleeting party affiliation is due not to intense ideology, but to lack of an early learning of party identification. More of such research comparing the pattern of socialization is needed.

In addition, more research should be done to examine different socialization patterns within countries. An example of such a study is by Jaros and

---

7. Philip E. Converse and Georges Dupeux, "Politicization of the Electorate in France and the United States, "*Public Opinion Quarterly,* 26:1–23.

others.[8] They compared the orientations of children toward the President in two subcultures: black children in Chicago and white children in Appalachia. The Appalachian white children were considerably less trusting than the blacks. A problem with this study, however, is the fact that the samples were taken at different times. The Chicago sample was taken during Eisenhower's administration, and the Appalachian sample was drawn during Johnson's presidency. The differences may be due to the passage of time, rural–urban differences, popularity of each President, and so forth, rather than subgroup differences. Again, more work should be done to examine socialization differences between different groups within countries and to relate those differences to political orientations and behavior. In the absence of such research there can be little use of the concept of socialization to compare the type of learning.

A final problem of the research on socialization is that there needs to be more effort to use that research to develop empirical theory. Many interesting findings have been produced. And there has been some attempt to build a few generalizations, although most of these generalizations have yet to be substantiated adequately by research. There has, however, been little attempt to interrelate those generalizations in a logical order. It should be obvious that greater attention should be paid to making socialization studies more theoretical.

We hope we have not discouraged you with this list of the problems of the socialization research. You should realize that all we are saying is there is plenty of room left for political scientists to do research on political socialization. If all the answers were known, there would be no chance for the rest of us to play the game of solving the puzzle, which is really what is involved in theory building. And if we were not aware of the problems of the past research, then there is no way we could make our research better than what has gone before. With this in mind, let us now turn to a discussion of what we know about political socialization as a result of research. As you may have guessed, most of this research has assumed that socialization is an important determinant of our political attitudes and behavior. Therefore, the research, has focused on answering the two questions: How do we learn? What is learned?

How Do We Learn?

As we hinted in the discussion of how political socialization has been operationalized by political scientists, more attention has been focused on the question of what is learned in socialization than on the process of how it is learned. But long before political scientists were interested in socialization,

---

8. Dean Jaros, Herbert Hirsch, and Frederic J. Fleron, Jr., "The Malevolent Leader: Political Socialization in an American Subculture," *American Political Science Review*, 62 (1968), p. 568.

researchers from other disciplines were interested in the question of how we learn. While little political research has been directed precisely at this question, some findings are relevant to theories of learning developed by researchers from other disciplines, especially psychology. There are two prominent conceptions of how we learn, both developed by psychologists, and we will consider whether or not the research done by political scientists has supported these theories. The first of these conceptions is called *learning theory*.

Learning theory argues that learning takes place when we develop appropriate responses to particular stimuli. A stop sign may be seen as a stimulus; stopping your car is the learned response. Why and how do we learn such responses? Some learning theorists argue this learning takes place simply by associating one thing with another. (Cars always stop at stop signs.) Others believe that positive reinforcement must be given before the proper response is learned. Consider the example of a teacher asking you a question in class. If the response you give is the proper one, the teacher will give you such positive reinforcement as praise or a good grade. If the response given is not proper, then the teacher will give you a negative reinforcement (a lecture, a bad grade). Learning may take place either directly or indirectly. In a classroom, there is usually a very conscious attempt to provide stimuli and use reinforcement to create the desired response. Children also learn by imitating social models. For example, many children learn their party identification from their parents whether or not their parents set out to teach party identification to their children. Children probably become aware of their parents' party identification from conversation (stimulus) and decide to imitate that identification (response). This may result from the child simply hearing that party is always used in association with the word Republican or Democrat. Or it may be that this imitation pleased the parents and the pleasure acted as positive reinforcement for the response. In either event, this illustrates that much learning takes place by imitation.

Socialization research has produced information which would support learning theory. For instance, such research has indicated that much of our political learning takes place in school.[9] The school-learning situation is set up according to the social-learning model. Positive reinforcement (acceptance, praise, good grades) is given when you give the proper response (a salute) to a stimulus (the flag).

Research has also emphasized the importance of the family and of peer groups in our political learning.[10] What we learn from these groups is more likely to be indirect learning than what we learn in school. But we try to

---

9. Hess and Torney, *The Development of Political Attitudes in Children*, pp. 121-23.

70 THE SETTING OF POLITICS

imitate those around us and try to learn what are the "right" attitudes and behaviors because we want to be positively reinforced by receiving such things as praise from our parents, acceptance from our friends, etc. The learning theory approach can help us understand a situation which we mentioned at the beginning of this chapter: the tendency for the lower class to abstain from political participation. As we indicated before, the reason why the members of the lower class do not participate may be that they fail to learn civic attitudes such as interest in politics and belief in their ability to influence politics. This failure is probably due to the fact that their parents did not have these attitudes and to the fact that their peers do not value participation. This means that participation is not respected (positively reinforced) and may even be a subject for laughter and jokes (negatively reinforced). It may also be the case that previous participation was negatively reinforced by the system.

The other major theory of how we learn is *cognitive development*. This theory, which has been the focus of much research by the French psychologist Jean Piaget,[11] is not necessarily contradictory to learning theory. The basic idea of cognitive development theory is that there are definite stages in our learning. Certain kinds of things can only be learned when we reach a particular stage of our development. For example, the ability to learn about concrete things comes before the ability to understand abstracts.

Much socialization research has focused on the question of what is learned at what stage of development. As the cognitive development theorists believe, it appears that there is a definite developmental pattern in how we learn about politics. As young children, we first learn about very concrete, "real" things. For instance, some researchers found that the first political phenomenon of which we are aware is the idea that we are a member of a particular political community. That is, we learn we are Americans, or French, or Filipino, or whatever. There seems, however, to be no real conception of what that membership really means. Children identify this membership by the concrete symbol of the flag. The first awareness children have of government comes from recognizing the President. Only later do they become aware of Congress, or the Supreme Court, or of other levels of

---

10. On the influence of the family, see Hess and Torney, *The Development of Political Attitudes in Children*, pp. 107–116; Herbert Hyman, *Political Socialization: A Study in the Psychology of Political Behavior* (New York: The Free Press, 1959), pp. 64–66; Kenneth Prewitt, "Political Socialization and Leadership Selection," *The Annals*, 361 (1965), 96–111; Herbert McCloskey and Harold Dahlgren, "Primary Group Influence on Party Loyalty," *American Political Science Review*, 53 (1959), 757–76. On the influence of peer groups, see: Dean Jaros, *Socialization to Politics* (New York: Holt, Rinehart & Winston, 1973), chap. 6; Hess and Torney, *The Development of Political Attitudes in Children*, pp. 120–25.

11. Jean Piaget and Barbel Inhelder, *The Psychology of the Child* (London: Routledge and Kegan Paul, 1971).

government. Obviously, it is much easier to grasp the existence of the President than of Congress. The President, as a single man in charge of the country, is analogous in many children's minds to another very familiar authority figure: a father in charge of the family. Congress, as an institution composed of 535 men and women, is an abstract which children cannot grasp until later in their development. Thus, there definitely seem to be stages in a child's learning process which would support the cognitive development theory.[12] The question still remains whether what is learned in the early stages influences our later political values and behavior more than learning after childhood.

Related to the question of how we learn is that of who teaches us. For the most part researchers agree that the family and the school are two of the most important agents of political socialization, although they disagree about which of these two is more important.[13] Obviously, we learn much of our knowledge, our values, and our behaviors from our parents. It makes sense, therefore, to believe that our political learning also comes from our parents. In fact, research has substantiated that much political learning does take place in the family. From the family we tend to learn basic orientations, such as our attitude toward authority, our identification with our country, and, often, our identification with a political party.[14]

Most of these things, you will notice, are basically emotional orientations. However, some research has indicated that the ability of the family to transmit attitudes and values beyond these basic orientations may vary. For instance, it has been found that in families of low socioeconomic status, there is little interest in politics and, therefore, children learn little about politics from the family.[15] It appears that parental influence is greater if the parents are themselves interested in a particular political phenomenon and if the child accurately perceives how the parents feel.[16]

Other studies have found that other factors besides interest affect the transmission of political knowledge and values from parent to child. For instance, children are more likely to learn their party identification and voting patterns from the family if the family members are all in agreement on these choices, if there is frequent contact within the family, and if they share similar life styles.[17] All of this tends to corroborate the social learning

---

12. M. Kent Jennings and Richard Niemi, "Patterns of Political Learning," *Harvard Educational Review,* 38 (Summer 1968), 443–67. Fred Greenstein, *Children and Politics* (New Haven: Yale University Press, 1965); Hess and Torney, *The Development of Political Attitudes in Children.*
13. Greenstein, *Children and Politics,* pp. 44–46, 72–74; Hess and Torney, *The Development of Political Attitudes in Children,* p. 101.
14. M. Kent Jennings and Richard G. Niemi, "The Transmission of Political Values, From Parent to Child," *American Political Science Review,* 62 (March 1968), 169–84.
15. Hess and Torney, *The Development of Political Attitudes in Children,* p. 100.
16. Kent L. Tedin, "The Influence of Parents on the Political Attitudes of Adolescents,' *American Political Science Review,* 68 (December 1974), 1579–92.

process. If the parents are interested in politics and if the family is an important factor in the child's life because of frequent contact and strong affection, then children will probably receive positive reinforcement to adopt the political values of the parents. If the parents are not interested or the family is not important to the child, less political learning takes place.

The second major agent of political socialization is the school. The school makes a conscious attempt to transmit political knowledge and values, although its success in this effort is still being questioned. In general, it appears that the school has the greatest impact on children of lower socioeconomic background.[18] As we noted above, the family influence in such cases is usually weak because of a lack of political interest. The school apparently fills in this gap. But in all cases, the school appears to be most effective when it reinforces the child's orientations rather than when it transmits new values.[19] The level of education a person has obtained can be shown to be related to a variety of political characteristics, such as interest in politics, awareness of government impact, tendency to discuss politics, and so forth.[20] It is not clear, however, whether this is really the effect of education or whether it is due to the fact that those with high levels of education also tend to have high status backgrounds. More research obviously needs to be done on the effect of formal education on the child's political learning.

Two other factors are often mentioned as important influences on the political learning process: peer groups and the media.[21] The effect of peer groups seems to be dependent on two variables: how interested the child is in politics and how dependent he or she is on the family. The higher the interest and the lower the dependence on family increases the effect of the peer group. Much has been said about the effect of the media, but research findings have been contradictory. Some people, such as former Vice President Spiro Agnew, believed we were helpless pawns buffeted by an all-powerful media. This is an exaggeration since everyone watches, reads, or listens to various media from the vantage point of his own existing predispositions. The result, some researchers have argued, is that the media is more successful at reinforcing prior beliefs and less so at changing old beliefs or teaching new ones.[22] Yet some more recent research seems to indicate that the media may have an impact on some political orientations such as what roles

---

17. McCloskey and Dahlgren, "Primary Group Influence on Party Loyalty."
18. Richard E. Dawson and Kenneth Prewitt, *Political Socialization* (Boston: Little, Brown, 1969), pp. 147–55.
19. M. Margaret Conway and Frank B. Feigert, *Political Analysis: An Introduction* (Boston: Allyn and Bacon, 1976), p. 169.
20. Gabriel A. Almond and Sidney Verba, *The Civic Culture* (Boston: Little, Brown, 1965), pp. 371–78.
21. Martin L. Levin, "Social Climate and Political Socialization," *Public Opinion Quarterly*, 35 (Winter 1961), 596–606.

we expect from government officials.[23] Once again the need for further research is obvious.

What, then, are our conclusions? What do we know about how we learn about politics? Let us review the findings by phrasing them in the form of generalizations.

1. Children learn about politics by imitation of those around them and/or by the selective use of positive and negative reinforcements by those around them.[24]
2. Concrete knowledge (we are Americans; George Washington was our first President) is learned before abstract knowledge (federalism, separation of powers).[25]
3. The influence of the family in socialization is increased if the family is interested in politics.[26]
4. The influence of the family in socialization is increased if the family has frequent contacts, has close emotional ties, and shares a certain life style.[27]
5. The influence of the school is increased if it reinforces pre-existing orientations.[28]
6. The influence of the school is enlarged if the family has not been an important influence in the area of political learning.[29]
7. The influence of peer groups is enlarged if the child is interested in politics.[30]
8. The influence of peer groups is enlarged if the child is not dependent on his family.[31]

This list certainly should not be considered comprehensive. In general, it should be obvious that we do not really know very much at this time about how we learn about politics. We are not really sure what the effect of the media is. We do not completely know the relative influence of the various socializing agents. There also needs to be more work done on the process of adult socialization to discover if there are changes in an individual's political orientations once he becomes an adult. What is most obviously lacking is, perhaps, the existence of any theoretical structure. There is some connection between the learning theory approach developed by psychologists and many of the generalizations above. If the child or the family is interested in

---

22. Joseph T. Klapper, *The Effects of Mass Communications* (New York: The Free Press, 1960).
23. John Robinson, "Perceived Media Bias and the 1968 Vote: Can the Media Affect Behavior After All?" *Journalism Quarterly*, 49 (1972), 239–46.
24. Richard Merelman, "Learning and Legitimacy," *American Political Science Review*, 60 (September 1966), 548.
25. M. Kent Jennings and Richard G. Niemi, "Patterns of Political Learning."
26. McCloskey and Dahlgren, "Primary Group Influence on Party Loyalty."
27. Ibid.
28. Conway and Feigert, *Political Analysis*, p. 169.
29. Hess and Torney, *The Development of Political Attitudes*, p. 100.
30. Levin, "Social Climate and Political Socialization."
31. Ibid.

politics, more political learning takes place. Interest would make the learning satisfying and this satisfaction may be seen as positive reinforcement. The importance of the socializing agent to the child will increase the tendency of the child to learn from that agent. Obviously, the learning is pleasing to the agent in the sense that imitation is the sincerest form of flattery and that pleasure becomes positive reinforcement to the child. But more concerted effort should be made to conduct research on the socialization process with the conscious goal of theory building. The bottom line, then, is that much more research needs to be done on the question of how we learn about politics.

Let us now turn to the results of research on the second question concerning political socialization: What is learned in the socialization process?

What Do We Learn About Politics?

As we have said before, we know much more about what we learn about politics than how we learn it. But even here we will have to point to some significant questions left unanswered. A major problem of this research is that most of it has concentrated on socialization in the United States. Therefore, our findings may or may not be relevant to other countries.

Early research on political socialization produced findings which indicated basically that children learn very positive and supportive orientations to their government.[32] Again, the first thing children learn about politics is that they are members of a particular political community in the United States. They also learn that this is the best country in the world. Children later become aware of the President and tend to view him as being all wise and all good.[33] Some researchers have claimed that the President is seen as a father figure, that is, caring, wise, concerned, benevolent. Later, children learn about the other parts of the government, and the strong emotional attachment children originally felt only for the President is generalized to these other institutions. This means that participation, beyond the somewhat ritualized act of voting, or any form of oversight of the government is seen as unnecessary since the government is benevolent and will act for our best interests.

This is a very brief overview, but it does provide some basis for speculation about the permanence of our early learning and, therefore, about the possible effect of socialization on the functioning of government. Americans obviously do not maintain their idealized image of government all their lives. The early socialization process shields children from the more corrupt

---

32. David Easton and Robert Hess, "The Child's Political World," *Midwest Journal of Political Science*, 6 (August 1962), 229–46.
33. Ibid.

aspects of politics, but as children grow their perception of government may become increasingly more critical. Explanations for this contradiction have usually been based on the reasoning that while our early beliefs are accurate, we happen to be stuck at the moment with "crooks" in office. The supposed answer is simply to kick the rascals out and return the government to its prior, perfect state. Thus, the contradiction between early learning and the current situation is resolved. This pattern seems to persist even in the wake of actual governmental scandals.

The early learning also seems to impede our perception of wrong doing by some officials. We learn so early and so fervently about the goodness of the President that many find it difficult or impossible to believe a President could be wrong or even dishonest. This sort of strong emotional support for authority obviously could be one explanation for the stability of the United States government. If problems can be solved simply by replacing people in office, there is no reason to contemplate more drastic action such as revolution.

Of course, we have been talking about general patterns, patterns observed during early research on socialization from the 1950s through the 1960s. It has always been the case that some groups within the United States have not shared the general supportive attitudes toward government. As we indicated, Jaros found that Appalachian children were much less convinced of the benevolence of the President,[34] and blacks have had somewhat less supportive attitudes toward the government in general.[35] The basic question which must be answered now is whether the general pattern of support in the population as a whole which has been observed in the last two decades has changed in the 1970s. There is some evidence that all American children today are less likely to show the strong emotional support for their government which children in the 50s and 60s did. Intuitively, one might point to Vietnam and Watergate as possible reasons for the change. And one effect of television may be that children are no longer shielded from the harsh realities of politics.

The evidence of a change in what children are learning about politics is at the moment inconclusive. Obviously, more research is needed in this area as well as research on the reason for the change, if it has occurred. Such research may well help us know not only more about what we learn about politics, but also more about how we learn.

How can we evaluate the research findings concerning what we learn about politics? It appears that there is one basic generalization which this research has produced. Early political learning produces strong emotional support for the political system in America. We still need more research to

---

34. Jaros, and others, "The Malevolent Leader: Political Socialization in an American Subculture."
35. Edward S. Greenberg, "Orientations of Black and White Children to Political Authority Figures," *Social Science Quarterly*, 51 (December 1970), 561–71.

show the extent of influence the events of the last ten years have had on this pattern, and to what extent these supportive feelings persist as the child becomes an adult. As we said, this is the basic question of the socialization research. And once again, we need to aim such research at the goal of building theories. Too much of socialization research has been basically descriptive rather than theoretical.

More research is also needed on a comparison of patterns of political socialization in various countries. The cross-national research which has been done thus far indicates that the concept should potentially be very useful in explaining differences in attitudes and values of people in different countries. The basic political attitudes and values which people in a particular country learn are called *political culture* by some researchers. Let us now turn our attention to the research which has been done on the concept of political culture.

POLITICAL CULTURE

Political socialization research is concerned with political learning. In the process of examining this learning researchers also investigate what is learned. Researchers of political culture focus entirely on what is learned and, in fact, narrow their focus even more by looking at only those things which they believe to be fundamental political attitudes, values, and beliefs of a particular country. This means that those interested in political culture do not look at those political orientations which are constantly changing. For instance, they would not be primarily interested in examining what Americans may think at the moment about energy policy or what the Russians may feel about arms control. These more specific and fleeting political beliefs are called opinions. The researchers of political culture would argue that these opinions are conditioned and filtered through fundamental and enduring political beliefs. These fundamental orientations are the focus of political culture research. Perhaps this distinction can be made somewhat clearer by pointing out that the concept of culture, which is borrowed from the anthropologists, has been defined as ". . . the entire way of life followed by a people."[36] Thus, political culture is the political way of life of a people.

Although there is a consensus that political culture is concerned with fundamental political orientations of a people, there are, of course, disagreements about what exactly the components of these fundamental beliefs are. Each researcher seems to have a unique set of components which he believes comprise political culture. Walter Rosenbaum, however, has identified three "core components" which he believes are common to all definitions of political culture. We will rely on this list of components as the basic

---

36. Charles A. Valentine, *Culture ind Poverty* (Chicago: University of Chicago Press, 1968), p. 3.

definition for political culture. The components he listed are (1) orientations toward political structures, (2) orientations toward others in the political system, and (3) orientations toward one's own political activity.[37]

Let us consider what each of these means. Orientations toward government structures would involve a person's evaluation of government institutions and policies. Orientation toward others in the political system would refer to a person's identification with and trust in others, as well as his idea of rules governing political life. Orientation toward political activity is concerned with various kinds of participation in politics and whether or not such participation would be likely to produce any effects. With this general definition in mind, let us turn to the research questions suggested by the concept of political culture.

What Can Political Culture Tell Us?

America has existed and prospered for 200 years under a government based on the separation of power among executive, legislative, and judicial branches. Attempts to "export" that form of government to other countries (such as Vietnam) have often failed. Most Russians are fairly quiescent under the rule of the Communist Party, but in Hungary tanks have at times had to be used to quell citizens protesting the power of the Communist Party. These examples illustrate that the attitudes and behaviors of citizens are important to the functioning of governments, a point which we made before. These examples also illustrate that attitudes and behaviors of citizens of different countries often vary widely, and may well affect the stability of the political system.

Two primary research foci are suggested by political culture. In the first place, researchers wish to use the concept as a means of systematically studying the differences in basic political orientations. In other words, instead of researchers wandering around in different countries looking for numerous and sundry different pieces of information, the concept of political culture should provide some order to the research effort by providing all researchers with a common focus so that comparable information could be gathered. Once differences between countries have been established, the second focus becomes relevant. How do the basic political orientations of a population affect the functioning of the political system? The question is, therefore, what is the linkage between the attitudes and values of the people and the stability or instability of a country? One prominent study of political culture has given a somewhat more precise pharsing to this question. Almond and Verba, in their five-nation study, hypothesized that for a country to be stable, it is necessary to have a congruence between type of government

---

37. Walter A. Rosenbaum, *Political Culture* (New York: Holt, Rinehart & Winston, 1975), pp. 6–7.

form and the type of political culture.[38] Stated somewhat simplistically, they believe that it is impossible to successfully impose a democratic governmental structure on a population whose basic political orientations favor an authoritative government. In general, the concept of political culture asks the question of what are the basic patterns in the political orientations of people in different countries and whether the performance of the government can be traced to these patterns. Thus, the basic goal is to be able to use political culture to explain, for example, why government in the United States is relatively stable while the government of Vietman was unstable

Let us now examine how political culture has been researched and consider some of the problems encountered in trying to do research on political culture.

How Has Political Culture Been Studied?

The first problem encountered in trying to do research on political culture is, of course, the need to operationalize the concept. As an example of how this might be done, let us consider how the first component listed by Rosenbaum, orientations toward government structures, may be operationalized. For this purpose, we will look at what is, perhaps, the major study of political culture, the above-mentioned five-nation study by Almond and Verba. The data from this study were nationwide samples from England, the United States, Germany, Italy, and Mexico. To measure different orientations toward government, Almond and Verba asked people what they knew about their government (*cognition*) and how they felt about the government (*affect*). To discover political cognitions, they asked people if they believed government had an impact on their lives, if they followed accounts of political and governmental affairs, and if they could name party and government leaders. To measure political affect, they asked of what aspect of the nation people were the most proud, and what kind of treatment people expected from the government.[39] Let us consider some of the problems in operationalizing political culture in this way.

Perhaps the most obvious problem is that political culture is intended to be used to study differences between countries. Therefore, it is important that the same questions be asked in different countries so the responses can be compared. But how can the researcher be sure that the same question will mean the same thing in different countries? Even if the question were translated literally from one language to another, some words may have entirely different connotations in another language.

Consider, for example, the different meanings the term "political party membership" would have for someone in England and in the United States.

---

38. Almond and Verba, *The Civic Culture*, p. 20.
39. Ibid., chaps. 2 and 3.

In England being a member of a party means paying dues, and many British people do pay. Therefore, only the hard core dues-paying member would say he or she belonged to a political party in England. In the United States, on the other hand, many people identify with a party and consider themselves members but pay no dues. Most Americans would say they belonged to a party no matter how shallow the commitment. There is always the danger, therefore, that the researcher and the respondents may be working at cross-purposes.

Another problem is the question of just how widespread the orientations must be within the population in order to be considered a typical part of the political culture. Political culture, of course, refers to the dominant orientations of a people. But in any culture there are some people who do not conform to the dominant patterns. There may be individual "mavericks" or subcultures which share their own particular patterns. The researcher must decide if "fringe" cultural groups are indicative of a cross-section of the entire culture.

But there is an even more fundamental problem with this approach to studying political culture. The basic notion of the concept concerns fundamental political orientations of a people. In other words, it is a concept which refers to characteristics of a group. Yet it is being researched by asking questions of individuals. Proponents of using political culture see it as a bridging concept. That is to say, beliefs of an individual (an *individual-level concept*) can be put together (or aggregated) with those of other individuals to determine the general views of society (a *group-level concept*). It is always risky to combine the individual and group levels of analysis. Some researchers argue that political culture should mean something more than simply a collection of individual beliefs, just as culture should mean something more than individual life styles. The problem, though, is how to pinpoint what this "something more" is in such a way that it can be studied empirically. This fundamental debate about political culture research has yet to be resolved.

With these problems in mind let us turn to a brief examination of what information has been produced so far by research on political culture. We will divide this discussion between the two separate questions suggested by the concept. First, we will examine what has been discovered about different patterns of orientations in different countries. Secondly, we will examine what we know about the linkage between political culture and the functioning of government.

Patterns of Political Culture

There seems to be consensus among the researchers on political culture that it is, in fact, possible to use the concept to discover differences in the orientations of people toward their political systems. There have been many in-depth studies of the political cultures of individual countries.[40] However, since we do not have the space here to consider the findings produced in each of these separate countries, we will consider instead only the comparative findings produced in the landmark study of political culture by Almond and Verba.

As indicated, Almond and Verba conducted surveys with samples of people in five different countries: Italy, Mexico, the United States, the United Kingdom, and Germany. They found significant variations in the profiles of these countries.[41] They characterized Italy as an alienated political culture.[42] Italians, they found, were lacking in trust, in national pride, in the sense of obligation to participate, and the belief that such participation would have an impact. While Italy had a fairly homogeneous political culture, Mexico was found to have inconsistencies, characterized by Almond and Verba as "alienation and aspiration."[43] The Mexicans had a high belief in their ability to affect the government and a great deal of pride in their government, yet were not likely to actually participate in politics, perceived that the government had little impact on their lives, and did not expect equal or considerate treatment from the government. The German political culture was found to be one of "political detachment and subject competence."[44] Germans were very aware of government, tended to believe that they have a responsibility to vote, and expressed a high level of confidence toward the government. At the same time, however, the Germans were rarely active in other forms of political activity beyond voting and tended not to have a strong, emotional tie to the political system. They tended to be detached and passive about politics. This ambivalence may be a result of the socialization experience of the Nazi era. The United States was characterized as a "participant civic culture."[45] By civic culture, Almond and Verba mean one in which the orientations of disinterest, passive acceptance, and active participation all exist and are blended in the culture. In the United States, however, they believe there was some imbalance toward active participation. They state that Great Britain had what they call a "deferential civic culture."[46] They believe that the difference between the United States and Britain is that Britain has a more "effective" combination of those orientations leading to either passive or active participation.

This research and other research has, therefore, substantiated empirically that there are differences in political orientations among people of

---

40. See, for example, the series of country studies published by Little, Brown, including among others Richard Rose, *Politics in England*, 1964; Lewis G. Edinger, *Politics in Germany*, 1968.
41. These profiles are examined in depth in Almond and Verba, *The Civic Culture*, chap. 12.
42. Ibid., p. 308.
43. Ibid., p. 310.
44. Ibid., p. 312.
45. Ibid., p. 313.
46. Ibid., p. 315.

different countries. To a large extent, this aspect of research on political culture has been aimed at description rather than at the creation of generalizations. This is so partially because of the nature of questions asked, and partially because research on political culture is only in its initial stages. In the future, more attention should be paid to developing generalizations concerning why such differences exist.

More attention has been paid to creating generalizations in research on the second question which is suggested by the use of the concept of political culture. This question concerns how political culture affects the political system. The evidence from these generalizations is, however, more sketchy than that establishing the existence of differing political cultures. Let us turn to an examination of this aspect of political culture research.

The Impact of Political Culture on the Political System.

Basically, Almond and Verba assume that political culture affects the functioning of the political system. Their primary goal, however, was to discover what particular pattern of orientations would lead to stability in democratic governments. It should be pointed out that Almond and Verba not only assumed that political culture has an impact on government, but they also assumed the nature of that impact. They assumed that political culture must be congruent with the governmental structure or the political system would be unstable.

It is important to note that the research itself was not designed to establish the fact that incongruence between culture and structure will lead to instability. They initially designated the United States and Great Britain as stable countries.[47] They then argued that the cultural values present in those countries, what they called the civic culture, were necessary for the stability of those countries. This linkage was not directly tested. They did, however, examine empirically the pattern of orientations in the five countries, which are all structural democracies. They found the patterns in Britain and the United States to be similar and the patterns in the three other countries to differ significantly from the civic culture. Furthermore, the level of political instability has in the past been higher in those three countries than in Britain and the United States. Thus, there seems to be some support for the assumption that lack of congruence between the political culture and the political structure may be associated with instability.

Another study which did attempt to document empirically a relationship between political culture and the functioning of the political system was that by Donald Devine of the American political culture.[48] By an imaginative

---

47. Ibid., pp. 5–10.
48. Donald J. Devine, *The Political Culture of the United States: The Influence of Member Values on Regime Maintenance* (Boston: Little, Brown, 1972).

use of public opinion data, Devine showed how aspects of what he calls the liberal political culture "acts" to screen stimuli from the environment and thus "shapes" the opinions of Americans.[49] This shaping, he argues, will determine the expectations Americans have of their system, and will, in turn, affect the kinds of demands they make and the support they give to the system.

What is needed, however, is much more careful and rigorous testing of the nature of the relationship between political culture and the functioning of political systems. Such testing would necessitate looking at many countries. The difficulties in doing this are immense. Cross-national research is very difficult because of the language barriers we mentioned before. Such research is also very costly. And there is always a problem that some countries simply will not permit such research.

There are also other fundamental problems which are illustrated by the Almond and Verba study. In the first place, we have difficulty, when doing cross-national research, in avoiding the problem of seeing things from the perspective of our own national identity. It may be significant that Almond and Verba chose their own country as one with a civic culture to be emulated. Secondly, there is the problem in such research of finding what you expect to find. Having specified Britain and the United States as ideals, it is difficult to resist the temptation of concluding that the political culture in those countries is also ideal and that other cultures have problems which they must overcome. In both of these instances we can see the difficulty of disassociating research from values.

Once again, let us urge you not to be too discouraged by this list of problems. To say that more work needs to be done is not equivalent to saying it is hopeless. We are simply trying to warn you of the potential pitfalls of using the concept in research and to make you a careful and analytic reader of others' attempts at using the concept.

Let us consider some of the directions further research should take. Researchers should establish more of a consensus as to what the fundamental components of political culture are. (We relied on Rosenbaum's list, but this is not universally accepted by researchers.) Consideration should be given to how political culture is learned and how and why change may occur in this socialization process. More attention should be given to the crucial question of how political culture affects the political system. Perhaps Devine's approach of examining the effect of the culture on the political expectations of a people could be used as a guide.

So far we have been viewing these concepts from the perspective of a political scientist who will either conduct research or read the reports of such research. We have taken the perspective of objective political scientists looking down from our ivory tower and argued that these concepts would

---

49. Ibid., p. 31.

provide us with a better understanding of how and why people behave politically as they do. But it is also true that understanding these concepts is important to those who are actually involved in politics. Virtually every political leader is, or should be, concerned with the creation of citizenry with a supportive political culture because the existence of such a citizenry would make his or her job easier. As Almond and Verba argue, a supportive political culture may be different in different countries and at different times. In a democratic country, Almond and Verba argue that the political culture should include predominantly the values of citizen activity and involvement, while in an authoritarian country the political culture should be characterized by citizen passiveness and submissiveness.

In some countries, political leaders devote large amounts of the nation's resources to attempt to socialize their citizens into desirable political cultures. This is especially important and, therefore, especially common in the new nations in the world, such as the African and Asian countries which have just emerged from colonial rule. It is also the case in countries which have undergone a recent revolution, for example, Cambodia, Uganda, or Cuba in 1959. Citizens in such countries must learn a new political culture which would be supportive of new leaders, new political institutions, and new patterns of behavior.

This attention to affecting the political socialization of citizens sounds suspiciously like manipulation. Of course, that is exactly what it is. But it is not something that is necessarily evil or something limited to authoritarian countries or to revolutionary situations. In fact, it may interest you to know that the American system of free public education was developed, in part, because of the recognition by political leaders of the importance of socializing the vast waves of immigrants into the American political culture. Even now there is still a great amount of time and effort spent in the public schools teaching children about politics. Consider, for example, the Pledge of Allegiance in the mornings, the time spent learning about America's political heroes such as Washington and Lincoln, and the number of civics courses in the curriculum. This list is, of course, far from complete, but it should alert you to the number of ways our school systems consciously attempt to make us desirable citizens of our country or, in other words, attempt to socialize us into the American political culture.

SUMMARY
POLITICAL SOCIALIZATION

Core Definition:	The way that individuals learn about politics.
Operationalization:	1. The content of socialization is usually operationalized by the use of questionnaires, testing knowledge and attitudes.

84 THE SETTING OF POLITICS

	2. The process of socialization is usually operationalized by comparing attitudes, knowledge, etc., of those being socialized with those of various agents of socialization.
Basic Questions:	1. How do we learn about politics?
	2. What do we learn about politics?
Summary of Major Findings:	1. We learn by imitating those around us and/or by the conscious and unconscious application of positive and negative reinforcement.
	2. There are stages in our learning process. We learn about concrete things first (the President, the policeman) before we learn about abstracts (government, Congress).
	3. Traditionally, Americans have learned strong, positive feelings about their government.
	4. The major agents of socialization are the family, schools, media, and peer groups.
Directions for the Future:	1. More work linking the socialization process to characteristics of the government
	2. More work on comparing patterns of socialization
	3. More work on adult socialization
	4. More information on the impact of discontinuity in the socialization process
	5. More research on the relative roles of various agents of socialization (family, schools, etc.)
	6. Generally, more work on making generalizations and building theory rather than on description alone

SUMMARY
POLITICAL CULTURE

Core Definition:	The fundamental political orientations of a people
Operationalization:	The use of questionnaires to discover the knowledge, values, and emotions of a people concerning their government
Basic Questions:	1. What are the patterns of political culture in various countries?
	2. What is the impact of political culture on the government?

Summary of Major Findings:	1. Different countries can be characterized by different patterns of political orientations. 2. Some evidence supports the contention that a congruence between political culture and the structure of government leads to stability.
Directions for the Future:	1. More work to distinguish culture from a collection of individual attitudes 2. More work on how political cultures develop and change 3. More work on the effect of political culture on the process of government decision making, especially in the areas of what issues are raised and what decisions are made

STUDY QUESTIONS

1. Consider your own political socialization. a. How did you learn about politics? That is, think about the order or pattern in which you learned about politics. b. What were the primary agents (groups, institutions, people) who socialized you? c. What did you learn about politics? Consider what you know about politics as well as what your feelings about politics are. d. Make hypotheses about what you believe is the connection between the way you were socialized and how you are now oriented to politics.
2. There seems to be disagreement about whether the family or the school is the more important agent of socialization. Hypothesize which you think is more important (you might want to make conditional hypotheses, such as, the school is more important if certain conditions are present). Devise a way to test your hypothesis.
3. Make hypotheses concerning what you believe are the effects of the media and of peer groups in socialization. How would you test these hypotheses?
4. What problems might discontinuity in the socialization process cause for the individual? For the government?
5. What is the value of using the political culture approach to understand politics? Describe the political culture in your community in terms of Rosenbaum's three dimensions.
6. Give operationalizations of Rosenbaum's dimensions of political culture.

Political Interactions

Chapter Five

The last chapter examined two conceptual approaches to understanding the importance of the setting of politics. Political socialization and political culture provide us with frameworks for researching the values and beliefs of people in a political system, how people learn those values and beliefs, and the impact of this pattern of beliefs on the functioning of the political system. Now we will be moving our attention from the setting of politics to the processes of politics. We will examine how the interactions among political actors are structured, as well as the nature of those interactions. To do this we will discuss five basic concepts: power, group, conflict, system, and communication. These concepts are so basic that some researchers claim that they are *the* fundamental concepts of the discipline.

Some political scientists argue that politics is the exercise of *power*. Most believe, however, only certain kinds of power should concern political scientists. David Easton defined politics as the use of authoritative power to allocate the resources of society.[1] But this still means that power in some form is so basic that it defines the scope of the discipline of political science. Granted the fundamental importance of the concept of power, we still are

---

1. David Easton, "An Approach to the Analysis of Political Systems," *World Politics,* (April 1957).

faced with the problem of defining and operationalizing the concept so that it can be used in empirical research. Our discussion of power then will focus on these problems of using the concept in research.

The second concept is *group*. The importance of group in politics has been recognized for centuries. Madison, in fact, based his plan for the new American government in 1789 on an analysis of the nature and behavior of groups. But the modern emphasis on group was motivated to a large extent by Arthur Bentley's book, *The Process of Government*, published in 1908. Bentley argued that "When the groups are adequately stated, everything is stated. When I say everything I mean everything. The complete description will mean the complete science, ..."[2] David Truman, who "rediscovered" the concept of group in 1951, states in his book *The Governmental Process* that ". . . the acceptance of groups as lying at the heart of the process of government is unavoidable."[3] While Bentley and Truman may be the strongest proponents of the group approach, many other researchers have followed their lead and focused on groups in research. We will consider the kinds of questions such a focus would suggest and some of the advantages and disadvantages of using the concept of group in research.

The third concept to be considered in this chapter is *conflict*. And, sure enough, there have been claims by some political scientists that conflict is the fundamental concept of politics. As E. E. Schattschneider wrote in *The Semi-Sovereign People*, "At the root of all politics is the universal language of conflict."[4] The study of conflict has basically focused on such questions as the following: Why and how do conflicts arise? How do conflicts differ? How is conflict spread, or contained? How is conflict resolved?

The other two concepts, system, and communication, are the broadest approaches we will discuss. The concept of *system* focuses attention on the primary idea of this chapter: *interaction*. A system may be defined as a set of interactions among identifiable components. David Easton borrowed the concept of system from biology and cybernetics and adopted it for use by political scientists. He saw system as a unifying concept which would provide a framework for a general theory of politics. The concept of *communication* is closely related to system. It also emphasizes interaction among components. The major difference between the two approaches is the identification of components. The primary spokesman for the communications approach is Karl Deutsch.

---

2. Arthur F. Bentley, *The Process of Government* (Chicago: University of Chicago Press, 1908), pp. 208–9.
3. David B. Truman, *The Governmental Process: Political Interests and Public Opinion*, 2nd ed. (New York: Knopf, 1971), p. 46.
4. E. E. Schattschneider, *The Semi-Sovereign People* (New York: Holt, Rinehart & Winston, 1960), p. 2.

We will discuss each of these concepts in turn, but you should realize that it is impossible to totally separate these concepts from one another. A restatement of Easton's definition of politics should make this point clear. Politics, in this restatement, may be said to equal interactions which lead to the exercise of authoritative power to settle conflicts among groups concerning how the scarce resources of society will be allocated. With the understanding that they are intimately related, let us now turn to a separate investigation of each of these concepts.

POWER

The focus on power by political scientists seems to make intuitive sense. When you think of government you almost automatically think simultaneously of power. Government, or more accurately the representatives of government, can make you obey a stop sign while driving, demand and receive your hard-earned money in taxes, throw you in jail for refusing to obey its rules, and, in some instances, can even demand your life, either because you have committed what is considered a particularly distasteful action (murder, rape, and so forth) or because you are needed to fight a war. Intuitively, then, it is obvious that government has power. However, there are others in society who are also seen as exercising power. When the Lockheed Corporation, for example, requests and receives special financial help from the government, we say that Lockheed has power. When blacks succeed in securing passage of a civil rights bill, we say blacks are increasing their political power. Therefore, political scientists are interested in studying not only the power exercised by government, but also the relative power of those in society who use their power to attempt to affect the government's actions.

It should be obvious that our understanding of politics could be significantly improved if we could establish sound generalizations concerning the exercise of power. We could ask who possesses power; what tactics and strategies seem successful; and if it makes a difference, in terms of the policies and stability of a government, if different power structures exist. Before we can move to the stage of generalization, we first have to define our concept. So far, we have been talking about power in an intuitive sense. Researchers who wish to conduct empirical studies of power must go beyond the intuitive sense of power and clearly specify how we will know power when we see it. This means we have to define and operationalize the concept. One of the classic definitions of power is that developed by Robert Dahl: "A has power over B to the extent that he can get B to do something that B would not otherwise do."[5] Several points must be made about this definition.

---

5. Robert Dahl, "The Concept of Power," *Behavioral Science*, II (July 1957), 201–15.

In the first place, power is relational. This is to say, power can only be meaningful in an interactional setting. Because you were a big fourteen-year-old you may have been able to bully other kids on the block. You had power vis-a'-vis them. At the same time, you were probably unable to bully your parents. In this relationship you lacked power. Power does not exist in isolation, but only as a means of describing the interactions of two or more people, groups, or nations. As noted in our examples above, the characteristics of the "power holder" may not change, but it is the relationship which will determine if A can get B to do something he might not ordinarily have done.

This does not mean that capabilities or resources of power are unimportant, but that such resources are distinct from the exercise of power. In other words, power, here, is not defined as the possession of certain resources. Often, in common language, we would refer to someone like a heavyweight boxer as having a great deal of power because of his massive muscles. Or we would talk about a country having power because it has massive armaments. Dahl's definition, however, makes a distinction between resources of power (muscles, guns, expertise) and the actual exercise of power.

Resources and exercise of power may or may not be related. Referring again to Dahl's definition, it is clear that Muhammed Ali would be more likely to get you to do something that you would not ordinarily do than would, say, Don Knotts. But, then, Muhammed Ali, with all of his muscles, may not care what you do. That is, possession of resources of power does not ensure that it will be used in an attempt at coercion. Thus, resources are analytically separate from the use of those resources in the exercise of power. Another point which should be made about Dahl's definition is that power is considered a form of behavior. This point should be clear from the discussion of the difference between resources of power and the exercise of power.

Dahl's definition has, therefore, shed some light on the concept of power. Yet there are still problems in trying to use this definition as a basis for empirical research. For an action to be described as an instance of power, Dahl has required that B do something he wouldn't otherwise do. How, pray tell, are we to know what B was planning to do in the absence of A? Some researchers have tried to get around this problem by saying that power exists if A can achieve what he, she, or it wants without worrying about the prior intentions of those who comply. But does it really make sense to say that a person has power simply because everyone happens to agree with him and acts as he wishes they would act? One way around this is to require that there be some observed interaction between who is supposed to have power and who is supposed to be responding to it.[6]

---

6. For a discussion of this, see Alan C. Isaak, *Scope and Methods of Political Science* (Homewood, Illinois: The Dorsey Press, 1975), pp. 239-40.

And yet again there is trouble. If behavior has to occur to prove that a power relation exists, how does one handle a situation in which a person acts one way to ward off potential action by another? For example, many congressmen try to decipher what their constituents feel strongly about and vote in compliance because they fear that if they do not, they may be deposed in the coming election. The voters may not have taken any actions prior to the congressman's vote, but it would certainly appear that the voters do, in fact, have some influence over him.

Friedrich would call this "anticipated reaction."[7] Using common sense, we would say that the voters hold power over congressmen because they can induce the congressmen to vote as the voters desire. To test this empirically, however, would be very difficult. You would have to ask congressmen if their vote was different than it would otherwise have been because of fear of the voters. Of course, it would have to be assumed that the congressmen would answer you honestly.

Bachrach and Baratz raise another major problem in examining power. They argue that one very potent form of power is the ability to prevent certain situations from arising. They call this aspect of power *non–decision making*.[8] For instance, if Congress had to vote to raise its pay each year, the voters might organize yearly to fight the pay raise. Many congressmen might feel it is necessary to vote against the raise because of the fear of the voters' reaction later at the polls. In this case, the voters have power. On the other hand, Congress might pass a bill which provides an automatic pay raise each year for the next ten years. This means there is no debate in Congress after the first year and, therefore, no opportunity for the citizens to oppose the raise after the first year. The result is that the congressmen get what they want with no opposition. In this hypothetical example the outcome was determined by the fact that one party had the power to prevent an issue from arising.

The obvious problem for empirical research is to find situations which do not arise. Sounds difficult? It is. Let us look at an example of an attempt to study nondecisions empirically. Crenson, in a study of air pollution, found that such issues seldom received serious consideration if certain groups were against them.[9] Of course, the lack of consideration may have been due to the lack of concern on the part of the population. Yet in every case studied, once the issue did become the subject of widespread discussion, air pollution ordinances were passed. This is at least circumstantial evidence that the public wanted air pollution control, but that certain groups managed to delay consideration of the issue.

---

7. Carl J. Friedrich, *Constitutional Government and Democracy* (Boston: Ginn, 1950), p. 49.
8. Peter Bachrach and Morton S. Baratz, *Power and Poverty* (New York: Oxford University Press, 1970).
9. Matthew A. Crenson, *The Un-Politics of Air Pollution: A Study of Non-Decisionmaking in the Cities* (Baltimore: The Johns Hopkins University Press, 1971).

It should be obvious by now that while the concept of power has much intuitive appeal as an approach to analyze politics, it is very difficult to get a handle on the concept. You may also have noticed that one reason why it is difficult to research a power relationship is because, as Dahl defined it, it is a special case of a causal relationship. To meet Dahl's requirements, a researcher would have to prove that it was A who caused B's actions rather than any other cause. There are so many possible causes for an action by humans that it is very difficult to establish one factor (A's actions) as a cause. In addition, to research power empirically we must have some way to transform the relationship into empirical phenomena, that is, to operationalize it. But we have yet to develop acceptable indicators for those instances when we feel power is involved, but with no observable action. It is clear that defining and operationalizing power is something which researchers must still work on.

This problem of defining power is aggravated by the necessity of distinguishing power from a number of similar ideas. For instance, is there a difference between power and such terms as influence, manipulation, authority, and force? Many researchers do make distinctions among these concepts. But unfortunately, once again there seems to be no real consensus among researchers on what these distinctions are.

The existence of so much confusion about the definition of power obviously leads to great difficulty in using the concept in research. As you might expect, with so much confusion over the definition of power, there is also much disagreement over how to operationalize the concept. It is quite likely that using different measures to analyze data will lead to different interpretations of that data. Therefore, the research findings may appear to be highly contradictory. That, in fact, has happened in the research on power. For example, at one time there was considerable interest in researching the question of who has power in American communities. Two major studies of this question produced completely contradictory results. Floyd Hunter, in his examination of the power structure in Atlanta, concluded that a business elite existed which monopolized the city's power.[10] Robert Dahl, on the other hand, concluded that in the city he studied, New Haven, Connecticut, power was widely distributed and that different groups had power in different issue areas.[11] There are many possible explanations for the contradiction in these findings.

It may simply have been that the distribution of power in each city was different. Regardless of the real power structure, however, extensive research has seemed to indicate that the methods chosen to search for the "power holders" determines where they will be found.[12] Hunter used the

---

10. Floyd Hunter, *Community Power Structure* (Chapel Hill: University of North Carolina Press, 1953).
11. Robert A. Dahl, *Who Governs?* (New Haven: Yale University Press, 1961).
12. John Walton, "Discipline, Method and Community Power: A Note on the Sociology of Knowledge," *American Sociological Review* (October 1966), 688.

reputational approach, which relies upon knowledgeable "judges" in the community listing the people they believed had power. Dahl, on the other hand, examined those who participated in various decisions.

The problem with Hunter's method is that the "judges" may ascribe power to people who really do not hold it. On the other hand, Dahl would attribute power to people who participated in decisions, whether or not they were able to get others to comply. He also only looked at specific issue areas rather than trying to look at power in general as Hunter had done. These two techniques could, therefore, obviously lead to contradictory conclusions. It is also noteworthy that, in all probability, power structures change over time. Therefore, the time frame in which the study is done will affect the findings.

Many researchers have ignored the stage of definition to make generalizations using power. Some generalizations derived from the community power literature are the following:

1. The larger the size of community, the greater dispersion of power.
2. The stronger the labor unions, the greater dispersion of power.
3. The more socially heterogeneous the community, the greater the distribution of power.
4. The more competitive the party structure, the greater the distribution of power.[13]

International relations specialists have also focused extensively on power as a tool to understanding the behavior of nations. The arms race between the United States and the U.S.S.R. is rooted in, among other things, the notion of balance of power.[14] The basic idea of balance of power is the belief that if one nation becomes more powerful than the other, war will result. This again raises the problem of measuring power. In international relations power has generally been operationalized in terms of the resources of power, that is, military expenditures, size of armed forces, GNP, energy consumption, urban population, and so forth.

Until researchers can develop a consensus concerning how to define and operationalize power, tests of such generalizations will be inconclusive since each researcher may mean something entirely different than his colleagues. As we indicated with our example of Hunter and Dahl, many reputable researchers do not even agree on such a basic question as who has power in a particular area. There is a major debate concerning who holds power in America. Hunter's and Dahl's studies, cited earlier, are part of the literature on this debate. Hunter argued that power in Atlanta was monopolized by an elite.[15] Others, notably C. Wright Mills, believed that the

---

13. Robert L. Lineberry and Ira Sharkansky, *Urban Politics and Public Policy*, 3rd ed. (New York: Harper & Row, 1978), pp. 183–5.
14. For a discussion of balance of power, see Inis L. Claude, Jr., *Power and International Relations* (New York: Random House, 1962).
15. Hunter, *Community Power Structure*.

elite model also characterized the whole American political and social system.[16] The notion that power is dominated by a few is known as *elitism*. Dahl argued, on the basis of his study of New Haven, that power is spread widely among various groups in society.[17] Much of his other writings show that he believes that the pattern in New Haven is mirrored in America as a whole. The belief that power lies with many groups in society is known as *pluralism*. Obviously any conclusion on whether elitism or pluralism most accurately describes the power structure in America is dependent, once again, on establishing a consensus on a definition of power.

Much of the work using the concept of power is termed theory. For example, people talk about pluralist theory, or elitist theory. But there is not yet a structure of knowledge which really deserves the title of theory. The primary reason for this is the problem we pointed to earlier: the definition and operationalization of the concept of power. Until that can be resolved we can't move to the stage of making empirical generalizations. At this point, the generalizations are only statements of tendencies rather than statements of relationships that occur with a known probability. The centrality of the idea of power in politics means that researchers must devote more effort to definition. Much more work is needed on defining the concept and developing generally acceptable indicators. Only then can studies of power be used to move beyond intuitive analyses to developing scientific generalizations. One thing that must be avoided is a rather common tendency among many political observers of a definite circularity in thinking about power. Many will observe that some people seem to get what they want from government. The observers characterize these people as having power. The fact that these people have power is then used to explain why they get what they want. This sort of circular reasoning is called *tautological*. No new information has been produced. It is equivalent to saying that one plus one equals two and then turning around and explaining that something is two because it equals one plus one.

Power, obviously, is an elusive concept. It was partly to avoid the problems of dealing with such elusive ideas that Arthur Bentley argued for a focus on groups. Let us turn to a consideration of the problems of doing research on groups.

GROUP

At face value, group is an easier idea to deal with than power. It would seem as though a group is empirical, and, therefore, it would not be difficult to define and operationalize precisely. In fact, Arthur Bentley, the political scientist who first introduced the concept of group to the discipline in 1908,

---

16. C. Wright Mills, *The Power Elite* (New York: Oxford University Press, 1956).
17. Dahl, *Who Governs?*

94 POLITICAL INTERACTIONS

argued that the advantage of focusing on group was to get away from research on nonempirical things such as "sovereignty," and "the state." He called such abstract ideas "ghosts." Bentley also argued that group could form the basis for a general theory of politics. As we indicated before, he believed that all political activity is group activity. In his words, ". . . there are no phenomena except group phenomena. . . ."[18]

These arguments of Bentley's should sound familiar to you. More than seventy years ago he was arguing for the importance of empiricism and the construction of empirical theory. The concept which he believed would form the basis of such theory is one of the few concepts which has been developed primarily by political scientists rather than being borrowed by them from other disciplines and adapted for political analysis. What, then, has happened to the development of a group theory of politics? For the most part, attempts to build a general theory based on groups have failed. Bentley's work generated some research, but for the most part was forgotten until David Truman "rediscovered" it in 1951.[19] Truman, who developed his ideas from Bentley's work, again called for group to be the basis for a general approach to political analysis. Again, research was generated, but there still is no general theory. Let us consider why there has been trouble in developing such a general theory.

Ironically enough, the problem once again seems to be defining just what is meant by group. Bentley himself turned up his nose at the problems of definition.[20] But others who followed Bentley's path tried to specify the nature of the concept of group. To them a group has to do with interests and actions. Let us look at some examples. For instance, David Truman argued, ". . . interactions, or relationships, because they have a certain character and frequency, give the group its molding and guiding powers. In fact, they are the group, and it is in this sense that the term will be used."[21] Charles Hagan, in an echo of David Easton, talked about that ". . . mass of human activity out of which was to be abstracted that which is relevant to the authoritative allocation of values."[22] And Harry Eckstein said that ". . . masses of activity have common tendencies in regard to decisions; these masses of activity are groups."[23]

Now, what does all this mean? Unlike the concept of power, the concept of group is empirical. A "mass of activity" is empirical since activity can be observed. But how are we to distinguish the mass of activity which

---

18. Bentley, *The Process of Government*, p. 222.
19. Truman, *The Governmental Process*.
20. Bentley, *The Process of Government*, p. 199.
21. Truman, *The Governmental Process*, p. 24.
22. Charles B. Hagan, "The Group in Political Science," in *Approaches to the Study of Politics*, ed. Roland Young (Evanston, Illinois: Northwestern University Press, 1958), p. 44.
23. Harry Eckstein, "Introduction: Group Theory and the Comparative Study of Pressure Groups," *Comparative Politics: A Reader*, eds. Eckstein and David E. Apter (New York: The Free Press, 1963), p. 391.

constitutes a group from any other mass of activity? A concept which cannot be used to distinguish among various phenomena is not very useful since the basic function of concepts is to point to certain phenomena which share certain characteristics and are differentiated from other phenomena. It is probably because the concept of group, as so defined, is so vague that researchers have had problems using it as a basis for a general theory of politics.

Why, you may be wondering, do people devise such a vague definition? The answer probably is that they want the concept to be broad enough to be used to analyze all political activity. The dilemma seems to be that if the concept is broad enough to apply to all political activity, it is too broad to distinguish among kinds of activities and to provide a basis for generalizations. Therefore, it is impossible to develop a series of established generalizations which can form a theory.

David Truman tried to get around the problem of the concept of group being too vague by developing a classification of groups. He identified four types of groups: *categoric groups, interaction groups, institutional groups,* and *potential groups.*[24]

Categoric groups are simply categories of people who share some common characteristic(s). The people in this group may or may not be aware of the shared property. That characteristic may be nothing more than a demographic or a physical trait. For instance we may talk about people with high socioeconomic status or people with blue eyes as groups. Such groups, however, may not be anything more than the way a researcher decides to categorize people. Categoric groups would be of interest to the political scientist only if this shared trait were related to another commonality that political scientists study, such as the way these people think and behave politically.

Interaction groups are those collections of people who get together because of their shared characteristic but do not have a formal organized structure. Mothers who meet in the park would be an example of this type of group. An institutional group is characterized by formality and structure. Institutional groups range from families to legislatures to the U.N.

The hardest type of group to deal with empirically is the potential group. It is here that we encounter serious difficulties for theory construction. A potential group is a collection of individuals with a shared characteristic who may at some time interact or organize. Although the potential group is nonexistent at a given point in time, the group theorists argue that other groups react to this potential group. Many people say that American consumers form a potential group. The government has been expanding its consumer protection, perhaps in response to the possibility of consumers organizing in the future. Herein lies the problem for the empirical theorist.

---

24. Truman, *The Governmental Process,* pp. 23–35.

How can we establish empirically that a potential group exists? It is conceivable that any collection of individuals may sometimes see itself and be seen as a group. So, we are basically back where we started. Anything may be a group and, therefore, we cannot distinguish a group from a nongroup.

It is these problems of definition and operationalization which have plagued the efforts to develop a general theory of politics based on the concept of group. But while we do not have a group theory, we do not want to imply that the concept of group has not been useful for understanding politics. Perhaps one of the most useful contributions of the concept of group was that it shifted the attention of researchers from a focus solely on the legal/institutional aspects of politics. After Bentley's book, increased attention was paid to the role and influence of groups which Truman would call interaction and institutional groups. Of particular concern were political interest groups, or pressure groups.[25] While Bentley and the other group "theorists" might be displeased with such research, it has the definite advantage of dealing with an empirical and easily identifiable subject matter. Such research has produced some valuable findings. Let us now examine the questions which have been asked in the research on political interest groups.

What Questions Have Been Asked?

Political scientists, who have used the group concept, have basically tried to understand two aspects of political reality. The two basic questions they ask are: (1) How, and to what extent, do groups have an impact on the attitudes and behavior of their members? and (2) How, and to what extent, do groups have an impact on the functioning of the political system? To answer the first question, political scientists are interested in those groups which become reference groups.[26] Reference groups are those groups to which members look for cues for their attitudes and actions. It should be obvious that not all groups become reference groups. Blue-eyed people may be a categoric group, but it is probably unlikely that this shared characteristic will affect attitudes and behavior. On the other hand, people of higher socioeconomic status or members of a labor union may be aware of common interests and look for appropriate cues. Investigators of the second question have focused primarily on political interest groups. Interest groups can be defined as a combination of individuals who have organized around shared interests to attempt to affect the political process. Both of the questions listed above have led to an abundance of research. Let us consider some of the findings which have been produced by that research.

---

25. See, for example, the following: E. Pendleton Herring, *Group Representation Before Congress* (Baltimore: The Johns Hopkins Press, 1929); Peter H. Odegard, *Pressure Politics: The Story of the Anti-Saloon League* (New York: Columbia University Press, 1928); E. E. Schattschneider, *Politics, Pressures, and the Tariff* (New York: Prentice Hall, 1935).
26. Bernard R. Berelson and Gary A. Steiner, *Human Behavior: An Inventory of Scientific Findings* (New York: Harcourt Brace Jovanovich, 1964), p. 558.

Effects of Groups on Individuals. We have already answered part of the question of how groups affect an individual's attitudes in our discussion of political socialization. We noted that the family usually teaches a child such fundamental political attitudes as national identity, attitude toward authority, trust of the system and, in America at least, party identification. We also noted that as the child grows older, peer groups, which are also *primary groups,* may also influence a child's political attitudes. Both the family and peer groups may be considered primary groups because of the frequent face-to-face interaction which occurs among its members. As we mentioned before, there is some research which indicates that the learning from such primary groups has an enduring influence on the child as he matures.

Beyond childhood, the individual may also develop other group identities. These may be called *secondary groups* because the frequency and intimacy of contact is not as great as in primary groups. Many of these may be more formalized than a peer group. Some people will join organized groups which act to represent particular interests, such as the Man-Will-Never-Fly Memorial Society International and the National Goldfish Society (both of which do exist). Many will join more than one of these groups. For instance, it is quite conceivable that a person could love both flying and goldfish.

What is the influence of such group memberships on an individual's attitudes and behaviors? One of the classic studies of voting behavior, *The American Voter,* has examined this question. The answer seems to be, simplistically stated, that it all depends. In general, the group's influence on an individual seems to vary with the degree to which the individual identifies with the group.[27] The closer the identification, the greater the influence of the group on the individual. Influence in specifically political matters involves another important factor. Groups have greater influence on the political attitude of their members if the group is seen as being related to the world of politics.[28] For instance, the National Goldfish Society would probably have less influence on its members' political attitudes than would, say, the League of Women Voters or the Public Affairs Council.

Thus, there are two broad generalizations which have resulted from this focus on groups: (1) If member identification is high, groups can have an impact on individuals, and (2) If the group is seen as being related to politics, it can have an impact on individuals.

The influence of the group can be of two kinds. Groups can influence how people think and feel about political issues. The group can become a source of trusted political cues. Therefore, interaction with the group can facilitate access to political information. Secondly, group membership can encourage political participation. This is probably due, in some cases, to efforts by groups to encourage members to contact government officials. It

---

27. Angus Campbell and others. *The American Voter* (New York: Wiley, 1964), p. 168.
28. Ibid., p. 171

is also probably due to the perception that an individual's action may have more impact because his effort is backed by the other group members. Another reason may be that groups increase access to political information and studies have shown that those who are more informed tend to participate more. In any event, membership in a group seems to have an impact on individuals' political attitudes and behavior, especially if he identifies with the group and sees the group as politically relevant.

Effects of Groups on Government. The second question concerns the extent to which groups have an impact on a political system. Again, the answer must be conditional. Obviously, some groups have no impact because they make no, or infrequent, attempts to influence politics. Other groups may attempt to influence government and be unsuccessful. Political scientists have attacked the question of the influence of groups by asking what characteristics are likely to make a group successful.

A key idea in determining the potential success of a group is its "access" to government.[29] Access basically means the degree to which particular groups have access to government officials. But the idea of access has not really helped us understand why some groups do and others do not have access. To understand this we have to examine characteristics of groups as well as the techniques they use. Researchers have found several characteristics which seem to increase the probability of a group being successful in achieving access. For example, they have found that the greater the cohesion, the larger the size, the better the leadership, the higher the status, the better the organization, and wealth, the greater the possibility of a group achieving political access.[30] These are the major generalizations concerning the impact of groups on the government.

Researchers have also identified the effective techniques for groups to use. Much of this research has been done in the context of legislatures. It appears that the most effective technique is for group representatives to form close, personal relationships with legislators. This has also been found to be used often and effectively with bureaucrats. It also helps if the group representatives can point to some relationship between themselves and the legislator's constituents.[31] Contrary to popular belief, hard pressure tactics were less often used to convert opponents than attempts at reinforcing predilections of friendly legislators. Providing information and testifying at hearings are also tactics which seem to be effective.

Overall evaluations of the impact of groups on the political system vary. The "elite theorists," of course, would argue that only a very few homogeneous groups monopolize the power of the country and make the key deci-

---

29. Truman, *The Governmental Process*, p. 264.
30. For a summary of such generalizations, see Isaak, *Scope and Methods of Political Science*, p. 211.
31. John W. Kingdon, *Congressmen's Voting Decisions* (New York: Harper & Row, 1973), p. 143.

sions.[32] To them the group struggle exists, but has an impact only on minor issues. The pluralists on the other hand argue that politics *is* the group struggle. In this debate we see the overlap between the power and group approaches.

Some argue that government simply umpires the struggle and then ratifies the decisions produced by the groups.[33] Others believe that the government itself is another group which participates in the group conflict.[34] Some see the group conflict as good since it distributes power widely and helps to give everyone a piece of the action.[35] Others see it as bad, pointing to the fact that some can't compete equally in the group struggle (primarily the lower class), and the struggle tends to lead to the government delegating decisions rather than acting authoritatively.[36] But all tend to believe that, at least on some issues, groups can and do have an influence on the decisions of government.

Group has also been used to explain political stability. It is argued that groups provide a safety valve for dissatisfied individuals by providing a linkage to the political system.[37] In the United States, it is further argued that since many individuals belong to many groups and since cleavages between groups vary with the issue involved, there are few deep-rooted cleavages in the society. Therefore, the society can reach a dynamic equilibrium based on coalitions of groups, each with some stake in orderly change.[38]

The focus on organized interest groups has produced some valuable information about politics. Examining such groups has given us a better understanding of the informal aspects of politics. The group approach has focused our attention on an important influence on the attitudes and behavior of the people in the United States and a primary way people attempt to affect the functioning of the political system. Such investigations should be extended to other countries as well. But this does not mean that we have or can develop a general theory of politics based on the concept of group, since organized interest groups are only a part of the political world. The information produced by this research may, however, become an important part of an attempt to develop such a theory.

Let us now examine a concept which is often used in conjunction with groups: conflict. Both group theorists and conflict theorists see politics as the process of conflict among groups. Groups in isolation would not be of importance to government. But when their interests differ and when con-

---

32. Mills, *The Power Elite.*
33. Truman, *The Governmental Process,* p. 350.
34. Schattschneider, *The Semi-Sovereign People,* p. 17.
35. Robert Dahl, *A Preface to Democratic Theory* (Chicago: University of Chicago Press, 1956).
36. Theodore J. Lowi, *The End of Liberalism* (New York: Norton, 1969), chap. 3.
37. William Kornhauser, *The Politics of Mass Society* (New York: The Free Press, 1959).
38. Truman, *The Governmental Process,* pp. 159–61.

100 POLITICAL INTERACTIONS

flict arises, the government must make authoritative decisions in an attempt to resolve those conflicts. Let us see how conflict has been, and can be, used as a central focus for political research.

CONFLICT

As with the above-mentioned concepts, there is not a total consensus on a definition of the concept of conflict. But fortunately, unlike the situation with power and group, there is a widespread agreement on the basic idea. Conflict is a pattern of interaction which occurs when there are disagreements concerning the allocation of scarce resources. The relevance of this to Easton's definition of politics should be obvious. Easton believes the function of the political system is to resolve such disagreements by making authoritative decisions. To a group theorist the primary sources of such disagreements are the differing interests which form the basis of group activity.

Many of us tend to see conflict as something bad. There is no doubt that under some conditions some forms of conflict are extremely disruptive and destructive. This may obviously be seen as bad by some people, especially by those who come out on the short end of the stick or by those authorities who have to attempt to resolve the dispute. But, except in the visions of utopian thinkers, conflict is also an inevitable fact of life. It is not only inevitable, but it may also have positive effects.[39] For instance, conflict may be the process by which change occurs. Thus, it is important to move from the condemnation of conflict to a fuller understanding of the nature of conflict. We will first consider ways of describing conflict and then will examine what we know about the three basic questions which form the basis of research on conflict: How do conflicts arise? How do conflicts expand? and How are conflicts resolved?

How do Conflicts Arise?

Cobb and Elder have listed three crucial dimensions of a conflict situation.[40] The first of these is the *scope of conflict*. This refers to the number of people who are involved in a conflict situation. As Schattschneider argues, scope is very important because ". . . the balance of forces in any conflict is not a fixed equation until everyone is involved."[41] Schattschneider believes that the scope of the conflict will eventually determine its outcome. The second dimension is the *intensity of the conflict*. Intensity refers both to the commitment the parties have to the issues at stake and to the degree to which

---

39. Lewis Coser, *The Functions of Social Conflict* (New York: Free Press, 1956).
40. Roger W. Cobb and Charles D. Elder, *Participation in American Politics: The Dynamics of Agenda-Building* (Boston: Allyn and Bacon, 1972), p. 43.
41. Schattschneider, *The Semi-Sovereign People*, p. 5.

the positions of those involved are mutually contradictory. One hypothesis which may be made is that it is more difficult to resolve conflicts characterized as having high intensity. The final characteristic listed by Cobb and Elder is the *visibility of conflict*. This refers to the number of people who are aware of the conflict. These characteristics are obviously interrelated. As Cobb and Elder see it, the visibility of a conflict is dependent on its scope and intensity.[42]

Another way of describing conflicts is to consider the *pattern of the conflict*. In some conflict situations two groups of people constantly oppose each other. This pattern of conflict may be likely to be characterized by high intensity in Cobb and Elder's terms. This is especially likely to happen if one group consistently perceives itself as losing the battles. An example of this would be the situation in Ireland where Catholics are always allied with Catholics and Protestants with Protestants—and the Catholics consider themselves consistent losers. Many argue that such a situation will lead eventually to violence, as, in fact, it has in Ireland. Another pattern is one of cross-cutting cleavages in which different issues divide people in different ways, and there are no permanent blocs of opponents. For example, in the United States, some women may support the Equal Rights Amendment and some do not. And some women's groups may be allied with business groups on some issues (lower taxes) and against them on other issues (affirmative action). It is believed by many that such a pattern will be less likely to lead to violence. Today's enemies may well be tomorrow's allies. And in a shifting situation like this there are less likely to be permanent losers. This assumes, of course, that there is not one issue which creates a very intense conflict situation and which the opponents will not tolerate losing.[43]

These descriptive dimensions should be used as a basis for more research aimed at establishing relationships. For example, it would be important to know what factors are likely to produce high intensity in a conflict situation. What form of conflict resolution is likely to occur in a situation of high intensity? Is it the case that, as Cobb and Elder hypothesize, visibility is dependent on the scope and intensity of a conflict? Is it the case that an overlapping pattern of conflict is less likely to lead to high intensity and violence? Once again more research is needed.

How do conflicts arise? It follows from the definition of a conflict, that conflicts arise when people become aware of their differing interests concerning the allocation of scarce resources. Cobb and Elder have argued that the primary step in the initiation of such a conflict is the creation of an issue. They see three different goals which motivate people to create issues.[44] In the first place, issues may be manufactured by those who feel they are not

---

42. Cobb and Elder, *Participation in American Politics*, p. 44.
43. Schattschneider, *The Semi-Sovereign People*, p. 67.
44. Cobb and Elder, *Participation in American Politics*, p. 83.

receiving a "fair deal" in the allocation of various resources. They may attempt to "readjust" the situation. An example of this would be the issues created by blacks or women to obtain equal rights. Secondly, individuals or groups may attempt to advance themselves by creating an issue. For example, political candidates seek to develop issues to catch public attention. In other cases, people may create issues to further what they see as the "public interest." Many environmental groups use this as their motivation. Thirdly, initiation of issues may also be dependent upon various unforeseen events. Examples of these "triggering devices" would be riots, natural catastrophes, or technological innovation. Cobb and Elder argue that some link has to be made between these triggering devices, which suggest grievances, and an initiator who can convert the grievances into an issue which will form the basis of conflict.[45]

Another line of inquiry in attempting to discover how conflicts arise is followed by political scientists studying violent and revolutionary conflict. The magnitude of political violence is measured in terms of the extent of participation (scope), destructiveness (intensity), and time frame (duration).[46] The work of James C. Davies, Ted Robert Gurr, and others indicates that violent conflict in a society is usually the result of frustration. This frustration results from rising expectations which remain unfilled by the political system. The more one feels deprived relative to other groups in the society, the more likely it is that violent conflict will ensue. Quantitative studies across a number of nations would tend to support this thesis.[47]

Many researchers have pointed to the crucial role that groups play in this process of creating issues which engender conflict. Groups also serve to rally various interests on opposing sides of the conflict. It is also the case that the perception of an issue may serve as the basis for the creation of new groups.

Expansion of Conflict

Once an issue has arisen, it is quite likely that various significant developments will occur. The process of conflict expansion has received much attention from researchers. Coleman has focused on stages of community conflict and has argued there are seven stages in the development of conflicts:

---

45. Ibid., p. 85.
46. Ted Robert Gurr, *Why Men Rebel* (Princeton: Princeton University Press, 1970), p. 9.
47. Ibid., James C. Davies, "Toward a Theory of Revolution," *American Sociological Review,* XXVII (February 1962), 5-19; Crane Brinton, *The Anatomy of Revolution* (New York: Norton, 1938); Hugh Douglas Graham and Ted Robert Gurr, eds., *Violence in America: Historical and Comparative Perspectives* (Washington, D.C.: National Commission on the Causes and Prevention of Violence, 1969).

1. Initial issue arises.
2. Equilibrium of community relations is disrupted.
3. Previously suppressed issues (against opponents) appear.
4. Opponent's beliefs increasingly enter into the disagreement.
5. Opponent appears totally bad.
6. Charges made against opponent as a person.
7. Dispute becomes independent of initial disagreement.[48]

Coleman emphasizes the role that groups play in this developmental sequence. This focus is buttressed by Schattschneider's argument that the audience is a crucial factor in the development of any conflict.[49] As different individuals and groups are pulled into the conflict situation, each brings along a different set of interests. These interests are allied on one side or the other of the conflict and thus serve to alter the balance of power. It follows, therefore, that a crucial strategy in any conflict situation is control over the numbers and types of individuals and groups who will become involved with the issue.

Those who are initially on the winning side will, of course, attempt to stop others from joining the conflict. Schattschneider calls this limitation of the scope of conflict *privatization*.[50] The initial losers in the conflict will, on the other hand, attempt to recruit others in the hope of gaining allies. Schattschneider calls this the *socialization* of conflict.[51] Schattschneider and Cobb and Elder realize the importance that language plays in controlling the scope of conflict. If the conflict is to be expanded, the issue at its base must be defined in ways which will be meaningful to large numbers of people. Cobb and Elder have posited five generalizations concerning how issues should be defined to assure the socialization of the conflict.[52]

1. The more ambiguously an issue is defined, the greater the likelihood that it will reach an expanded public.
2. The more socially significant an issue is defined to be, the greater the likelihood that it will be expanded to a larger public.
3. The more an issue is defined as having extended temporal relevance, the greater the chance that it will be expanded to a larger audience.
4. The more nontechnical an issue is defined to be, the greater the likelihood that it will be expanded to a larger public.
5. The more an issue is defined as lacking a clear precedent, the greater the chance that it will be expanded to a larger population.

---

48. James Coleman, *Community Conflict* (New York: Free Press, 1957), p. 11.
49. Schattschneider, *The Semi-Sovereign People*, p. 2.
50. Ibid., p. 7.
51. Ibid., pp. 7-8.
52. Cobb and Elder, *Participation in American Politics*, pp. 96-97.

Another important part of the language of conflict is the use of symbols. Symbols can be very powerful because they evoke strong emotions.[53] The use of alternative symbols to characterize the opposing sides of a conflict may determine to what extent the conflict will be socialized. Consider the example of a conflict over establishing a national health insurance. Proponents may try to affix the symbol of equality to the proposal, hoping that that basic democratic value would appeal to large numbers of people. On the other hand, opponents of the measure may try to label the idea as socialism, in the hope that potential supporters would be frightened away.

In general, it appears that conflicts develop as increasing numbers of people, either as individuals, groups, or nations become involved. This happens as a result of attempts to define the issue in generally meaningful terms. At the same time one side of the conflict is attempting to expand the conflict, the other side may be trying to narrow the scope. Their strategies are based on attempts to define the issue narrowly. Each will attempt to associate positive symbols with their side of the conflict and negative symbols with the other side.

Resolution of Conflict

A final question to be asked about conflict concerns conflict resolution. Obviously, the expansion of conflict, which we have just considered, is motivated by the goal of achieving a favorable status for the final resolution of the conflict. Therefore, the strategies involved in the development of the conflict are also relevant as strategies of conflict resolution. Schattschneider has also pointed to another strategy of conflict resolution: *displacement*.[54] Displacement refers to substituting one conflict for another in the public's eye. Such substitution, in essence, resolves the initial conflict even if it only has the effect of maintaining the status quo.

William Gamson has developed another perspective on conflict resolution. He is only interested in the conflict between authorities and those who wish to influence those authorities. He argues this conflict must be viewed both from the perspective of the influencer and the influenced. The influencers, whom he calls "potential partisans," are attempting to achieve favorable decisions from the authorities. At the same time, the targets of the influence, the authorities, are attempting to maintain social control.[55] Gamson argues that the strategies that each will use are determined by the key variable of trust. He develops six hypotheses concerning what strategy will be used when.

---

53. For an insightful discussion of the importance of symbols, see Murray Edelman, *The Symbolic Uses of Politics* (Urbana: University of Illinois Press, 1964).
54. Schattschneider, *The Semi-Sovereign People*, chap. 4.
55. William A. Gamson, *Power and Discontent* (Homewood, Illinois: The Dorsey Press, 1968), pp. 36–37.

"A confident solidary group will tend to rely on persuasion as a means of influence."[56]

"A neutral solidary group will tend to rely on inducements as a means of influence."[57]

"An alienated solidary group will tend to rely on constraints as a means of influence."[58]

"Authorities will tend to rely on persuasion as a means of control over confident solidary groups."[59]

"Authorities will tend to rely on sanctions and particularly on inducements as a means of control over neutral solidary groups."[60]

"Authorites will tend to rely on insulation as a means of control over alienated solidary groups."[61]

Gamson also argues that the success or failure of these strategies may affect the levels of trust and thus alter the strategies chosen in the future. Gamson's hypotheses illustrate once again how closely related are the concepts discussed in this chapter. He recognizes the centrality of groups to conflict and he sees the basic conflict as a power relationship between groups in society and the authorities who attempt to control them.

Further evidence for the interrelation of the power, group, and conflict perspectives can be had by examining how Gamson's hypotheses mesh with other points raised previously in this chapter. When discussing power we mentioned that Bachrach and Baratz argued that one "face of power" which is often ignored is that of the control over nondecisions. In other words they argue that a significant form of power is the ability to determine what issues will and will not be considered in a political system. This control over the political agenda is precisely what Schattschneider and Cobb and Elder are considering when they discuss the effect of issue definition on expansion of a conflict. And Gamson is essentially looking at the same phenomenon when he hypothesizes that authorities will attempt to insulate, or close out, those groups in society they perceive as being alienated. This has significant long- and short-term consequences. The central question in each of these cases is why some groups do not succeed in the political allocation game. Simply stated, the answer is that these groups are unable to achieve access to the system. And the question of who achieves access is, as we noted before, a central concern of those who research groups.

Another way of looking at conflict resolution is to examine the decision-making process in a political system. We will consider the concept of decision making in the next chapter. For now, let us consider the value of

---

56. Ibid., p. 164.
57. Ibid., p. 168.
58. Ibid., p. 169.
59. Ibid., p. 180.
60. Ibid., p. 181.
61. Ibid., p. 182.

conflict as an approach to analyzing politics. Conflict, as we have seen, has generated a large amount of theoretical analysis. Attempts have been made to move beyond description to develop hypotheses concerning the nature, development, and resolution of conflict. Now what is needed is more rigorous testing of these hypotheses. This will require attempts to specify in operational terms the stages of conflict development. These stages, as of now, are much clearer analytically than they are empirically. Testing will also require specifying much more precisely the population to which the hypotheses refer. As of now, the impression, for the most part, is that conflict is conflict, whether it occurs within groups, cities, nations, or international systems. It may be that there are differences in the nature of conflict depending on where the conflict occurs. Coleman argued that the size and characteristics of cities affect which issues become the basis of conflict and how the people participate in the conflict.[62] It may, therefore, be reasonable to ask if the different sizes and characteristics of a city versus a nation or an international system may similarly result in differences in the nature, development, and resolution of conflict. Once again, we conclude that more research is necessary. But there has been a useful start on the use of conflict as a basis for analyzing politics.

We are now going to examine two concepts which differ somewhat from the concepts we have discussed so far. The goal of most of the concepts we have discussed is to help you analyze politics by focusing your attention on only one aspect of the political world. The idea is to tear the pieces of the puzzle apart to permit intensive study of each of the pieces. The goal of the concepts of system and communication is essentially the opposite of that: to help you fit all the pieces together again. Because these are inclusive frameworks, most of the questions which are suggested by other concepts can be integrated within analyses based on systems or communications. The basic idea of both of these concepts is to provide a broad framework for analyzing the whole political process rather than just one part of the whole, although they can also be used to examine parts of the total political process. Let us begin by examining the concept of system.

SYSTEM

Although each systems researcher has a slightly different definition of the concept, the common thread which runs through all of these definitions is the emphasis on interaction. A basic definition of system is interaction among identifiable units to achieve some purpose.[63] Obviously, such a broad definition can be used to refer to many things, political as well as nonpoliti-

---

62. Coleman, *Community Conflict,* chap. 2.
63. Leroy Rieselbach, *The Congressional System: Notes and Readings* (Belmont, Cal.: Duxbury Press, 1970), p. 2.

cal. For instance, a chair may be conceptualized as a system since it is composed of separate components (legs, seat, back) which interact to achieve a purpose (to support someone in a sitting position). The basic idea of a system was developed in disciplines other than political science and borrowed by political scientists who were looking for a basic framework to guide and to organize political research.

By examining the basic definition of a system we can see that there are four basic questions which a systems analysis should suggest to political researchers. In the first place, we would want to identify the primary purpose of a political system. Secondly, we would want to identify the components or units of the system. Once we identify the units of the political system, it is necessary to establish boundaries which separate the political system from other phenomena. This leads us to the third question which concerns the relationship between the political system and phenomena outside the political system, that is, the environment. And finally, we would want to examine the patterns of interaction among those components of the system.

Let us see how two political scientists have answered these questions which are suggested by systems analysis. First, we will examine the model of a political system developed by David Easton. Next, we will examine the work of Gabriel Almond, which is often seen as a development and extension of the basic systems framework.

Easton defined politics as ". . . the authoritative allocation of values. . . ."[64] He thought of his definition of politics as part of his broader definition of a political system. Easton defines a political system as "a set of interactions, abstracted from the totality of social behavior, through which values are authoritatively allocated for a society."[65]

Several points should be made about this definition. In the first place, Easton specifies the ultimate purpose of a political system: to allocate values for society. And he also specifies the components of a political system. He explicitly states that he will include in the political system interactions "abstracted from the totality of social behavior." This indicates that the primary components of the political system will be behavior, presumably by both individuals and institutions. But not all behavior will be considered part of the political system. Only when behavior is aimed toward the purpose of allocating values for society will it be considered part of the political system.

By abstracting certain aspects of behavior he is essentially saying that a political system can be distinguished from other kinds of systems and other forms of interactions. Those other systems will compose the environment of the political system. The pattern of interactions which compose the political

---

64. Easton, "An Approach to an Analysis of Political Systems."
65. David Easton, *A Framework for Political Analysis* (Englewood Cliffs, N.J.: Prentice-Hall, 1965), p. 57.
66. Ibid., pp. 63-69.

system will be distinguished from the environment by a boundary.[66] This boundary obviously does not exist as a physical entity. It is not even real in the sense that individuals say to themselves "Now I am going to act as part of the political system and allocate some values." As Easton indicates, behavior is a "totality," but researchers distinguish certain forms of behavior to study, and by this distinction they analytically create boundaries between that behavior and other kinds of behavior.

Expected patterns of behavior in specific social locations are known as *roles*. Thus, the isolated sets of behavior which compose the system are political roles. As noted earlier, we all perform many activities each day. Some are political, while others are not. Some actions which we do not think of as political at the time may well have political implications, such as reading "The Midnight Ride of Paul Revere." Each researcher has to determine what he wishes to know and then decide where to set the boundaries of the system on the basis of what will best serve the purposes of his research.

Let us give an example of how we may attempt to draw such a boundary for the American political system. We may decide to examine the behavior of the occupants of the three primary branches of government: the President, the Supreme Court Justices, and the Congressmen. But we would only be interested in those people when they are behaving as occupants of those positions, not when they are behaving as parents, church members, veterans, or any other such role.

We should also make clear that for the purpose of his particular research, a researcher may choose to draw his boundaries around a small subunit of the system. Such a subunit is known as a *subsystem*. For instance, he may examine the Congress as a system. Or it is possible that he may want to examine the interactions among various nations, in which case each nation is a subsystem. The point is that the researcher establishes the boundaries to suit his purposes.

In his definition of the political system, Easton has answered analytically two of the questions suggested by systems analysis. He has specified that the purpose of the system is to allocate values and has indicated that the components of the system are human behaviors which are aimed toward that purpose. The third question which systems analysis suggests concerns the nature of the interactions between the political system and the environment. This question is based on the assumption that the boundaries of the political system are permeable. In other words, factors from the environment can have an effect on the political system, and the political system in turn will have an effect on the environment around it.

The effects coming from the environment are referred to by Easton as *inputs*. Inputs can be broken down into two types: *demands* and *supports*.[67]

---

67. Ibid., pp. 112-113.

The demands from the environment create stress for the political system.[68] An example of such a demand from the environment is a request by the American Agricultural Movement that the government assure crop prices at 100% of parity. Easton assumes that a goal of the political system is persistence.[69] Therefore, the system must attempt to process such demands in a way which will be satisfactory to those in the environment making the demands.

The second form of input from the environment is support. Supports are essential if the system is to respond successfully to demands. One form of support is the taxes we pay. Obviously, if the system is to respond to any demands for material benefits, taxes are a necessary resource. Another form of support is our belief that the political system is a legitimate authority. If we think the system is legitimate, we believe it has the right to make laws regulating our behavior. We are, therefore, more likely to obey those regulations. This reduces the necessity of the system to use its resources to assure compliance with the laws and frees the use of those resources to respond to demands.

The effects of the system on the environment are known as *outputs*.[70] Easton classifies outputs into two types: *decisions* and *policies*. We will discuss both of these in the next chapter. For now let us simply say that such outputs are actions taken by the system to respond to stress in the environment. This does not mean that the outputs are simply a one-to-one response to the demands. The political system does not operate that mechanistically.

There is one other form of interaction with the environment which is mentioned by Easton: *feedback*.[71] Once the system has produced an output, the story is far from over. The results of decisions made by the system may be the creation of entirely new and unforeseen problems. Or the decision may simply not resolve the original demands. For example, the system may respond to demands from the American Agricultural Movement and assure crop prices at 90% of parity. But this may lead to increased inflation and/or it may encourage the AAM to press for 100% of parity. It is also possible that the output may satisfy the group or resolve problems. In either event, the reaction to the outputs of government forms the basis for new inputs on the system, both demands and supports. This influence of the outputs of a system on the inputs of that system is called feedback. It is in this way that Easton provides for dynamism, or constant movement and change.

We can summarize these various interactions by the schematic drawing in Figure 5-1.

---

68. Ibid., pp. 80-81.
69. Ibid., pp. 98-100.
70. Ibid., p. 126.
71. Ibid., pp. 127-130.

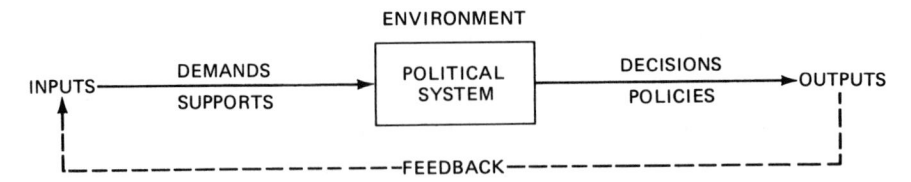

```
                    ENVIRONMENT
          DEMANDS    ┌──────────┐  DECISIONS
INPUTS ─────────────→│ POLITICAL│────────────→ OUTPUTS
        SUPPORTS     │  SYSTEM  │  POLICIES   │
   ↑                 └──────────┘             │
   │                                          │
   └──────────────────FEEDBACK────────────────┘
```

Figure 5-1 CONCEPTUAL SCHEME OF A POLITICAL SYSTEM (Source: Adapted from Easton, *Framework for Political Analysis*, © 1965, p. 112. Reprinted by permission of Prentice-Hall, Inc., Englewood Cliffs, New Jersey.)

The final question suggested by systems analysis concerns the nature of the interactions among the components of the system. Unfortunately, Easton is considerably more vague here. In fact, in the schematic drawing of the systems model you will notice that the political system is indicated by a box. This box is often referred to with more than a little frustration as "the black box" since so little is known of the processes within it.

Before discussing some of the problems and prospects of Easton's model of systems analysis we will examine Gabriel Almond's approach to systems analysis. Let us first consider Almond's definition of a political system:

> ". . . the political system is that system of interactions to be found in all independent societies which perform the functions of integration and adaptation by means of the employment, or threat of employment, of more or less legitimate physical compulsion. . . . Legitimate force is the thread which runs through the inputs and outputs of the political system."[72]

There are some similarities between Almond's and Easton's definitions of a political system. In the first place, both emphasize the importance of interactions. Both also distinguish the political system by its use of legitimate force (authority in Easton's terms). The major difference, however, between these two definitions is the specification of the purpose of the political system. To Almond, the purpose is integration and adaptation as opposed to the allocation of values.

A more fundamental difference between the two approaches becomes clear in Almond's identification of the basic functions of the system. While Easton argues only that a system will strive to persist, Almond specifies eight functions of the system. A *function* may be defined as an activity which must be performed to assure the persistence of the system. Almond breaks these functions into five input functions and three output functions. Thus, in his specification of the functions of the system, Almond also covers the question of how the system interacts with its environment.[73]

---

72. Gabriel A. Almond, "Introduction: A Functional Approach to Comparative Politics," in *The Politics of the Developing Areas*, eds. Gabriel A. Almond and James S. Coleman (Princeton: Princeton University Press, 1960), p. 7.
73. Ibid.

The five input functions are *political socialization, political recruitment, interest articulation, interest aggregation,* and *political communication.* Political socialization, as we indicated in the last chapter, is the process by which political learning takes place. Political recruitment is the means by which political leaders are selected and trained. Interest articulation means the transmission of demands from the environment to decision-makers in the political system. Interest aggregation is the process by which the demands are filtered and grouped to facilitate response by the political system. Political communication concerns the transmission of messages both within the system and between the system and its environment. The three output functions parallel the three branches of government in the United States. *Rule-making* obviously is the legislative function. *Rule application* parallels the executive function, and *rule adjudication* is the judicial function.

Almond later reconceptualized these eight functions. He included six under the category of *conversion functions.*[74] By conversion function he meant the process by which inputs are transformed into outputs. The six he included were interest articulation, interest aggregation, rule-making, rule-application, rule-adjudication, and communication. The remaining two functions, socialization and recruitment, he categorized as *system-maintenance* and *adaptation functions.*

Almond also differs from Easton in his identification of the basic components of the political system. Easton argues that the political role is the primary component and, in fact, explicitly argues that it is unnecessary to discuss structures except for purposes of illustration.[75] Almond, on the other hand, gives structures an important place in his work. He defines structures as a set of interrelated roles.[76] A single structure may perform several of the functions while one function may be performed by several structures. To Almond an important basis for the comparison of political systems is a determination of the relationship between functions and structures.[77] Because of his emphasis on the importance of structures and functions, Almond's approach is often called *structural–functionalism.*

Almond also argued that the degree to which structures specialized in the performance of a single function was one aspect of the process of political development. The second aspect of development, he believed, was an increase in the secularization of the culture, which he defines as the development of an empirical orientation and an increase in the specificity of orientations in the political culture. Both structural specialization and cultural secularization are believed to increase the system's capabilities to deal with problems or challenges.[78]

---

74. Gabriel A. Almond and G. Bingham Powell, Jr., *Comparative Politics: A Developmental Approach* (Boston: Little, Brown, 1966), p. 14.
75. Easton, *A Framework for Political Analysis,* p. 49.
76. Almond and Powell, *Comparative Politics,* p. 21.
77. Ibid., p. 31.
78. Ibid., pp. 22-25.

We realize that this has been a very brief overview of both Easton's and Almond's use of the concept of systems, but we hope we have given you enough of a basis to consider some of the problems and prospects of research on systems. Let us first emphasize the positive aspects of their approaches. In the first place, both of the approaches are admirable for their ambition. Political science, like all disciplines, would be greatly benefited by the development of an overall framework to organize and to direct research. Before a discipline can begin to develop theory, the research must become cumulative. That depends on agreement on a common research focus and on a means to relate and compare research findings. Both Almond and Easton have provided frameworks which are broad enough to integrate research findings. In addition, the frameworks have directed our attention to significant research questions. We mentioned four basic questions above. In addition, we can list other questions which the concept system suggests: How do systems maintain themselves? Are there universal functions? How do systems cope with stress?

To illustrate the utility of the system framework, let us look at an example of the use of system in political analysis. Richard Fenno used the system framework to analyze the Appropriations Committee in the United States House of Representatives.[79] The first question suggested by system concerns the purposes or goals of the political system. Easton, of course, argues that the political system allocates values. But we can still ask what values are allocated and to whom. Fenno defined the purpose of the Appropriations Committee as the allocation of money.

He then dealt with the second question, which concerns identifying the units of the system. Answering this was easy because the committee has an established membership. The third question concerns the relationship between the system and the environment. The committee was highly effective in dealing with the entire House of Representatives, which is a significant part of the committee's environment. Fenno attributed this effectiveness to the bipartisan solidarity on the committee. Finally, Fenno considered how the units of the system interact. He found that high membership stability, consensus on goals, and an egalitarian attitude led to a great deal of integration among committee members. This brief discussion of Fenno's study illustrates some of the advantages of the systems approach. The system framework can provide organization for both the process of research and the presentation of research findings.

Despite these benefits, the systems approach can be criticized. One fundamental criticism concerns the difficulty in operationalizing the con-

---

79. Richard F. Fenno, Jr., "The House Appropriations Committee As a Political System: The Problem of Integration," *American Political Science Review,* 56 (1962), 310–24.

cepts involved. We have a common sense understanding of the concepts of inputs, output, boundary, interaction, etc. But beyond that, specifying indicators that enable us to "know it when we see it" is considerably more complex. This difficulty in providing clear operationalizations leads to another problem which plagues both approaches. The lack of empirical concepts makes it difficult, if not impossible, to empirically develop testable hypotheses. No such hypotheses have yet been produced. Systems can be used to suggest areas of research but cannot provide a basis for deriving hypotheses. We can hypothesize such things as "inputs affect outputs." But this is obviously too vague to be of any use. What this means is that these approaches cannot be classified as empirical theory.

The inability to operationalize the concepts also means that it is impossible to substantiate Almond's basic contention that there are eight functions which must be present for a system to maintain itself. With no operationalization it is impossible to determine if the functions are indeed being performed. Given the vague nature of the concepts, there is a tendency for a researcher to see what he wants to see. For example, a village idiot could whisper something into the ear of a tribal chieftain in a primitive society and a researcher would exclaim, "Aha! Interest articulation!" At the same time, another researcher could watch the members of the American Agricultural Movement drive their tractors around Washington, D.C., and also be pleased to see interest articulation. Obviously, more precise definition and operationalization are needed.

Besides the lack of empirical substance, there is another criticism which can be made of systems. The basic question which underlies both approaches concerns how systems are maintained. This means that both approaches have a definite normative bias in favor of the status quo. This becomes a special problem in the Almond approach since the status quo bears an eerie resemblance to the American political system.

Besides being an admirably ambitious attempt, as we indicated above, have there been any contributions of the use of systems in political science? The answer is undoubtedly yes. In the first place, the system framework has been useful as a teaching technique. It has been used frequently in texts and classes to organize into a meaningful pattern the mass of information to be presented. Secondly, the system framework has spawned empirical research in new fields. For example, the research on political socialization and political culture was a result of the questions raised by systems analysis concerning the maintenance of systems. And finally systems analysis has helped to switch the attention of researchers from traditional institutional and legalistic concerns to more general and theoretically relevant research. All in all, while systems has not produced the elusive goal of empirical theory, it has been a useful step in that direction.

COMMUNICATIONS

We have said that the major weakness of the systems approach is the inability to tie its component concepts to empirical indicators. This means that it is impossible to develop testable hypotheses and, therefore, it is impossible to develop theory. That problem is overcome in the communications approach which is closely related to systems analysis. Because of the empirical base of communications research many researchers see communication as a promising foundation for theory building.

The basic idea of communication is to investigate the transmission of information. The information then takes the place of inputs and outputs in a systems analysis. Information is defined by Karl Deutsch, a primary proponent of communications analysis, as a "patterned relationship between events."[80] Information is not the events themselves, but what is communicated concerning the events. Information is empirical and it can, therefore, be identified and measured.

From the raw data of the events themselves, individuals or groups select certain aspects and transform those aspects into symbols. This is the process of *encoding*. The resultant message is transmitted via communications channels.[81] The original events may be distorted either by the encoding process or by the process of transmission along the channel. For example, competing messages, or noise, may effectively block certain parts of the message. Or, in fact, the entire message may be blocked, either because of interception by others or because of *overload*, which means the number of messages exceed the capacities of the communication channel. Distortion may also occur when the message is received and the receiver *decodes* it.[82]

Information is not only sent and received, it is also stored. This capability is known as *memory*.[83] Also important in transmission of information is *feedback*.[84] Feedback in communications analysis is essentially the same as in systems analysis. With feedback, the individual or group or system becomes aware of the consequences of its actions and corrects for them.

These basic components of communication can be used at any level of analysis. Let us look at questions we might ask of various levels, both to make that point and to illustrate further the use of communications to analyze politics. We may examine communication at the level of the individual. There has been a significant amount of research which is relevant to the study of interpersonal communication. For instance, we know that humans tend to perceive phenomena selectively.[85] That is, there is a tendency to see

---

80. Karl W. Deutsch, *The Nerves of Government* (New York: The Free Press, 1966), p. 84.
81. Ibid., p. 6.
82. Ibid., pp. 147-150.
83. Ibid., p. 80.
84. Ibid., pp. 88-91.
85. Ibid., p. 148.

what they want to see. (We mentioned this before in the context of the difficulty of determining if Almond's eight functions are actually universal.) Such selective perception will obviously be a source of distortion, both in the process of encoding and sending information and the process of receiving and decoding the information. Unpleasant information, or information contrary to one's own values or attitudes, may simply not be received.

Further light has been shed on the process of selective perception by the psychologists who have done research on the phenomenon they call *cognitive dissonance*.[86] They argue there are three components to any opinion situation: your own opinion, the opinion of the other person with whom you are communicating, and your evaluation of the other person. The idea of cognitive dissonance is that these three elements should be in balance. That is, we want to be in agreement with those we like and in disagreement with those we do not like. If this is so, it would point to the importance of the sender and the receiver of a communicated message.

This has led to a series of generalizations concerning the source of the message and its impact on the receiver. Many of the generalizations discussed concerning the influence of groups on individuals could be considered in communications terms. For instance, the greater the importance of the group (in your mind), the more likely it is that you will listen to its dictates. The more frequently you interact with people, the more likely you are to make your values congruent to theirs. Communications can also help in the understanding of socialization. Messages from the family (especially at an early age) are likely to have a greater impact than messages from other sources.

At the level of a single nation, we may consider the question of what information is transmitted to political authorities. Communication analysis can provide a framework within which many of the questions suggested by group, power, and conflict can be analyzed. For instance, the process by which groups achieve access to authorities may be conceptualized as a process of transmitting information via various communication channels. Those groups with access, that is, those which are most successful at transmitting their messages without distortion and without blockage, are most likely to be effective and powerful (that is, able to get what they want). Another way of looking at the impact of communications on power is from the perspective of the research by Bachrach and Baratz. As we indicated, they argue that one form of power involves the ability to determine what issues will be decided. This control over the agenda of the political system is achieved by controlling what information is communicated to the authorities. Control over communication is also essential in order to control the expansion of conflict.

---

86. Leon Festinger, *A Theory of Cognitive Dissonance* (Stanford: Stanford University Press, 1957).

An important factor in determining what information will be communicated in a political system is the mass media. There is much need for more research on the impact of the media. It is clear that the media is not as powerful as some have claimed. Individuals are not "blank slates" who can be buffeted by any information transmitted by the media. Selective perception and cognitive dissonance are as important when Walter Cronkite speaks as when Joe from the corner bar speaks. But at the same time, it is clear that we get most of our political information from the media. This means that the question of what information is transmitted and how much distortion there is in the transmission are obviously important. The media is also seen as an important influence in the processes of nation building in the case of new nations; maintaining absolute, centralized control in the case of totalitarian nations; and solidifying power in the case of revolutionary governments.

Finally, we can look at communication at the international level. It is possible to compare political systems on the basis of how the function of communication is performed. For example, Almond, who included communication as one of the eight universal functions of political systems, listed four variables which could serve as a basis for comparison:

1. Homogeneity of political information
2. Mobility of political information
3. Volume of political information
4. Direction of flow of political information[87]

Lester Milbrath has argued that it is possible to use communications patterns as criteria to evaluate the responsiveness of democratic systems to public opinion. He has listed three factors which are important: (1) a two-way channel of communication between political leaders and the public; (2) open channels of communication; and (3) access to alternate sources of information.[88] Similar listings of variables could obviously be developed to categorize and evaluate other types of political systems.

Let us now consider how we would evaluate the concept of communication as a basis for an empirical theory of politics. In the first place, as we have noticed, many of the questions which we considered in our discussion of other concepts can be reconceptualized in terms of communication. This indicates that the concept may have the potential of becoming a broadly inclusive framework for analyzing politics. In this way it is similar to systems. Communications, however, has a significant advantage over systems. Unlike the rather vague concepts which indicate the components of a system (inputs, outputs, and so on), communications deals with components which are empirical. It is possible to identify messages which are transmitted and to

---

87. Almond and Powell, *Comparative Politics*, p. 50.
88. Lester Milbrath, *Political Participation*, 2nd ed. (Chicago: Rand McNally, 1977), p. 151.

determine who sends the messages, who receives them, what the informational content is, how much distortion occurs, and so forth.

It would appear that communications, therefore, has the potential of forming the basis of an empirical theory. However, it is far from the stage of theory at the moment. Once again, more research is needed to build generalizations at various levels of analysis and to interrelate those generalizations into theoretical structures. However, in this process of theory building, researchers must try to avoid focusing on only the most trivial aspects of communication because they are easily measured. For instance, simply counting messages will probably tell us little. Merely looking at the words used in the communication may not be adequate to fully understand what information is communicated. In addition to the words, such things as the intensity of the message should be considered. Obviously, these aspects of information arc less easily handled empirically than are other aspects. They should not, however, be ignored. What we are saying is that here, as in all theory building, we should be careful not to sacrifice substance for empiricism.

Now that we have discussed some of the concepts which aid us in understanding the setting for politics and political interactions, let us turn in the next chapter to two of the concepts concerned with the products of the political process: decisions and policy.

SUMMARY
POWER

Core Definition:	The ability to get someone to do something he or she would not otherwise do
Operationalization:	There have been three main ways used to operationalize power: 1. Some studies use resources of power (guns, muscles, and so forth). 2. Some studies relied on informed "judges" to locate who has power. 3. Some studies have operationalized power as participation in decision making. None of these operationalizations is totally satisfactory.
Basic Questions:	1. Who has power? 2. How is power distributed? 3. How does the distribution of power both in a country and in the international setting affect the policies of government?
Summary of Major Findings:	1. The larger the size of the community, the greater the dispersion of power.

118 POLITICAL INTERACTIONS

	2. The stronger the labor unions, the greater the dispersion of power. 3. The more socially heterogeneous the community, the more pluralistic the power structure. 4. The more competitive the party structure, the more pluralistic the power structure.
Directions for the Future:	1. More precise definition and operationalization 2. More work discovering the consequences of various power structures 3. More work on nondecisions

SUMMARY
GROUP

Core Definition:	Two or more individuals who share some common characteristic(s). Political scientists are concerned with these individuals when their common characteristic(s) affect political behavior.
Operationalization:	1. Bentley's concept of group as a mass of activity has never been successfully operationalized. 2. The most frequently used operationalization is an institutionalized structure. 3. Reference groups could also be operationalized by the use of questionnaires.
Basic Questions:	1. How and to what extent do groups have an impact on the attitudes and behaviors of their members? 2. How and to what extent do groups have an impact on the functioning of the political system?
Summary of Major Findings:	1. If member identification is high, groups can have an impact on individuals. 2. If the group is seen as being related to politics, groups can have an impact on individuals. 3. Group membership increases participation and efficacy (effectiveness) of individuals. 4. Characteristics of groups, such as size, cohesion, and prestige, affect how much political impact groups have.

Directions for the Future:	1. Better distinctions between groups and nongroups (especially important in dealing with potential groups) 2. Continued research on the impact of groups on individuals and the political system

SUMMARY
CONFLICT

Core Definition:	A pattern of interaction which occurs when there are disagreements concerning the allocation of scarce resources
Operationalization:	The presence of two or more actors expressing divergent claims
Basic Questions:	1. How do conflicts arise? 2. How do conflicts expand? 3. How are conflicts resolved?
Summary of Major Findings:	1. Conflicts may be characterized in terms of intensity, visibility, and scope. 2. Issue definition affects the expansion of conflict. 3. The level of political trust of various groups will affect what strategies they use to resolve conflict with the political system. 4. The political system will use different strategies to resolve conflict with groups, depending upon the extent to which the groups are perceived as trusting the system.
Directions for the Future:	1. Attempts to discover if patterns of conflict differ in different settings 2. More comparative and systematic empirical research to confirm the generalizations above

SUMMARY
SYSTEMS

Core Definition:	An interaction among identifiable units to achieve some purpose
Operationalization:	No satisfactory operationalization has been found for the general systems framework.
Basic Questions:	1. What are the primary purposes of a political system? 2. What are the units of the system?

	3. What is the relationship between the environment and the system?
4. What is the pattern of interaction among the components of the system?
Summary of Major Findings:	Systems has been used as a basis for analyzing politics, but it has not produced empirical generalizations.
Directions for the Future:	1. If possible, operationalization of system and the components of system
2. More attention to interaction among the components of the system—the black box problem
3. More consideration for how change occurs as well as how systems persist
4. More work on how to establish boundaries and what interactions occur across boundaries
5. Development of means to test Almond's assumption that certain functions are necessary and universal

SUMMARY
COMMUNICATIONS

Core Definition:	The ability to transmit messages and react to them
Operationalization:	Messages, that is, exchanges of information, in written and oral form are empirical.
Basic Questions:	1. What factors affect the receipt of information by individuals?
2. What factors affect the receipt of information by political systems?
3. How does communication affect the functioning of political systems?
Summary of Major Findings:	1. People receive communications selectively.
2. The more powerful the source of the message, the more likely the message will be received by the political system.
3. Patterns of communication can be used to distinguish among different political systems.
Directions for the Future:	1. More attention to operationalizing the meaning of the message

2. More work on specifying relationships between the source of the message and the impact of the message
3. More work on the processing of messages

STUDY QUESTIONS

1. Discuss the problems of operationalizing the following concepts: power, group, and system.
2. Using a system perspective, describe the United States Congress.
3. What hypotheses might you test with each of the following concepts: group, conflict, and communications.
4. Consider how you would devise a means to answer the question of "Who has power?" on your campus.
5. Consider in what ways conflict between Russia and the United States may differ from conflict between two mayoral candidates in your home town.
6. Consider the groups with which you identify or to which you belong. What impact have these groups had on your attitudes and behaviors? Make hypotheses about the impacts to be tested empirically among many people.
7. Apply Almond's categories of functions to the relationships among nations.
8. Use Almond's categories of functions to compare three countries.

The Products of Politics

Chapter Six

In this day of increasing governmental responsibility, it is virtually impossible to escape the impact of government decisions and policy on our lives. The big businessman, regardless of his faith in free enterprise, worries about import and export policies and the corporate tax structure. The independent farmer, plowing his fields in solitude, worries about parity prices and government set-aside programs, both of which affect the prices for the crops he will eventually harvest. The elderly retiree worries about social security benefits and whether he can qualify for the food stamp program. Even the hermit living peacefully in his cave should worry about policies to protect the wilderness in which he lives. All of these policies are determined by the government. No one, we reiterate, can escape the impact of government. Therefore, no one should be disinterested in understanding all he can about the result of political interactions: the decisions and policies of government.

In this chapter we will consider two concepts which are important for understanding the results of politics: decision-making and policy. Actually decision-making is a process and, therefore, it might seem that it should have been considered in the last chapter rather than in this one. We have decided to consider decision-making in this chapter for two reasons. In the first place, we feel that decision-making is the last step in the process of creating policy. It is the point toward which all the other factors which we have discussed are aimed. All of the factors discussed in the last two chapters affect the decision-making process. The need for decision arises because of conflicts among the interests of various groups in society. The interests may differ because of differing socialization or differing circumstance. The socialization of the decision-makers, the dominant values of the political culture, the relative power of the conflicting groups, and the amount and kinds of information communicated to the decision-makers may all affect the decision which they make. The decision results from inputs from the environment, and the decision itself is an output of the political system. Decision-making, thus, is a final step of the political process, at least temporarily, and results from the impact of the other factors we discussed.

The second reason why we decided to discuss decision-making in this chapter is that there is a close relationship between the concepts of decision-making and policy. Political researchers have often argued that the process by which decisions are made has a very significant impact on the type of decisions which result.[1] Thus, there is a strong relationship between the findings of decision-making research and that classified as policy research. The close connection between the process of decision-making and the policy which results is another reason why we have decided to discuss the two concepts in this chapter.

Although, as we indicated, research on the two concepts is closely interrelated, we will attempt to discuss each separately. We will first look at the process of decision-making.

DECISION-MAKING

How and why do political officials make the decisions they make? These are basic questions which are suggested by a focus on the concept of decision-making. Stated in such a way, the questions seem to be quite simple. Unfortunately, this simplicity is deceptive. To understand the complex set of internal and external interactions which result in particular kinds of behavior is the fundamental aim of all social sciences. And yet achieving this goal of explaining behavior, which is what is involved in the study of decision-making, has so far eluded social scientists.

Despite the difficulties involved in explaining how and why decisions are made, it should be obvious that such an explanation could be extremely valuable both to scientists searching for knowledge and to those who wish to have an impact on political decision-making. Decision-making is at the essence of the political process. So, let us consider the amount of success researchers have had in answering these fundamental questions.

---

1. Perhaps the most provocative example of this argument is Theodore J. Lowi, *The End of Liberalism: Ideology, Policy and the Crisis of Public Authority* (New York: Norton, 1969).

The first step, of course, is to consider exactly what is meant by decision-making. Unfortunately, in many studies the meaning of the term is left undefined. Perhaps, this is because researchers believe that the concept has a widely understood meaning. But leaving a definition implicit is never a good idea because a researcher can never really know if others have the same understanding of a concept as he does. One researcher who did define the concept of decision-making was Richard C. Snyder. Snyder was the political scientist who first formulated a framework for analyzing politics based on the concept of decision-making. He gave the following definition of the concept:

> Decision making results in the selection from a socially defined, limited number of problemetical, alternative projects (courses of action) of one project to bring about the particular future state of affairs envisaged by the decision makers.[2]

As we will see later, there are some researchers now who might quibble with Snyder about the degree to which "future states of affairs" may be the predominant motivation in decision-making. Yet, we feel that all would agree with his statement that the essence of decision-making is choice. If there were no alternatives, there would be no need for decisions to be made. For the purposes of our discussion here, therefore, we will rely upon part of Snyder's definition and define decision-making as follows: the process of choosing among alternative courses of action. We hope that this definition narrows down the field of study adequately so that we may begin our inquiry, and yet is broad enough to encompass the large amount of research which has been done on decision-making.

Now that we have given some brief consideration to the problem of definition, let us consider some of the particular questions we can ask using decision-making as a basic focus. The first thing which we should know about decision-making is who is involved in making the decisions in which we are interested. Answering this question will mean that you must identify those individuals or groups of individuals that you feel are the most important participants in making the choices in which you are interested.

You will then probably want to know which factors are important influences on those involved in the decision-making. In the systems terminology, we are asking what are the inputs on the decision-makers. This means that we are making the assumption that the decision-making does not exist in a vacuum, and the environment and the individual's psychological make-up do have an impact on decisions. Therefore, we must look both to the overall setting as well as to the immediate context of decision-making.

---

2. Richard C. Snyder, "A Decision-Making Approach to the Study of Political Phenomena," in *Approaches to the Study of Politics,* ed. Roland Young (Evanston, Illinois: Northwestern University Press, 1958), p. 19.

Next we would probably want to know something about how decisions are made: are there general patterns of decision-making and are there basic rules which govern the decision-maker's reaction to, and choice among, the various alternatives which confront him and the influences which affect him. If general patterns and rules could be found, then decision-making could start to produce generalizations and advance toward becoming the basis for a theory. Let us now examine the research which has been done on each of these questions.

Who is Involved?

Obviously, no research can answer this question for all instances of decision-making. Some consideration has been given, however, to how a researcher should direct his effort to identify the participants in decision-making. In the first place, you should realize that identifying the participants, what Snyder calls defining the decision unit,[3] is equivalent to defining boundaries in systems analysis. As we said before, decision-makers do not exist in a vacuum. They are influenced by inputs from the environment. Therefore, a researcher must judge which are influences and which are actual participants in the decision-making.

Snyder argued for including in the decision unit only those who could make authoritative decisions.[4] In essence, then, he would only include as decision-makers public officials. Other researchers would disagree with this position. The researchers who focus on the role of groups in politics often argue that it is the interaction among groups which produces the decisions for society. In their view, the role of government, and, therefore of the public officials, is simply to ratify the decisions reached by the groups.[5] Focusing on public officials, they would argue, would mean ignoring the most important decision-makers.

Many researchers who are interested in community power structures would agree with the group theorists on this point. Many, including Robert Dahl, operationalize the concept of power by participation in decision-making.[6] As we indicated before, Dahl found different groups in society participated in making decisions in different policy areas. He is, therefore, saying that decision-making includes others besides public officials. Whether or not people other than public officials should be included as participants in decision-making, rather than as inputs on the decision-makers, must be a judgment made by each researcher.

---

3. Ibid., p. 20.
4. Ibid., p. 16.
5. See especially David B. Truman, *The Governmental Process: Political Interests and Public Opinion,* 2nd ed. (New York: Knopf, 1971).
6. Robert Dahl, *Who Governs?* (New Haven: Yale University Press, 1961).

Still another question must be answered about those involved in decision-making. There are three possible levels of participants which could be the focus of researchers. On the one hand, it is possible to focus on the individuals as decision-makers. Alternatively, it is possible to focus on an organization and its role in decision-making. Finally, it is possible to consider a whole system as a decision-maker. Graham Allison points out that different factors must be considered as important influences on decision-making depending upon which level of analysis the researcher selects.[7] We will use the classification of individual, organization, and systems levels in the next section when we consider influences on decision-makers. We should point out, however, that although researchers may focus on one or another level, it is quite probable that to understand the entire process of decision-making it may be necessary to examine all three levels of analysis.

Influences on Decision-Making

Individual. Richard Snyder, in his initial decision-making framework, was perhaps the first researcher to direct attention away from the state as an actor to the role of the individual official in political decision-making.[8] The basic assumption behind the focus on the individual is that not all decision-makers will respond similarly to the same situation. Individuals vary, and these differences will affect how individuals perceive influences and pressures in the environment and, therefore, how they will respond. Snyder argued for the importance of understanding the individual's perception of his setting and environment in order to explain the decisions he or she makes.[9] There are three basic factors which can help us understand an individual's perception of the environment: personality, socialization, and organizational position.

The importance of personality in understanding how a decision-maker will react to his environment is illustrated by Allport's definition of personality: "... the dynamics of organization within the individual of those psychological systems that determine his unique adjustments to his environment."[10] Researchers normally use the concept of personality to refer to a deep-rooted system of predispositions. These predispositions are presumed to underlie a person's attitudes. Personality has been used to explain both what kind of people will be recruited to political activism (that is, will become decision-makers) as well as how such people will behave in decision-making situations.

---

7. Graham Allison, *Essence of Decision: Explaining the Cuban Missile Crisis* (Boston: Little, Brown, 1971).
8. James S. Rosenau, "Premises and Promises of Decision-Making Analysis," in *Contemporary Political Analysis,* ed. James C. Charlesworth (New York: The Free Press, 1967), p. 197.
9. Snyder, "A Decision-Making Approach," p. 22.
10. Gordon Allport, *Personality: A Psychological Interpretation* (New York, Holt, 1937), p. 48.

In *Psychopathology and Politics,* Harold Lasswell suggested that there was a particular personality type who became political leaders. He explained the development of this personality type by the following formula:

$$p \} d \} r = P$$

The p stands for the private motives of an individual which are developed from early childhood. The symbol $\}$ indicates "transformed into." The second component of the formula, $d,$ indicates that the private motives are displaced onto public objects. The r indicates the displacement is rationalized by reference to the public interest. Finally, P indicates the creation of political man.

What Lasswell is saying is that people find an outlet for their psychological tension in politics and then rationalize the political involvement by referring to the public interest or developing a political ideology.[11] The implication is that political activity is the result of an unhealthy personality. Researchers have discounted this argument as at best a partial explanation.[12] By no means do all political activists have unhealthy personalities, but further research on personality may yet help us understand why some people become active in politics.

In addition, research on personality may help us understand how those activists will behave in decision-making situations. Perhaps the most extensive study of the effect of personality on decision-makers is James David Barber's examination of *Presidential Character.*[13] Barber argued that there are two dimensions of personality which are crucial. One dimension concerns how active or passive a President is in office. The other dimension is how positively or negatively a President feels about the activity. From these two dimensions, Barber constructs four personality types: active–positive, active–negative, passive–positive, and passive–negative. He uses these dimensions to classify Presidents and claims he can then predict presidential performance, according to the personality classification (see Table 6-1).

Table 6–1 Barber's personality classification scheme for presidents

	Active	Passive
Positive	Active–Positive	Passive–Positive
Negative	Active–Negative	Passive–Negative

11. Harold D. Lasswell, *Psychopathology and Politics* (New York: The Viking Press, 1960).
12. Rufus Browning, "The Interaction of Personality and Political System in Decision to Run for Office: Some Data and a Simulation Technique," *Journal of Social Issues,* 24 (July 1968).
13. James David Barber, *The Presidential Character* (Englewood Cliffs, N.J.: Prentice-Hall, 1972), pp. 6–8.

A second factor which is important at the individual level is political socialization. This might also help us understand which people will become political activists. As we indicated in our examination of political socialization, researchers have pointed to certain characteristics of socialization experiences which tend to increase a person's interest and involvement in politics. For example, it was found that those people who come from a family which is close and which share interests and which is interested in politics are themselves more likely to become interested in politics.[14] It may well be that particular characteristics of the socialization experience can be shown to predict future decision-makers.

There are also other ways that political socialization may help us understand decision-making at the individual level. The socialization process is how we learn our values and our orientations to the world around us. A decision-maker is buffeted by a variety of influences and pressures from the environment. If we could understand more fully the kinds of orientations and values the decision-maker had learned, we would be better able to predict his reaction to the various influences from the environment.

A final factor which is important to consider at the individual level only becomes significant after a person has been recruited to a decision-making position. That factor is the influence of the organizational or institutional setting of the decision. By organizational setting, we simply mean that a decision-maker is part of a structure which includes formal and informal ranks, has other members, has patterns of authority and hierarchy, etc. A person's position in an organizational setting can affect how he or she sees the world. It was this aspect which was predominant in Allison's examination of the individual level of analysis. According to Allison, the most important determinant of individual decision-making behavior is the position one holds in an organization. Getting to the heart of the matter, he states ". . . where you stand depends on where you sit."[15] Basically Allison's point is that an individual's position in an organization will affect her perspectives. This position will affect the amount and kinds of information she receives and what she sees as her self-interest. For example, what the Secretary of the Department of Defense sees as a top priority for the country is probably not the same as what the Secretary of the Department of State may decide is top priority.

Other factors may be listed that are important in individual decision-making behavior. But the basic argument of those who focus on the individual is that influences from the environment are perceived differently by individuals. If we could understand the individual thoroughly, we could predict how he or she would perceive the influences and thus predict the decisions he or she would make.

---

14. Herbert McClosky and Harold Dahlgren, "Primary Group Influence on Party Loyalty," *American Political Science Review*, 53 (1959).
15. Allison, *Essence of Decision*, p. 176, attributed to Don K. Price.

Organization. We have previously discussed the effect of the organizational context on indvidual decision-making. Now we will examine the organization as a whole as an actor in decision-making. An organization, of course, is a collection of individuals. And yet we frequently talk as though an organization per se has acted. For instance, we say that "Congress passed the energy bill," or that "the Department of Defense protested its appropriation for the next fiscal year." To some researchers, there are certain characteristics or properties which can only emerge when there is a collectivity of individuals. For such researchers, examining individual decision-making alone would be inadequate.

In examining the decision-making of organizations, Allison has argued that organizations, like the individuals who compose them, have limited perspectives. There are several reasons why organizations develop such limited perspectives: (1) development of routines, (2) selective perception of information, (3) selective recruitment, and (4) value congruence.[16] In the first place, organizations establish certain routines and "standard operating procedures." The reason for such routines is to enable the organization to make decisions quickly by referring to precedents. But such routines may also have the effect of limiting the situations to which the organization will respond. Organizations may follow the routines so closely that they find it difficult to react to situations for which there is no precedent. Therefore, such new situations may be simply ignored in the decision-making process.

Another reason for the limited perspective is the fact that organizations respond selectively to information. That is, the Department of Defense does not concern itself with problems of eliminating poverty in the United States. Its responsibility is defense, and it is to defense issues that it addresses itself. The third reason for the limited perspective is the fact that organizations selectively recruit their personnel. Organizations normally have certain standards and expectations of what kinds of personnel should be hired. Pacifists would probably not apply to the Department of Defense and would probably not be hired. Finally, once personnel have been hired, organizations attempt to socialize the individual into the perspectives of the organization. This socialization can be accomplished by a variety of means. For instance, salary decisions, promotion decisions, internal pressures, and training sessions can all be used to teach and/or reinforce certain perspectives and values.

This all sounds very manipulative, and, in fact, it is. But if you think about it, the organizations with which one deals all have some means of trying to assure uniformity among their members. Fraternities and sororities use "rush" to recruit their members selectively and then use initiation and various forms of informal social pressure to make sure that members assume certain values. Colleges and universities usually have selec-

---

16. Ibid. pp. 67-96.

tive admissions procedures to recruit the kinds of students they want and then use grading to encourage the values of learning and study, or they may simply remove those students who do not fulfill the expectations of the organization. Why do organizations attempt to manipulate their membership? The answer is that uniformity of values and perspectives in some ways makes the organization more effective and efficient. Think of the problems the Department of Defense might have if a large portion of its membership were pacifist. Internal conflict would almost necessarily make it difficult for the organization to take any action.

What effect does this limited perspective have on decision-making? On the one hand, as we said above, the limited perspective makes it more likely that the organization can act as a unit. On the other hand, however, the limited perspective of the organization can have numerous negative effects on the organization's decision-making. Information which might be useful may be ignored if it is not seen as relevant. For instance, it might be very useful for the Department of Defense to know something about negotiations being conducted by the Department of State. But Defense might ignore such information because it is not directly tied to defense issues. Another possibility is that State may refuse to share the information since it may be jealous of its own responsibilities and powers. In either case, coordinated decision-making is difficult.

Another effect of this limited perspective is that decisions may not be examined thoroughly either before or after they are made. Irving Janis calls this phenomenon *groupthink*. Groupthink refers to "a mode of thinking that people engage in when they are deeply involved in a cohesive in-group, when the members' strivings for unanimity override their motivation to realistically appraise alternative courses of action."[17]

And, finally, by ignoring situations which do not fit the established routines, an organization may fail to adapt to new pressures and demands. The decisions made may, therefore, be irrelevant. In general, then, while the limited perspective is intended to increase the efficiency of the organization, the effect may actually be to limit the effectiveness of the organization's decisions in some cases.

System. The final level of analysis that Allison lists is the system level. By focusing on this level, the conflicting values, interests, and perspectives which are examined at the individual and organizational levels are ignored. At the level of the system as a whole, the researcher assumes that the interacting parts operate smoothly together. He further assumes that there are certain ends or goals which decision-makers have in mind and decisions are made by considering all alternatives and then choosing that alternative which will be most effective and efficient in achieving these goals. Such a comprehensive and goal-oriented process is known as *rational decision-*

---

17. Irving L. Janis, *Victims of Groupthink* (Boston: Houghton Mifflin, 1972), p. 9.

making. At the system level, the factors which influence decision-making are the acceptance of certain goals and the comprehensive range of alternative means to reach these goals. We will examine rational decision-making in more depth in the next section.

How are Decisions Made?

There are two approaches researchers have used to learn how decisions are made. One approach is to identify the various steps involved in decision-making. Different researchers, of course, break up the decisional pie into different slices.[18] It is, however, possible to point to some aspects which tend to be frequently included. First, there must be a recognition and definition of the problem. Both may be crucial determinants of a final decision. As Bachrach and Baratz have argued, failure to recognize certain problems may be the most important form of power.[19] And how an issue is defined will determine the amount and kind of support or opposition for various alternatives.[20] (Is poverty a problem of "lazy good-for-nothings" or "social injustices"?) Next there must be some gathering of information and formulation of alternative solutions. In the third step some form of recommendation or prescription will be made which may be accompanied by attempts to gather support by bargaining or persuasion. Finally, a decision is made, perhaps based on some set of decision rules. After the decision, attempts will be made to evaluate the decision. This may lead to further decisions, a point we will discuss later.

Although the categorization of steps may be useful as a guide to research, it does not help us explain how decisions are actually made. To do this, the second line of research might be more helpful. This research is aimed at finding basic premises or decision rules which decision-makers use.

In the last section we considered some of the factors which might be important influences on the decision-making process. By listing such factors we can provide some guidance to those who wish to research the process of decision-making. But simply listing such factors is only the first part of developing a theory of decision-making. Some way must be found to make generalizations about how and when such factors will be important. If we could find some general patterns in decision-making, then we could make generalizations and begin the development of a theory. To do this, some

---

18. See, for example, Charles O. Jones, *An Introduction to the Study of Public Policy,* 2nd ed. (North Scituate, Massachusetts: Duxbury Press, 1977), p. 12; James E. Anderson, *Public Policy-Making,* 2nd ed. (New York: Holt, Rinehart & Winston, 1979), p. 25; Snyder, "A Decision-Making Approach to the Study of Political Phenomena," p. 10.
19. Peter Bachrach and Morton S. Baratz, *Power and Poverty* (New York: Oxford University Press, 1970).
20. Roger W. Cobb and Charles D. Elder, *Participation in American Politics* (Boston: Allyn and Bacon, 1972), p. 96.

researchers have attempted to develop basic frameworks into which the separate influences and factors could be integrated. One of these basic frameworks is rationality. This is the premise which Allison argued was predominant at the system level of analysis. Let us consider in more depth what is involved in rational decision-making.

Rational decision-making is presumed to proceed logically through a series of steps.[21] The first step is the recognition of a problem. Secondly, the problem is clearly defined. Next, all possible goals are listed and ranked in the order of preference. The next step is to survey all possible means to reach the goals in the order ranked and to determine the costs involved of each alternative means as well as the expected benefits it would produce. The final step, then, is simply to select that means which will achieve the desired goal with least cost and maximum benefit.

This, of course, is an idealized characterization of the rational decision-making process. Students of rational decision-making borrow heavily from economists and mathematicians in order to understand the process. The basic assumption, from economics, is that people try to maximize benefits and minimize costs. Individuals are willing to bear costs of acquiring information, spend time that could be used on other activities, and so forth, as long as the benefits outweigh the costs. When the costs of making "the best" decision equal the possible benefits to be derived, further investment becomes "irrational." As the value of the goal increases, the burden we are willing to bear also increases.[22]

An example of the use of rational decision-making to analyze politics is William Riker's study of coalition formation.[23] Coalition formation is rational to the extent that coalitions help their members maximize their gains and minimize their losses. Riker has argued, however, that by trying to include all factions, rewards to any one faction are diluted while costs of negotiations are apt to increase. Therefore, he tells us, parties will attempt to win elections by creating "minimum winning coalitions." In this way rewards need not be distributed equally to 70% plus of the electorate. The bulk of the rewards can go to the 55% or 60% which were part of the winning coalition. To be totally rational the winning coalition would be 50%+ one in an election with a decision rule of majority victory. However, in a world with uncertain knowledge it is usually better to dilute the rewards slightly rather than risk receiving none at all.

The effect of this "size principle," as Riker calls it, is visible in national

---

21. See Anthony Downs, *An Economic Theory of Democracy* (New York: Harper & Row, 1957), pp. 4–11; Charles E. Lindblom, *The Policy-Making Process* (Englewood Cliffs, N.J.: Prentice-Hall, 1968), p. 13.
22. William H. Riker and William J. Zavoina, "Rational Behavior in Politics: Evidence from a Three Person Game," *American Political Science Review*, 64 (March 1970), 53.
23. William H. Riker, *The Theory of Political Coalitions* (New Haven: Yale University Press, 1962), p. 32.

elections.[24] When we have a President who wins by a landslide, it usually is a short time before supporters become disenchanted because they don't feel the benefits they are being allocated are greater than the costs they have borne.

Another problem of making rational decisions when more than one person is involved is the decision rule which is used. In cases where a majority is required, problems of rationality may result if more than two alternatives are presented. With three people and three alternatives it is possible that no alternative will be preferred by two, that is, a majority.[25] In the real world this becomes even more complicated. The problem is apt to be solved through trade-offs or bargaining. It may also be resolved by considering if one party has an intense preference and the other two only mildly support their choices. The questions of how and if the intensity of individual preferences should be considered in decisions is a question of values. One problem of dealing with intensity is that it may be difficult to measure intensity empirically.

Using the rational decision-making framework, several researchers have been able to explain various individual political decisions and some political patterns. Snyder, whose definition of decision-making we cited at the beginning of the chapter, together with Glenn D. Paige, analyzed the decision by the United States to resist the invasion of South Korea by North Koreans.[26] A very simple statement of their basic argument is that Truman intervened in Korea because he believed that intervention was the best way to achieve the goal of preserving the national security of the United States.

Perhaps one of the most thorough examples of an analysis based on the assumption of rationality is *An Economic Theory of Democracy* by Anthony Downs. Using the assumption that men are rational as a basis of his study, Downs manages to explain such disparate political phenomena as the similarity of American parties and some people's indifference toward voting. For example, to explain why the parties are so similar, Downs argues that "Both parties agree on any issues that a majority of citizens strongly favor."[27] Downs is arguing that the parties both want to represent public opinion in order to win elections. When that opinion is consensual, the parties will take the same stands. To explain why people do not vote, Downs argues that participation decreases greatly when the costs of voting (time, effort) are substantially increased.[28] The decision to vote is, therefore, the result of

---

24. Ibid.
25. This is a gross simplification of Arrow's Paradox in Kenneth Arrow, *Social Choice and Individual Values,* 2nd ed. (New York: Wiley, 1963).
26. Richard C. Snyder and Glenn D. Paige, "The United States Decision to Resist Aggression in Korea: The Application of an Analytical Scheme," *Administrative Science Quarterly,* 3 (December 1958), 376 ff.
27. Downs, *An Economic Theory of Democracy,* p. 297.
28. Ibid., p. 299.

weighing costs and benefits. Both of these hypotheses assume decisions are made rationally. That is, there are goals (winning election, the benefits of voting), and actions are based on determining what is a favorable cost/benefit ratio. Both hypotheses seem plausible and deserve rigorous testing. To test them, of course, such terms as "strongly favor," "substantially," and "agree" would have to be given precise meaning.

A very sophisticated use of the assumption of rationality is in the field known as game theory.[29] Game theory gets its name from the fact that models of political interaction are set up based upon an analogy of a game. That is, there are players identified who have differing goals and differing amounts of resources. Certain rules are specified. Then strategies for obtaining the goals are developed taking into consideration various alternative moves of the opponent. The criterion for choosing among the strategies is that of maximizing benefits and minimizing costs. Given all of these components the researchers can then predict by simple deduction which strategy will be chosen. Some researchers have developed these games to the stage where the steps can be expressed by mathematical equations, and the solution to the game can be determined by solving the equations. Riker's work, discussed above, is an example of the game theory approach. In many cases, computers are programmed to work through the game and predict the outcomes.

Obviously, game theory takes the assumption of rationality to its logical extremes. Game theory is often criticized because it lacks one necessary characteristic of empirical theory: correspondence to reality. In the real world, people do not always play according to the rules. Resources of the opponents may not be known. And yet as a result of using games, several hypotheses have been suggested which could form the basis for empirical research in the future.

What is the value of assuming that rationality is a basic premise of decision-makers? In the first place, such an assumption can lead to a framework for analyzing decision-making. It can help to organize the various influences on the decision-making process and can, therefore, begin to provide a basis for predicting and explaining decisions, as Downs' examples illustrate. There are, however, several criticisms which can be made of using rationality to organize decision-making analysis.[30]

The first criticism may already have occurred to you. Man is not always rational. Presumably, you are reading this book as part of the requirements of a college course. Presumably you are planning to pass this course. Passing the course, perhaps even with a good grade, is, therefore, your goal. To

---

29. For an introduction to game theory, see Martin Shubik, "Game Theory and the Study of Social Behavior: An Introductory Exposition," in *Game Theory and Related Approaches to Social Behavior,* ed. Martin Shubik (New York: Wiley, 1964).
30. For an in-depth critique of the rational model, see David Braybrooke and Charles E. Lindblom, *A Strategy of Decision* (New York: The Free Press, 1963), Part I.

maximize the attainment of that goal it is necessary for you to read and study this book and the other course materials carefully. That goal and the optimal way to achieve it will be constant throughout the term of the course. That means that a rational decision would be for you to spend any available time studying this book. We have our doubts, however, that you would be found on any given Friday night holed up in your room, studying the pearls of wisdom contained in this text.

Let us assume that next Friday night you spend relaxing with your friends at the local watering hole. Now why would you "waste" Friday night like that if your goal is to pass the course? Well, we might say that people do not always make rational decisions, and, therefore, assuming rationality will not always enable us to explain or predict human behavior. Of course, you might tell us that your goal Friday night is to relax and, therefore, it is rational for you to spend the night having a few beers with your friends. That may well be true. But that interpretation of your action does not help us as scientific researchers to explain or predict your behavior. All you are really saying, then, is that there is some reason for every decision you make. However, that does not really help us as researchers to identify the causes and explain the various decisions.

Another criticism of assuming rationality is that men may not be capable of performing rational decision-making. As we indicated, rationality assumes the existence of goals which can be ranked in order of preference. We may not have the information necessary to determine what our goals should be, let alone to determine some sort of absolute ranking of those goals. We often simply do not have the resources necessary to see that far into the future. Even if we have some goals in mind, the goals and their ranking may be different in different situations, as our example of your Friday night plans illustrates.

If we did, in fact, have goals in mind, we do not often have the information necessary to determine how to reach those goals, let alone what means will assure us maximum benefits and least costs. For instance, if your primary goal is passing this course, there may actually be many means you could use to attain that goal. You could, of course, study this book. But on the other hand you may find it is better to attend the classes since the instructor can explain the material more clearly. Or you may decide that the only way to learn the material well is to spend your time conducting a research project rather than poring over this book. Or, what is more likely the case, the best way may be to combine all of these means in some unknown quantities. We probably do not have to tell you that deciding the best way to go about passing any individual course is no simple process.

So far we have been using examples of decision-making on an individual basis. Consider the massive increase in problems and complexity which results when we shift our focus from individual decisions to the kind of decisions the government will have to make to allocate the budget in the next fiscal year. All of the problems are intensified. How do you determine the goals for the political system of a country, and then how do you rank those goals in some absolute way? Any country encompasses large numbers of people with conflicting interests and values. Different people will demand different goals for the country. Who can decide what goals and what ranking will predominate? Usually we simply do not know for sure how to achieve any goals we can specify, and it is, therefore, impossible for us to know the best means. What is the best way to maintain peace? What is the best way to end poverty?

Recognition of these limits on rational decision-making has led to the development of another framework: *incrementalism*.[31] The basic idea of incrementalism is that, since rational decision-making in its ideal form is impossible, we develop other guidelines or cues for our decisions. Since we cannot see into the future to set ultimate goals we tend to focus instead primarily on various alternative means and attempt to evaluate those means. Because we do not have the information necessary even to be aware of all possible alternative means, we tend to use what has been done in the past or alternatives which differ very little from those of the past. Since we focus on means rather than ends we can no longer evaluate the alternatives on the basis of which best achieves the desired goal. The criterion of "good," therefore, becomes that alternative on which there is agreement. Many researchers who study American politics seem to believe that incrementalism provides a more accurate description of decision-making of the American government than does the rational model.

Perhaps the most thorough application of the incremental frame as a basis for analyzing decision-making is Aaron Wildavsky's study of the budgetary process. He demonstrates that the best predictor of how much money will be allocated for various departments, agencies, etc., is the amount that was allocated in the prior year.[32]

There are still criticisms that have been made of the incremental model. The rational model was criticized for overstating the ability of decision-makers to plan for the best way to achieve a desired future. On the other hand, the incremental model may be criticized for its tendency to ignore any goal-oriented decisions. Amitai Etzioni has argued that both incremental and rational decision-making occur in the political system. He argues that rational decision-making is used to set basic directions, and incremental decision-making is used after the basic directions have been set. He calls this integration of the two approaches *mixed-scanning*[33] To test

---

31. For a description and defense of incrementalism, see Charles E. Lindblom, "The Science of 'Muddling Through,' " *Public Administration Review,* XIX (1959) 79-88.
32. Aaron Wildavsky, *The Politics of the Budgetary Process,* 3rd ed. (Boston: Little, Brown, 1978).
33. Amitai Etzioni, "Mixed Scanning: A 'Third' Approach to Decision-Making," *Public Administration Review,* XXVII (December 1967), 385-92.

Etzioni's argument, of course, we would have to have some means of empirically distinguishing rational decisions from incremental decisions.

Once again, much more research is necessary to determine if either of the two frameworks, or if some combination of the two, can be used to explain the decision-making process. Such research is essential if decision-making is to be used as a basis for the development of theory. James S. Rosenau has argued that the primary contribution of Snyder's initial decision-making framework was that it switched the attention of researchers from abstract entities, such as the state, and focused their attention on the behavior of individual decision-makers.[34] Yet, if decision-making is going to develop into a theory, research must produce generalizations which can explain the behavior of those decision-makers. For this reason uncovering basic patterns and premises of decision-making is essential. In addition, there is one other problem which must be solved. The individual is obviously an important focus. But if our goal is to explain the decision-making of a social system we must go beyond looking at individual decision-making alone. We must also consider how these individual decision-makers interact to produce decisions for the society. Once again, more work is needed before decision-making becomes more than a concept directing our attention to particular phenomena, that is, before it becomes the basis of a theory.

Let us now turn to an examination of the results of the decision-making process: policy.

POLICY

Up to now we have discussed concepts which could be seen as the products of the behavioral revolution in political science. This is not to say that the concepts were all created during this revolution. Many of the concepts had been part of political analysis for centuries. Power would be a good example of such an enduring concept of political analysis. Yet, all of the concepts we have listed became the focus of new and much more rigorous research in the aftermath of the behavioral revolution. Since that revolution was aimed at, among other things, making scientific investigations predominant in political science, most of the research which has developed from these concepts has attempted to produce value-free explanations of political phenomena rather than to prescribe political choice.

The concept of policy differs somewhat from the previously mentioned concepts. Policy, as a specific field of study, is a relatively new concern for political scientists. This means that the concept of policy came of age during the postbehavioral era when many political scientists, students, and practitioners alike were demanding a discipline which was more relevant. It is probably the case that the concept of policy became of interest to political

---

34. Rosenau, "Premises and Promises of Decision-Making Analysis," p. 197.

researchers because of their attempt to engage in research which they and others believed to be relevant. Relevance, of course, is a highly subjective idea, and nothing is relevant to everyone. But the basic argument made for a focus on policy is that the results of research could in some way be of practical use to society. The result of this heritage is that the research on policy is more likely than other research we have considered to include consideration of normative issues. This does not mean that all policy research is normative. It does mean, though, that research on policy has represented in many cases a conscious attempt to blend normative and scientific research in the discipline of political science.

What exactly is policy? There seem to be all too many definitions of the concept. Thomas Dye defines policy as ". . . whatever governments choose to do or not to do."[35] Richard Hofferbert defines it as ". . . visible products of decisions taken by identifiable actors for public purposes."[36] Many other researchers have argued that it is not possible to give a single definition of policy. Rather, they believe it necessary to list various elements and ingredients of policy, such as goals and implementation of programs, or such considerations as various aspects of direct and indirect benefits and costs of policy.[37]

Despite the large number of different definitions, we feel again, that there is some basic consensus on the meaning. We believe that James Anderson pointed most accurately to this core meaning with his definition of policy: "A purposive course of action followed by an actor or set of actors in dealing with a problem or matter of concern."[38] Let us consider in somewhat more depth what we feel Anderson is talking about here. In the first place, the phase "purposive course of action" refers to the fact that policy is a vague and abstract set of goals that decisions are supposed to further. In decision-making we are considering the process in which a choice among specific alternatives is made. Policy indicates a series of decisions which deal with one particular area of concern, such as foreign relations or poverty or conservation. For instance, we have a policy of defending Europe from Soviet aggression. We make a number of decisions to further that goal, such as the development of cruise missiles, the creation of a rapid deployment force, and so forth. This is an important point. Earlier we pointed out that a decision was the culminating stage in a political process, the point toward which the various influences and pressures were aimed. We indicated that

---

35. Thomas R. Dye, *Understanding Public Policy*, 3rd ed. (Englewood Cliffs, N.J.: Prentice-Hall, 1978), p. 3.
36. Richard I. Hofferbert, *The Study of Public Policy* (Indianapolis: Bobbs-Merrill, 1974), p. 4.
37. George C. Edwards III and Ira Sharkansky, *The Policy Predicament: Making and Implementing Public Policy* (San Francisco: W.H. Freeman & Company, Publisher, 1978), p. 2; Larry L. Wade, *The Elements of Public Policy* (Columbus, Ohio: Chas. E. Merrill, 1972), pp. 11–15; L.L. Wade and R.L. Curry, Jr., *A Logic of Public Policy: Aspects of Political Economy* (Belmont, California: Wadsworth, 1970), pp. 5–8.
38. Anderson, *Public Policy-Making*, p. 3.

that particular culmination may be only temporary. Problems which reach the government can very rarely, if ever, be resolved finally by a single decision. The decision may or may not have an impact on the problem. The impact may or may not be what was intended. Other aspects of the problem become apparent. In any event, government response must be a continuous process. In systems terminology, we could say that, as a result of feedback, new decisions must be made. Policy in an area is composed of a series of decisions. It is because of this that there is such a close relationship between decision-making and policy. Let us now consider the kind of research which has been done on policy.

We can divide the research on policy into two separate areas: *policy-making* and *policy analysis*. Research on the policy-making process closely parallels research on decision-making, for obvious reasons. In fact, the questions asked are the same: Who is involved? What are the influences? How is policy made? There is, however, one difference between the research on policy-making and that on decision-making. The research on decision-making tends to emphasize what leads up to the decision. This is equivalent in systems terms to the imputs to a decision. On the other hand, the research on policy-making tends to emphasize the outputs of the decision-making process. Such research examines the content of the decisions which are made. In addition, research is focusing increasingly on what happens to the decisions after they are made, that is, the way in which the decisions are implemented.

This emphasis on the outputs has led to a second strain of research: policy analysis. Policy analysis does not focus on the process of decision-making, but solely on an examination of the characteristics of the policy produced. The central concerns of this research are examination of the impact of the policy and evaluation of the policy. We will now look at each of these areas of policy research in more depth.

Policy-Making

We indicated that there are two concerns of policy-making research. The first is the content of the policy. Researchers have examined content by trying to distinguish types of policy and the process by which each type is made. The second concern is the way the policies are carried out, or implemented. Let us begin by looking at attempts to classify policy types.

One way in which researchers have distinguished types of policy is by their functional area. In other words, they categorize policy by the substantive areas of concern with which the policies deal. Examples of such a functional categorization would be welfare policy, foreign policy, agriculture policy, etc. This categorization can provide a basis for an in-depth study of one area. These studies have primarily produced description of the policy and the way it is made rather than generalizations. Almond and Powell have developed a four-fold typology of public policy: extractions, regulations, allocations, and symbols.[39] Extractions are the resources that government demands from its citizens, for example taxes. Regulations are controls which the government places on an individual's behavior, for example stopping at red lights. Allocations are the resources which government distributes to its citizens, for example snow removal. Finally, symbols are a special form of allocation which is ritualistic and involves little or no material goods or services—Memorial Day or National Vietnam Veterans Week.

Theodore Lowi has suggested another typology in which he attempts to consider type of policy as well as styles of policy-making. He divides policy into three types: distributive, redistributive, and regulatory.[40] He argues that each policy arena is characterized by a distinct style of policy-making. Distributive policies are those that allocate the resources of the society to many diverse groups. It seems like there is a little something for everyone and no one gets stuck with a big bill for the government services. Veteran's benefits, job training, college loans, farm subsidies, and business loans are examples of the breadth of resources our government divides up out of general tax revenues. Lowi says that this type of policy can be seen as logrolling. That is, decision-makers more or less agree to help others get something if they see that there is something for them too.

Redistributive policies are those which allocate benefits to certain groups, but there are other identifiable groups which must bear the costs. Welfare issues tend to be of this type. The middle class and rich are expected to pay high taxes to provide services to those who need them and can't afford them. Since there is not something for everyone and those who benefit and those who pay are well defined, this policy arena will cause conflict and will be characterized by stable coalitions between the haves and the have-nots. As in the Almond and Powell schema, regulatory politics deals with government controls. Lowi says that policy-making in the regulatory arena will be characterized by intense conflict and unstable coalitions. For example, airlines fight other forms of transportation for favorable freight rates, yet they fight each other for concessions from the government.

We now have three generalizations concerning the relationship of the type of decision-making and the type of policy from Lowi's schema. This is by no means a comprehensive list of all the ways researchers have categorized policies. But this list should be adequate to provide a basis for a discussion of the uses and limits of creating policy types. You may think all such attempts only lead to the creation of jargon and nothing more. There is no doubt that jargon does result. But the reason researchers try to create such categories is to try to create some order out of chaos. There are vast numbers of policies in any country. Before we can begin to make generaliza-

---

39. Gabriel A. Almond and G. Bingham Powell, Jr., *Comparative Politics: A Developmental Approach* (Boston: Little, Brown, 1966), p. 27.
40. Theodore J. Lowi, "American Business, Public Policy Case Studies, and Political Theory," *World Politics,* 16 (July 1964), 677-715.

tions about these policies we must have a firm grasp on the nature of the policies themselves. We must decide if all policies are fundamentally the same, or if there are differences among policies. If there are differences, we must attempt to specify the differences. That is what is involved in developing categories or types of policies.

The problem is that it is very difficult to develop categories which can be used to classify policies with no ambiguity or overlap. For instance, the functional classification seems to make sense, especially considering the fact that the organization of the American government follows functional lines: the Agriculture Department for agriculture policy, the Transportation Department for transportation policy, and so forth. Yet, there are policies which overlap these functional lines. For instance, the policies of federal assistance following natural disasters include housing assistance, handled by the Department of Housing and Urban Development, the granting of loans for renewal, handled by the Small Business Administration, and emergency aid, handled by the Red Cross which is a private organization. Neither the Almond and Powell nor the Lowi typology can assure unambiguous classification of policies. For instance, Almond and Powell themselves list honors as forms of allocative policies, yet a good case could be made for classifying such policies as symbolic since they involve such a low material cost. Both the Almond and Powell and Lowi typologies ignore the fact that many policies combine aspects of regulation and distribution. For instance, agriculture policies often guarantee some minimum price level for crops in return for agreement to allow the government to regulate the number of acres to be planted. And Lowi himself admits that in the end all government policies are redistributive.[41] Regardless of the problems, however, these typologies are an important first step in sorting out and organizing the confusing variety of policies as a basis for building generalizations.

The second question in policy-making concerns how policy is carried out. This question has commanded more attention since the book *Implementation* by Pressman and Wildavsky.[42] Students of policy realize that policy-making is an on-going process which does not end with the establishment of a program. The constant sets of decisions necessary to carry out policies are quite important for the final outcome. To date, no generalizations have been established that are directly related to implementation. Political scientists, however, have reinvestigated some generalizations concerning organizations since most policy implementation is done by public bureaucracies. One example of a hypothesis might be that decentralized bureaucracies are able to adapt policy to changing circumstances more quickly than can centralized bureaucracies.

---

41. Ibid., p. 690.
42. Jeffrey L. Pressman and Aaron B. Wildavsky, *Implementation* (Berkeley, California: University of California Press, 1973).

Policy Analysis

A second emphasis in policy research has been on two aspects of policy analysis: What is the impact of policy? What is the evaluation of policy? We design policies under the assumption that they will achieve some purpose. Research is now increasingly directed to discovering if that purpose was achieved, if the policy had any unintended consequences, and how costly the policy was. Let us consider some of the steps involved in identifying policy impact.[43] In the first place, it is necessary to identify the target population involved. In other words, we have to specify on whom or what the policy was expected to have an impact. Next, we must identify what were the desired effects of the policy. For instance, is a welfare policy intended to provide a certain minimum standard of living for the poor or is it supposed to provide them with the resources necessary for them to improve their lives? If there are many goals of a given policy these goals should be ranked.

Having identified the intended effects of the program, the next step is to identify the actual effects. In doing this, we must keep several things in mind. First, we must realize that government outputs are not the same as outcomes. Outputs are the activities of government. Outcomes, or impacts, deal with the changes which have resulted from the policies. Outputs are easy to identify and measure, and, therefore, it is very tempting to use these outputs as proxy measures for policy impact. For instance, we may be tempted to determine the impact of educational policy by identifying the amount of money the government spends on schools. But research has shown that the amount of money spent, or output, may or may not have anything to do with the impact of the educational policy on children.

A second thing one should keep in mind is that policies may have unintended outcomes which should also be identified. For instance, a welfare program may achieve its intended impact of assuring the poor a minimum standard of living. But it is possible that such a policy may also have the unintended impact of reducing their incentive to work. A third factor to keep in mind is that policies may have impacts on others besides the target population. For instance, consider again the poverty policy we have been using as an example. The impact on the poor may be an increased standard of living, but the impact on the middle class may be increased taxes which will lead eventually to a tax revolt.

This last example also illustrates two other points. First, policies may have both short-term effects (increased taxes) and long-term effects (a tax revolt). Secondly, we must realize that policy impacts include both benefits (minimum standard of living for the poor) as well as costs (taxes and the tax revolt). Part of the cost to be considered includes the other activities that must be sacrificed in order for the policy to be implemented. This cost of

---

43 For a review of policy impact see Anderson, *Public Policy-Making*, pp. 153–156.

foregone opportunities is known as "opportunity costs." If we had not put the poverty policy into effect we might have been able to subsidize mass transit systems to alleviate the energy problem.

The examination of policy impacts is generally part of the broader process of evaluating policy. As the term implies, policy evaluation involves drawing some conclusions about a policy.[44] Is it good? Is it bad? Is it doing what it is supposed to be doing? Do the benefits outweigh the costs? As these questions indicate, policy evaluation is a normative process since criteria first have to be specified before a program can be evaluated.

We have always performed some sort of policy evaluation. We complain that a city's snow removal is inadequate when we can't get out of our house after a blizzard. We complain that the welfare policy is rotten when told of the many welfare cheaters. We say the government's energy policy is failing because the price of gas keeps rising. Such evaluation, of course, is a rather haphazard, impressionistic process. One of the major changes in policy evaluation is to make evaluation a much more rigorous and systematic process. This involves thorough research aimed at identifying policy impacts rather than relying on hit-or-miss evidence. It is here that the research skills of social scientists are being applied to practical problems. But evaluation also involves some specification of the criteria to be used to determine if the impacts are satisfactory. One of the major problems of evaluation research is the question of who should specify these criteria. Should it be the researcher or the political leaders? Should the program administrators be responsible, or perhaps the target population?

In many cases, the researcher is expected to specify criteria. He, of course, may feel uncomfortable with such a responsibility because his training as a scientific researcher has not prepared him for the job. Some researchers, however, have begun to include in their work analysis of what criteria should be used to evaluate government policies. One of the most prominent examples of this is the research on political economy.[45] This research melds the study of politics with the techniques, concepts, and the assumptions of economics.

In analyzing policy it is necessary not only to measure costs and benefits, but to determine such things as whether free-market activity (assuming a free market can exist) is superior or inferior to government regulation in serving public needs. It is also necessary to consider such things as the cost of public goods, who pays for what services, etc., if we wish to analyze public policy thoroughly. The relationship between citizens and their government is conceptualized as basically a bartering relationship in which the demands of citizens are met in exchange for the citizens' willingness to be taxed and

---

44. For an examination of the problems and prospects of policy evaluation, see Alice M. Rivlin, *Systematic Thinking for Social Action* (Washington, D.C.: Brookings Insitution, 1971).
45. Wade and Curry, *A Logic of Public Policy*, especially chapters 3 and 6.

regulated by the government. The assumption is made that the rational citizen will demand efficient supplies of public goods, fair distribution of income, and economic stability. The burden of taxes is then to be distributed equitably. An equitable distribution may mean either those who benefit from the public good pay or that those who have the ability to pay will assume the burden. Efficient, fair, and equitable are all criteria which could be used to evaluate the impact of public policy. Of course, operationalizing these criteria is easier said than done.[46]

Even if the problem of establishing criteria can be resolved, there are still many practical problems involved in doing evaluation research.[47] In the first place, one must realize that to ask what is the impact of a policy is to ask what kinds of effects it causes. As we said several times before, it is very difficult to gather enough empirical evidence to establish that one thing causes another. This is especially difficult when experiments cannot be set up that control the effects of other factors which may be confusing the situation. And in most cases we simply can't set up experiments to evaluate policies. It would be neither politically popular nor morally acceptable to withhold food stamps from some poor people and not others in order to see what impact the food stamp program has. This does not mean that experiments can never be used, but only that their use is limited. We will discuss experiments in political science more thoroughly in Chapter Eight.

This leads to another problem with performing evaluations. In general, it is very difficult to gather information. Even if we rely on experiments we still must find some way of measuring benefits and costs. How do we measure the benefits of an education policy? Is it measured by the increased amount of income the students will eventually make? Of course, that would not account for the intangible benefits that result from education, such as the increased quality of life, the enjoyment of reading, etc.

So what measures can be used? The point is that the costs and benefits of social programs cannot be measured easily. But to determine if the benefits outweigh the costs (a frequently used criterion of good policy), somehow measures must be found. One thing which especially complicates the measurement process is the fact that policies often have symbolic benefits. The policy may really be designed primarily to prove to some group of people that the government cares for them. How do you measure the benefits of such symbolic policies? Another problem of gathering information is the fact that people involved in the policies are sometimes reluctant to cooperate fully with the evaluators. This may be because they believe strongly in the policy and are afraid any negative information might endanger it. Or they may simply be afraid that negative information may make them look bad and endanger their jobs.

---

46. Rivlin, *Systematic Thinking for Social Action*.
47. For practical guides for performing evaluation see Harry P. Hatry, Richard E. Winnie, and Donald M. Fisk, *Practical Program Evaluation* (Washington, D.C.: Urban Institute, 1973); and Edward A. Suchman, *Evaluative Research* (New York: Russell Sage Foundation, 1967).

Another problem of evaluating policies is determining the goals of a policy. The policy might be described and justified in one way when it is actually aimed toward something else. For instance, a job-training program may be justified in terms of its impact on improving the life of teenage dropouts, when the real goal is to get them off the streets so they won't cause trouble. The researcher must dredge through the various stated and unstated goals before confronting the other problems of gathering data. To do this, we must, in some cases, be a "mind reader" to be successful.

Another place where a "sixth sense" would help is in determining the impact the policy had on people other than the target population. Such impacts are obviously unintended; so, how does the evaluator know where to look for them? Such impacts may be as important, or, perhaps, even more important than the impacts on the target population. For example, as we said before, a welfare program could conceivably result in a tax revolt among the middle class which may be more important than whatever effects the policy had on the poor. So, a little guesswork would also help in determining the potential long-range impacts of policy when the evaluation must be done now rather than in the future.

Evaluation research is obviously an important new field. It makes use of the advances in techniques and methods in the social sciences and blends those advances to discover which government policies work and which do not. Researchers performing evaluations face a double set of obstacles. First, they must wrestle with problems of measuring intangibles (the benefits of education) and of gathering data, as must all social researchers. But in addition, they face the problem of values. What should the values be? Who should determine the values? Facing such obstacles is the frustration, as well as the challenge, of research.

By now you have a background in a wide variety of concepts political scientists use to try to understand politics. Each is helpful in answering questions about different aspects of the political process. You should have some questions on some aspects of the political process which you find particularly intriguing and wish to answer. The next section will help you get down to the "nitty gritty" of political research, from the choice of a topic to preparation for analysis.

SUMMARY
DECISION-MAKING

Core Definition: The process of choosing among alternative courses of action
Operationalization: 1. Observation of individuals in choice positions
2. Questionnaires to determine calculations and behavior in choice positions
Basic Questions: 1. How do political officials make decisions?

	2. Why do political officials make the decisions they do? 3. Who is making political decisions?
Major Findings:	1. Presidential decision-making appears to be related to personality type. 2. Characteristics of organizations affect decision-makers and, therefore, affect the decisions which are made. 3. Rational decision-making rarely exists in the real world.
Directions for the Future:	1. More precise specification of factors shaping decisions 2. More precise linkages between the factors which affect decisions and the actual decisions which are made 3. More work on ways of dealing with nondecisions

SUMMARY
POLICY

Core Definition:	Purposive course of actions in dealing with a problem
Operationalization:	Usually an investigation of a series of decisions in a given functional area
Basic Questions:	1. What are types of policies? 2. How are policies implemented? 3. What is the impact of policies? 4. How are policies evaluated?
Major Findings:	1. Policies have unintended as well as intended impacts. 2. Different styles of policy-making occur on different types of issues.
Directions for the Future:	1. Work to specify the relationship between the type of policy and the type of policy-making process 2. More extensive and rigorous investigation of policy implementation 3. More work on the measurement of policy impact

STUDY QUESTIONS

1. Distinguish between a decision and a policy.
2. What concepts from the last two chapters might be helpful to understand decision-making?
3. Choose a current decision made by government. Analyze the decision-making process in terms of actors, influences on those actors, and rationality.
4. List three governmental decisions you believe were made using rational decision-making and three decisions you believe were made incrementally.
5. List five hypotheses you could test to examine policy-making.
6. Policy evaluation is often based on the criteria of efficiency, fairness, and equity. Operationalize these concepts.
7. What are problems you would be likely to encounter if you tried to do evaluation research?

Political Research

Part Three

Having looked at the components of political theories and major concepts, the building blocks of theory, let us now look at the ways in which political scientists actually go about trying to build theories by conducting political research. Actually, research performs two functions in the process of theory building. In the first place it provides us with knowledge about the political phenomena in which we are interested. If we want to make statements about commonalities among events we need to have information on those events. Research provides us with that information. Secondly, after statements about the patterning of political events have been formulated, political scientists need to know if those statements are accurate. Research is the way political scientists test the accuracy and utility of their theories or generalizations.

In this section we will give you a "Cook's Tour" through some of the procedures involved in doing research. We will list some sources at the end of the book which cover the techniques of political research in greater depth. There are several reasons why we feel it is important to examine the steps involved in doing research. In the first place, of course, it is quite possible that you may be called upon to perform political research in this course or other courses. The steps involved can be used as guidelines whether you are doing research for a college term paper or a paper for publication. Obviously, if you are researching a term paper you may not have the resources necessary to conform to all the standards we will discuss. All research requires compromises to some extent. However, trying to meet as many of these standards as possible should improve the quality of your research.

A second reason for investigating the process of research is that you may very well be called upon to read or listen to a report of a political research project even if you yourself never do research. These guidelines can give you some standards to evaluate the quality of that research. Finally, we believe you may have a better idea of the things political scientists actually do with their time by learning about the process of doing political research. And teaching you about what political scientists do is exactly what this book is about.

Doing research is a multistage process. Chapter Seven will discuss the first step in this process, the task of selecting a problem for investigation. Once the research question is specified, the next step is to plan research. This plan is known as the research design. Chapter Eight deals with gathering data. You have to select people or events to study in order to attempt to answer the question you have posed. It is also necessary to devise a way of selecting evidence. That is, you must decide if you will administer a questionnaire, which means writing questions which measure what you are looking for. Or you might gather data through observation. In this case you must set criteria for evaluating your observations. Once your data are collected, you must organize and store the data in a usable form. This is the topic of Chapter Nine, the last chapter in this section.

The fourth section of the book will explain how to analyze and draw conclusions from the data you have collected.

Planning Research

Chapter Seven

So far we have exposed you to "the stratosphere" of the research process by considering the philosophy of scientific research and the conceptual analysis of political phenomena. Now we will get down to the "nitty gritty" of the research process—the steps involved in actually conducting empirical research. Although we are shifting gears, it does not mean that we are changing topics. The assumptions of the philosophy of science and the questions raised by conceptual analysis are essential to the design and process of research.

We think this will be quite clear by the time you finish this chapter on planning research. In this chapter we will consider how you can get over the first two hurdles of a research project: specifying the hypothesis and devising your research strategy. These steps may seem very mundane and not worthy of much discussion, but they are really the most important steps of any research project. A hypothesis which is poorly thought out will, at best, mean the research will take more time because of the various false starts and detours which will inevitably occur. At the worst, a poorly thought out hypothesis may mean that the time is wasted in the end since you may conclude that the topic is simply not researchable.

Even if the hypothesis is well thought out, a sloppy or sketchy research plan could also doom your research. A poorly planned research project could easily mean that you fail to gather enough of the right kind of information to answer your research question. What we are saying is that failure to specify your topic clearly and to plan in detail your research strategy could doom the research from the start.

To help you specify a research hypothesis we will discuss three steps to follow. First, we will consider some things to keep in mind when choosing a general topic for research. We will then give you some hints to help you do some digging to discover what other research has been done on the topic. And finally, we will consider how you can narrow the topic and phrase it precisely so that it can be tested. Then at the end of the chapter, we will begin our discussion of planning the research project. We say "begin our discussion" because such planning is the subject of the rest of this third section of the book. Let us now turn to the first of the steps in specifying a research hypothesis: selecting the topic.

SELECTING THE TOPIC

Unfortunately, selecting a topic is one of the toughest parts of the research process. When professors try to be "nice" and tell students to go out on their own and select a topic that interests them, invariably panic sets in. And those who have gone through this process and lived to tell about it are not much help. Ask a political scientist why he has chosen to study the tension between the U.S.S.R. and the People's Republic of China, or the election of 1980, and you will probably get an answer similar to Edmund Hillary's response to the question of why he climbed Mt. Everest, "Because it was there." What we are saying is that there is no nice and simple formula to aid you in choosing a research problem. But we can give you two basic guidelines to keep in mind in this process. First, the topic should interest you. This is quite important. You will, of necessity, be spending a significant amount of time on the project if you do it justice, so you might as well enjoy it. And you will probably do a better job if you are dealing with something that appeals to you. Secondly, you should try to pick a topic which has some significance both in practical and theoretical terms. In other words, the topic should provide information to help you and others better understand the political environment. Of course, this question of what is significant is both very subjective and closely related to the question of what interests you.

With these two guidelines in mind, let us consider where you should start your search for a topic. There are many potential sources for topics of research. Something may interest you in the readings you do. Books, magazines, and newspapers all focus on political events which could provide a basis for further research. Or there may be some event in your own immediate environment which will stimulate your interest. A campus demonstration may get you interested in the tactics of organizing to make political demands or in strategies leaders use to resolve conflict. The point is that we are essentially a very political society. Like it or not, the government has been constantly reaching into more and more areas of our lives. This means the number of topics for political scientists to study is constantly increasing.

To help you choose among various topics, you might want to consider what goals you are trying to achieve in your research. The research may be intended to achieve academic, social, or personal goals.[1] Of course, research may also be intended to achieve all or any combination of these goals. Let us consider each in turn.

To achieve the academic goal of research you should choose a topic that allows you to build on existing knowledge. The development of knowledge is cumulative. That is to say, we want to examine what things we know and go on from there. Building a body of knowledge is quite important. We do not want to start from scratch every time a question arises. Knowledge is built and laws are established by replicating, that is, by redoing studies in new situations. We would want to know if the findings are unique or if they can be generalized. If the findings of the studies are similar, we can be more certain of a universal condition. If the findings differ, then knowledge can be furthered if reasons for the divergence can be found.

Let us consider an example of how replication could be used in building knowledge. We have previously mentioned Hunter's study of the power structure of Atlanta, Georgia. He found that it was not the political leaders, but a group of big businessmen who held the real power in Atlanta. We might wish to redo the study today to see if there have been changes with the passage of time. Or we might want to know if big business rules all Southern cities, or all cities, or maybe even the United States Government.

Unfortunately, studies too often ignore the goal of accumulating a body of knowledge. Prestige in the discipline often comes from being unique, and, therefore, there may be few rewards for replicating studies. Another problem is that the discipline often goes through fads. The authors of this book went through graduate school in the era of systems analysis and survey research. Before a body of knowledge could be built based on these approaches, the discipline moved on to other interests. In general we are arguing that the discipline would be helped by more effort on replicating studies.

The second reason given above for selecting a topic is to aid in solving social problems. A given end is stipulated as a societal goal, and the question for the political scientist becomes how one can most easily reach that goal. For instance, we might select as a problem the issue of how to eliminate racial discrimination. The researcher may or may not be involved in the normative process of specifying the goals. The postbehavioral political scientist sees it as

---

1. David C. Leege and Wayne L. Francis, *Political Research* (New York: Basic Books, 1974), pp. 4–18.

his or her duty to apply expertise to specifying "good" ends for society. On the other hand, the researcher may try to divorce himself from the value of a specific goal of society and merely attempt to determine what activities foster the achievement of that goal, be it a "good" or "bad" goal.

The last reason for selecting a problem area may be for personal reasons. If you are a black or a Jew or a woman you may wish to discover for yourself why some people discriminate against you. This may help you understand them and perhaps even give you ways to change their attitudes. You might also be interested in an issue solely for the sake of individual curiosity. If you were a railroad buff, for example, you might be interested in how government regulation affects the economic well-being of railroads. Also for personal reasons, you may choose a topic which you feel is of interest to your instructor or boss, as it may be a means of getting ahead.

Considering these various goals may help you choose a general topic or area for research. Once you have the topic, you are ready to proceed to the next step.

BACKGROUND LIBRARY RESEARCH

After you have decided on a general area of inquiry for your paper that seems both interesting and significant to you, you will need to find out what else has been written on the topic. A good place to start is with a basic textbook. Look up the chapters or subsections which discuss your topic. Reading this should give you a general background. More importantly, the footnotes and bibliography will start you on your way to collecting references to other sources. You should check each source for other sources as well. Of course, not all of these references will be relevant to you. They may not even be easily available. This is one reason to begin research projects early. Many sources may not be available in your library but may be available through inter-library loan or directly from the author or publisher. This, however, often takes time.

Eventually you should make your way to the library to look for the books cited in your textbook, or to look for other textbooks to get more citations. These works will refer to previously written material. If the citations you are dredging up refer to material which is relatively old (more than three or four years), you may wish to get more current citations. These may be obtained through the *Social Science Citation Index*. Check in this index for the materials you have uncovered. The index will list other works which cite that material. Some of these may be more current than what you are familiar with.

The next step is to find these sources in the card catalog. In addition you should also look for books under subject headings relevant to your topic. The National Union Catalog lists virtually all books available in the United

States. For instance, if you are interested in United States foreign policy, look in the subject catalog under that topic. It will probably be broken down into regions, such as the Middle East, and even by country, for example, Egypt or Israel.

Another place to look while at the library is the list of journals being received. You may be familiar with some journals, such as *Time Magazine, American Political Science Review,* or *Foreign Affairs,* but you may discover many other potentially relevant journals. Journals, such as *Time, Newsweek,* and so forth, are probably less valuable for serious research because they use journalistic, as opposed to scientific, analysis, and it is difficult to find a precise use of concepts and methods. Nonetheless, these sources may provide excellent background material and may suggest questions for scientific testing. A look at their yearly indexes may alert you to relevant articles.

Much of the information found in journal articles may be beneficial because it is apt to be more current and more narrowly focused than material available in books. There are comprehensive indexes such as the *Public Affairs Information Service* (P.A.I.S.) and *A Reader's Guide to Periodical Literature.* In addition, there are specialized social and political science indexes, such as the *International Bibliography of Social Science: Political Science*; *The Advanced Bibliography of Content: Political Science; The Universal References System: Political Science*; and *Government and Public Policy Series,* to name a few of the most useful indexes. There are also a variety of specialized subject indices. For instance, in the area of Urban Studies, the United States Department of Housing and Urban Development publishes a bulletin with urban references. The National League of Cities does likewise. The United States Government publishes the *Monthly Catalog of U.S. Government Publications.*

There are still other sources of information, such as *International Political Science Abstracts,* which give you summaries of articles. Book reviews, indexed in the *Book Review Abstracts,* may help determine if a book will be useful. Depending on your topic, newspapers may be relevant. There are also some general reference books which you should be aware of, such as the *Municipal Yearbook, Congressional Quarterly,* U.S. Bureau of Census publications, and many others.

As you work in a given area you will find yourself becoming more and more familiar with reference material which will help you research a topic. A beginning researcher should consult a reference librarian for assistance. After you have compiled a list of books and articles which look relevant to your topic, the next step is to sit down and read through them. Of course, you might not have to read all of the material you have gathered. A quick check of the index and table of contents may tell you that only certain parts of a book will be helpful to you. And skimming the first few pages of an article may make clear to you that it is of little or no use to you. The point is that you want comprehensive knowledge about your topic but you do not want to waste more time than necessary gathering information which is of little use to you. Read selectively. When you first start reading, of course, you won't be too sure what is relevant or irrelevant. However, as you continue to read, your topic will (or should) become more clearly defined in your mind. Throughout this process, you would be taking down important points and information on note cards so that you won't have to return constantly to the original sources when you want to refer to the information.

If possible, you should try to organize your findings into a "propositional inventory." A propositional inventory is a listing of generalizations found in the literature. These need not be interrelated as a theory would be, but by organizing your literature review in this way you will become attuned to causes, effects, and relationships which have been established or at least investigated. You may wish to reinvestigate some of these propositions, attempt to find new relationships, or interrelate propositions for your own research. Be sure to write down bibliographic information so that if you use this information in your report you will know where it came from and how to properly refer to it. Remember, that as footnotes and bibliographies are beneficial to you in finding out background information, they are also important to those who read your work. Your work will be unique in terms of the way you put together previous research and, perhaps, in some new information and methods. It should be related, though, to the existing body of knowledge. At some point when you feel at least fairly confident of your knowledge of the topic, you should stop your library research for a while and proceed to the next step of research: formulating the question.

FORMULATING THE QUESTION

When you began your library research, you probably had only a vague idea of your topic. As you become more familiar with the subject, however, you should notice that on some aspects of the topic there seems to be substantial agreement. But on other aspects there is probably significant disagreement. In all likelihood you will select one of the points on which there is disagreement as the basis for your research. You do not necessarily have to select a topic on which there is the most disagreement. As we said before, there are now no universal laws in political science, and there is always a benefit in consistently testing and retesting generalizations. We may discover in greater depth under what circumstances they hold and under what circumstances they do not. Or we may find that changing conditions produce different conclusions. However, it is probably more likely that the controversy and conflict surrounding some issues will stimulate your interest.

Karl Popper notes three bases for selecting problems based on inconsistencies. These are inconsistencies (1) within theories, (2) between theories, and (3) between theory and reality.[2] If a theory is incorrectly or incompletely specified it is possible that derived hypotheses may be contradictory. Here is a source of a problem to be investigated. An example might result from using cross-pressure theory. Simply stated, cross-pressure theory is based on the notion that individuals often receive contradictory stimuli with respect to events and expected behavior. If these contradictions are strong, it is expected that one will withdraw from activities where stress is created. This is one explanation given as a reason for nonvoting by some citizens. On the other hand some people ignore the contradictions and do participate. The problem then is to determine under what conditions the theory will hold.

A second contradiction is one between two existing theories. While not deductive theories, pluralism and elitism are often used as theoretical explanations of public policy. Elite theory argues that governments pursue policies which benefit the "rich, well-born, and able" because these are the men who actually rule. Pluralist theory argues that policy is the end result of the interplay of diverse interests in society. Obviously, a research problem would be to investigate a policy arena to determine which explanation is more plausible.

The third contradiction noted is between theory and reality. Marxist theory predicted a workers' revolution beginning in industrialized societies. Observations of reality indicate that Marxist revolutions occurred in underdeveloped and developing nations. The problem here is to determine if any parts of Marxist theory are valid in explaining the real world or if the entire theory must be reformulated. Can Marxist theory be used to explain Communist revolutions in developing states?

These three types of inconsistencies provide us with an infinite supply of problems to be studied. We should point out again that in this book we are concerned with defining and analyzing empirical problems. There are also other types of problems: normative and analytic. Normative problems are based upon value judgments. For example, they are usually concerned with what "ought" to be done or what is "best." Answers to these problems cannot be found empirically but rest upon a search for essential truths and values. These problems may offer future directions and solutions for society. Analytic problems are those which are based solely on the logical structure of the argument. Once certain assumptions are made, the rest of the argument can be logically deduced. All mathematical problems are analytical. Since such analytical statements are verified by the use of logic rather than by the observation of the empirical world, they are not really scientific. But analytical statements may help us achieve the goal of science, which is understanding the real world. For example, Downs in *An Economic Theory of Democracy*

---

2. Karl Popper, *Conjectures and Refutations: The Growth of Scientific Knowledge* (New York: Harper & Row, 1963), p. 222.

assumed that men always act rationally. This assumption is obviously not realistic. But from that assumption of rationality he logically deduced explanations for such questions as voter indifference and similarity of party platform.[3] These explanations are not universal since men do not always act rationally. We could though, direct our empirical research to determining when and how often men do act according to Downs' predictions and looking for reasons why at times the predictions are not accurate.

Empirical problems, our main concern here, can be divided into three types: descriptive, relational, and causal.[4] The first type of problem is one of description. This type of problem can be a quite simple question, such as: What proportion of the electorate favor lower taxes? Or it may be quite complex: How does Congress operate? The essence of a descriptive empirical study is to get a picture of *what is*. A descriptive study does not answer the question of why things appear as they are. Before we can ask these why questions, though, we must be certain we have a valid conception of reality.

If we feel we know what is, we can raise relational problems. That is, we can make systematic comparisons between two or more variables or events. The question here is whether or not certain occurrences happen together. In other words, we wish to know if the events are in some way connected. For example, how is one's religion related to party affiliation? How does increasing education relate to earning power? These are relational questions which are empirically testable.

The more we know about the relationships, the more clearly we can specify how the variation in one characteristic will be reflected in the variation of another characteristic. As noted above, one can never definitely prove one event causes another. If, however, certain conditions can be met, it is possible to infer that the relationship is causal. For instance, how is police maltreatment of blacks, or any group for that matter, related to social unrest or ghetto violence? Some political scientists have developed mathematical models to attempt to deal with the problems of causation. Different kinds of conclusions and statements could be made depending upon whether the research was aimed at description, relation, or causation. So you should be very clear what you will do in your research.

With this background you are now ready to turn your general topic into a problem statement or question. Once again, while there are no hard and fast rules for determining what is a "good" problem, there are four criteria to be considered. The application of these factors tends to be somewhat subjective. These factors are: (1) scope (how narrow or broad); (2) clarity (simple

---

3. Anthony Downs, *An Economic Theory of Democracy* (New York: Harper & Row, 1957), passim.
4. Leege and Francis, *Political Research*, pp. 19–29.

and explicit); (3) significance (academic and societal); and (4) scientific testability (empirical).[5]

Scope

Determining the scope of the problem is one of the greatest dilemmas facing the prospective researcher. Actually, the scope of the problem varies with the reason for the research. If you are asked to write a ten page term paper you have to choose a fairly narrow topic. On the other hand, if you are writing a book, the topic should generally be quite broad. It is a common fault of beginning researchers to define issues too broadly so that they will be sure of having something to say. All too often because of an extremely broad topic, the researcher never gets to "say" anything since there is so much information to search out. Ten pages is certainly too little space in which to specify an energy policy for the United Staes for the remainder of the century. By the same token, if you are asked to write a 50-page paper it might be a good idea to look at a broader problem than voter turnout on your street in the 1980 election. To help you determine the proper scope of a problem you should consider (1) the reason for doing the research, (2) the amount of time you have to do the research, (3) the expectations concerning the length and depth of the finished product, (4) the amount of prior research done in the area, (5) available resources such as money, time, and so forth, and (6) your expertise.

Clarity

It is extremely important that the problem be stated as simply as possible. One obvious reason for this is so other people will know exactly what you are investigating. A reason which is not so obvious but equally important is the fact that it helps you to focus your energies. For example, if your interest is in the general area of electoral campaigns and advertising, you should have a clear and explicit statement or statements concerning your exact problem. You should not say that many factors affect voting, including advertising, demographic factors, etc. With such a statement, a reader certainly would not have a clear idea what you were saying. And such a vague statement may also cause you to go far afield looking for the effect of many factors rather than focusing your research on what might be the most

---

5. There are many criteria established. See, for example, Dickinson McGaw and George Watson, *Political and Social Inquiry* (New York: Wiley, 1976), pp. 99–104; Fred N. Kerlinger, *Foundations of Behavioral Research,* 2nd ed. (New York: Holt, Rinehart & Winston, 1973), pp. 17–18.

important factors. You should state explicitly what you want to know. For instance, you should state that you want to know the impact of political advertising on voting. While this statement is explicit, it still may not be clear enough to begin your research. You might want to limit the types of political advertising you wish to investigate, that is, TV ads, newspaper ads, handbills, etc. Or you may want to know if different types of campaign advertisements will affect different segments of the population differently. You will also have to clarify what you mean by voting. Do you mean the amount of voting or the choice of candidate people vote for? Does increasing advertising, in terms of dollars spent, increase participation? How do certain techniques or symbols favor one candidate over another? All of these are questions you might want to ask about the impact of advertising on voting. The key point is that before you start your research you should clearly state exactly what you will be asking. Do not try to be fancy. Just be as explicit and clear as you can. One further note, keep jargon to a minimum. Use it only when necessary.

Significance

As noted above, there are many reasons why individuals select research problems, but generally speaking, the greater the significance and relevance, the better the topic. If you can contribute to building new knowledge or even reevaluating old beliefs, you can help an academic discipline to develop. If you can at the same time help society gain insights on some pressing issues, it is better still.

Scientific Testability

The last criterion for problem selection may be the most difficult to satisfy. Problems should be scientifically testable. That means that above all, they must be empirical. As noted above, there are many very important questions which cannot be studied empirically. Such things as ethical, moral, and theological matters fall into this category. If you want to be a scientist, however, you cannot deal solely with questions of values. It is sometimes possible to cast value questions into an empirical mold. For example, while you cannot verify empirically whether democracy is the "best" political system, you can test whether democracy leads to higher per capita income, more consumer goods, freedom from fear, and so forth—although most believe that establishing these relationships does not prove democracy is good.[6]

---

6. Some have labeled this the "naturalistic fallacy" and have argued that value questions cannot be made interchangeable with empirical questions. See McGaw and Watson, *Political and Social Inquiry,* pp. 93–94.

Another thing to keep in mind about testability is whether data to solve the problem are either already available or can be collected within the time and resource boundaries of the study. You could probably think of many problems which could be empirically tested if you had unlimited time and/or resources. But it is important for you to realize your limits and avoid such problems. You are now ready to proceed to the next step: the research outline or research design.

RESEARCH DESIGN

Once you have decided precisely what problem you will focus upon in your research, you must decide exactly what you want to know from the research. What we are saying here is that research involves more than just gathering together information from various sources and reporting it. Research involves gathering information to use in testing your guesses—or hypotheses—concerning the patterning of political events. In other words, research involves answering questions, not just reporting on the results of other research. This does not mean that you necessarily have to go into the field and gather new data. It just means that regardless of what data you use, your research should be organized around providing information to aid in substantiating the generalizations which are so fundamental to theory building.

Therefore, it is necessary to plan your research before starting out blindly. This plan or outline of the procedures you will use to answer your research question is an essential step to be performed before actually conducting your research. You will often be tempted to skip this step in research, but it is not a good idea. There are many problems that can be caused by not thoroughly planning your research before you start your project. By not thinking through the necessary procedures thoroughly, you may find at the end you have asked the wrong questions, gathered the wrong kind of data, or not gathered sufficient data to test the accuracy of your generalization.

Fred Kerlinger defines research design as "the plan, structure, and strategy of investigation conceived so as to obtain answers to research questions and to control variance."[7] This broad notion of research design will be used here. The "plan" is the overall outline, beginning with choosing and operationalizing variables, and continuing to the strategy for the final data analysis. The "structure" of the design deals with the logical structure of your argument. In setting your structure you must specify the relationship between your generalizations. The "strategy of investigation," as set forth

---

7. Fred N. Kerlinger, *Foundations of Behavioral Research,* p. 300.

in the research design, entails the specification of what data are to be collected, how it will be collected, how it will be analyzed, and what the standards of verification will be (that is; how will you know if you must accept or reject your hypothesis). Many texts only consider this strategy of investigation in their discussion of research design, but we feel that it is necessary here to see the research design as an important aid in doing political research from beginning to end.

The research design should be written to provide you with answers to the following questions:

1. What concepts or variables will you use and how will they be operationalized?
2. What relationships (building generalizations) do you believe exist among your concepts?
3. How are your generalizations related to each other?
4. What data will you need to test your theoretical formulation and how will you collect it?
5. How will you store your data?
6. How will you analyze your data and what standards will you apply to accept or reject your hypotheses?

The first three questions will be discussed in the remainder of this chapter. Much of this discussion will draw on what you learned in Chapter Two about the role of theory building in research. A more in-depth discussion of question four—research strategy and data collection—will be provided in the next chapter. The last chapter in this section will provide alternative answers to question five: data storage. The next section of this book will answer the last question: analyzing and interpreting data.

CONCEPTS AND OPERATIONALIZATION

The first question to be faced is "What concepts or variables will you use and how will they be operationalized?" The first section of this text introduced you to the importance of concept formation in theoretical scientific inquiry. As we indicated before, concepts are words which abstract common elements from disparate phenomena. You should also remember that a variable is a concept which can take on more than one value. Perhaps the most important thing to keep in mind in dealing with concepts is that they must be clearly and precisely defined so that they aid—not hinder—communication. Of course, the most precise way to define concepts is to go beyond simple definition by specifying some empirical indicator or indicators of the concept. Many people feel that this precision is gained at the loss of much richness. Regardless of how you feel about operationalization, you should keep in mind that concepts, which will be the basis of your research, should be clearly defined.

When operationalizing concepts, there are several things to keep in mind. In the first place, you should make sure that the operationalization is congruent with the definition. For instance, if you define democracy as a form of government characterized by competition, then you should look for regular elections in which at least two parties compete. Given that definition, it would not make sense to use as an operationalization a questionnaire which asks citizens how satisfied they are with their government.

A second thing you should keep in mind when operationalizing concepts is to make sure you don't measure both the independent and dependent variables with the same indicators. For instance, in our discussion of power we mentioned that people at times use as an indicator of power the ability to obtain desired goals from the government. But if that is how power is measured, it makes no sense, then, to hypothesize that power leads to the ability to obtain desired results from government. That would be equivalent to saying that A leads to A. Such a circular statement is a tautology.

Thirdly, you should make sure that you enumerate in any report of your research how you operationalize the concepts. This is to fulfill the requirement of intersubjectivity. Remember, one of the characteristics of science is objectivity. But it is often very difficult for scientists to be totally objective especially when they are dealing with a subject such as politics. Therefore, they have imposed on themselves the requirement that they specify very clearly and in detail all of the procedures they followed in a research project. In fact, the procedures should be specified so clearly that anyone else could precisely duplicate the research project. This is the requirement of intersubjectivity.

Intersubjectivity can help overcome the problem of values in two ways. In the first place, if the researcher's values led him to "stack the deck" by his choice of procedures, either knowingly or unknowingly, it should be apparent to anyone reading his research report. For instance, a researcher might hypothesize that college-educated people are liberal. If he tested his hypothesis by interviewing only college graduates who were members of the Socialist Workers Party we would know something was fishy.

The second way intersubjectivity overcomes the problem of values is by making it possible for researchers to duplicate research. If one researcher exactly duplicated what another researcher had done but drew different conclusions, then we might suspect that the researcher's values were affecting the conclusions. If different researchers consistently duplicate research and consistently report the same findings, then we can be fairly sure that values are not affecting the conclusions.

Reliability and Validity

You should also consider whether the operationalization is reliable and valid. Reliability refers to whether the indicators you have selected consistently produce the same results. Validity refers to whether the indicators are actually measuring what you think they are measuring. Let us consider how we can attempt to establish the reliability and validity of our indicators.

To establish reliability, we must determine that the indicators we have selected for our operationalization consistently produce the same results. That is, if we measure patriotism by asking if people always salute the flag, do some people respond "yes" consistently and others "no" consistently, so that there is no confusion about how to classify them? The most obvious way to determine reliability is the *test–retest method*. In other words, observe a group of people and at some later time observe the same people. If the indicators are reliable, then the results of the two observations should be similar. Unfortunately, they will almost inevitably not be identical.

There are many sources of unreliability that a researcher cannot control. People may "feel" different one day than another. People may actually have changed from the first test to the second. In that case, the indicators are not unreliable, but the people are. And, of course, the research may actually cause people to change. For instance, if we were basing our research on a test, people may have been upset that they didn't know the answers and searched them out before the second test. Or they might have remembered the answers they gave on the first test and may have given the same ones on the second to make themselves look consistent—or even different ones on the retest to deliberately confuse the researcher. There is a real dilemma here. If you give the second test soon after the first one, people are more likely to remember their answers and respond accordingly. If you wait a long time, people are likely to change. So the test-retest method will never produce absolutely identical results.

There are also some sources of unreliability that researchers can control, and this is where the results of a test–retest method can help. For instance, the wording of the question may be ambiguous. If we ask people if they always salute the flag, they may not know if we really mean always, always during the Pledge of Allegiance, always during parades, or whatever. Making questions clear and unambiguous is one way to make measures reliable.

Another way to improve reliability is to make the test situation as similar as possible for all respondents. That means trying to administer the tests to all the subjects over a short period of time so that things in the environment don't change. It also means training the interviewers so that they will administer the tests as consistently as possible. If an interviewer gets bored with a question and shortens the wording, it is only natural that people will respond differently.

Reliability is hard to achieve, but it is even harder to achieve validity. Validity refers to whether we are really measuring what we think we are measuring. For instance, it is possible that people will always say they salute the flag because they believe that is the socially acceptable thing to say. If this were the case, saying that you always salute the flag does not actually measure whether or not you are patriotic but whether or not you are worried about social acceptability. A reliable measure is not necessarily valid. It may consistently measure something besides what you want it to measure.

There is no totally satisfactory way of determining the validity of measures. You could try to decide if, in fact, the measure seems to be an accurate indicator of the concept. This kind of validity, which is called *face validity*, obviously relies on subjective judgment. Alternatively you could investigate whether the indicator is related to other phenomena in the same way that the concept is related to those phenomena. For instance, if you knew that patriotic people always vote, you could observe whether those who say they always salute the flag also always vote. Schematically, what we are saying is that if A is related to B, then "*a*," which indicates the existence of A, should be related to B in the same way:

$$\begin{array}{c} A \longrightarrow B \\ \updownarrow \nearrow \\ a \end{array}$$

This type of validity is known as *predictive validity*. Of course, using this method to establish validity depends on being certain that A is always related to B. In our example, we would have to be certain that patriotic people always vote. Obviously, we very rarely have such certain knowledge about the relationships among political phenomena. So validity remains a thorny problem.

It is important to realize that since most concepts can be operationalized in may ways, you must be certain how others have used the concept if you wish to make comparisons between works. One author may operationalize patriotism by the use of two indicators: saluting the flag and participating in government decisions. In that case we may conclude that New Englanders are the most patriotic people in the United States because they not only salute the flag but participate directly in government through town meetings. Another author, operationalizing patriotism solely in terms of saluting the flag, may find that the Midwest is more patriotic. This situation may lead to confusion. This is why you must point out how you are operationalizing your concepts before you begin your research. It will serve as a guide to what data must be collected. It will also aid you in relating the findings of others (and, perhaps, contradictions in the literature) to your research.

Index and Scale Construction

Another thing to consider in the process of operationalizing is how many indicators you will use, and, if you are using more than one indicator, how you will relate the indicators. Sometimes a single indicator is quite sufficient. For instance, if you want to know someone's party identification, it might be quite adequate to ask "What party do you identify with?" But if you are dealing with a very complex concept, you may feel that a single indicator is simply not adequate. By using more than one indicator you may increase validity. For instance, you may feel that there is no way a single indicator can adequately operationalize the concept of prejudice. You may decide to use several statements to indicate prejudice. Examples of such statements might be the following:

A. I wouldn't mind living next door to a black.
B. I oppose equal rights for blacks.
C. I wouldn't mind if my sister dated a black.

Now you have to decide how you will handle these statements. There are many techniques for combining these separate indicators into a composite measure. Perhaps the first question you will have to answer is how precise you want your measurement to be. Although the terms are frequently used interchangeably, the difference between an *index* and a *scale* is the degree of precision. An index is constructed by simply combining the values of various indicators of an underlying dimension. In other words, we are trying to measure different aspects of *one* phenomenon. For instance, to construct an index of political participation we may include items on voting, fund raising, campaigning, and so forth, but not items on religion. While religion may be related to political participation, it is not an aspect of political participation as are the other variables. No assumptions are made about the nature or structure of the relationship among the indicators. The only assumption is that the indicators are related. To devise a scale, some criteria are established concerning the structure of the relationship among the indicators. The structure is usually seen as having to do with different levels of intensity.

To create a simple index, you merely add the responses to the separate indicators. For example, let us consider the three statements we listed to indicate prejudice. We can say that a person who gave a nonprejudiced response to all three statements is less prejudiced than one who gave a prejudiced response to any of them. If we numbered a prejudiced response as 2, and a nonprejudiced response as 1, individuals could be ranked from 3 indicating low prejudice, to 6 indicating high prejudice.

Two important decisions have to be made about the construction of such indexes. First, you have to decide what indicators to include. Much of the time, researchers rely on face validity to determine what indicators should be used. In other words, they decide what makes sense for them to include. Remember, all the indicators are supposed to be measuring one underlying dimension; therefore, all the indicators should seem to be related to that dimension. If you are measuring prejudice you should not include a question which is an indicator of party identification.

Another way to decide which indicators to include in an index is to examine how people respond to the statement in a pretest. If two statements both indicate prejudice, then the same people should tend to respond to both in the same way. Of course, if everyone responds to both statements in exactly the same way, there is no need to include both of them. One of the statements, then, would group the respondents in exactly the same way as both the statements together would. This means you are only wasting your and the respondent's time. Another thing to consider is whether different people respond differently to the same statement. That is, if everyone agreed to a particular statement about prejudice or if everyone disagreed with that statement, then it is impossible to use that statement to determine people's prejudices.

The second question you have to consider about building indexes is how to weigh the indicators you include. In our example above, we weighed each statement equally. We were saying implicitly that we thought each statement is equally important as an indicator of prejudice. So, for each statement we indicated agreement by 1 and disagreement by 2. It might be possible that we believe one statement is an especially important indicator. We would want to count that response more than the responses to other statements. If we thought one statement was twice as important as the others we might indicate agree by 2 and disagree by 4. Usually, we simply don't know enough to weight various questions in this way; therefore, we weight them all equally.

The second way to create a composite measure from a group of questions is to scale them. To create an index we summed the responses to individual statements. To create a scale, we examine the response pattern across several statements. That is, we assume there is some logical or empirical pattern or structure to the statements.

There are a variety of scaling techniques available. Two of the most common will be discussed here: Likert Scaling and Guttman Scaling.

Likert Scale. A Likert Scale is a simple additive measure which provides a score based on the number and intensity of responses to a series of statements.[8] A Likert Scale for prejudice of whites could be set up based on the following questions: "Do you strongly agree (1), agree (2), neutral (3), disagree (4), or strongly disagree (5) with the following statements:

---

8. Rensis Likert, "A Technique for the Measurement of Attitudes," *Archives of Psychology*, 140 (1932).

	SA	A	N	D	SD
A. I wouldn't mind living next door to a black.	1	2	3	4	5
B. I wouldn't mind going to school with a black.	1	2	3	4	5
C. I favor equal rights for blacks.	1	2	3	4	5
D. I wouldn't mind my sister dating a black.	1	2	3	4	5
E. I wouldn't mind if my sister married a black.	1	2	3	4	5

In our example the least prejudiced person would have a score of 5 and the most prejudiced a score of 25, with a wide variety of possible scores and degrees of prejudice possible. If you are more comfortable with the least prejudiced getting a 25, there is no reason the values could not have been reversed as long as they remain consistent. In an actual study you would reverse at least one of these questions and adjust the scoring accordingly as we did in the previous example. This is to prevent "response set." This will be discussed in Chapter Eight. With the Likert Scale you are assuming implicitly that all statements are of equal "difficulty," that is, there is no ordering of the statements. You are also assuming that they are all measuring prejudice. After responses are collected, one uses what is known as item analysis to validate the index. A comparison is made of the relation of the index to each indicator which composes it. The index should be able to predict responses to the individual indicators. If that is the case, then we can be fairly sure that the indicators are, in fact, measuring one underlying variable. For instance, we would expect a high degree of relationship (correlation) between our indicators of prejudice (see correlation in Chapter Thirteen). If our indicators are not very closely related, we may be measuring more than one dimension. If they are too closely related, we may not need all the items. Experience and the degree to which you are willing to tolerate errors will determine what are acceptable relationships.

Guttman Scale. Unlike Likert Scales, Guttman Scales do not measure intensity of each response. Instead, the Guttman Scale orders the *statements* in terms of intensity. Like an index or Likert Scale, A Guttman Scale assumes that there is one underlying dimension which is being measured. In addition, it assumes that there is an ordering to the statements. The Guttman Scale procedure provides a way to check empirically if these assumptions are valid. Let us look at an example of a Guttman Scale to measure prejudice. We will use five questions, with the possible responses being either agreement or disagreement.

A. I wouldn't mind living next door to a black.
B. I wouldn't mind going to school with blacks.
C. I favor equal rights for blacks.
D. I wouldn't mind my brother dating a black.
E. I wouldn't mind if my brother married a black.

We would assume that a person who is very unprejudiced would agree with all the statements, and one who is very prejudiced would uniformly disagree. But with a Guttman Scale we also assume there is an order to how people see these statements. We assume these statements can be ordered in terms of "hardness." As the statements increase in difficulty, we expect more and more people to begin to disagree. In other words, we think the scale statements will be seen by the respondents as differing in intensity. We believe that if a person can agree with a statement of medium intensity, or "hardness," he should also be able to agree with "easier" statements, but not necessarily agree with any of the more "difficult" statements.[9]

One thing that should be made clear about Guttman Scales is that they are only considered to scale if the respondents themselves reply to the statements in a cumulative pattern. This means that what may be considered a scale for one sample may not be considered a scale for another sample. For us to agree that a Guttman Scale exists, the responses from each sample must be evaluated in order to determine if enough respondents saw the statements as ordered in intensity. Let us see look at a hypothetical ordering of responses of ten individuals to these five statements: (see Table 7-1).

Table 7-1 Hypothetical Guttman Scale Responses (Raw Data)

Respondent	Statements				
	A	B	C	D	E
1	O	X	X	O	O
2	O	O	O	O	O
3	X	X	X	X	O
4	X	X	X	X	O
5	O	O	X	O	O
6	X	X	X	O	O
7	O	X	O	O	O
8	X	X	X	X	X
9	O	X	O	O	O
10	X	X	X	X	O

X = agree; O = disagree.

The statements and the respondents should be reordered to determine if the people responded to the statements cumulatively (see Table 7-2). The first step is to reorder the statements according to the number who responded positively to each statement. Eight people responded positively to Statement B, so it becomes the first, or "easiest," statement. This statement is followed by statement C (seven agree), statement A (five agree), statement D

---

9 Louis Guttman, "The Quantification of a Class of Attributes," in *The Prediction of Personal Adjustment*, ed. P. Horst and others. (New York: Bulletin no. 48, Social Science Research Council, 1941), pp. 319-44.

Table 7-2 Hypothetical Guttman Scale Responses (Reordered)

Respondent	B	C	A	D	E	Score
8	X	X	X	X	X	5
3	X	X	X	X	O	4
4	X	X	X	X	O	4
10	X	X	X	X	O	4
6	X	X	X	O	O	3
1	X	X	O	O	O	2
5	O	[X]	O	O	O	1
7	X	O	O	O	O	1
9	X	O	O	O	O	1
2	O	O	O	O	O	0

X = agree; O = disagree

(four agree), and finally statement E (one agrees). In addition to reordering the questions, the respondents must be reordered. Respondents 8 and 3 each agreed with all five statements, so they are listed first. Since respondents 4 and 10 agreed with statements B,C,A, and D but disagreed with statement E, they are placed after respondents 8 and 3. They are followed by respondent 6 who agreed with the first three statements, and so on until all the respondents are ordered according to the way they responded to the questions.

We can see that respondent number 5 has one "nonscale response." He agreed that blacks should have equal rights, but opposed going to school with blacks, a statement which other responses show is generally considered to indicate less prejudice. To determine if we have a valid Guttman Scale we must calculate the Coefficient of Reproducibility (CR). It is calculated by dividing "correct" or consistent responses by total possible responses. In our example, it would be as follows:

$$CR = \frac{Correct}{All} = \frac{49}{50} = 0.98$$

The 0.98 indicates a very good scale. This means that if you knew the respondents' scale types and the ordering of the statements, you could predict 98% of their responses correctly. Political scientists generally establish 0.90 as an arbitrary value which must be met or exceeded before a Guttman Scale can be accepted.

In addition to calculating the Coefficient of Reproducibility, it is also important to calculate the Coefficient of Scalability. This is based on comparing the number of errors to all possible errors. If everyone agreed, or if everyone disagreed with all statements, there could be no errors. To determine the number of errors that could possibly occur, we add up the number of "less frequent" responses on all items and then on all cases.

First we will look at the responses to the individual questions and determine the number of times the "less frequent" response was given. For statements B and C in our example, "no" was the "less frequent" response and the total number of "no" responses for those two statements was 5. For statement A there was no "less frequent" response since there were five "yes" responses and five "no" responses. Therefore either the number of "yes" responses or the number of "no" responses may be counted. For statements D and E, "yes" is the "less frequent response," and the total number of "yes" responses for those statements is 5. The total for all the statements is thus 15.

The second way to calculate total possible errors is to examine each respondent and to calculate how many "less frequent" responses each gave. Respondent 8 answered "yes" to all statements, so there are no "less frequent" responses. Respondents 3,4, and 10 answered "no" once each and respondent 6 answered "no" twice. The total for them is therefore 5. For respondents 1,5,7, and 9, "yes" was the "less frequent" response, and the total number of "yes" responses they gave was 5. Respondent 2 answered "no" to all questions. The total number of "less frequent" responses when examining each respondent is 10.

When calculating the Coefficient of Scalability, you compute the number of less frequent responses in both of the ways we demonstrated and select the smaller number. In this example, the smaller number is 10, which resulted when looking at the responses of individuals. This number is then compared to the number of errors in responses. As we determined above, the number of errors in these hypothetical data is 1. The formula for the Coefficient of Scalability (CS) is:

$$CS = 1 - \frac{\text{actual number of errors}}{\text{maximum number of errors possible}}$$

For this data we would have the following:

$$CS = 1 - \frac{1}{10} = 0.90$$

In this case, only 10% of all possible errors occurred, producing a CS of 0.90. The smaller the number of errors compared to the maximum possible errors the better. Researchers have established that the CS must be 0.60 or higher. What this means is that if more than 40% of all possible errors occur, your scale would be inadequate.

There are two advantages of using a Guttman Scale rather than an index. In the first place, since we say a scale exists only if at least 90% of the responses fit the cumulative pattern and less than 40% of all possible errors occur, we can confirm empirically that the questions should go together. Secondly, unlike an index, the intermediate scores on a scale are meaningful. With the index we constructed before, the scores could range from 3 to 6. We know exactly what those scores mean: complete agreement or complete disagreement. But what does it mean if someone scored 4? We have no idea with what questions he or she agreed or disagreed. With a Guttman Scale, the score tells us exactly how an individual answered each question.

We have one final point to make about selecting concepts to be used in research. Be sure that they are meaningful. This, of course, is another guideline which is primarily subjective. But many traditionalists have argued—and often with good cause—that in the effort to be empirical, many researchers have focused only on trivial ideas because such concepts could be easily operationalized. Obviously, if we are to increase our knowledge about political phenomena we must do research on important questions, even if it is difficult or perhaps impossible to operationalize the concepts involved. We should also point out that concepts need not be operationalized in quantitative terms. Where possible, quantitative concepts allow greater precision and are more amenable to statistical manipulation. This is so because a meaningful numerical value can be attached which will allow us to compare and relate concepts. But where necessary, qualitative concepts may be meaningful and provide important insights. Qualitative concepts are those which make distinctions based on a quality or characteristic rather than quantity. It is impossible to operationalize sex in quantitative terms; but by using the qualitative distinction of men and women, we can make meaningful statements about distinctions in political activities of the sexes. We need not be stymied by the feeling that everything must be quantified.

BUILDING GENERALIZATIONS

Once you have chosen the concepts with which you will deal and defined them clearly, you must consider the second question of your research design. "What is the expected relationship among your concepts?" In other words, you must link your concepts to create generalizations. You should clearly think through and specify your assumptions and hypotheses. An assumption is a condition which you believe exists and which you will not be testing empirically. However, you will be testing the hypotheses. Your library research should be helpful in determining what beliefs are commonly accepted. By examining what others have found about your topic, certain patterns should suggest themselves. Your statement of patterns you believe to exist and wish to examine empirically is a statement of the hypothesis. You may wish to study these patterns because the relationship is less certain than the relationships you use as assumptions.

There are a few pitfalls to be avoided in hypothesis writing:

1. Since it is a form of generalization, the hypothesis must be a general statement applying to classes of properties and people.

2. The hypothesis must not be true by definition (tautological).
3. Relationships should be clearly specified.
4. Statements should be empirical and, therefore, not normative.[10]

Let us look at each of these in more depth.

Make General Statements

Remember, you are supposed to be doing this research to aid in theory building. This means that you should choose a generalization for research which has a broad enough scope to be significant. Here again is a fairly subjective criterion. All this really means is that our generalization should not deal with single individuals. To say "President Carter is liberal" is not an example of a generalization with sufficient scope since it refers to only a single individual. "American Presidents are liberal" or "American Presidents for the last two decades have been liberal" are examples of generalizations since they deal with the concept "President" rather than the unique individual, President Carter. Remember concepts are words which abstract commonalities from disparate phenomena. The Presidents of the last two decades have been men with very differing characteristics. The concept "President" expresses one commonality which they share. Generalizations are always associated with such commonalities.

Avoid Tautologies

You must also beware of using two concepts which describe the same thing as the components of your hypothesis. For instance, to say that "Liberals are likely to favor change," is not really a hypothesis to be tested. It is one definition of what we generally consider a liberal to be, that is, liberal = favoring change. A better hypothesis might be "Liberals tend to vote Democratic," or "Low-income people tend to be more liberal, or favor change." This latter hypothesis may or may not be true in the United States but may be true in other societies. At any rate, it can be tested.

Specify Relationship

Generalizations, remember, are statements of the relationships between two concepts. That is, *if* one characteristic is present, *then* another characteristic will also be present. Since you will eventually want to establish the accuracy of these generalizations, you must be sure that they can be

---

10. Robert A. Bernstein and James A. Dyer, *An Introduction to Political Science Methods* (Englewood Cliffs, New Jersey: Prentice-Hall, 1979), pp. 10–12.

phrased to permit testing. This will involve not only using concepts which have some empirical referent but also phrasing the generalization as clearly and precisely as possible. For instance, to say "political participation is related to trust in government" is a satisfactory generalization, as long as there is some way of handling political trust empirically. On the other hand, to say that "increased political participation is related to increased trust in government" is even better since the nature of the relationship is made much more specific by specifying the effect on trust.

Be Empirical

The last pitfall to avoid is to make sure your hypothesis is nonnormative. It should not specify that something "ought" to be done or something is "better or worse" than another alternative. It is not possible to test a statement such as "Liberals ought to vote Democratic," or "Democrats make better Presidents." Both of these statements are normative and, therefore, not empirical or testable. To make these statements empirical you might say "People favoring increased welfare expenditures vote Democratic," or "Democratic Presidents support increased welfare expenditures." Both are testable.

Once you develop a series of testable generalizations you are ready to proceed to the next step. First, we had to develop usable concepts. Then we sought to relate concepts together. Finally, we seek to relate a series of generalizations to each other.

BUILDING THEORIES

At this stage you should try to relate your assumptions and hypotheses to each other. This will enable you to answer your questions in a theoretically significant way. This is the heart of theory building. As noted in Chapter Three, these generalizations may be related in two ways. If you create a series of hypotheses in the same subject area, you are working toward a concatenated theory. For instance, we could say that: (1) Increasing trust is related to increasing political participation; (2) Increasing income is related to increasing political participation; and (3) Increasing alienation is related to decreasing participation. If you could relate these hypotheses in a deductive theory you would have a more powerful explanation of political participation. We could say that (1) Increasing income is related to increasing trust; (2) Increasing trust is related to decreasing alienation; and (3) Decreasing alienation is related to increasing political participation. From here we can deductively derive that increasing income is related to political participation. Thus, we do not only know how income, trust, and alienation are related to political participation, as in our concatenated theory, but we also know the relationships between each of these statements.

Now that your concepts are clearly specified and related to each other in generalizations and you have related the generalizations into a theoretical structure, you are ready to proceed to the next step. You must develop a research strategy to determine the correctness of your hypotheses and the utility of your theoretical framework. How to plan a strategy and gather data will be discussed in the next chapter.

STUDY QUESTIONS

1. What are the most important considerations to keep in mind when selecting a topic and formulating a question?
2. If you wished to do a study of power in your community, find ten citations which might help you get a background of the power literature. What indexes might provide more citations?
3. Discuss the major stumbling blocks to operationalizing concepts.
4. How might you operationalize the following concepts: income, political participation, efficacy, self-esteem, and radicalism?
5. Prepare an index of liberalism. What assumptions and procedures would you use to create a scale of liberalism?
6. Choose a problem area and construct five hypotheses. Be sure to consider the criteria for establishing good hypotheses.
7. Choose a problem area and write both a scientific and a normative statement with the same variables. Briefly discuss the differences.

Gathering Information

Chapter Eight

Once you have clearly specified your hypothesis and fit it into a theoretical structure, the next step is to test it empirically. By testing the hypothesis, remember, you are not only determining its accuracy, but you are also testing the theory which produced the hypothesis. The way to test a hypothesis is to see if the relationship which you hypothesize actually does exist in the real world. There are many ways to gather data to test theories. This chapter will consider how you can gather the data you need.

We will consider three different topics about data collection. In the first place, we will consider how you can decide what data and how much data to collect. Secondly we will discuss how you can set up an outline or blueprint for the data-gathering process. And, finally, we will examine various techniques that can be used in gathering data. We will first consider how you decide what data to collect.

DECIDING WHAT DATA TO COLLECT

Before you start to collect data, you should first know exactly what data you will need. This involves considering both the nature of the data you need to collect as well as how much data you will need to collect. Only by clearly thinking these questions through before you start gathering data can you be sure that you have enough of the right kind of data to test your hypothesis.

The first thing you should decide about the data is the level of your analysis. The *level of analysis* refers to whether the properties to be considered in your generalizations pertain to individuals or collectives. It is methodologically incorrect to attribute group characteristics to specific individuals and vice versa. If you wish to determine the relationship between the degree of belligerence of a nation, operationalized in terms of number of wars in the last thirty years, and the number of negative votes in the United Nations, you would be dealing with a nation as an aggregate of its citizens. It would be wrong to say that specific individuals in belligerent countries were belligerent. On the other hand, to determine the relationship of aggressive behavior and the tendency to engage in criminal behavior you would be dealing with individual level properties.

Another thing you must consider is the units of your analysis. By *unit of analysis* we mean the actual object to be examined. In our examples above, we were focusing on national behavior and votes at the collective level of analysis. At the individual level, we were focusing on individual behavior. Other things that might be used as units of analysis are attitudes, roles, opinions, and so forth. You should be very clear about what your unit of analysis is. If you are interested in, say, attitudes, you should gather data on attitudes, not on roles, or opinions, or whatever.

The third thing to determine about data collection is the *population,* or *universe.* By the term universe we mean the total collectivity to which your generalizations or hypotheses apply. If your hypothesis was concerned with voting behavior in democracies, your universe would be all eligible voters in all democracies. If you were only interested in voting in the United States, then the eligible voters in the United States becomes your universe. If you have made a hypothesis which concerns voting behavior in the United States "farm states," you must first define "farm states" (for example, in terms of numbers employed in agriculture or percent of Gross State Product from agriculture), and then every eligible voter in those states will compose your universe. Finally, once the universe is specified, you now must decide how much of the universe will be examined in the research. In some cases, the whole universe can be included. For instance, if we are interested in the voting patterns in the United States Senate, it is quite conceivable that we could question all 100 Senators in our research. However, if we are interested in the voting patterns of the entire United States voting population, it is inconceivable that we could question the several millions of people who compose that group. Out of that universe we will want to select a sample of voters which we hope will be representative of the voting populace as a whole. Whether we will examine the universe or only a sample is determined by the size of the population in question and the resources of time and money possessed by the researcher.

One point should be made very clear. When we select a sample from our universe, we do not necessarily mean selecting individuals. Nor do we mean to suggest that data for all samples are gathered through survey research or interviews. The data to be collected depends on the unit of analysis of your inquiry. If the unit is individual attitudes you would probably use survey research. On the other hand, if your unit of analysis were Senate votes, you would probably draw a sample from the votes which are reported in the *Congressional Record*.

If you decide to sample, you want to try to draw a sample which is representative of the universe. There are two factors which will affect how representative the sample will be. The two factors are the size of the sample and the way it is selected. Let us first consider how you should decide the size of a sample.

Sampling

When we hear that a pollster has conducted a poll of 2000 people, we figure there is no way his small sample can accurately reflect the opinions of 230 million Americans. Actually, the size of the population has very little to do with how large the sample must be to be representative. There are three things which will determine how large the sample should be: variation, risk, and accuracy.[1]

Variation. By variation we mean the amount of differentiation we expect among the cases. If all the cases had the same value on a given variable, a sample of one case would be representative of the population. While it is unlikely that everyone in a population would have the same value on a variable, it is quite possible that there would be few values. The less the variation, the smaller the sample needs to be. For instance, if you wished to examine the hypothesis that Republicans vote more than Democrats, you would need a relatively small sample. This is because the variable party identification can have only two values (Republican or Democrat), as can the variable vote (yes or no). On the other hand, specifying that those with higher incomes have higher political interest may involve much variation in the values of the variables. In this case you would need a large sample to help insure the variation in the universe is accurately represented in the sample. In addition to the possible range of alternatives, the distribution of these values in the population may vary. If the values in the population were divided 50/50 instead of distributed less equally, you would probably need a larger sample to make sure you did not overrepresent one value in

---

1. E. Terrence Jones, *Conducting Political Research* (New York: Harper & Row, 1971), p. 52.

your population. Since the amount of variation is not usually known in advance, it is usually determined by "rule of thumb" or through the use of a limited pretest.

Risk. Risk involves the degree to which you are willing to tolerate error in generalizations about the population from the findings in the sample. Any time you are generalizing about the population from a sample there is some chance of making mistakes. No matter how careful you are about drawing the sample, there is still the possibility that it would not be an exact reflection of the population. If you want the chance of being wrong to be very small, then you will need a large sample. In general, the less the risk of error you are willing to accept, the larger the sample needs to be. For example, if you were predicting the Presidential election for a national network, you would probably not tolerate much chance of error. Normally a political science researcher will tolerate a 5% chance that his findings are in error. That is to say, 95 times out of 100 your findings from the sample will be reflective of what you would find in the population as a whole, but 5 times out of 100 you may be wrong. (We will discuss the concept of risk in greater detail in Chapter Eleven.)

Accuracy. The accuracy is the degree of precision you desire. If you interviewed the entire population your findings would be 100% accurate of the views of that population. The smaller the sample the less accurate you can expect it to be. When surveys are reported you may frequently hear that they are subject to a plus or minus three (or any other number) percent error.

The 1948 election indicates how this plus or minus range can be important. The major pollsters indicated that Dewey would beat Truman by a slight margin plus or minus a few percent. Many of their predictions were accurate within that range. Unfortunately for them, that margin produced a Truman victory. In summary we can view the three major factors affecting sample size as follows:

↑ Variation → ↑ Sample size

↑ Accuracy → ↑ Sample size

↓ Risk → ↑ Sample size

We want a sample large enough to have some confidence that our results are meaningful. Where possible, we also want a sample which is large enough to allow us to examine subclasses of individuals and still have large enough numbers to make meaningful statements. For instance you might wish to know if blacks or whites are more militant. Since blacks have higher birth rates you are more likely to have a disproportionate number of young blacks. Since an alternative hypothesis is that the young are more militant, you may wish to divide your racial samples into young and old to determine whether it is race or youth or both which affect militance. At the same time you want a sample to be small enough that the data can be gathered efficiently.

While there is a formula to determine sample size, the usual criterion used is based on resources and "rule of thumb." The Gallup Poll, which has over time established a reputation for accuracy, has a sample size of about 2,000 to represent a United States population of 230 million people. A good "rule of thumb" for a national sample would be 1,500 to 2,500. For a smaller study with an average amount of subgroup analysis, 500 to 1,000 is usually used.[2] Special circumstances may dictate a larger sample or allow the use of smaller samples. Regardless of the size of the population, you are quite limited in the ability to generalize from a sample smaller than thirty because it does not easily lend itself to statistical manipulation.

The second factor which determines how well the sample represents the population is how the sampling is performed. Reputable researchers usually reject the kind of sampling known as "nonprobability" sampling. An example of this kind is sampling the man-in-the-street interview often done by TV and radio stations. In a situation like this researchers have little or no control over who is included in the interviews since they cannot determine who will walk down the street at any given time. Any control they have will probably create a bias since they might only interview people who look intelligent, or weird, or whatever trait appeals to them. Therefore, there is really no basis for our believing that those interviewed in such a process are at all representative of the population with which the research is concerned.

Probability sampling, on the other hand, gives the researcher some basis for believing the sample selected is representative. The basic idea of a probability sample is that everyone or everything in the population that is the focus of research must have an equal, or at least a known, chance of being selected. There are many ways of trying to meet this requirement, but all techniques are offshoots of the basic process of simple random sampling.

Simple random sampling. To perform a simple random sample, the researcher must first have a list of all of the individuals in the population. This, of course, is no easy task and many a sampling procedure has failed at this stage. Where would you go to get a list of all the voting population in the United States—or even in your own city or town? Actually, it would not really matter if some people were not on the list, as long as there was no bias involved in determining who was on the list and who was not. But there is almost always some bias involved. For instance, one frequently used list is the telephone book. But the telephone book is not a perfect source because it does not include people who are too poor to own a phone, or who, for

---

2. Seymour Sudman, *Applied Sampling* (New York: Academic Press, 1976), pp. 86–87.

whatever reason, do not want their names listed. It may well be that these groups of people would have political attitudes that would be different from those whose names appeared in the phone book. If so, those attitudes would not be represented in a research project using the telephone book as a basis for sampling.

Once a list has been decided upon, the next step is to number the individuals on the list consecutively. Next you go to a table of random numbers which can be found in the back of any statistics text. A table of random numbers (see Appendix) has been generated in such a way that there is no patterning in the order in which the numbers appear. It is as though the numbers have been selected by successively flipping dice and writing down the numbers which turn up. You may begin at any point in the table, and by going across the rows, or down the columns of a table of random numbers, you can pick a list of numbers equivalent to the desired size of your sample. The final step, then, is simply matching the numbers selected from the table of random numbers to the numbers you have assigned to the list of individuals with which you began. Those whose numbers turn up are selected for the sample. Therefore, everyone has an equal chance to be chosen. This is another way of saying there should be no reason why certain people would be more or less likely to appear in the sample. You, therefore, can hope that the sample is representative of the population as a whole.

Let us reiterate that we do not mean to imply that random sampling is only useful in gathering data from individuals. You may wish to study service delivery in United States cities with populations over 25,000. In this case your universe would be all those cities and your sample would be selected at random from the list of all those cities.

As we indicated previously, other forms of probability samples are simply developments of this basic process of simple random sampling. While the examples we use refer to survey sampling of individuals, these strategies are applicable to any kind of data gathering. Let us briefly look at some other types of probability sampling. We will consider (1) systematic sampling, (2) proportionate stratified sampling, (3) disproportionate stratified sampling, and (4) cluster sampling.

Systematic sampling. Systematic sampling is often easier and more convenient than simple random sampling. Before you begin you decide that you will survey every Kth element on your list. For instance, if you have a population of 10,000 people and you desire a sample of 100 people, you would begin at a random place, such as the fiftieth person or element, and select other persons at an interval of 100. You would select numbers 50, 150, 250, . . . , 9,950 and would thus have a sample of 100. This method is fine unless the list of this population is organized on a cycle which corresponds to your sampling cycle. If, for example, the population of 10,000 in our example represented the student body in your college, and if, in addition, all living units contained fifty students listed in order by grade-point average, then by sampling students 50, 150, and so forth, we are always getting the smartest or dumbest student in each group. These students would probably not be a fair representation of the student body. If you know that no systematic bias is introduced by your interval, though, this method may simplify the process of selecting your sample.

Proportionate stratified sampling. Proportionate stratified sampling involves dividing your population into subgroups, or strata, and selecting samples from each subgroup. Obviously, you would only do this if you thought the subgroups were related in some way to the relationship you are investigating. For instance, you may want to investigate the relationship between ethnicity and political partisanship. If you think religion will affect that relationship, you might want to stratify on the basis of religion. But if there is no reason to believe that sex has any effect on the relationship, there would be no reason to stratify on the basis of sex.

Let us look at how you can stratify a sample. If you wish to determine the impact of religion on political partisanship, you might stratify on the basis of religion. If you were interested in Protestants, Catholics, and Jews, you might make three lists, one for each group. If the population as a whole were 80% Protestant, 15% Catholic, and 5% Jewish, your sample should also be 80% Protestant, 15% Catholic, and 5% Jewish. That is, if you wanted a sample of 1000 you would randomly select 800 Protestants, 150 Catholics, and 50 Jews. That is, the proportions of each group in the sample should be equal to the proportions in the population. Why stratify? Since such a small segment of your population is Jewish, a simple random sample might underrepresent them and, therefore, make it impossible to generalize about that stratum. By stratifying you can be sure you will be able to generalize about all the strata.

Disproportionate stratified sampling. Like proportionate stratified sampling, disproportionate stratified sampling involves dividing your sample into subgroups and selecting samples from each subgroup. With proportionate sampling, the sample size from each subgroup is determined by the size of each subgroup compared to the population as a whole. This is not the case with disproportionate stratified sampling. It might be that you would randomly choose the same number of people from each stratum. Or you might select a larger number of people from one stratum. The goal of disproportionate sampling, like proportionate sampling, is to make sure that all strata are included in the sample in large enough numbers to permit generalizations. But since you do not have to maintain the same proportions as the population as a whole, you may be able to achieve the goal with a smaller sample size. If, for instance, you were afraid to generalize about the partisanship of the Jews in the last example because there were only fifty, we might want to select more Jews. If time and money were no object, we could double all the samples. But time and money are almost always objects of concern. If we could double the number of Jews in the sample, the time and cost increase is held down, and it might allow us to have more confidence in our generalization. If we double the Jewish sample, it is then necessary to introduce a weighting factor, if we wanted to generalize about the whole population rather than just about each separate stratum. In this example, we would have to count each Protestant and Catholic in your sample twice so that the proportions in the sample are equal to the proportions in the population.

Cluster sampling. Cluster sampling is the process of dividing your population into geographical areas and sampling from these areas. If you wanted to test the hypothesis that income leads to satisfaction with urban services, you could divide the city into census tracts, randomly select ten of say, fifty census tracts, then you might select at random two blocks on each census tract, and interview each head of household on those two blocks. Cluster sampling is used for two reasons. First, it is used to save transportation costs and travel time. This means that it is quite efficient and because of this, frequently used. Second, it is used when an overall list of the population does not exist. For example, there may not be a list of all households in a city, but there may be a list of city blocks. Therefore, to sample households, you would first sample blocks from the list and then sample households from those blocks.

A problem with cluster sampling is that you are, in essence, taking two samples. That is, first you are sampling the clusters and then you are sampling the elements for the research. This means that the possibility of sampling error is increased and it may be necessary to increase the sample size. In addition, the clusters may contain different numbers of people. Unless corrections are made, this may lead to oversampling or undersampling of certain groups.

To avoid over- or undersampling, you should select the first sample based on the size of the clusters and then sample equal numbers of cases from each cluster. For example, assume a given town has ten blocks with the following number of households:

Block	*Number of Households*	*Cumulative Households*
1	10	1-10
2	5	11-15
3	15	16-30
4	7	31-37
5	11	38-48
6	6	49-54
7	10	55-64
8	9	65-73
9	4	74-77
10	20	78-97

Let us say you want to sample three of these blocks. If you simply numbered the blocks 1 through 10 and then randomly selected three blocks and three households on each block, you would be giving the households in the smaller blocks a higher probability of eventually being sampled. Instead you should number the blocks cumulatively, according to the number of households on each block. Then you could use a table of random numbers to select three two-digit numbers between 1 and 97. Assume you get 35, 70, and 5. You would then look at the cumulative list of households and pick the blocks in which households 35, 70, and 5 are located. These are, respectively, blocks 4, 8, and 1. The blocks with larger numbers of households have a higher probability of being selected. Since you have already compensated for the differing sizes of the blocks, you then can take equal numbers of households from each block.

As noted above, all these sampling techniques are variations of simple random sampling. Each of these methods may increase convenience and lower costs. They also may lead to increased sampling errors which the researcher should be aware of and take steps to prevent. The important thing to keep in mind is that any time you are drawing a sample, you should try to make sure that every case in the population has an equal or at least a known chance of being selected for that sample. This basic principle of random sampling is crucial in the next step of data gathering: designing your research.

Once you have decided what data and how much of that data you will need to test your hypothesis, the next step is deciding how to gather it. The first thing you must do is set up a blueprint or outline of your research project. At this stage you will consider your overall strategy for attacking the research problem. Let us look at some alternate research strategies.

CHOOSING A RESEARCH STRATEGY

To understand how to plot your research strategy, you should be very clear about the evidence you need to test hypotheses. The hypothesis states that the independent variable (that is, the values are independent of anything under consideration) has some effect on the dependent variable. The only way you can determine if, in fact, the independent variable does have an effect is by examining what happens to the values of the dependent variable as the values of the independent variable change. If the values of both are constant, you can tell nothing about the relationship. This is why in hypothesis testing one must deal with concepts that are variables (those that assume various values). To test hypotheses, you must establish by how much the independent and dependent variables covary (vary together). That means that in plotting the research strategy you must make sure that both variables have a maximum opportunity to vary. In other words, you want to maximize the variance of the variables in the hypothesis.[3]

At the same time, however, you must be aware of the fact that some other factor besides the independent variable may be affecting the dependent variable. You want to try to eliminate the effect of variables besides those in the hypothesis you are testing. To eliminate the effect of other variables you try to hold them constant, that is, you try to control the variation of other extraneous variables. You should understand that if the value of a variable is held constant, it cannot be the source of any change or variation in other variables. Of course, it is impossible to control the effect of all other variables. But the goal is to control the effect of as many other variables as possible. Control may be achieved either physically or statistically. An example of a physical control would be a laboratory experiment on liquids in which we could manipulate the physical setting by maintaining a constant air pressure, varying heat, and determining the boiling point of water. If we could not physically control the air pressure, the best way to determine the impact of heat on water is to measure the temperature required to heat water at a variety of pressures, but only compare the temperature at equal pressures. Since the comparisons are at the same pressure, we can establish the temperature necessary to boil water at each level of pressure. In each instance, the pressure is a constant. This is the logic behind statistical control. Physical controls are limited in the social sciences so we often depend upon statistical controls.

The twin aims, then, of a strategy for conducting research are (1) to maximize the variance of the variables in the hypothesis and (2) to eliminate or control the variation of all other variables. The way scientists try to achieve this is by setting up a situation where they can manipulate the independent variable and can observe what changes occur in the dependent variable as a result of changes in the independent variable. Such a situation is known as an *experiment*. In political science the opportunity to control variation is quite limited, as we will discuss in greater depth below. It is important, though, to understand what kinds of extraneous variables might affect our studies and the conclusions we draw from them. By understanding these factors we may be able to minimize their effects. To illustrate some of the kinds of factors which might affect the research findings, let us examine a hypothetical research project.

Let us assume that we want to examine the effects of political science courses on the political interest of the students. We decide that to do this we will examine the level of political interest of students before and after they

---

3. This section draws heavily on the seminal work of Donald T. Campbell and Julian C. Stanley, *Experimental and Quasi-Experimental Designs for Research* (Chicago: Rand McNally, 1963), passim.

have taken a course in American Government. On the first class of the semester we give the assembled students a questionnaire to determine their existing level of interest. This measurement at the beginning of a study is known as a *pretest*. Now we sit back while the experimental variable, the American Government class, is administered to the students throughout the semester. Finally, at the end of the semester, we give the students the same questionnaire. A measurement at the end of a study is known as a *posttest*. To determine if the level of political interest has changed, we simply compare the responses on the pretest and the posttest.

We will assume that the responses on the posttest generally indicate a much higher level of political interest than was previously present. Can we conclude that it was really the course which caused the increase? Remember, to establish causation we have to try to eliminate the possible effect of other factors. In our study we managed to manipulate the experimental variable (the course), but we have not designed the research to eliminate the effect of other factors.

Let us consider what factors other than the course may have produced the change in political interest. First, something in the environment might have occurred between the time of the pretest and the posttest, for example a Presidential election campaign, and that might be the real cause of the increased interest. This factor is known as *history*. People may simply become more interested in politics as they grow older; in this case the real cause of the change is *maturation*. Perhaps, the pretest had sensitized the students to the fact that they were not very interested in politics, and they resolved to become more interested. The change was due to *testing*, not to the course. The change might be due to the unreliability (inconsistency) of the questionnaire and, therefore, is a result of poor *instrumentation*. Alternatively, the people who took the course may not have been interested in politics initially, but were predisposed to become interested, which is why they decided to take the course. This factor is known as *selection*. Finally, it is possible that those who were the least interested in politics, or at least the least predisposed to become interested, dropped out of the course, leaving only those interested to take the posttest. This is known as *experimental mortality*.

What we are saying is that we may observe changes in the dependent variable, but these changes may not be due to the effect of the independent variable but rather to the way we designed the experiment. In other words, we are not really observing a valid effect of the independent variable. Campbell and Stanley call this a problem of *internal validity*.[4] That is, something internal to the design of the research might lead to an invalid conclusion. Campbell and Stanley present a more thorough list of threats to internal validity in their book, *Experimental and Quasi-Experimental Designs for Research*.

---

4. Ibid., p. 5.

There are basically two things which researchers should do to attempt to reduce the problems of internal validity. In the first place, they can use two groups in the experiment. One group will be subjected to the manipulation of the independent variable (the political science course in our example above), and the other one will not. If the hypothesis is accurate, the group subjected to the course should be more interested than the other group. The group which is given the experimental treatment is the *experimental group* and the other group is the *control group*. That should help to uncover any problems due to history, testing (assuming both were given a pretest), and instrumentation, since those things should happen to both groups.

We can be even more sure about controlling for the effects of history, testing, and instrumentation if we could be relatively sure that the two groups were equivalent. In addition, making sure that there was no systematic bias in the selection of the two groups would help in controlling the problems caused by maturation, selection, and experimental mortality. The procedure that can be used to be relatively sure the selection process is not biased and that, therefore, the experimental and the control groups will be equivalent is the process of random sampling which we discussed above. In random sampling, every case in the population has an equal chance of being selected for the sample. This reduces the chance that there is a bias in the kinds of cases in the sample. Unfortunately, though, we can never be absolutely sure there is no bias. In other words, we are never totally sure there is no bias in the sample, but there is no reason to expect bias.

Therefore, the best way to set up a research project to avoid the problems of internal validity is to choose two groups by the process of random sampling, pretest each, expose one to an experimental manipulation, and then test each again. This classic experimental design can be diagrammed:

1. R   0   X   0

2. R   0   0

where R = random selection; 0 = pretest and posttest; and X = experimental treatment. If the two groups differ in the hypothesized direction on the posttest, then we can be fairly confident that the difference was not due to the way we set up the research project.

Even with this design we may not be able to conclude that we can generalize this finding to the population as a whole, that is, we may not be able to ascertain its *external validity*. The basic threat to external validity is the artificiality of the experimental situation. To a large extent, there is no real solution to these problems of generalizability. One recommendation which has been made is to increase the number of groups in the research design to four. In diagram form, this design would look as follows:

1.	R	0	X	0
2.	R	0		0
3.	R		X	0
4.	R			0

In this case, groups 1 and 3 would both receive the experimental treatment. Only group 1 would be given a pretest. But since both are chosen randomly we should expect them to be equivalent. This means that if the pretest had no effect, the scores of groups 1 and 3 should be similar on the posttest. By the same reasoning, groups 2 and 4 did not receive the experimental treatment. Group 2 was pretested but group 4 was not. If the pretest had no effect, the scores of 2 and 4 on the posttest should be similar.

This design, called the Solomon four-group design, is an attempt to discover the effect of testing and pretesting on the values of the dependent variable. It is at the moment the research design most preferred by scientists.

Consider, for a moment, how often you can remember seeing this design used by political scientists. It would not be surprising for it to be unfamiliar to you. Unfortunately, it is rarely used. And, for that matter, the classic experimental design with two groups is also rarely used. This should raise two questions in your mind: (1) Why, if these designs are so useful, are they so rarely used by political scientists? (2) If these designs are so rarely used by political scientists, why are we wasting your time talking about them? Let us take each question in turn.

In general, political scientists rarely have the resources necessary to conduct experiments. In the first place, we usually cannot randomly assign people to the different groups which we will be studying. If you wanted to test different teaching techniques, you could probably assign students randomly to four classes. But if you wanted to test the impact of different forms of urban government, it would create quite an outcry if you tried to randomly assign people to live in those communities.

Secondly, you certainly could not command those cities to alter their forms of government to conform with the requirements of your research hypothesis. That is, we often cannot manipulate the independent variable at will. In addition, we cannot develop an environment where the effects of extraneous variables can be controlled as can a physicist who can establish a vacuum for atoms or even a psychologist who can isolate white rats. There is another problem that exists when dealing with human subjects: Human nature may have an impact on your study. The experiment itself, by focusing special attention on a group, may become a variable which has an effect on behavior. This is known as the *Hawthorne Effect*. Under normal circumstances it is unlikely that people will put their hands in a box of poisonous snakes. In an experimental setting, however, many research participants were willing to do just that.[5] The Milgram experiment, where participants willingly administered supposedly lethal shocks to others, is another example which shows that people may not behave normally in an experimental setting.[6] A final problem, noted in our earlier discussion of the Milgram experiment (see Chapter Three), is the question of ethics. If by some stroke of fate we were granted the power to randomize and to manipulate, we would probably hesitate to use the power because we felt using it might be unethical.

Given all those reasons why a good experimental design is not very feasible in political research, why have we spent so much time talking about it? We talked about it for the same reason we talked about building theories. The experimental research design we discussed is the standard against which other research designs are compared. We may not be able to reach the standard of an experimental design 100%, but our goal should be to approximate the standards of that design as closely as possible given the nature of political research. That is why we want you to understand completely why experiments are set up as they are. Understanding the nature of standards should also make you understand the problems with most political research procedures. This rather depressing knowledge should make you much more careful and realistic about the kinds of conclusions that can be drawn from that research.

Now let us consider how political scientists usually design their research. There are some circumstances in which political scientists can use a "natural experimental design." This means that a researcher may become aware of some change which is going to be implemented in some area or for some group. For example, a researcher may find out that a city is planning to change its form of city government. Researchers cannot manipulate the independent variable but can make use of the fact that others are essentially manipulating it for them. The most rigorous way to conduct research in that case is to try to find another group which seems similar to the group involved in the change, for example, another city of similar size and composition. It might even be possible to give both groups a pretest. This is known as a *nonequivalent control group design.* Now there are two groups, an experimental group and a control group. But without randomization there is no way to assume that the groups are really equivalent. This natural experiment is really a *quasi-experiment* since the researcher cannot control the manipulation of the independent variable and cannot randomize the members of the groups. Another example of a quasi-experimental design frequently used by political scientists is *time series* studies. The researcher accumulates a series of

---

5. Martin T. Orne and Frederick J. Evans, "Social Control in the Psychological Experiment," *Journal of Personality and Social Psychology,* I (1965), pp. 189–200.

6. Stanley Milgram, "Behavioral Study of Obedience," *Journal of Abnormal and Social Psychology,* 67(1963), pp. 371–78.

data prior to a stimulus and takes readings afterward. If a change occurs at the time of the stimulus we may attribute the change to the stimulus. The before and after readings give us reason to believe the stimulus caused change, but without experimental controls we cannot be certain that other events did not interfere. For example, we might choose to monitor spending in City X 10 years prior to a change in government structure and five years after this change. Following the change in government we might notice that the rate of budgetary increase was cut from an average of 10% per year to 2% per year. It would seem that the change in governmental structure resulted in decreased expenditures. There are alternative explanations that might be offered, though. For instance, other levels of government may have taken over some service responsibilities, spending limits may have been instituted, or a different party or individual with a different philosophy may have come to power at the time of the changeover. Interpretation might be further complicated if the spending increase went down to 2% in the year following the change and back up again, or if fluctuations occurred throughout the 15-year period under study. In the absence of controls you must consider and try to account for alternative explanations. *Multiple time series* comparisons with cities not undergoing structural change may help here.

Still other quasi-experimental designs are a variety of *separate sample pretest-posttest group* designs which can be used when you are unable to do a pretest on your experimental group. In these designs you use existing data as a point of comparison with data gathered for your research. The existing data may be used in place of a pretest. You may find in your literature search that someone has done a random survey which you might use in lieu of a pretest. After a stimulus you might do your own random survey. You might attribute any changes between the existing data and your findings to the intervening stimulus. In this case, though, there may again be alternative explanations. Slight differences may be due to sampling error. Also, other events and maturation between the pre- and posttests may have caused changes which you are unable to control for. The separate pretest does provide a baseline or starting point which may aid in presenting evidence to verify or disprove your hypothesis. There are a variety of other quasi-experimental methods which political scientists use when they are unable to randomize, create control groups, or use pretests.

Often political researchers must use designs which are even weaker than the quasi-experiment. We might call these research designs *pre-experiments*. For instance, in some cases, researchers do not have the time or resources for any pre-measurement. Or, they may actually only become aware of the change after it occurred. Such research after the fact is called *ex post facto* research. If researchers attempt to use a control group, they cannot be sure that the control and experimental group are comparable. This means that the researchers would not know whether differences observed in any posttest resulted from the experimental treatment (the change in city government) or if the changes had always existed.

Often researchers not only lack a pretest, but may also lack any group to use as a control. They may just observe what happens after the experimental treatment and attribute any changes to the treatment. Of course, there is no way to know if the changes would have occurred regardless of whatever experimental treatment was used. For example, if a city changed its form of government, we might observe that the level of citizen participation increased. We cannot know, without a control group, if the increase is due to the change in government or to the fact that after the change a Presidential election campaign was starting and people were more interested in politics.

We might also use this design for ex post facto research. That is, we might observe an increase in citizen participation and then look in the past for some reason for the increase. But there are always many things changing in a city. There is no way we can control ex post facto all of the other changes in order to observe the impact of one of them. Therefore, there is no way we can be sure which of the changes is the reason for the increase in citizen participation.

A study of citizen participation which examines one case in great depth and does not make any rigorous attempt to compare that case with a control group is known as a *case study*. Often these case studies result in the gathering and reporting of great quantities of data. It should be clear to you that any conclusions about the relationships among variables based on case studies must be extremely tentative. Such research, though, may be valuable for suggesting possible relationships which could form the basis for future, more rigorous testing.

The types of experiments, quasi-experiments, and pre-experiments discussed here are meant merely to be suggestive of various approaches to designing research. Campbell and Stanley discuss a variety of other methods which might be applicable in certain situations. Regardless of the format chosen we must be aware of the costs and benefits of each. The basic point of our discussion of strategies to use in doing research is that before we can make any conclusions about the relationships between two variables, we must ensure that the variables themselves assume different values, and we must try to control the effects of other variables. An experiment is the best way to achieve both of these goals. For many reasons, political researchers are limited in their ability to use experiments. You should always be alert, though, to situations where you could take advantage of the natural experiment. And where possible, you must try to use control groups. For example, you might be able to use data gathered by others as a form of control group. Of course, you should try to find groups which are as similar as possible. Be

194 *GATHERING INFORMATION*

imaginative about designing your research to come as close as possible to the experimental model. But don't give up if you can not match that ideal precisely.

Once you have decided on your research strategy, you have to decide how to collect the data you will need to test the hypothesis. There are numerous potential sources of data for use by political scientists. We will examine these data sources in two categories: gathering new data and sources of existing data. There are obvious advantages of using existing data sources. It is almost always cheaper to use existing data than it is to gather data on your own. In addition, using existing data also usually shortens the time necessary for a research project. However, to counter these advantages, there are some definite disadvantages of using existing data. In the first place, the data source may not contain the kind of information you would like to have or may not contain enough information for you to perform what you consider to be an adequate test of your hypothesis. Another problem is that such information, while relevant, may be out of date.

We will discuss four sources for primary data collection, that is, collecting original information. These sources are observation, content analysis, survey research, and simulation. In addition, we will briefly discuss two common sources of secondary data (existing information). These are library sources and data archives.

PRIMARY DATA GATHERING

Observation

While it may be more costly in terms of both time and money, gathering your own data gives you the advantage of great control over the kinds of information which you will have available to test the hypothesis. There are several ways that you can proceed to collect your own data. The first way is to use various kinds of *observational techniques*. For example, you might want to study how Presidential nominating conventions work in the United States. You could perhaps manage to get yourself appointed as a delegate to a convention. In this case you would be a participant–observer since you are actually taking part in the process which you are studying. The advantage of being a participant–observer is that you can probably understand much more intimately the conflicts, pressures, and excitement of a convention—or any political process—if you are actually taking part in it. The disadvantage is that by being a participant you may lose your objectivity and not be able to analyze the event without bias.

Alternatively, you might simply go to the convention and observe as a bystander. Of course, the advantages and disadvantages here are exactly the opposite of those mentioned above. You may not gain as much comprehensive understanding by simply observing, but you are more likely to maintain your objectivity. In either case, you should specify as clearly as possible before you begin your observations exactly what kinds of actions you will be looking for and how you will classify these phenomena. This is often a very difficult task. Without such a precise framework—which should be specified in your research design—you may waste your time looking at totally irrelevant things, and you may find at the end of your research that you do not have the information necessary for answering your research question. And you certainly cannot call the convention delegates back into session to rerun the convention for your benefit. Specifying precisely what should be observed and how it will be recorded is especially important if other observers will be working with you.

In addition to deciding whether or not you will actually participate in what you are observing, you must also decide whether you will tell those you are observing that you are planning to use them as data in your research project. In deciding this you should first consider the ethics of the situation (see Chapter Three). Is it really ethical to sit as a participant in a conference in the proverbial "smoke-filled room" without first warning the others present that what they say and do may potentially come back to haunt them via your research project? But there is also another consideration. People who know they are being observed have a definite tendency to behave differently than they would normally. If your fellow convention goers "put on a show" for you—either consciously or unconsciously—the utility of your eventual report will be seriously affected. Your report will reflect what convention goers want other people to think about their actions, not what their actions normally are.

As an observer, you can gain many insights by looking beyond the obvious. It is likely that events will leave physical traces after the actual event is over. For instance, by checking where a state delegation was sitting and looking at discarded campaign literature, you may be able to deduce the popularity of various candidates. You might also want to buttress your observations through the use of archives by checking past records for clues to present behavior. For instance, a check of Congressional voting records might indicate what candidate a congressman is most likely to support at the convention.[7]

One more point has to be made about this observational technique. In our example, our researchers went to one Presidential nominating convention. They probably will not wait around the necessary number of years to observe several such conventions before reporting the research, but instead

---

7. Eugene Webb and others, *Unobstrusive Measures: Nonreactive Research in Social Sciences* (Chicago: Rand McNally, 1966), passim.

will probably make a report after attending the single convention. You must realize that our ability to make meaningful generalizations is severely limited because our researchers have observed only one nominating convention. In other words, they used the case study approach. It is only a single convention, and it takes quite a leap of faith to generalize about all conventions on the basis of information on one convention. Although there are many more people involved, this is analogous to generalizing about all Presidents on the basis of what one knows about President Jimmy Carter. Then, why use observational techniques such as this?

There are several reasons why case studies can be an important and useful research technique. In the first place, case studies can provide very comprehensive information about what is being studied. This may be a good place to start developing generalizations which can later be tested by examining many other similar cases. Sometimes a case study may be the only practical way to do research on certain phenomena. A good example of such a phenomenon would be the above-mentioned case of the nominating conventions. As we said, most researchers do not want to wait long enough to attend several such conventions before making a report of the research. In such circumstances, case studies can be very useful. A collection of several such studies can be built up over time which are comparable enough to be used to substantiate generalizations.

Of course, not all observational studies are case studies. You might want to do a study of city councils. With sufficient resources you could conceivably travel to several cities to observe the city councils. In this example, the researcher could legitimately use his observations of these several city councils to make or to confirm generalizations. Here you might be able to set up a quasi-experimental situation. The cities may not be selected at random but attempts may be made to match, that is, to select cities which appear to be similar. Or you might be able to use a study done by another researcher as a sort of pretest. This part is secondary analysis. You might then go out and make your own observations of the same universe (primary data gathering) and draw conclusions.

Content Analysis

A second way of gathering data is content analysis. Actually, content analysis is nothing more than a very rigorous way of surveying existing communication, such as historical records, books, videotapes, letters and so forth. However, we have listed this procedure under new sources of data because we feel the rigor of the technique actually produces new information which would not be obvious by merely reading, listening to, or viewing, the material. The basic procedure in content analysis is first to specify clear categories or codes and then organize the relevant aspects of the material into those categories.

For instance, you may hypothesize that Democratic Party candidates consistently make more appeals for minority group support during elections than do Republican Party candidates. To test this hypothesis with content analysis, you would first establish categories of words or phrases that would indicate to you an appeal for minority group support. This process is similar to specifying operational indicators for the concept of appeals to minorities. For instance, you might include as a code "mention of minority group leaders or heroes." Then, whenever any candidate were to mention, for example, Rev. Jesse Jackson, head of the black group PUSH, when talking to blacks, or Cesar Chavez, head of the United Farm Workers Union, when addressing Hispanic Americans, the mention could be listed as an appeal for minority group support.

The use of content analysis can often uncover some patterns of appeals and emphasis in documents which would not otherwise be obvious. But there are, of course, problems in the use of content analysis. The first problem is that, as with any attempt to specify empirical indicators, you must consider whether or not the indicator is a valid measure of what you are trying to investigate. Does the mention of a minority group leader really constitute an appeal for support? A second concern is whether the codes are precise enough to permit consistent—or reliable—classification. In our example there are numerous sources for potential confusion in the process of classifying campaign material to determine if it contains appeals to minority groups. Even if we agree that the mention of a minority group leader constitutes an appeal for support from that group, we still have some important factors to consider. For example, we have to decide exactly what constitutes a "mention." Does merely saying the name qualify, or must there be something additional said about the leader? What if the statement is negative? Secondly, we have to decide who would qualify as a leader of the particular minority group. Specifying such things clearly is especially important if the researcher is having other people do at least some of the categorizing of the material.

After representative campaign material from both Republicans and Democrats has been examined and categorized, it is then possible to add up the number of appeals made to minority groups to see if there is a difference between the parties. Of course, you should have clearly specified before you began your research how big a difference between the parties would be sufficient to substantiate your hypothesis.

Counting the frequency or amount of time and space given to our key words (appeals to minorities in this example) is a quantitative measure. We may also be concerned with the intensity of meaning, or a qualitative measure. Using quantitative information enables us to maximize reliability since, if key words, phrases, ideas, etc., are clearly specified, all researchers at any given time would find the same thing. Such quantitative measures suffer from problems of validity, though, since the mere mention of a word may not signify what we have assumed it does. In dealing with qualitative content analysis we will generally increase validity. By examining how an idea is used we have a better idea if it does indicate what we think it does. However, reliability often suffers since measures are usually subjective. Something which seems very intense to one researcher may be considered moderate by another. There are a variety of techniques which are used to increase reliability. Some require using many judges. In this way there is a consensual basis for dealing with intensity. Others establish a range of values to be given to words depending on their usage, from slightly intense to moderately intense to extremely intense.

As with any form of collecting data, there are advantages and disadvantages to the use of content analysis. One very major advantage is that contrary to the observational techniques we just discussed, content analysis is an unobtrusive way of gathering information. That is, there will be no interaction effects since the documents already exist before the researcher makes use of them; there is no danger that the research itself will affect the behavior of those being observed. On the other hand, there is no real assurance that the documents are at all representative of the values, beliefs, behaviors, and so forth, of who wrote them. This is so because there may very well be a reluctance to put into written form and circulate the kinds of things in which researchers might be most interested. For instance, there is a story of Harry Truman walking into a room to find his wife Bess throwing old letters to her from her husband into the fireplace. When Mr. Truman protested that the letters may be of interest at some time to historians, Mrs. Truman retorted that that was precisely why she was burning them. The point is, the kind of documents which survive may be the very ones which are not representative. In addition, the kinds of documents to which researchers have access may be atypical. For example, what might appear in intragovernmental memos may be quite different from official government announcements. Content analysis often involves a case study which is aimed at uncovering and organizing critical information about a specific event, person, or place. It might also be possible to use quasi-experimental techniques. For instance, we might examine changes in the level of racial hostility in two cities, only one of which had experienced a race riot. We might do this by performing a content analysis of the major newspaper in each city before and after the time of the riot.

Survey Research

Another form of generating new data is survey research. This is perhaps the most frequently used way of collecting new data in political science. Survey research involves responses of certain people to specific questions. It is most useful to gather data dealing with people's reactions to their environment. For example, if we want to know what people know about something, how they feel about it, whether they value it, and so forth, the best way to find out may well be to ask them. That is the basis of survey research. Of course, as you might expect, there are disadvantages to the process of survey research. As is often the case with the observational techniques, in survey research the respondents will know they are the subject of investigation. The fact may significantly affect their responses. Survey research also tends to be quite costly in terms of time and money.

Despite its drawbacks it is used extensively by political scientists because it is one of the best ways to determine what people know and believe. Observation and content analysis allow us to look at specific behavior. Survey research does not look at behavior but, rather, asks questions about it. Thus, it is probably not the best way to study actual behavior. It is, however, quite useful in addressing the question of *why* people behave as they do. In using survey research, the first step is to define your universe and select a sample, as indicated earlier in this chapter. Once the manner of selecting your sample is determined, the researcher must decide what questions should be asked and how these questions will be asked. The resources available will affect how the questions will be asked. This, in turn, may affect what questions are asked.

Types of Interviews

There are three basic ways of administering questionnaires, no one of which is necessarily the best. The three ways are (1) self-administered, (2) telephone interviews, and (3) face-to-face interviews. Given unlimited resources the last method may be the best, but rarely does one have unlimited resources. Therefore, it is necessary to understand the costs and benefits of each alternative.

Self-Administered. In many ways this technique is the easiest way to administer a questionnaire. This, of course, is a definite plus. Once you have drawn your sample and written your research instrument (questionnaire), you can let the individual respondent take over. Self-administered questionnaires are often used in a group setting, thus enabling you to obtain many responses at one time. Perhaps the most frequently used type of self-administered questionnaire is the mail survey. This is very efficient in terms of time and is a relatively cheap way to reach a large sample. In addition if no name is required, you may receive more candid comments.

There are, however, many pitfalls with self-administered questionnaires, especially mail surveys. The major problem is the low response rate and biases of the respondents. The return rate on mailed questionnaires is quite low—frequently less than 50%. And it is often the case that those who take the trouble to respond are those who have some prior interest in the subject. In addition they are usually better educated. The attitudes of these respondents are not necessarily representative of the population as a whole. Another problem with a mailed questionnaire is that you have absolutely no control over who actually has answered the questions, the order in which the questions are answered, whether or not the respondent actually understood the question, and so forth. In addition to the low response rate, the major problem with self-administered surveys is that you can never be sure that the respondent understands the question. Being sure the respondent understands the question is a major benefit of interactive interviews. The response rate on mailed questionnaires can be improved by providing return postage, writing follow-up pleas to nonrespondents, and even offering to pay respondents. Misunderstanding of questions can be minimized by taking great care in writing questions (see below) and thoroughly pretesting the questionnaire.

Telephone Surveys. If you have access to a phone and can get the information you need by asking only a relatively few questions, a telephone survey may be the best approach. Generally a telephone interview should take no more than ten or fifteen minutes. If you are not making long distance calls (and even this may be cheaper than travel costs), the cost is relatively low. Also, response rates are usually good and time is used efficiently. If respondents obviously misunderstand a question, you can clarify it for them. A telephone survey also often produces relatively high response rates, takes little time, and is convenient. As with all interviewing methods, there are biases introduced by phone surveys. For example, if you use a phone survey, naturally you can only talk to those who have a phone. As we indicated previously, there are some who cannot be reached by phone and there is no way for us to know whether their attitudes can be accurately represented by those who can be reached by phone. There is some reason to suspect that those who are too poor to own a phone may have significantly different political attitudes than do those who own phones, since socioeconomic status has been shown to affect political attitudes and behavior. There are also problems with those who do not have listed phone numbers. There is however a way to deal with this problem. After dialing the three-digit prefix for the exchange, the last four digits can be selected from a table of random numbers. Therefore, whether the number is listed or unlisted is irrelevant. It is also conceivable that the way the questions are asked by the interviewer may bias the results. Proper interview techniques will be discussed below.

Face-to-Face Interviews. As noted above, if resources are not a restraining factor, you would choose face-to-face interviewing in most instances. The response rate is usually quite high. It is usually highest if you contact the respondent by mail using official stationery. This establishes credibility for your project. If you just appear at someone's door and start asking questions, the respondent might be somewhat suspicious. In the letter contact you should explain the nature of your project, why you need respondents' help, if they will be paid, how long the interview will take, and that you will call to set up an appointment for a time convenient to them. The mailing and phone call adds to the work and cost, but if these are not constraints, this approach pays dividends. Interviewers have more control over the situation in a face-to-face interview. They are more likely to be sure the questions are understood by the respondent, answered in a particular order, without outside "coaching" from others, etc. On the other hand, face-to-face interviews take much more time than do other procedures and may also cost more because of transportation costs and/or the necessity of hiring additional interviewers. Another problem with using several interviewers might be bias because different interviewers interpret the questions differently. Another problem with face-to-face interviewers is that the nature of the interviewer may become a significant factor in determining the kind of answers given by the respondents. The interviewers' personality, how tired they are, how they read the question, etc., may determine to a large extent how the respondent replies to the questions. It is quite important that the interviewer dress appropriately (normally a tie and jacket for men or skirt and blouse for women, but probably overalls to interview a farmer at work), be courteous, friendly, and not inject their own "two cents" or ad lib.

Questionnaire Construction

Once you have decided how your questionnaire will be administered you must sit down and write it. It should be obvious that the phrasing of the questions asked could be crucial to the success of the research. Great care must be taken to ensure that the questions are not ambiguous and that they will not irritate or alienate the respondent. There should be adequate questions to elicit the necessary information but at the same time there should not be so many questions that the respondent becomes bored or tired. There are several issues to consider: (1) you must decide what types of questions you will use; (2) your questions and instructions must be clear and unambiguous; (3) you must make sure you don't embarrass the respondent; (4) you must be sure the respondent is capable of responding accurately; (5) you must decide if you wish to use some questions to establish indexes or scales such as we discussed in the last chapter; and (6) you must make some technical decisions on format, length, and order of questions. You must guard against response set, which refers to a situation in which a respondent replies the same way to all questions without carefully determining what the questions mean.

Types of questions.. There are basically two types of questions: those with fixed responses and those which are open ended. In a fixed response the alternatives are set. For example:

Column 7 1. *Did you vote in the last presidential election?*
　　　　　　　1. ( ) Yes
　　　　　　　2. ( ) No

or

Column 8 2. *What do you think was the major issue in the last campaign?*
　　　　　　　1. ( ) Peace
　　　　　　　2. ( ) Energy
　　　　　　　3. ( ) Economy
　　　　　　　4. ( ) Candidates' personalities
　　　　　　　5. ( ) Defense
　　　　　　　6. ( ) Other, specify ————————————

Notice in question 2 there is an "other" category. This is often useful in close-ended questions because it allows for some flexibility and does not force the respondents to say something they don't mean. Questions with fixed responses help you ensure that all responses are comparable. On the other hand, to the extent that respondents feel constrained to fit their thoughts into predetermined categories results may be biased. In addition, even the most imaginative inquisitor can rarely think of all possible alternative responses to many questions. If many responses are lumped in the "other" category, there will not be much differentiation, and it is likely that some important possible responses may have been overlooked. (The column number in the left-hand column facilitates computer storage of the data you are collecting. This will be explained in the next chapter.)

Open-ended questions, such as the example below, may allow more accurate responses from the interviewee.

Column 9–10 3. *How do you feel about black/white relations?*

Such open-ended questions may create problems of consistency, though, if you wind up with 100 similar but somewhat different responses. They may be difficult to organize and code for later analysis. The next chapter will discuss this problem further. You must categorize responses after getting them, whereas with fixed responses, you establish categories before the questionnaire is administered. The type of questions you use depends on the nature of the question and how well it lends itself to structured responses.

Ambiguity. To avoid ambiguity try to use ordinary language. If you have a specific idea in mind, ask direct questions and don't rely on the respondent's interpretation. Questions should be clear to the respondent. Don't ask "Do you think that procedures are institutionalized?" or ambiguous questions, such as "Are you interested in politics?"

Be clearer:

Column 11   4. *Are there regular procedures which are followed?*
             1. ( ) Yes
             2. ( ) No

Be more specific:

Column 12   5. *Do you read about politics weekly?*
             1. ( ) Yes
             2. ( ) No

Column 13   6. *Do you talk about politics weekly?*
             1. ( ) Yes
             2. ( ) No

Embarrassment. Since the questionnaire seeks to elicit honest answers, questions should be carefully worded to avoid embarrassing the respondent by implying a proper answer or a socially correct answer. For instance, if you ask the question, "Did you vote in the last election?" you will probably get a number of positive responses well above the actual voting rate. This is because, in the United States, we are taught that voting is a civic responsibility and people do not want to admit freely they did not vote. One way to get a more truthful answer is to structure the question in a more tactful manner. For instance, the Survey Research Center at the University of Michigan asks about voting as follows:

Column 14   7. *Sometimes people find it hard to vote in elections because they cannot get away from work or something like that. In your own case did you happen to vote in the November election or didn't you have a chance to vote?*
             1. ( ) Yes
             2. ( ) No

Accuracy. While many things may affect the accuracy of the responses, two common problems occur because respondents have forgotten past occurrences or because they lack the knowledge to respond to your question but are reluctant to admit it. It is virtually impossible to know if someone is responding incorrectly because of a faulty memory. If possible, you might double-check. Perhaps the best way to avoid this problem is not to expect respondents to remember too far back in the past and to word questions in such a way to allow the respondents to gracefully admit they forgot. For instance, you might say:

204 GATHERING INFORMATION

Column 15   8. *I realize that the 1972 election was a long time ago, but can you still tell me who you voted for?*
        1. ( ) Yes
        2. ( ) No; skip to question 10.

Column 16   9. *If yes, was it:*
        1. ( ) Nixon
        2. ( ) McGovern
        3. ( ) Other, specify ─────────────

To make sure a respondent is answering knowledgeably you should use a "filter question." You might ask:

Column 17   10. *Will you list the countries that participate in the SALT negotiations?*

If the person responds correctly you might then ask:

Column 18   11. *Are you for or against the SALT Treaty?*
        1. ( ) For
        2. ( ) Against
        3. ( ) Don't have an opinion; skip to question 12.

One final word on accuracy is in order. It is very difficult to prevent a case in which a respondent sets out to deceive you deliberately. If the respondent's statement can be verified from other sources, you might double-check it, especially if you feel you are being deceived. For example, if someone says he or she is a registered voter, this can usually be checked. Another way to prevent deception is to scatter similar questions throughout to see if the respondent is consistent. If the person is a persistent liar, this check will fail. You can only hope that if you are inoffensive, most people will be honest.

Indexing or scaling. You must decide if you will be using single or multiple indicators of your concepts. If you are using multiple indicators you must decide what kind of scale or index you wish to construct. If you wish to establish an index of political activism you might use the following format.

12. *In the past 5 years have you (circle number in column of correct response):*

		Yes	No	Don't Know
Column 19	1. *Written your congressman*	1	2	3
Column 20	2. *Voted*	1	2	3
Column 21	3. *Campaigned*	1	2	3

Technical matters. Throughout this section we have tried to provide a model of how questions might be set up for easy reading and marking. Questions 3 and 11 are examples of open-ended questions. The others are fixed-response questions. In all but question 12 you would check the box corresponding to the proper answer. In question 12 you are asked to circle the answer. Either format is acceptable although the circling may be a little more confusing and might be avoided in self-administered questionnaires. You might also note that questions 8 and 10 provide a format for "filter" or "contingency" questions. One type of response elicits another question while other responses indicate that certain questions can be skipped. In the margins we included column numbers. This will aid you if you will want to use a computer to analyze the data. This will be explained in the next chapter. The key should be ease of reading, understanding, marking, and coding (to be discussed in the next chapter).

Another consideration in preparing a questionnaire is how many questions are needed to get necessary information. There is no hard and fast rule. It really depends on your hypotheses and the depth of your research. If you hypothesize that liberals are Democrats, you could merely ask two questions: "Are you a liberal?" and "Are you a Democrat?" the term liberal is often ambiguous. You might operationalize liberal as those who favor social change. You might then ask "Do you favor social change?" If your research is more complex you might wish to have more complex indicators for the term liberal. You may wish to create an index or scale to measure the degree of liberal attitudes, in which case the questionnaire becomes larger.

Another point which might affect decisions on the length of the questionnaire and the kind of questions to be asked is the way the questionnaire will be administered. Telephone questionnaires must be short. Responses to self-administered questionnaires will probably decrease as the length increases. For face-to-face interviews you should generally take about one half-hour. Only rarely can you expect respondents to give you an hour of their time.

You should also consider how you will order the questions in the questionnaire. Generally speaking, you must be careful to begin the questioning with easy nonthreatening questions. This will put the respondent at ease. If you are using a self-administered questionnaire, you must start with some interesting questions or the respondent will be unlikely to continue. Beyond this there are no easy rules for ordering questions. Some researchers group similar questions together to allow the respondent to think things through logically. Other researchers randomize to make it easier to test for consistency. In most cases, the former way would seem to be favorable.

The last major technical pitfall we mentioned was the problem of response set. By response set we mean that the respondent gets in the habit of answering the same way regardless of the question. For example, "Are you for civil rights?"—Yes; "Are you for freedom?"—Yes; "Are you for repression?"—Yes. Anyone who is really for civil rights and freedom could not logically favor repression. A response set has occurred and these responses would have to be discarded. The three questions above also illustrate how you can determine if a response set has occurred. You should examine how individuals respond to questions. If they respond the same way to all questions regardless of how illogical it is, there is a problem of response set. This means that you should always word the questions so that a respondent cannot answer the same way and be logically consistent. That is, if you are measuring liberalism, you should not word the questions so that a yes always indicates liberal. If you did you would not know if people answered yes to all questions because they were very liberal or because of a response set.

Interviewing

Once the questionnaire is prepared it must be administered. If it is not to be self-administered, this will mean some type of interview. If all the previous work is not to be wasted, it is important that the interview be designed to minimize bias. The key to a good interviewer is common sense. It also helps to have a good research instrument. The interviewer should appear to be like the people to be interviewed. This may aid in putting the respondent at ease since people often do not respond well to others who appear different. Although it is unfortunate, respondents take cues and form judgments from such clues as dress, race, sex, hair, and so forth. Some of these things are not possible to change but it is important to realize that it may have a bearing on the interview. Therefore, we may wish to change what we can to be as inoffensive as possible. The interviewer should be pleasant and friendly and *neutral* with respect to the questions which are asked. Most people like to please and will attempt to respond the way they think the interviewer wants them to respond.

To avoid a respondent answering in a manner to please the interviewer, the interviewer must avoid providing cues as to what is the "right" answer. Questions must be carefully worked to avoid implying a "correct" answer. You should not say "Are you for civil rights or are you a bigot?" Less obvious, but also problematic, would be to say "Do you agree that the civil rights movement is going too far?" You should always provide an option. "Do you agree or disagree that the civil rights movement is going too far?" You must also beware of inflections which may imply a preferred answer.

Needless to say the interviewer must understand the questions. This is especially important if there is more than one interviewer. All similar questions must be read exactly as written and responses recorded exactly as given. This may aid future interpretation. If respondents do not understand a question or provide an obviously inappropriate answer, the interviewer must carefully explain without influencing the respondent. A good interview technique is an art as well as a science, and practice is the best way to learn it.

As with other types of data collection, probably the most common use of survey research is in case studies. But obviously survey research could also be used to gather information before and after an experimental treatment.

Simulation

The final technique which we will discuss for gathering primary data is simulation. In a simulation certain real world conditions are artificially created. This means that a simulation is a form of experiment. For example, we might provide a group of people with the goal of planning a city's development and provide them with resources such as a set amount of money, time, rules, and so forth and then observe what decisions they make. As an experiment it suffers from all the threats to validity discussed above. However, simulations do provide a means by which certain properties of the real world can be controlled, sped up, or slowed down while we examine the consequences. Given the caveats which are present with all experiments, simulation can provide us with actions and reactions of real people which may enable us to better see and understand patterns of behavior in the real world. Simulations can be quite simple; usually real world conditions are simplified and only key variables are included. Researchers observe behavior in this simulated setting to determine what patterns of behavior occur. For instance, if you wish to test a hypothesis about rational choice you may supply selected pieces of information to participants and determine whether or not their decision is "rational." During a debriefing you may obtain more information about the decision process. Simulations can be made more complex by increasing the number of players or the number of relevant variables.

The growth of computer technology has greatly expanded simulations as a data-gathering technique. The use of computer technology has allowed for more complex simulations by including more variables. For instance, a computer program might create a situation where a city manager must choose between allocating funds for specific urban services. Based on previous probabilities, the program might predict riots or bankruptcy or prosperity as a result of various allocations. Through this simulation, then, it might be possible to relate expenditure patterns to well-being and then look for similar relationships in the real world. These simulations usually are based on prior trends and, therefore, may not be very useful in predicting change. However, results of simulations often lead to revision of hypothesized relationships which make them more compatible with reality.

For the reasons discussed above, it is usually impossible to do political science experiments in the real world. These simulations, or "laboratory experiments," may aid us in predicting, and perhaps further our understanding of, patterns of empirical reality.

We have provided a brief introduction to primary data-gathering techniques. As noted above, it should facilitate the collection of the most relevant data to your study. However, it is apt to be costly in terms of time and money.

SECONDARY DATA GATHERING

Library Sources

Let us now examine some potential sources of existing data. First, of course, there are library sources. As long as you are looking for information to confirm or disprove a hypothesis and not just planning to repeat what others have said, it is perfectly legitimate to turn to such secondary sources as books and journals. Using these sources would involve procedures similar to those you used to begin narrowing down your research topic. The major difference would be the extensiveness of your search.

In addition to published research, there are historical records. There are also a number of books which present large bodies of statistical information. This information may be useful in comparing aggregates or groups because the data is not often presented for individuals. If, for instance, you wish to test if the proportion of blacks in cities is increasing, you could look in *U.S. Census Data* to determine the percentage of blacks in the central city population from 1930 to 1970. The federal government collects many statistics. These are indexed in the *American Statistical Index*. Census data is indexed in the *Catalog of U.S. Census Publications*. Below is a list of some major sources of raw data:

1. *U.S. Census of Population*—demographic information
2. *U.S. Census of Housing*—housing characteristics
3. *County and City Data Book*—local government characteristics
4. *Guide to U.S. Elections*—voting returns
5. *Gallup Opinion Index*—polling data
6. *Congressional Quarterly*—Congressional roll-call voting
7. *U.N. Statistical Yearbook*—International data
8. *World Handbook of Political and Social Indicators,* ed. Charles Taylor and Michael Hudson—International data

This list of sources just scratches the surface. Many interest groups, international organizations, other nations, newspaper archives, court records, pollsters, and so forth collect information which can be obtained by writing directly or through your library.

The statistics reported in these sources usually differ from those obtained in survey research. In survey research the unit of analysis is usually the individual. You would know if individual A were a Catholic and voted

Democratic. You could determine how many individuals who indicated that they were Catholic were also Democratic. Statistics reported in the sources above tend to be aggregated, that is, lumped together. By perusing these data sources we could probably find the number of Catholic church members in each state and the percentage of Democratic votes in each state. If there appears to be a correlation we might wish to surmise that Catholics vote Democratic, but we could not know for sure. We have no way of knowing whether the Catholics are the ones who are the Democrats. This is known as the *ecological fallacy*—an attempt to attribute the characteristics of aggregates to individuals. All we can say is that Catholic areas also tend to vote Democrat. We might be on firmer ground to suspect that Catholics vote Democrat if we could also use survey research as another data source. If this is impossible, the study would be more useful if we had a theory to support the findings. If we had logical reasons to expect the pattern we discovered empirically, the results would become more credible.

Aggregate data analysis has been used extensively in all aspects of the discipline. Its usage ranges from policy analysis to political behavior to political structures. It is probably most frequently used in Comparative and International Politics because the unit of analysis is often the nation-state rather than the individual. For instance, propensity of a nation for political violence can be shown to be related to such aggregate variables as rise/decline in GNP (Gross National Product), extensiveness of mass media, and so forth. When dealing with aggregate data, it is best to study aggregate phenomena and avoid the leap of faith necessary to deal with individual events. This constitutes a limiting factor in the use of aggregate data. On the other hand its low cost, ease of access, and range of information make it highly attractive for much research.

Because of the wide variety of data available any of the pre- or quasi-experimental research strategies might be applicable. For instance, you may do readings and get statistics concerning a specific place as part of a case study. Alternatively, you might use Gallup Poll data from two different time periods to use in pretest and posttest. For instance, if you hypothesize that major international events increase presidential popularity, you would select time frames which bracket major events and compare the differences in presidential support.

Data Archives.

In addition to published sources of data for secondary analysis there are archives which make available raw data for you to process and reanalyze. The archive which probably has the most data of relevance to political scientists is the Inter-University Consortium for Political and Social Research (ICPSR) at the University of Michigan. The ICPSR collects researchers' primary data and allows others to do secondary data analysis. The questions, sample, and time frame, may not be exactly what you might wish, but the available data is cheaper in terms of time and costs. You would analyze the data in the same manner as survey research or aggregate data. Once again this secondary data may be used with a variety of pre- and quasi-experimental strategies.

We hope that this has served to give you some familiarity with the data gathering techniques used by political scientists and has introduced you to some of the advantages and disadvantages involved in the use of each of these techniques.

This chapter has focused on the fourth question in your research design: "What data will you need to test your theoretical formulation and how will the data be collected?" The first section dealt with the problem of choosing data. The second section dealt with your research strategy. Would you use a true experiment or a pre- or quasi-experiment? The advantages and disadvantages of various research strategies were discussed in terms of threats to the validity of your findings. The last section discussed ways you could collect information for the strategy you have chosen. The next chapter will explore the fifth question on your outline, "How will you store your data?"

STUDY QUESTIONS

1. Besides individuals, list five other possible units of analysis.
2. What factors determine the size of sample you should select from a universe?
3. Compare the pros and cons of simple random sampling, systematic sampling, proportionate stratified sampling, disproportionate stratified sampling, and cluster sampling.
4. The purpose of experiments is to maximize the experimental variance while minimizing the extraneous variance. Discuss factors which may threaten the validity of your experiment.
5. Give examples of research projects in which you might use the following kinds of designs or strategies: experimental, quasi-experimental, or pre-experimental.
6. If you wished to do a study of student protest movements, discuss how you could use observation, content analysis, survey research and simulation to gather your data.
7. Distinguish between primary and secondary data gathering. What are the benefits and limitations of each? How might the two forms be combined in one study?
8. Discuss why different subfields might be more or less likely to use certain techniques of data collection, sampling, and sources.

Storing Data

Chapter Nine

By now you should have a good idea how to choose a topic, establish hypotheses, and collect information. As you begin to collect your data you will begin to realize that you are now faced with another problem. What are you going to do with all the information? How can you keep the material organized? Where are you going to keep all the information? Is there a way to keep it which will make it easier to use the data? This chapter will help you answer those questions. We will discuss the use of computers as well as less complex ways to store data when computers are either not available or not efficient. We will also discuss synthesizing and cataloging your information by coding (substituting numbers for words) and developing a code book (a "dictionary" to define numbers in words).

A few introductory remarks about the use of computers in political science should be made before continuing. In recent years computer technology has greatly assisted the political scientist in storing his data. For this reason much of this chapter will provide an introduction to the use of computers in political science. It is essential to understand, however, that there are other ways to store information and that computers are not always the best way.

Very often students respond in irrational ways when introduced to the computer. Some people react with "computer anxiety." They develop an irrational fear of this machine. They believe that a computer is super intelligent and is, therefore, sabotaging their projects. At the same time they lament the stupidity of the machine because "it did not know what I really meant."

Another irrational response to an introduction to the computer is to view it as the answer to everything. The student who believes this will constantly turn to the computer whether it is appropriate or not and expect the "truth" to fall out. A computer will help us store and organize data. It will perform mathematical calculations at an incredibly fast speed. The analysis of what this all means is still in the hands of humans. The computer analogy to the cliché "you can't get blood out of a stone" is "garbage in–garbage out." In other words what comes out is directly related to what you start with. This chapter will try to remove some of the mystique and fear surrounding the use of computers. We are not attempting to create computer programmers out of you but merely to introduce data processing as a tool for political scientists.

Before discussing computer-assisted forms of storing data, it should be made clear that there are other ways of storing information. It is not always beneficial or even possible to use computers. The degree to which the computer will be useful will depend on three factors: (1) the type of data to be collected; (2) the amount of data to be collected; and (3) the type of analysis to be used.

Type of data: If you are using qualitative data, it might not readily lend itself to computer storage and processing. Of course, qualitative data can be stored. If, for example, you are doing a literature review or using observational data, you will probably take notes on 3 x 5 cards or notebook paper. If you are using newspaper clippings for data, you may simply wish to file them and perhaps index them. You could place the information from your file cards or clippings on the computer using words instead of numbers, that is, in alphanumeric form. Usually, it is not worth the trouble. While this information could be translated into quantitative form for computer use, much of the richness might be lost. On the other hand, if you are gathering quantitative data or responses from large numbers of people, a computer would probably be helpful not only for storage but for later manipulation.

The amount of data: How much information you will be collecting will also determine if computers will be useful. Converting information to a form which is usable by a computer adds another step to the research process; therefore, you should be sure that the data is cumbersome before you undertake this step. If you are planning to write a short paper, do brief interviews with a few people, or look at characteristics of a few nations, the information can probably best be stored on cards and processed by hand.

However, if you have mountains of material which is difficult to wade through time and time again, putting the data on a computer is probably a wise investment of time.

Type of analysis: If your project involves political philosophy or other kinds of qualitative analysis, it may not be worthwhile to use computers. If, on the other hand, your research involves statistical manipulation, computers could be of great value.

CODING

Whether you will be using a computer or processing your information by hand, one of the important considerations is reducing the amount of space necessary for storage. When using computers, this is not only a matter of convenience but also one of cost. Since computer time is quite expensive, the more cumbersome the data you store the larger the space it takes on the computer and the more time consuming and costly the study becomes. The standard way that political scientists reduce data is by coding. Coding is the process of using numbers to represent places, attitudes, qualities, etc. In other words, it substitutes numbers for more complex verbal descriptions. In this way qualitative information can be made more concise.

Let us give an example of how this may be done. You have conducted a study of citizen participation in five cities. You wish to store information on the cities you have studied concerning the successfulness of their citizen participation programs. Note that as used above "successful" is an extremely vague and normative term. Let us assume that you have established a criterion for success. In our example let us say that you studied the following cities: New York, Atlanta, Fort Worth, Seattle, and Detroit. Hypothetically, let us say that New York was moderately unsuccessful, Atlanta and Seattle was very successful, Fort Worth was moderately successful, and Detroit was very unsuccessful. If you were to use numbers you might assign them as follows:

1. New York
2. Atlanta
3. Fort Worth
4. Seattle
5. Detroit

1. Very Successful
2. Moderately Successful

3. Some success, some failure
4. Moderately Unsuccessful
5. Very Unsuccessful

Thus, New York (moderately unsuccessful) becomes 1,4; Atlanta (very successful) becomes 2,1; Fort Worth (moderately successful) becomes 3,2; Seattle (very successful) becomes 4,1; and Detroit (very unsuccessful) becomes 5,5.

Besides making data storage more efficient in terms of taking less space, there is one other important advantage to coding information. If you plan to use statistical techniques to test your hypotheses, the numbers are ready to be used in the appropriate formula. The next section of this book will explain the use of statistics to aid in verifying hypotheses.

The numbers you assign to each category may have no meaning in and of themselves. In our example we assigned the number 1 to New York. It could just as easily have been assigned any other number. The important thing to remember is that you must keep a record of what each number stands for. If you are doing survey research as discussed in the last chapter, you can establish the categories even before the data is gathered by using closed-ended questions. If, on the other hand, you have used open-ended questions, it is at the storage stage that categories must be created. To do this you must first read through all your responses. As you do this you are looking for common responses that can be grouped together. For instance, if you asked ten people "What is best about the U.S.?" you might get these responses:

a. "You can do whatever you want."
b. "My son can become President."
c. "Freedom."
d. "It is beautiful with its lakes, mountains, and forests."
e. "The land of plenty."
f. "Chance to become rich."
g. "All men are equal."
h. "Nothing."
i. "Standard of living."
j. "Independence."

Since all ten responses are somewhat different we could have ten categories and assign each a number from 1 to 10. This would certainly condense the information. However, for future processing we may wish to create more general categories. You might use the following:

	Statements
1. Freedom	a,c,j
2. Opportunity	b,f,g
3. Natural resources	d
4. Good way of life	e,i
5. Nothing	h

Alternatively the responses could be categorized as follows:

	Statements
1. Economic conditions	e,f,i
2. Political conditions	b,c,j
3. Social conditions	d,g
4. Other	h
5. Missing	a

There is no one right set of categories. The best set will be the one that organizes your data in a way that it can easily be used to answer the questions you are asking. It may be impossible for you to categorize all responses. You may need a miscellaneous category. Of course, if you start to put everything in this catch-all category you will be defeating your own purpose. Some questions may go unanswered or contain responses which are totally inappropriate. You may code these as missing data.

Another problem may be deciding which category is most appropriate for a particular response. This is often quite difficult. In our example above we coded "You can do whatever you want" as missing. Alternatively we might have coded it as a political statement, thinking the respondent was referring to political freedom. It may also be possible that the respondent may have meant he or she was socially free. The coder has to try to understand what was really meant or code the information as missing so as not to distort the meaning of responses and findings of the study.

There may also be times that you will want unique codes rather than categories. If, for instance, you wanted to identify individual respondents, each person must have a unique number. We should also point out that in our first example—studying citizen participation—a literature or newspaper search could have been the data source. In the second example sample survey information was coded. All too often a student associates coding only with survey responses.

216 STORING DATA

Once a coding scheme is developed it is essential that it be recorded. If you cannot remember what your numbering code stands for, your data is useless. The format for recording your code is called a codebook.

CODEBOOK

A codebook is a listing of all information, where it is being stored, and what each number represents. It need not take the form of an actual book, but it should not take the form of little scraps of paper which are easily lost.

Generally, the first thing you will note in the codebook is the data source. If you are doing library research and a literature review, each source can be noted. For instance, if you are doing a review of voting behavior literature, you might establish codes for the various books you read:

01—The American Voter
02—Voting
03—Participation in America

That way you could identify what information came from what source. In the example of the citizen participation study used above, the city could become the identifying focus. If you were doing a sample survey of individuals, then you would want to provide an identification number for each individual. It may not be necessary to list a name next to every number since most surveys stress anonymity as a means of obtaining unbiased results. The identification number may be important, though, as a means of keeping a single respondent's answers organized or if you wish to compare specific respondents with each other. If you will be using a computer, it is especially important to make sure the respondents or cases stay in sequence. Table 9-1 provides an example of the first part of a codebook.

Table 9-1 Partial Codebook—Citizen Participation Study

Column 1-3	Identification #
Column 4	Card #1
Column 5	1. City
	(1) New York
	(2) Atlanta
	(3) Fort Worth
	(4) Seattle
	(5) Detroit
Column 6	2. Is there a neighborhood organization in your community?
	(1) Yes
	(2) No
	(3) Don't Know

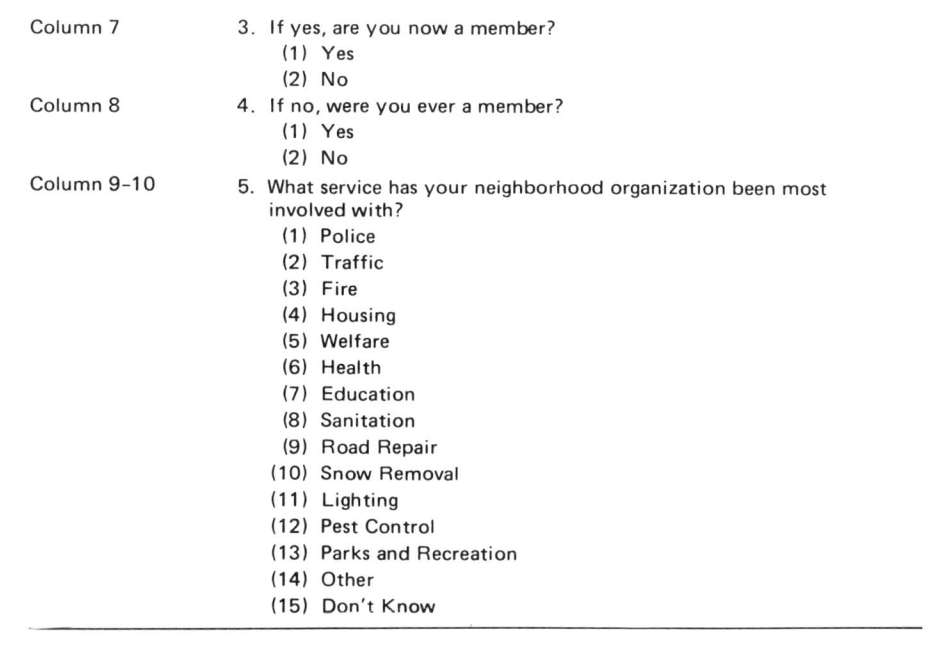

Column 7	3. If yes, are you now a member?
	(1) Yes
	(2) No
Column 8	4. If no, were you ever a member?
	(1) Yes
	(2) No
Column 9-10	5. What service has your neighborhood organization been most involved with?
	(1) Police
	(2) Traffic
	(3) Fire
	(4) Housing
	(5) Welfare
	(6) Health
	(7) Education
	(8) Sanitation
	(9) Road Repair
	(10) Snow Removal
	(11) Lighting
	(12) Pest Control
	(13) Parks and Recreation
	(14) Other
	(15) Don't Know

It is also important that you specify the location of the information. Computers cannot distinguish one set of numbers from the next. You must tell it where to find the specific set of numbers you wish to study. This is what column numbers stand for.

INTRODUCTION TO COMPUTERS

So far, we have discussed how data may be coded and catalogued for storage and eventual analysis. While we have stressed that computers are not always necessary or even helpful in all cases, we find the use of computers in political science is increasing. There are many reasons for this. In the first place, developments in computer technology make computers easier and cheaper to use all the time. In addition, the advent of this technology led to the development of more complex research strategies which require the use of computers. Lastly, the emphasis in the discipline of political science has stressed increased empirical verification and with it large bodies of information which are often impossible to process adequately by hand.

    The introduction of computers has not been an unmixed blessing. By freeing us from manual manipulation of our data, we can use more sophisticated techniques and process more data. The negative side of this is that researchers are often induced to use techniques they do not fully understand. This may lead to inaccurate conclusions. This is all the more serious since we tend to attribute a false validity to our studies because we have used a computer. In addition, when doing analysis by hand you may discover interesting patterns which might be overlooked had you only analyzed the results produced by the computer.

One further problem which is sometimes the result of overzealous use of the computer is the so-called "fishing expedition." Since it is almost as easy to do a thousand computations as five, there is a tendency to try everything and see what comes of it. That is why we are introducing data processing now after having discussed the importance of theoretical justification. It is not enough just to discover patterns (although this may be a valuable exercise in descriptive studies). We must try to understand why those patterns have emerged. Without a theoretical framework we cannot be sure if the patterns emerge by chance or because of some other factors. Thus, while the use of computers may lead us to see new patterns, we must be skeptical investigators. We can make computers work for us as long as we remember who is in charge.

At the beginning of the chapter we noted that you should not be in awe of the computer nor should you be timid in using it. We believe that the one aspect which frightens students most when they are told they will be working with the computer is the introduction of a new terminology and the awe-inspiring equipment. It is also our belief that things which are not understood are feared.

Each discipline develops its own language or jargon so that terms will contain a precision not ordinarily found in common usage. There are also terms which are created for special disciplines since they exist nowhere else. If you can understand the basic language you can communicate with the specialists. So it is with "talking" to the computer. Here we will present the key terms you are likely to encounter in dealing with computers. Let us begin with the computer itself.

A computer is a device which is programmed with a set of instructions to calculate arithmetical and logical functions. Computers range from hand-held calculators to the new "toy" computers for home and small business use to massive IBM and CDC machines. Generally speaking, the larger the machine the more manipulations it can do and the faster it can do them. Most large computers can do various things at the same time and can accommodate multiple users. While smaller units usually have more limited capabilities and are slower, they may be adequate for our purposes.

There are two types of computers: analog and digital. Analog computers were the first type developed and are still used to solve engineering problems. They register quantities in a physical state and then translate them into numbers. An example of an analog device is a thermometer which measures heat by a changing level of mercury which is then recorded in numerical terms.[1] A digital computer is the type in most common usage today. The remainder of our discussion considers only digital computers. Values are directly translated into numbers or digits for manipulation. A desk calculator with wheels that click into place for each number is a rudimentary example of a digital computer. Most digital computers convert information into binary numbers. Binary systems use only two digits: 1 and 0. All numbers, letters, and symbols are converted to 1s and 0s. Electronic computers work on electric impulses. Whenever the machine encounters a 1 it emits a positive charge. A 0 generates a negative charge.[2]

Hardware

A computer system contains four essential components: (1) an input device, (2) a storage unit, (3) a processing unit, and (4) an output device. Components 2 and 3 are the actual computer. All these elements constitute computer hardware. The term *hardware* refers to the actual physical devices used to transform raw information into processed results.

Input devices. The most common form of input is the *punched card*. A punched card is eighty columns wide (see Figure 9-1). If you will be using

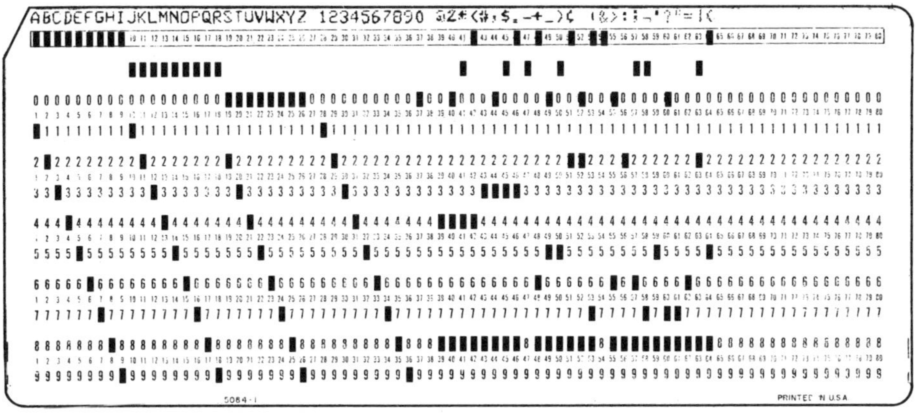

Figure 9-1 HOLLERITH OR PUNCH CARD

punched cards to enter your data into the computer, you should use coding paper when coding your data. Coding paper, like a punch card, is also eighty

---

1. Donald J. Veldman, Fortran Programming for the Behavioral Sciences (New York: Holt, Rinehart & Winston, 1967), p. 2.
2. Ibid.

220 *STORING DATA*

columns, and it makes it easier to keep the numbers in the right place when punching the cards. The coding paper contains many rows, each representing a new card (see Figure 9-2). Your codebook should note what column or columns on which card contain which pieces of information. For instance, a person's sex might be coded on card 1, column 19, his age on card 1, columns 20–21, and so forth. The data is transformed from coding paper to the punched card by the use of a *keypunch machine*.

A keypunch machine looks like an elaborate typewriter; each time a number, letter, or symbol is struck, holes are punched in a computer card. Therefore, one cannot erase. In order to verify what has been typed, the numbers, letters, and symbols usually are typed across the top. Computers do not read these. Instead, electronic sensors scan each card and generate electronic impulses to be used by the computer. The device used to input the punched card is the *card reader*. Another input medium similar to the punched card is punched paper tape. In principle it operates the same as the punched card but may well be longer than eighty columns wide.

A third widely used input format is *magnetic tape*. Generally speaking, the tape is made during one run of a computer program and stored for later or continued entry. The tape looks similar to that used in home tape recorders. It is much more efficient than punched cards when data will be used often or when the data set is large. These tapes are read by the computer by interpreting the direction of the magnetism as the tape moves along. An input medium similar to the tape is the *disk pack*, which is more or less like a stack of records. Again, the disk is magnetized during one computer run and data is then stored to be input at a later date.

Still another input medium is the *optical scanner*. Whenever you have taken a test which required a No. 2 pencil, you may safely assume that those marks were read by a computer. Researchers are currently developing input devices which will "understand" the human voice and "read" the printed page without the necessity of other input media.

One additional type of input medium which should be mentioned is various keyboard stations. These keyboards may be like teletype machines or they may have cathode-ray television screens. This type of input is generally used with *time-sharing* or *interactive input mode*. This means that you are "talking" directly to the computer. You may edit your input as you go along or you may respond to output from the computer. The advantages of this are obvious. You can get your results immediately. You can quickly correct errors. Also, some results may suggest further analysis which you may do immediately. This last advantage may also be a disadvantage since you may not take time to think things through clearly, and you may, thus, be tempted to go on the proverbial "fishing expedition." Also, on many interactive systems, it is not possible to store the data. If you are dealing with a large data set, you may not want to enter the data with each computer run. Finally, not all interactive systems provide for a written record, so results may have to be copied by hand.

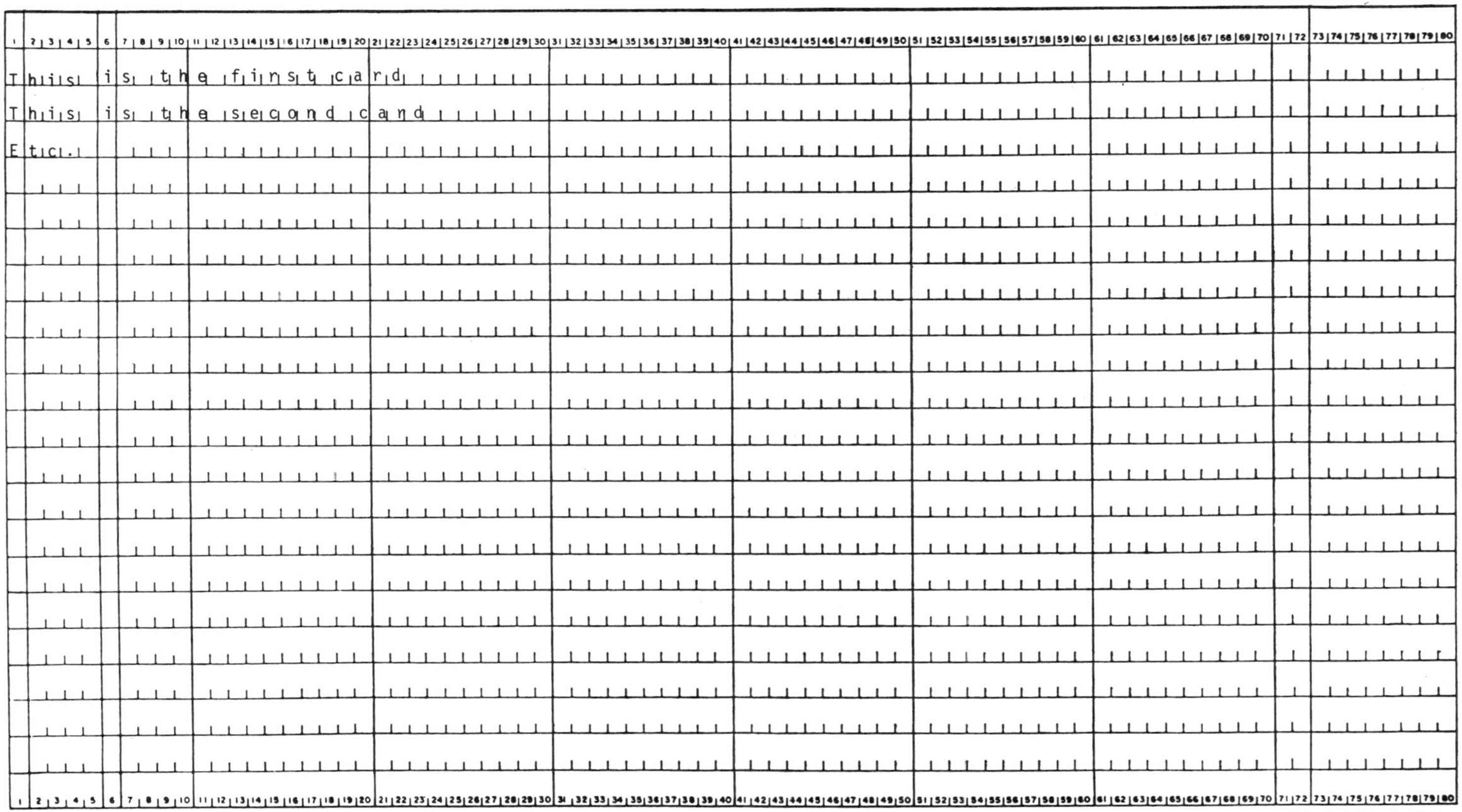

Figure 9-2 CODING PAPER

The first five input devices are generally not used with the interactive mode, but with the *batch mode*. This means that jobs are read into the computer and stored until the computer can process your data. This usually works better if many people are using the same data sets. Because the jobs can be processed by the computer at off-peak hours, the batch mode is often used in schools. Batch is usually more efficient if there is a lot of output. It is slower than interactive, though, and one mistake may require you to resubmit the whole job and wait again.

Storage units. Computers have two basic types of storage units: *core* and *auxiliary*. The core is an integral part of the computer and stores basic information for use by the computer in processing your program. It is also used to provide a temporary storage facility while the computer is executing your program. The larger the capacity of the computer, the more core it will contain. This generally allows it to perform more complex functions since it has a large repertoire of routines in its memory. It will be able to process more jobs at the same time by dividing its work space between jobs. The capacity of a computer is measured in terms of K bytes. A *byte* is the amount of space required to store one character. One K equals 1024 bytes. A simple program may require only 60 K or 61,440 bytes. A more complex analysis might require 220 K or 225,280 bytes. Generally speaking, the more core you will need, the lower the priority you will get on the computer and the longer you will have to wait for your results.

If you have devised a program, or are using someone else's program, or have a large data base which will be used repeatedly, you will probably want to make use of auxiliary storage devices. Auxiliary storage devices are used to supplement the computer's direct storage capabilities. The two most common devices have already been discussed as input devices. These are magnetic tape and magnetic disk. Data, programs, and so forth, may be imprinted and stored to be used later as input.

Processing unit. The *Central Processing Unit* (CPU) is the part of the computer which performs the actual manipulations you have requested. This is the fastest part of the process. That is why several jobs can be input at once, stored, quickly executed, and then output. Often there will be many input and output devices attached to one computer. Earlier we stated that computers are not as "smart" as many people think. It should also be stated that computers seldom are responsible for errors. The CPU follows routines and sequences which have been stored in the core. It has no mind to think or innovate. It is a "dumb" but "faithful" machine. If a computer is programmed incorrectly (by a human), it will produce incorrect answers. If you ask it to do something for which it has not been preprogrammed, it will not do what you ask. Your improper command may be caused by an error in logic which prevents a computer from acting as you requested, by a typographical error which results in a command which the computer does not recognize, or by your requesting it to do something beyond its capacity.

The CPU has three basic components: (1) a control unit which implements your instructions; (2) an arithmetic–logic unit which performs the actual operation; and (3) temporary storage which holds intermediate computations which may be needed later. The CPU is extremely complex in operation, but since we are not computer professionals, it is unnecessary to provide more detail here.

Output devices. The most common output device is the *printer*. The printer operates like a teletype by translating electronic impulses from a computer into letters, numbers, and symbols and printing them on paper. Another common output device is the cathode-ray tube. The cathode-ray tube allows the student to input information and then receive output on the same machine. Output can also take the form of punched cards or can be recorded on tape or disk for future use. Elaborate plotters are often available to produce graphical displays.

Miscellaneous hardware. Since we are trying to introduce and explain the basic components and jargon of computer technology which you may well encounter in your first experience with computers, we should discuss three more pieces of hardware which might prove useful. A *reproducer* will duplicate a stack of cards and may be set to even rearrange or omit certain punches. While a reproducer will punch holes, it does not print at the top of the card. An *interpreter* is a machine which will translate the punches and print at the top of each card. As noted above, this is not necessary for the computer but may help you spot any errors. A *countersorter* is a device which stacks cards on the basis of punches in a preselected column. This might be useful if you wish to remove a specific group of cards before a computer analysis or if you merely wish to tabulate the number of cases in each category of a specific item.

Software

While the machinery or computer hardware facilitates data storage and eventual analysis, it is useless without a means of communicating to the computer to tell it what to do and how to do it. The instructions necessary to get a computer to perform its tasks are called *software*. Computer experts prepare basic programs which allow computers to follow the instructions of the user such as yourself. Up until a few years ago, if you wished to use a computer, you had to be able to "speak" a computer language and give fairly detailed instructions to produce results. Learning a computer language became just another requirement to be able to perform analyses expected of political scientists. A variety of languages were developed. The most common language and one that many of you may have heard of is known as Fortran. Other common languages are COBOL (used extensively for business applications) and PL-1. Using any of these or other languages, one could confront a problem and then "speak" to the machine in the form of a program. This would then be translated into machine language and processed.

The contemporary political scientist is more fortunate than the pioneers of computer analysis. It is nice to know a computer language since that might enable you to solve simple problems more efficiently as well as special problems, but knowledge of a language is usually not necessary. We are generally able to use what are known as "canned programs." These programs are written by experts and are capable of doing a variety of storage and manipulative tasks. Basically what the user has to do is to call up a specific program out of the computer center library. Once the program is plugged into the computer, you then have to identify your data so the computer knows where to search for what information and what operations you wish to have performed. Not all computer centers have all possible packages in their libraries any more than your school library has every book. Your computer center may have some programs written locally which are useful. You should check with your computer center to see what is available. There are also programs prepared by the computer manufacturers known as "utility" programs which require little computer knowledge and allow you to do such simple and common tasks as transferring data from cards to tape, duplicating a tape, and so forth. What has made the use of canned programs even easier is the development of "packages" of such programs. That is, a group of programs to perform several different procedures are written, using a standard format and criteria.

Of all the packages of "canned" programs which are generally available, the four you are most likely to encounter are BMD,[3] SAS,[4] OSIRIS,[5] and SPSS.[6] BMD stands for Biomedical Computer Programs. It was developed at UCLA for medical research, but has been extensively used by social scientists. It is quite easy to use and offers many complex statistical manipulations. Even though these and other packaged programs will do the complex computation for you, it is essential that you understand statistics if you are to use the programs properly. That is why the next section introduces statistics even though you may eventually use the computer to do your actual calcula-

---

3. W. J. Dixon, ed., *BMD Biomedical Computer Programs* (Los Angeles: University of California Press, 1970).
4. *SAS76: Statistical Analysis System* (Chapel Hill: University of North Carolina, 1976).
5. *OSIRIS III: An Integrated Collection of Computer Programs for the Management and Analysis of Social Science Data,* vols. 1–6 (Ann Arbor, Mich.: Institute for Social Research, 1973).
6. Norman Nie and others, *SPSS: Statistical Package for the Social Sciences,* 2nd Ed. (New York: McGraw-Hill, 1975).

tions. BMD is the oldest package. SAS, or Statistical Analysis System, developed at the North Carolina State University, is one of the newest packages available. It, too, is fairly extensive and easy to use. OSIRIS, which stands for Organized Set of Integrated Routines for Investigation with Statistics, was developed at the University of Michigan. The University of Michigan is the home of the Inter-University Consortium for Political and Social Research (ICPSR) which makes raw data available for analysis, as was noted in the last chapter. This data may be obtained in a manner formatted for use with the OSIRIS package for ease of analysis. Statistical Package for the Social Sciences (SPSS) was developed at Stanford and the University of Chicago. It generally requires a larger computer than the other packages but is one of the simplest to use and most versatile. It is also one of the most extensively used packages by political scientists and can also be used with OSIRIS.

Control cards. Before you can begin to use a packaged program, it is necessary to understand a few more terms and procedures. The first thing you will probably have to do to use the computer is to establish an account at the computer center. In many instances, your professor will do this for you. Once you have an account number you should be ready to go. The first thing you will have to know is the Control Cards necessary for your system. This identifies you to the computer, tells it what parts and how much of the computer you will be using, where to find your data, and what it should do with your results or output. The basic Control Cards are (1) the *Job Card,* which identifies you and establishes your basic requirements of the computer resources; (2) the *Execution Statement,* which notifies the computer which "canned" program you wish to use; and (3) the *Data Definition Statement,* which identifies the input source and where you want your output recorded, that is, printer, tape, and so forth. Many systems do not require this statement if input is by punched cards and output goes on the printer. The terms Execution or EXEC Statement and Data Definition or DD Statement are terminology used for IBM computers. If your system is not IBM, you may use other forms of Control Language, but the information required and the purpose are the same.

The exact format of these cards will vary for each computer installation and type of equipment. Each installation is also likely to establish different *default options.* A default option is the standard set of instructions given to the computer. If you wish to use different specifications, you would then specify to override the default option. For instance, a default option might set a limit of 10,000 lines of printed output (print out) per job. Since the printer is usually the slowest part of the computer operation, this will limit the time any one person can tie up the printer. If you override the option to get more lines printed, the additional lines will be printed, but usually the computer will be programmed to lower your priority, forcing you to wait rather than making others wait. Default options are also put in place to prevent wasted time caused by errors. If you forget to end a program, it might continue forever unless some fail-safe device is set up to intervene.

By now you have had a brief introduction to control language. You are now familiar with some computer jargon, and you should be ready to select a set of packaged or "canned" programs and begin your analysis. Each package will include instructions for its use and will allow you to perform the statistical procedures which will be explained in the next section.

SUMMARY

In this chapter we concerned ourselves with the problem of storing the information gathered to do research. There are many ways to organize the data that will make it compact and easily accessible. Note cards, newspaper clipping files, indexes, and computers all aid in organizing information for later use. While the computer is not the answer to all storage problems it is becoming more useful for the type of research political scientists are doing. At times it is beneficial to make data more concise by coding it and providing a codebook to act as a dictionary for the codes. If you are using a computer, coding will almost certainly be necessary. Coding refers to the substitution of numbers for verbal descriptions. In some cases you wish to assign a different number for each unique variable, for example, an identification number. In other instances you wish to establish a few codes to allow you to categorize your information. In any case a codebook must be established so that the meanings of the numbers assigned are not forgotten or can be interpreted by others.

If you wish to place your coded information on a computer for storage it is essential to understand how to communicate with the computer. Using a computer is not really difficult if you are not afraid of the jargon. You must be aware that a computer can perform many tasks quickly and efficiently, but it can only do what some human has already told it.

You should be familiar with the hardware or machinery which is part of computer technology. You should also understand the importance of software or instructions which make the system work. While it is no longer necessary to know computer programming to use a computer effectively, it is helpful to know some terminology. This will allow you to be somewhat independent and permit you to communicate to those who work with computers. There are a variety of packaged programs which facilitate storage and processing of data. It is necessary to learn how to use these as well as some Control Language which will help you instruct the computer.

The next section of this book will deal with statistics which can be used to process your information and aid in testing your hypotheses. That is the final step before you write your research report.

STUDY QUESTIONS

1. Discuss the pros and cons of using computers to store data.
2. Under what conditions would you normally wish to avoid using a computer to store your data?
3. Discuss the procedures involved in coding open-ended questions into a few general categories. Make up and develop an example.
4. Distinguish between computer hardware and software.
5. Distinguish between the use of Control Language and canned programs.
6. What are the basic types of control cards and what purposes do they serve?

Statistical Analysis

Part Four

In the last section we tried to guide you through the process of planning research and gathering and storing data. At this point, if you were actually doing a research project, you would be at the stage where you have all sorts of bits and pieces of data neatly tucked away on computer cards, or notecards, or whatever. The question is, what does all that data mean? To answer that we have to consider the last question of the research design: How can we analyze the data?

In empirical research, which is aimed toward building theory, we very often have great quantities of data. We need all that data because we want to go beyond making statements about unique individuals and unique events to making generalizations of significant scope. The more data we have, the more sure we can be that a general pattern exists, but also the more difficult it is to organize and make sense out of it all. This is where statistics come in handy. Social scientists use statistics to organize data and to summarize the patterns found in the data.

We mentioned in the last section that many people approach the computer with great fear and awe. It is also the case that people approach statistics with great wariness, to say the least. All too often students decide they cannot understand statistics and give up before they even try. We hope that you won't do that. The only math you need to understand this section on statistics is addition, subtraction, multiplication, and division. Beyond that a little common sense is useful.

We should immediately point out that this section will not make high-powered statisticians out of you. There are many statistical techniques. We will discuss only a few of the most common and most basic statistical procedures. There are three goals we have tried to achieve in our brief discussion of statistics. In the first place, we have tried to introduce you to the basic uses of statistics in data analysis. Some statistics help you describe the patterns in the date. These are called *descriptive statistics.* Some statistics help you decide if you can infer patterns in the population as a whole from the patterns you find in your sample. These are called *inferential statistics.*

Secondly, we have tried to familiarize you with some statistics which you are most likely to run across in your reading of political science literature. And, finally, we have tried to discuss statistics in such a common sense way that you will overcome any fear of statistics you might have.

Chapters Ten, Twelve and Thirteen in this section are primarily concerned with descriptive statistics. Chapter Ten is concerned with describing a single variable. Chapters Twelve and Thirteen discuss how to describe the relations between two variables, and, in addition, Chapter Thirteen considers how to describe relations among more than two variables. Chapter Eleven is primarily concerned with procedures you should use to predict if the patterns in your data appear in the population as a whole. Once you can understand the fundamental reasoning in these chapters, you should be able to understand other, more sophisticated statistical analyses.

Describing the Data

Chapter Ten

After the data have been gathered and stored, you must then turn to analyzing them. The data at this stage are similar to the pieces in a jigsaw puzzle which has been dumped on the floor. There is a great deal of information, but until it is fit together in some meaningful way it can make very little sense to us. We must have some way of summarizing all that information and organizing it in such a way that we can use it to answer the questions which started us on the research project in the first place. Summarizing and organizing data is the function of statistics.

Some statistics require knowledge of higher math. We will not be concerned with such sophisticated techniques here. You should be willing to think about the logic which underlies the techniques we will be discussing. All too often, it has been our experience that the subject of statistics has been treated as though it were simply a matter of memorizing a few formulas. That approach is almost always doomed to failure. Unless you really understand the steps involved in a statistical technique, you will never be able to know when to use it or to understand what the results mean when you do use it.

This chapter is concerned with some of the most basic and simple kinds of statistical techniques. These are called *descriptive statistics*, and that name tells you exactly what the purpose of these statistics is. Statistical techniques provide means of describing a particular set of data. In the process of giving you means to describe the data, they give you a way of summarizing the information contained in the data. As always, by summarizing or generalizing, some information is lost. But without some summarizing we could make little or no sense out of the immense number of bits of information which are gathered in any empirical research project. We use concepts, generalizations, and theories to summarize conceptually commonalities among phenomena. We use statistics to summarize bits of empirical information we gather in research.

What you must understand first before we discuss any of the descriptive statistical techniques is the idea of the distribution of your data. Remember, in research we deal with a particular kind of concept called a variable. We use this term to indicate that a concept can assume different values. That is, not all the units possess the same amount of the particular property which is expressed by the concept. Sex is a variable because it has at least two values: Some people are male and some are female. Income is a variable since different people make different amounts of money. Type of government is a variable since some are democratic, some are authoritarian, and some are totalitarian.

It is because our research deals with variables which have a distribution of values that we need some means of summarizing data. If every unit under study possessed properties with constant values, it would be very easy to describe the data. For instance, we would easily be able to describe the property of sex among a group of people if they were all male. No summarizing of that data would be necessary. If everyone in a particular study made exactly the same amount of money, again no summarizing would be necessary. But it is rarely the case that a particular property assumes constant values. And, as we indicated in the chapter on gathering information, we do not want those variables we are studying to have constant values. It is only by observing the pattern in which the values change that we can attempt to establish the existence of a relationship among concepts. Therefore, since we necessarily study concepts which assume different values, we need some means of summarizing and describing the particular distribution of the values we observe among those units we are studying.

There are several techniques which summarize and, therefore, help us describe the distribution of values in the data. In the first place, we will discuss three measures which refer to a central tendency in the values which a particular variable assumes. These are called, appropriately enough, *measures of central tendency.* Secondly, we will consider how much the values of a particular variable vary. These are called *measures of variation.* With one exception, these types of measures will produce a single number which will summarize the underlying distribution of values. There are also means by which the exact nature of a distribution can be described. To do this it is necessary to indicate how many of what values for a variable occur in the data. This description of the distribution is called a *frequency distribution*. We will consider ways of discussing frequency distributions as well as ways of picturing these distributions on graphs and tables.

Before we begin to discuss these means of describing the data, we should consider the idea of the *level of measurement* of the data. Level of measurement basically refers to how precisely the data can be measured. There are four different levels of precision involved in measuring the values of a variable. The first level of measurement is the *nominal* level. Unfortunately, this is the same word which we used in our discussion of defining concepts. In that context it was a definition that suited our research purposes. We define the concept in name only, hence the term nominal. Here nominal means that we have assigned numbers to the values a variable assumes, but those numbers simply act as a code for the values. The values have those numbers in name only. Such numbers do not imply anything additional about the values. They only provide a number identification for each value. For instance, for the variable sex, we could assign the number 1 as a code for male and the number 2 as a code for female. These codes would in no way imply that males were in some way better or worse, or higher or lower, than females. It simply allows us to sort our data into categories. In fact, many people do not even consider nominal a form of measurement, but only another way of classifying the values. However, there are ways of using those numbers in statistical manipulation, and, hence, we will consider nominal as a level of measurement.

The second level of measurement is called the *ordinal* level. In this case, when numbers are assigned to the values, the numbers are not just a code but also indicate that the order of the categories is important. For instance, if we were interested in examining the height of people in a classroom, we could line them all up in order of height. We might assign 1 to the tallest person, 2 to the next tallest, and so on down to the shortest person. By doing this we can look at the number assigned to an individual and know how his or her height compares to others in the class. By being able to order, we can therefore communicate more information about the distribution of values for a particular variable. We can not only classify the values, as we did with the nominal level of measurement, but we can also say something about how the values compare to each other. The number 1 indicates that the person so identified is taller than is the person who was identified as 2. The numbers indicate that the unit has more or less of a particular property. In our example, the number 2 indicated that the person so ranked had less height than did person 1 and more height than person 3. We know there is a relative difference between people but we do not know exactly what that difference is. Person 1 may be two inches taller than person 2 who may be only one-half inch taller than person 3. With ordinal measurement, then, we know the order but not the precise difference between the units.

If we also had some kind of absolute standard for measuring the property under investigation, we could make very precise statements concerning the values. For instance, in our discussion of the height of the members of a class, if we happened to have a ruler handy, we could state precisely everyone's height according to the measuring standard of feet and inches. Now we can go beyond simply saying that person 2 is shorter than person 1 and also say precisely how much shorter he is. In other words, we know how much one category differs from another. A scale which provides this much precision is called an *interval* scale since the standard used for measuring is composed of precise and uniform intervals, in this case inches.

A fourth level of measurement which is often specified is *ratio* measurement. It is similar to interval measurement in that the distance between each unit on a scale is equal to the distance for any equal unit, for example, the distance between one and two inches is the same as the distance between two and three inches. Ratio scales allow us added precision over interval scales because they have an absolute zero point. This allows us to consider precise relationships (ratios) between two values. Age can be measured on a ratio scale. There is an absolute zero. A person who is eighteen years old is twice as old as a nine-year-old and half as old as a 36-year-old. On the other hand, temperature on the Celsius scale is interval but not ratio. Zero degrees does not indicate the absence of heat. Therefore, we cannot say that 50°C is twice as hot as 25°C or half as hot as 100°C. For statistical purposes all the procedures we discuss which are applicable to interval level variables are also applicable to ratio variables. For that reason, when we say a statistic is applicable for the interval level you should understand it can be used for ratio data.

The reason why this discussion of levels of measurement is important is that the level of measurement will determine what statistics can be used to summarize and analyze the data. It should be obvious, if you think about it, that when numbers are only used as a form of identifying code, as they are in the nominal level of measurement, they cannot be treated the same way as can numbers which are derived from an interval scale. Statistics appropriate for a particular level of measurement can be used at that level and for all levels which are more precise. That is, statistics appropriate for the nominal level can also be used at both the ordinal and interval levels. However, this is rarely done, since statistics designed for higher levels of measurement will usually provide more information than will those appropriate for lower levels of measurement. That is a reason why, when possible, it is usually best to measure things at the highest level possible. This is so both because of the increased precision provided and because of the more powerful statistics available for that level of measurement. It should be obvious that statistics designed for one level of measurement cannot be used on data measured at lower levels, with the exception of interval and ratio variables where techniques we discuss are interchangeable. All of this means that the first step in any statistical analysis is to decide how precisely the data can be measured since that will affect what type of analysis can be used. With that in mind, let us now turn to examining statistical techniques which summarize and describe data distributions.

The first thing we will consider is how the central tendency of a distribution can be measured. In this, as in the entire discussion of various statistical techniques, we will consider for what level of measurement the technique is appropriate, how it is computed, what information it gives us, and what its advantages and disadvantages are.

MEASURES OF CENTRAL TENDENCY

There are three measures which are used to indicate the central point of a distribution, one for each of the three different levels of measurement. As we indicated above, all three measures could be used on the interval level. But it is usually best to use the measure designed for the interval level. The measure of central tendency which is specifically designed for the interval level of measurement is the *mean* or average. The mean is computed by adding the values of a set of numbers and then dividing by the number of values involved. This is expressed by the following formula:

$$\text{mean} = \frac{\Sigma x}{n}$$

Σ indicates that the quantities are to be summed. The x represents the values of the separate quantities, and the n indicates the number of values involved. If the mean is that of a sample, it is indicated by the symbol $\bar{x}$. If it is the mean of a population, it is indicated by the symbol μ. Let us compute the mean for the following set of numbers (assuming, of course, that they represent at least an interval level of measurement): 5, 3, 6, 2, 4. First these values are added together. $\Sigma x = 5 + 3 + 6 + 2 + 4 = 20$. Then the result of this addition is divided by the number of values involved: $\frac{20}{5}$. The mean $\bar{x}$ of this distribution of values is thus 4 (or $\bar{x} = \frac{\Sigma x}{n} = \frac{20}{5} = 4$).

This measure of central tendency has several desirable properties. In the first place, it is familiar to most people and, therefore, it can be easily and meaningfully communicated. Secondly, the mean always exists and is always unique. (This is not the case with the mode, as we will soon see.)

238 DESCRIBING THE DATA

Thirdly, the mean is based on the value of each individual item, and thus it takes into account all available information. Finally, the mean lends itself to further statistical manipulation. There is, however, one major disadvantage of the mean. A single extreme value can have a large impact on the value of the mean. The effect of this may be that the mean does not really give a good "feeling" of what the central point of the distribution really is. For instance, consider the problems using the mean to measure central tendency of income distribution in many countries. It may be, for instance, that 100 people made $4,000. But there might be two potentates who had yearly incomes of $1,000,000. That means total incomes would be (100 × $4,000) + (2 × $1,000,000) or $2,400,000. If we divide $2,400,000 by our total population of 100 + 2 or 102, the mean income would be $23,529.41. Sounds good. But this figure hardly gives an uninformed observer a good "feel" for income levels in the country.

In a situation like this, where the value distribution included a few extreme values, it may be better to include a measure of central tendency which has been designed for use for ordinal level data: the *median*. The median is the value of the middle item when data are arranged in an increasing or decreasing order. For example, consider the following distribution of nine values arranged in order: 3, 4, 6, 9, 9, 10, 10, 12, 13. The formula for determining the middle value is $\frac{n+1}{2}$, where n equals the number of values in the distribution. Thus, in this example: $\frac{9+1}{2} = \frac{10}{2} = 5$. The median of this distribution is the fifth value, or 9. If there is an even number of values in a distribution, there is never a middle value. In that case, the median is defined as the mean or average of the two middle values. For example, in a distribution of six values, there is no single middle value (3, 6, 8, 10, 13, 15). Using the formula for determining the position of the median we would have $\frac{6+1}{2} = \frac{7}{2} = 3.5$. We know, therefore, that the median falls between the third and the fourth values. Therefore, we average these values: $\frac{8+10}{2} = 9$. Nine is thus the median value.

You should notice that the formula for the median establishes not the value of the median, but its position. It divides the distribution in such a way that the values of one-half of the items are less than or equal to the median, and the values of the other half are greater than or equal to the median. This emphasis on position rather than value is both an advantage and a disadvantage of the median. Since it does not use values in its computation it obviously cannot be affected by extreme values, as can the mean. That is why, as we indicated above, even if the data is interval, you still may want to use the median along with the mean, as a measure of central tendency. But since the median ignores the values of the items, it in essence throws away information if the items are measured at the interval level. Also, it has been found that the mean varies less from sample to sample than does the median. Therefore, if you have interval data, the mean is a more desirable measure of central tendency than is the median, unless you know the distribution has extreme values.

For ordinal data, however, the mean is totally inappropriate. Remember the ordinal level of measurement only means that you can order items in ascending or descending ranks. At the ordinal level, you do not have a precise measuring instrument which can tell you precisely how many intervals separate one item from the other. The ordinal level of measurement, thus, only deals with the positioning of items. Since the median is concerned only with the position of the middle item in a distribution, it is the most appropriate measure of central tendency for the ordinal level of measurement.

For the nominal level of measurement, the only appropriate measure of central tendency is the *mode*. The mode is simply the value which occurs with the highest frequency. One advantage of the mode is the ease with which it is computed. All you have to do is to count the number of units in each of the categories or number codes. The code which has the largest number of units is the mode. For instance, to discover the modal category for the variable sex, you count the number of males and females in your data. If there happen to be 45 males and 55 females, then female is the modal category. Another advantage is that the idea of the mode is easy to grasp and, thus, it can be easily communicated to others.

There are, however, two disadvantages of the mode. In any given distribution there may be more than one mode. Consider the following distribution: 3, 5, 8, 3, 6, 3, 5, 9, 8, 5, 8. There are three modes in this distribution: 3, 5, and 8. Another disadvantage is that there is no mode if no two values are alike. For instance, there is no mode for the following distribution: 1, 2, 3, 4, 5.

MEASURES OF VARIATION

In addition to specifying the central point in a distribution, you may also want to know how much variability there is among the values of the items. Let us consider why this is so. If you were interested in buying a stock, you would probably be pleased to know that in the past year it had an average value of $100 per share. But before you bought the stock, you might also want to know whether that mean had resulted from the value of the stock varying from $90 to $110 or whether the values had, in fact, varied from $10 to $190. In both cases the average value may be $100, but probably only a gambler would want to buy a stock whose values would fluctuate wildly. In essence, knowing the variability of a distribution will give you some idea as to what extent you can rely upon the measure of central tendency as a reliable measure of the values in a distribution.

There really is no way to discuss the variability in a nominal distribution since the numbers do not really mean anything. One very simple measure of the variation in either an ordinal or an interval distribution is the *range*. The range can be indicated either by specifying the two extreme values in a distribution, or by specifying the difference between these two values. For instance, consider the following distribution: 1, 2, 11, 15, 17, 18, 29, 30. The range can be expressed by the extreme values (1 and 30) or by the difference between those values (29). This example points to one disadvantage of the range. Since the range depends by definition on the extreme values, it may not give an accurate picture of the dispersion of the values between those extremes. This is especially a problem with ordinal data, since any set of numbers may be used to indicate the ranking of items. If the data are ordinal, the numbers 1, 5, and 18 are equivalent to 1, 2, and 3 since the numbers indicate only the ranking rather than the precise intervals which differentiate the cases.

At the ordinal level, a measure of variation which is more useful than the range is the *interquartile range*. This measure is composed of the end points of the middle 50% of the entries in a distribution. It may be computed first by dividing the distribution into quartiles. A quartile is a positional measure like the median. Whereas the median indicates the midpoint in a distribution, a quartile divides a distribution into four groupings. The first quartile is the value below which 25% of the cases occur and above which 75% occur. The middle quartile is the median. The third quartile is the value below which 75% of the entries occur and above which 25% occur. After having determined the quartiles, the top and bottom quartiles are dropped. Then the range is computed for the middle fifty percent of the cases. The formula is:

$$Q = Q_3 - Q_1$$

where Q = the interquartile range; Q_3 = third quartile value; and Q_1 = first quartile value. For instance, consider the distribution above. Since there are eight values in this distribution, each quartile will contain 25% of them, or two values. We, therefore, will drop the top two values and the bottom two values. This leaves the following distribution: 11, 15, 17, 18. The next step is to compute the range for these values. The range is 11 to 18 or 7. The interquartile range may, in some instances, eliminate the problem of a few extreme scores giving an unrepresentative picture of the variability in a distribution.

If the data involved are measured at the interval level, there are other measures of variation which take into consideration not only the order of the units but also the actual values. One of these measures is called the *mean deviation*. The basic idea of the mean deviation, as the name implies, is that the amount of variation in a distribution is expressed by computing a mean of the amounts by which the values differ or deviate from the mean. The mean deviation, thus, is the average amount by which each value differs from the mean of the distribution. This measure makes use of the idea that if the variability of the values is small, the numbers are bunched closely around the mean, but if the variability is large, the numbers deviate widely from the mean. The formula for mean deviation then is:

$$\text{Mean Deviation} = \frac{\Sigma |x - \bar{x}|}{n}$$

where | | indicates the absolute value (signs are ignored); x = the value of the variable; $\bar{x}$ = the mean of the sample; and n = total number of cases.

To compute the mean deviation you would first compute the deviations, or the degree to which each value differs from the mean of the total distribution. Then, as in the formula for the mean, you divide by the number of entries. Therefore, the first step is to compute the mean of the distribution. Consider the following distribution: 2, 5, 10, 7, 6. The mean is $\frac{\Sigma x}{n}$, or 2 + 5 + 10 + 7 + 6/5 = 6. The next step is to compute the amount by which each value deviates from the mean value. Assuming we are dealing with a sample, we would indicate these calculations by $x - \bar{x}$. In this example

$$\begin{aligned} x - \bar{x} = \quad & 2 - 6 = -4 \\ & 5 - 6 = -1 \\ & 10 - 6 = 4 \\ & 7 - 6 = 1 \\ & 6 - 6 = 0 \end{aligned}$$

To compute the mean of these deviations, we would want to add up the value of the deviations and then divide by the number of entries. But as you can easily see, these deviations would sum to 0. This will always be the case since, by definition, the mean is the midpoint of the distribution of values, and some deviations will be negative and some positive. These deviations will always cancel each other out and adding them will always result in 0. One way to get around this problem is simply to ignore the signs. In this case the mean of the absolute deviations will equal (4 + 1 + 4 + 1 + 0)/5 = 10/5 = 2. This value is called the mean deviation. The larger it is, the larger is the variability of values in the distribution. This measure tells us that on the average, the values in this distribution vary from the mean by 2. The advantage of the mean deviation is that it has a direct intuitive meaning. The disadvantage is that since we have altered the values by ignoring the signs, it cannot easily be used in any other algebraic manipulations. For this

242 DESCRIBING THE DATA

and for other reasons which we will consider later, the mean deviation is rarely used, although it may be useful for the purpose of simply describing a distribution.

The measure of variation which is most frequently used with interval data is called the *standard deviation*. The first steps in computing a standard deviation are the same as those for the mean deviation. First the mean of the distribution is computed, and then the mean is subtracted from each of the values to determine the deviations. The difference between the mean deviation and the standard deviation concerns the problem of the deviations summing to 0. To compute the standard deviation, the deviations from the mean are squared instead of ignoring the signs. As you may recall from algebra, when two negative numbers are multiplied, the results are positive. To return to the example above, you would have the following: $(-4)^2 + (-1)^2 + (4)^2 + (1)^2 + (0)^2 = 16 + 1 + 16 + 1 + 0 = 34$. Then this quantity would be divided by the number of values in the distribution: $34/5 = 6.8$. This quantity is called the *variance* of a distribution. The final step in computing a standard deviation is to adjust for the fact that the values have been squared. To do this it is necessary to take the square root of the variance. Therefore, in this case, the standard deviation would equal $\sqrt{6.8}$ or 2.61 (S.D. = $\sqrt{v} = \sqrt{6.8} = 2.61$). As with the mean deviation, if the standard deviation is small, the values in the distribution are concentrated near the mean. If the standard deviation is large, the values are spread over considerable distances from the mean. Unlike the mean deviation, the standard deviation can be used in further statistical manipulations, as you will see in the next chapter. In summary then, the calculation of the standard deviation is given by the following formula

$$s = \sqrt{\Sigma(x - \bar{x})^2/n}$$

The symbol s indicates the standard deviation of a sample; σ indicates the standard deviation of a population.

With the exception of the mode, the measures of central tendency and measures of variation have produced a single number which summarize the distribution of values for a single variable. Now let us consider how we can describe more fully the distribution of values by creating frequency distributions. Once again we must consider the level of measurement when discussing frequency distributions.

FREQUENCY DISTRIBUTIONS: NOMINAL AND ORDINAL DATA

With both nominal and ordinal data, you may want to describe the distribution of values more precisely than a measure of central tendency or measure of variation permits. If the number of categories is not large, it is possible to go beyond the use of summary measures like the mode, median, and range to present a picture of exactly how the cases are distributed among the various values. This precise picture of the distribution is called a frequency distribution. The simplest kind of frequency distribution for both nominal and ordinal data is computed simply by counting the number of cases in each category. For example, a frequency distribution for party identification might look like Table 10-1. Depending on how you intend to use the table, you may or may not wish to exclude those cases whose party identification you do not know. If you wish to examine how people distribute themselves between the two major parties, then the "Other or None" category, and perhaps even the "Independent" category, could be dropped. But if your purpose, for example, is to demonstrate the decline in party identification in America, then it would be better to retain all the categories. In this, as in most decisions which must be made in doing research, there is no absolute guideline or answer. You must always consider what you think will be best given the questions you are asking and the resources available to you. That is why your research must be thoroughly planned before the data are collected. All statistics are meaningless if the data have been collected or organized incorrectly.

Table 10-1 Hypothetical frequency distribution of party ID

Democrat	Republican	Independent	Others or None
425	150	225	75

It is often more useful to express frequency distributions in terms of percentages rather than in the actual numbers of cases in each category. This is so because the percentages make it easier for you to compare frequency distributions which are based on different-sized samples. For example, you may want to compare the distribution of party identification in Table 10-1 to the distribution which was reported in research ten years earlier (see Table 10-2). Table 10-1 had 875 cases. Let us assume that the earlier research had been based on a sample of 1000. Try to compare these two distributions. As you can see, it is difficult to determine changes in the

Table 10-2 Hypothetical frequency distribution of party ID, 1969 and 1979

	Democrat	Republican	Independent	Others or None
1979	425	150	225	75
1969	510	320	150	20

244 DESCRIBING THE DATA

distribution because of the different sample sizes. Now let us transform these numbers into percentages by dividing the number in each category by the total number of entries in the sample (for example, 425/875, 150/875, and so forth) and multiply by 100. Now let us compare the two distributions (see Table 10-3).

Table 10-3 Hypothetical frequency distribution of party ID, 1969 and 1979, in percentages

	Democrat	Republican	Independent	Others or None
1979	48%	17%	26%	8%
	(425)	(150)	(225)	(75)
1969	51%	32%	15%	2%
	(510)	(320)	(150)	(20)

Now it becomes quite clear that there have been two major changes in the hypothetical distribution of party identification in the ten years between 1969 and 1979. The number of Republicans has declined and the number of Independents has increased. You should always include the actual frequencies with the percentages. A percentage based on 30 cases is obviously less valid than one based on 1,000 cases, and your readers should be told how many cases are involved.

You may also want to give a graphic picture of the frequency distribution. You may do this by developing a *bar graph*, or *histogram*. A bar graph is composed of a bar for each of the categories in the distribution. The height of the bar corresponds to the number of cases in that category. For instance, for the 1979 data on party identification, see Figure 10-1. Another

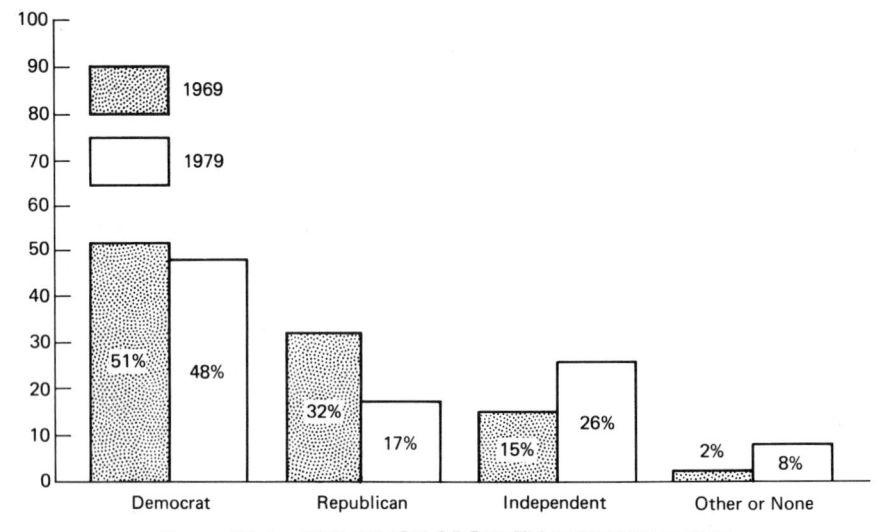

Figure 10-1 BAR GRAPH OF PARTY IDENTIFICATION

way to present the data graphically is to prepare pie-shaped graphs in which the sizes of the "slices" correspond to the number of cases in the categories (see Figure 10-2). Newspapers often use a pie-shaped graph to illustrate the government's budgetary allocations.

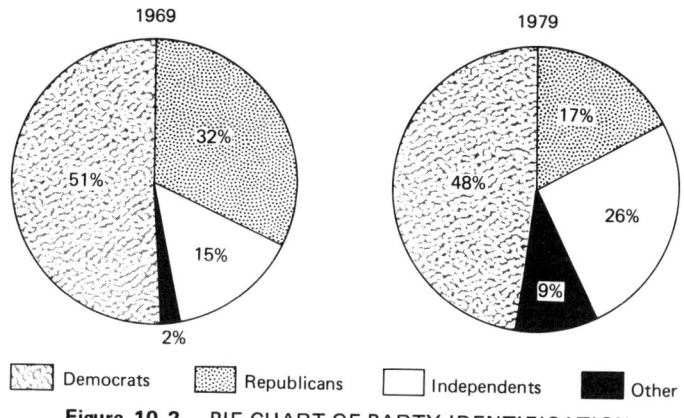

Figure 10-2 PIE CHART OF PARTY IDENTIFICATION

FREQUENCY DISTRIBUTION: INTERVAL DATA

When a measuring instrument exists which permits the specification of the exact number of intervals which differentiate the cases, it will usually be useless to try to construct frequency distributions for the number of cases in each category. This is so because there will probably be few cases in each category and the resulting frequency distribution, whether based on actual numbers of cases or percentages, will probably be too large and unwieldy to be of much use. Consider, for instance, a frequency distribution of exact income levels for 1,000 people. There is a good possibility that there would be 1,000 different income levels. One solution to this problem is to group the data so that it could be handled exactly as nominal or ordinal data. For instance, in the example of income, we might create the following categories of income levels: 0–$5,000, $5,001–$10,000, $10,001–$15,000, and so forth. The categories you create will depend once again on your particular research purposes. A small number of categories is easier to conceptualize and easier to picture graphically. But to create such a small number of categories you will inevitably be throwing away much information. You would obviously have much more precise information on the income level of an individual if you had developed income categories based on $1,000 intervals (0–$1,000, $1,001–$2,000) than if you had used $5,000 intervals as in our example. If you do construct categories, you may compute frequency distributions, using either absolute numbers or percen-

246 DESCRIBING THE DATA

tages, as you would with nominal and ordinal data. You could also, therefore, picture the data distribution by bar graphs or pie-shaped graphs.

If, on the other hand, you do not group interval data, bar graphs will not be of much use to you since you will need a separate bar for each exact measurement. Instead of picturing interval data by a graph composed of a large number of separate bars, interval data is graphically presented by a line graph. A line graph is based on the same principle as a bar graph. If a variable is measured by a continuous scale, such as time, temperature, or income, there would have to be an infinite number of bars included in a bar graph of that variable. In a line graph, a line is drawn to approximate the top of an infinite number of bars. For instance, consider the bar graph in Figure 10-3. We could also picture this distribution by a line graph (Figure 10-4).

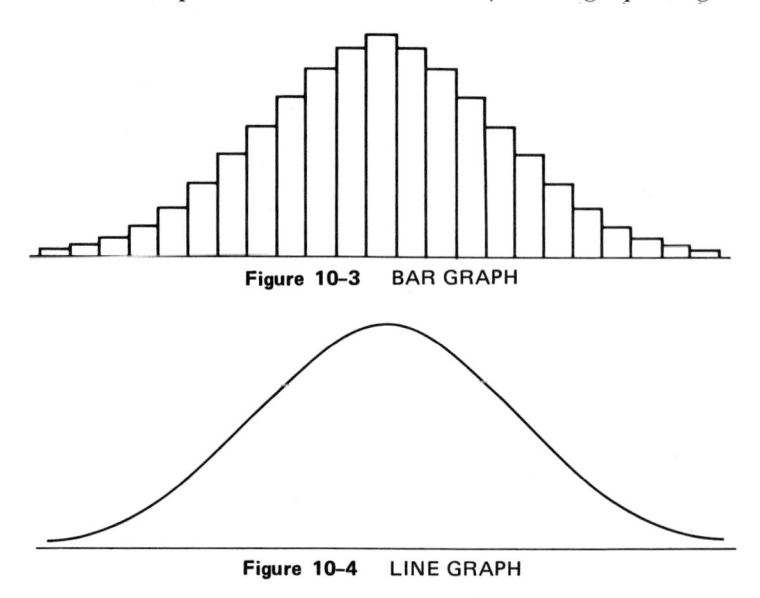

Figure 10-3   BAR GRAPH

Figure 10-4   LINE GRAPH

Variables, such as income, which might take on any value, are called *continuous variables*. Variables for which all values are not possible are called *discrete variables*. In the example above, party identification is a discrete variable, that is, it can take on only four values: Republican, Democrat, Independent, and Other. Other examples of discrete variables are number of children (one can have 1, 2, 3, etc., but not 1.63), marital status (you are or you aren't), and so forth. Where there are limited values, the bar graph can be used to represent the values. For a continuous variable, such as income or temperature, this would be impractical, and in those cases a line graph is used.

In a bar graph, the area of the bar represents the number of cases in that particular category. In a line graph, the area under the curve represents the frequency with which those values occur (the probability that a variable will assume values in that particular interval). For example, if we have a distribution such as in Figure 10-5, the shaded area represents the

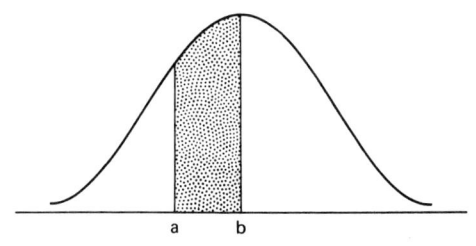

Figure 10-5 PROBABILITY DISTRIBUTION

probability that the variable with this distribution will assume a value between a and b. This distribution is called a probability distribution because of the information it gives you about the probabilities of particular values occurring. This particular characteristic of probability distributions will become important later when we discuss hypothesis testing.

A special kind of probability distribution is called a *normal curve*. A normal curve is a perfect, symmetrical, bell-shaped curve which is completely determined by its mean and its standard deviation. Such is not the case with curves which are *skewed*. By skewed we mean that there are extreme values on one end of the curve or the other (see Figure 10-6). If the

Positively Skewed   Negatively Skewed
Figure 10-6 SKEWED DISTRIBUTIONS

extreme cases are on the right tail, the curve is said to be positively skewed. If the extreme cases are on the left tail the curve is negatively skewed. One way to determine if and in what direction the curve is skewed is to compare the mean and the median for the distribution. The extreme scores will pull the mean in the direction of the skewness. The median, since it is not based on values, will be unaffected by the extreme scores. Therefore, if a curve is positively skewed, the mean will be larger than the median, and if the curve is negatively skewed, the mean will be smaller than the median. In a sym-

248 *DESCRIBING THE DATA*

metrical distribution the mean and the median will coincide (see Figure 10-7).

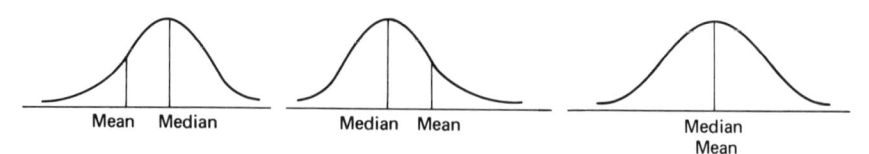

Figure 10-7 SHAPE OF DISTRIBUTIONS AND RELATIONSHIP OF MEDIAN AND MEAN

Thus far we have been considering how we can summarize and describe the distribution of a single variable. We will often want to display and compare more than one variable simultaneously. To do this it is necessary to construct a table. Such tables are called *cross-tabulation tables*, or *contingency tables* (crosstabs for short). Let us consider some of the guidelines to keep in mind when constructing tables to display the distributions of two or more variables.

CONSTRUCTING CROSS-TABULATION OR CONTINGENCY TABLES

In the first place, let us consider some of the terminology which is used in discussing tables. Let us start by looking at the very simplest form of cross-tabulation or contingency table in which you are dealing with two variables, each of which has two values. Such a table is often called a 2 × 2 table (Table 10-4). Cases which have a value of 1 for both variable x and variable y are classified together and counted. The number of such cases is put in the box in the upper left corner of the table. Those cases with a value of 1 for variable y and 2 for variable x are counted, and the number is put in the box in the upper right corner of the table. This process is repeated for those with a value of 2 for variable y and 1 for variable x the number being placed in the lower left box, and those with a value of 2 for both variable y and x the number being placed in the lower right box. Each of these boxes is called a *cell*. The total number of cases which have a value of 1 for variable y (the total number of cases in the top row of the table) is listed to the right of the top row. The total number of cases in each column is also listed at the bottom of that column. That is, the number of cases with a value of 1 for variable x is listed at the bottom of the column headed by 1, and the total with a value of 2 for variable x is listed at the bottom of the column headed by 2. These totals of row and column frequencies are called the *marginals* of the table, since they are listed on the margins.

Table 10-4 2 X 2 table

		Variable x (Independent) 1	Variable x (Independent) 2	
Variable y (Dependent)	1	Cell a	Cell c	Marginal
Variable y (Dependent)	2	Cell b	Cell d	Marginal
		Marginal	Marginal	N = Total

Such tables are often constructed for other purposes than just picturing the distribution of values on two variables. Such tables can also be used as one way of testing hypotheses. A hypothesis, remember, is a testable statement which specifies the relationship between two variables. To establish a relationship between two variables you must observe that the values on the variables change together, or covary in some pattern or order. If an increase of the values of one variable coincides with an increase in the values of the other, the relationship is said to be *positive*. If the values of one variable increase as the values of the other decrease, the relationship is said to be *negative*. In political science we do not usually have data which permits us to see changes in the values of variables. This is so because the data are gathered at one point in time. Therefore, all we can do is observe if cases with high values in one variable also consistently tend to have high values (positive relationship) or low values (negative relationship) on another variable.

If we are using a cross-table to test hypotheses, there are certain things to keep in mind in setting up the table. The row variable, which is always indicated by y as in our example, is always the dependent variable of the hypothesis. That is, that variable is the one which is believed to change in response to changes in another variable. The column variable, which is always indicated by x as in our example, is always the independent variable. That is, it is the variable which is believed to have an effect on the dependent variable.

In such a table the absolute frequencies should always be transformed into percentages. This is so because you will want to compare the distributions of both variables, and, as we noted above, it is always easier to use percentages rather than absolute numbers, especially if the groups to be compared are of different sizes. Let us now consider the steps you should follow to set up a percentage distribution table for the purpose of testing a hypothesis.

The first step would be to determine a hypothesized relationship. For example, let us hypothesize that the higher the income level, the greater the tendency to vote Republican. It may seem obvious to you that you would first specify a hypothesis and then seek confirmation, but there may be times when you would be tempted to construct tables to search for relationships. This "fishing expedition" may be acceptable in exploratory research. However, you cannot know if the relationships discovered in this way are anything more than a lucky discovery from the particular data available to you. By specifying the hypothesis prior to examining the data you have the extra verification of your theory to substantiate your findings.

The second step is to divide the data into the separate values of the independent variable. In our hypothesis, let us categorize income level as high, medium, and low. Of course, we must operationalize high, medium, and low, for example, $25,000+, $10–25,000, and $10,000−. If there were 875 people in our sample, we might find that 175 of them have a high income, 569 of them have a medium income, and 131 have a low income. You would examine the distribution of values of the dependent variable in each of the categories of the independent variable. That is, we could start by examining the distribution of party identification for the 175 people with a high income. Then we could examine the distribution of party identification among the 569 people with medium income and, finally, among the 131 with low income.

If we believe that different income levels are related to party identification, we should expect to find that the distribution of values of the dependent variable differ in each category of the independent variable. Therefore, the next step is to compare these three separate distributions, one for each category of the independent variable. Since each category of the independent variable has a different number of cases, we should transform the actual distribution into percentages to make it easier to compare the distributions in the three categories. To transform the data into percentages, we would simply divide the actual number of cases in each group by the total number of cases in that category of the independent variable and multiply by 100. Let us consider how these last two steps would be performed on our hypothetical data. First we look at the actual distribution in each category of the independent variable.

High Income	Medium Income	Low Income
131 Republican	228 Republican	26 Republican
35 Democrat	312 Democrat	99 Democrat
9 Independent or Other	29 Independent or Other	6 Independent or Other
175	569	131

Next we would transform each of those values into a percentage. For example, we would divide the number of high-income Republicans by the total number of high-income respondents (131/175 x 100 = 75%) and so on throughout each grouping. That would result in the following distribution:

High Income	Medium Income	Low Income
75% Republican	40% Republican	20% Republican
20% Democrat	55% Democrat	75% Democrat
5% Independent or Other	5% Independent or Other	5% Independent or Other
100%	100%	100%

The final step, then, is to place these three groupings together in Table 10-5. Notice that in this table the dependent variable is the row variable and the independent variable is the column variable. This is the way we previously specified how to arrange a table. Also notice that the table includes the number of cases in each column so that the reader knows exactly the number of cases on which these percentages were based.

Table 10-5 Hypothetical cross-table

Party Indentification	Income Level		
	High	Medium	Low
Republican	75%	40%	20%
Democrat	20%	55%	75%
Independent or Other	5%	5%	5%
Total Percent	100%	100%	100%
Sample Size	(175)	(569)	(131)

The most difficult part of constructing tables is yet to come: interpreting them. Up to now, the process has been purely mechanical. The interpretation requires your informed judgment as to whether the table does show the relationship you hypothesized to exist. The first part of the interpretation is simply to observe if, in fact, the percentage distributions do differ among the categories of the independent variable. Secondly, you should observe if the differences are in the direction you expected (hypothesized) them to be. Finally, you have to decide if the differences are large enough and consistent enough for you to be satisfied that your hypothesis has been supported by that data in the table. This final step is, of course, where your judgment comes into play, and there is no simple rule of thumb to guide your decision. You must have a realistic understanding that most relationships in the social sciences will not be perfect because of the effects of the many other variables which "get in the way" and befuddle the patterns we are attempting to discover. You must also not attempt to see relationships that do not exist just to save your hypothesis. What is called for here is hard-headed realism, based on your familiarity with your data, with prior research, and with your basic understanding of the phenomena in question. In the last two chapters of this section we will discuss statistical techniques which aid us in determining whether or not the relationships we observe are sufficient to support our hypotheses.

There are two other points we have to make about constructing tables: Be sure to divide the sample according to the categories of the independent variable, and then examine the distribution of the values of the dependent variable within each of those categories. This procedure is dictated by your initial hypothesis. You are arguing that the independent variable in some way affects the distribution of the dependent variable. Therefore, different categories of the independent variable should be characterized by different distributions of the dependent variable. In our example, we are saying that different income levels will have different distributions of party identification. Percentaging helps us examine these different distributions because percentaging actually controls for the different sizes of the categories we are comparing. By first dividing the cases according to the categories of the dependent variable and then looking for the distribution of the independent variable, we would actually be answering a different question. In our example, we would be asking if different party identifications are characterized by different income levels. This, in effect, has made party identification the independent variable. We would be implying that party identification affected how much money people make. This hypothesis is much less plausible than the one which implies income affects party identification. Since the percentages would then be based on the numbers in each category of party identification rather than each category of income, our final tables may look quite different. The point is you should first be very careful that your question asks precisely what you intended it to ask. Then you should always proceed by first dividing the sample according to the independent variable.

One final point should be made. Thus far, we have only discussed tables which display percentage distributions. If the dependent variable which you are studying has a large number of categories, it may be very cumbersome to look at the percentages within each of those categories. In that case you may want to use some measure of central tendency to summarize the distribution rather than looking at percentages. You should use the measure of central tendency which is appropriate for the level of measurement used for the dependent variable. The procedure for setting up such a table is the same as for creating a percentage table. First you should divide the sample according to the categories of the independent variable, and then examine the distribution of the dependent variable within each of those categories. The only difference is that the distribution of the dependent variable is expressed by the measure of central tendency (usually the median or the mean) rather than by percentages.

For instance, we might hypothesize that the form of urban government affects voter turnout. Since each city would probably have a unique voter turnout the mean could serve as a summary measure (see Table 10-6).

Table 10-6 Hypothetical cross-table using central tendency

	Type of Urban Government		
	Mayor	Commission	Manager
Mean Voter Turnout	42%	39%	23%
N	(191)	(23)	(203)

In this chapter we have examined ways of describing and summarizing distributions. We have also discussed some very elementary procedures for testing for relationships between two variables. The next chapter will consider in more depth the steps involved in the process of hypothesis testing. In particular, we will examine ways of attempting to eliminate the possibility that other factors have in fact affected the relationship we have specified between the independent and dependent variables.

SUMMARY
MEASURES OF CENTRAL TENDENCY

Level of Measurement	Statistic	Formula	Interpretation
Nominal	Mode		Value which appears most frequently
Ordinal	Median	$\dfrac{n+1}{2}$	Middle value
Interval	Mean	$\dfrac{\Sigma x}{n}$	Average value

SUMMARY
MEASURES OF VARIATION

Level of Measurement	Statistic	Formula	Interpretation
Ordinal	Range	high and low values	The extreme values in the distribution
Ordinal	Interquartile range	$Q = Q_3 - Q_1$	The end points of the middle 50% of cases
Interval	Mean deviation	$\dfrac{\Sigma \lvert x - \bar{x} \rvert}{n}$	Average amount by which values deviate from mean
Interval	Standard deviation	$s = \sqrt{\dfrac{\Sigma (x - \bar{x})^2}{n}}$	Average amount by which values deviate from mean

STUDY QUESTIONS

1. Give three examples of nominal, ordinal, and interval variables.
2. With what level of measurement would you use the median? mode? mean? Why might you sometimes report both the mean and median?
3. Find the mean, median, and mode for the following list of numbers: 1, 7, 5, 5, 2, 7, 3, 9, 6, 8.
4. What is the utility of the interquartile range?
5. Calculate the standard deviation for the following list of numbers: 1, 7, 5, 5, 2, 7, 3, 9, 6, 8.

Testing Hypotheses

Chapter Eleven

The primary function of statistics for a social scientist is to marshal evidence to support or to reject a statement of supposed relationship between two concepts. In other words, statistics are important to social scientists because they can help to test hypotheses. In actuality this chapter and the next two chapters will consider statistical techniques for establishing evidence that two phenomena are related. This chapter is entitled "Testing Hypotheses" not because it is the only chapter which is relevant to hypothesis testing, but because it will introduce you to the logic involved in phrasing hypotheses and in deciding whether to accept or reject a particular hypothesis.

    The most important thing to keep in mind before you accept a hypothesis is the question of whether there is some other explanation for the relationships you observe in your data. For instance, consider the hypothesis we were examining in the last chapter. We hypothesized that income level is related to party identification. When we examined the data in a cross-tabulation table, it was obvious that there was some pattern. High-income people were more likely to be Republicans, and low-income people were more likely to be Democrats. Before we accept the hypothesis that income level is related to party identification, we have to consider two other questions. In the first place we must ask if it is possible that the pattern we observed in that data was actually due to the influence of some other factor.

For instance, is it possible that some third variable, such as a higher occupational status, affects both the income level and the party identification of individuals. In that case, the relationship we think we observe in the data may be diagrammed income (A)→party identification (B), whereas the actual relationship may be diagrammed as follows

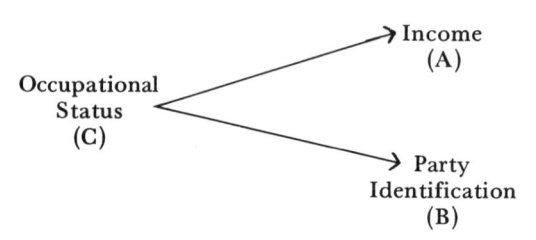

```
                              → Income
                                 (A)
         Occupational
           Status
             (C)
                              → Party
                                Identification
                                (B)
```

As occupation changes, it causes changes in both income and party identification. Therefore, both income and party identification vary together, even if they are not related to each other. The apparent relationship between income and party identification is in reality a *spurious* relationship. Before we can accept this relationship which we think was substantiated by the table, we have to attempt to reject the possibility that other factors are involved. Of course, it is impossible for any individual researcher to test for all of the alternative explanations. But all researchers should look for what they believe to be the most likely alternatives.

Secondly, we also have to consider if our observations are actually due to chance. In any set of data some of the variables will assume values that make it appear that there is a relationship when in fact there is not. This process is similar to what would happen if a monkey were put in front of a typewriter. There is a chance that he will type out a few meaningful words when actually he is doing nothing but pounding blissfully away at random. The reason why it is quite likely that we may get relationships where there really are none is that we generally study data from only a sample of the entire population.

Let us examine how sampling can make relationships seem to appear where there really is no relationship. In our example in the last chapter we found that of the 175 people with high income, 75% were Republican, and of the 131 people with low income, 75% were Democrats. This would seem to be fairly convincing evidence of a relationship between income and party identification. But we are dealing here with a sample of only 306 people, and we are presumably attempting to make statements about the population of the entire United States. Even if we have been very careful about drawing our sample randomly, there is still a possibility that, unbeknown to us, our sample is not representative of the population as a whole. Remember, we are dealing with variables which can assume differing values. And in the social sciences we almost never deal with universal statements. That is, we do not expect all rich people to be Republican and all poor people to be Democrats. We know that there will be a certain number of wealthy people who will have differing values on the variable of party identification. Therefore, we do not know if there really is a tendency for wealthy people to be Republican or if by chance we have drawn a sample which overrepresents the number of wealthy people who are Republican. If we were to accept the hypothesis that income is related to party identification we may be accepting a false hypothesis.

It is also possible that sampling error may result in our rejecting a true hypothesis. This is again due to the fact that we almost never deal with universal statements. We don't really expect all people with high income to be Republicans. We simply expect that a certain proportion of those with high income to be Republican. So, it is always possible that although there really is a tendency for people with high income to be Republican, we may see a disproportionate number of those who are not Republican due to sampling error, and, therefore, conclude there is no relationship between being rich and being a Republican. Rejecting a true hypothesis is known as a *Type I error,* and accepting a false hypothesis is known as a *Type II error.* Both types of error result from the effects of chance. We can never totally eliminate the possibility that what we are seeing is the result of chance, but we do have techniques which will be discussed in this chapter to determine the probability of chance.

Let us turn to discussing techniques we can use to try to eliminate the possibility that the relationship we observe may actually be due either to other factors or to chance.

ELIMINATING ALTERNATIVE EXPLANATIONS

The basic procedure used to eliminate the possible effect of other factors is to control for them. The simplest way to control for the effect of a variable is to transform it from a variable to a constant. Remember, the way we establish that two things are related is to observe that as the values of one change, the values of the other also change in some patterned way. If one of the variables has a constant value, and we still observe that the other variable assumes differing values, we would have to conclude there is no relationship. Let us return to our example of income and party identification to see how this basic principle can be used to eliminate alternative explanations for the relationship we think we are observing.

In our example we noticed that those people with high income tended to be Republicans and those with low income tended to be Democrat. We did not know if this relationship was actually due to the fact that a third variable, occupational status, was changing and causing the simultaneous change in both income and party identification. If we examined people who all had identical occupational status and we still observed a positive relationship, then we could safely conclude that occupation could not possibly be affecting the relationship.

There are various statistical procedures for controlling the effects of a third variable, the simplest of which is to divide the sample into groups with the same levels of occupational status. Then if income and party identification are still related within those groups, we can conclude that the relationship is not due to occupational status. (Although it still may, of course, be due to some other factor.) Let us look at some hypothetical examples of what may happen when we control for the effect of a third variable. First let us look at the relationship between income and party identification for some hypothetical data, without controlling for occupational status (see Table 11-1). Now let us

Table 11-1 Hypothetical relationship between income and party identification

	High Income	Low Income
Republican	75%	25%
Democrat	25%	75%
	100%	100%
	(55)	(105)

look at the relationship when we control for the effect of occupation by dividing the sample into groups which have homogeneous occupational status (see Table 11-2).

Table 11-2 Hypothetical relationship between income and party identification with occupation controlled—I

	High Occupational Status Income		Low Occupational Status Income	
	High	Low	High	Low
Republican	75%	25%	75%	25%
Democrat	25%	75%	25%	75%
	100%	100%	100%	100%
	(20)	(50)	(35)	(55)

It is obvious that occupational status has no effect on the relationship between income and party identification since the relationship remains strong even when the effect of occupation is controlled by holding it constant. (Of course it is highly unlikely, to put it mildly, that your data will ever be as clear as our hypothetical data here.)

Another possible result of controlling for a third variable is the disappearance of an observed relationship. For example, when we control for occupational status, we might see the following result (see Table 11-3).

Table 11-3 Hypothetical relationship between income and party identification with occupation controlled—II

	High Occupational Status Income		Low Occupational Status Income	
	High	Low	High	Low
Republican	75%	75%	25%	25%
Democrat	25%	25%	75%	75%
	100%	100%	100%	100%
	(20)	(50)	(35)	(55)

In this case it appears that the real determinant of party identification is occupation rather than income. Those with high occupational status are Republicans and those with low occupational status are Democrats, regardless of their income levels. The apparent relationship between income and party identification is shown to be spurious.

It is also possible that the control can in some way mask an actual relationship between the variables we are examining. If the effect of the confounding variable is strong, and if the effect is in a direction which is opposite to that of the independent variable, it is possible that controlling for the third variable may disclose a relationship which could not previously be observed or even reverse the original relationship which we observed. And, finally, it is also possible that each table produced by controlling for a third variable may display a different pattern. This would indicate that the overall relationship which we found in Table 11-1 is really a composite of two distinct relationships (see Table 11-4). By controlling for occupation we can

Table 11-4 Hypothetical relationship between income and party identification with occupation controlled—III

	High Occupational Status Income		Low Occupational Status Income	
	High	Low	High	Low
Republican	50%	50%	88%	2%
Democrat	50%	50%	12%	98%
	100%	100%	100%	100%
	(20)	(50)	(35)	(55)

see that each of our control subgroups exhibit different relationships between income (the independent variable) and party identification (the dependent variable). For people with high occupational status, income has no effect on party identification. On the other hand, for those with low occupational status, income has a marked effect on party identification.

In each of these examples, we are attempting to understand more fully the relationship which exists among the variables. We recognize that human behavior is affected by many factors. To understand these relationships we have to proceed one step at a time and examine each factor in turn. To do this we have to try to cancel out the influences of the other factors. Controlling in cross-tabulation tables is one way we attempt to cancel out the effect of other variables. Our examples control for only one variable. Theoretically, it is possible to control for many variables at one time. Practically, however, there are some serious limitations. In the first place, once we start to break down our sample into subsamples we may be faced with some tables with very few entries. It may often be the case that some cells of the tables will have no entries. It is obviously very difficult to make trustworthy generalizations based on tables with so few cases. This means that it is usually impossible to control for more than one variable at a time, unless we have a very large sample. A second problem concerns the interpretation of the tables. If the control variable has many categories or if we are controlling for more than one variable, we will undoubtedly be faced with a large number of tables. Such a wealth of data may well be overwhelming, and it may be difficult to sort out exactly what you have. One strategy which can be used to decrease the number of cells and increase the population in each cell is to collapse our categories. In our examples above, income has only two values—high and low. We may have begun with more than two categories, such as (1) less than $2,000, (2) $2,000–$3,999, (3) $4,000–$5,999, etc. By taking a cutoff point, for example $20,000, as the dividing line between high and low income categories and by collapsing many categories into two, interpretation is simplified. Fortunately there are other statistical procedures which can be used to control other variables. Since these techniques require interval level data we will delay a discussion of them until Chapter Thirteen.

Let us now turn to ways to evaluate the possibility that the relationship you observe is not due to other factors, but to chance.

THE EFFECTS OF CHANCE

To understand the problems that chance may cause for a social scientist, you must understand two things. In the first place, we deal with probabilistic relationships. This means that as the value of one variable changes, the value of another variable *tends* to change. But not all wealthy people vote Republican; only a certain proportion of them do so. Secondly, we rarely have the luxury of examining data on the whole population in which we are interested. When we say that wealthy people are Republican, we do not have data on all wealthy people in the United States today, let alone all people who have ever been or ever will be wealthy in this country.

Let us consider what is the effect of these factors. We make a hypothesis that A⟶B (the greater a peoples' wealth, the more likely they will vote Republican). We sample among the population of the United States. From this sample we look at all the wealthy people and ascertain if they voted Republican. If we observe what seems to be an inordinate number of wealthy people who vote Republican (say, 75%), we accept our hypothesis. If there seems to be no pattern in party identification among the wealthy (say, 50% Republican and 50% Democratic), we reject the hypothesis.

In both of these cases we may be making a mistake. Consider this: Despite the fact that we had religiously followed all the guidelines in drawing a random sample, we still have a certain probability of getting an unrepresentative sample. This probability is known as *sampling error*. Therefore, although being wealthy may not be related to being Republican, there is a certain probability that when we drew a sample from among the wealthy we happened to get an inordinate amount of those who happen to be Republican. And, likewise, although being wealthy may actually be related to voting Republican, we may have had the misfortune of drawing another sample of wealthy people who overrepresented those few who vote Democrat. All of this means that since we deal with samples and probabilistic statements we are limited to making inferences about relations. In fact, the statistics which help us in drawing these inferences are called *inferential statistics*. Let us consider the logic involved in these inferential statistics.

Consider the problems of estimating a mean income on the basis of a sample of a population. For simplicity, let us consider a population of only five people. Let us assume these five people have the following incomes: $5,000, $7,000, $10,000, $15,000, $25,000. The real mean of the income levels of this population is

$$\frac{\$5,000 + \$7,000 + \$10,000 + \$15,000 + \$25,000}{5} = \$12,400.$$

Now let us assume that we have decided for the purposes of efficiency we want to estimate this population mean on the basis of a sample of two people. (Obviously, in the real world there would be no need to sample with a population of five.) If we are very conscientious and do a simple random sample, each of the five people has an equal chance of being selected for the sample. That means that each of the five has a known chance of being paired with each of the other four people.

The total of all possible groups of two, selected from the five people, is the number of *permutations*. When we say all possible groups of two, we mean that we are considering each ordering of the two as a separate pair. For example, if we are considering groups of two letters chosen from the first five letters of the alphabet, we would count ab as one pair and ba as a second pair. In the case of the first five letters of the alphabet, there are 20 possible permutations: ab, ba, ac, ca, ad, da, ae, ea, bc, cb, bd, db, be, eb, cd, dc, ce, ec, de, ed. We have five choices when we pick the first letter: a, b, c, d, or e. But once one letter has been picked, we have only four choices remaining. Therefore, the number of permutations equals the number of initial choices (5) multiplied by the number of second choices (4) or 20. The general rule is that the number of permutations of a certain size, indicated by r, chosen from a set of n objects, is indicated by the following formula:

$$n(n-1)(n-2)\ldots(n-r+1)$$

In our example, n is 5, and $n-1$ is 4. The end term in the formula $(n-r+1)$ is also equal to $4(5-2+ = 3+1 = 4)$. Therefore, 5×4, or 20, is the number of possible permutations of two objects selected from five objects.

In most cases in political science, as with our example of estimating mean income, we are not concerned with the number of permutations. We only want to know how many ways the various units can be combined. That is, we are not interested in whether the order is ab or ba. We only want to know the odds of getting a and b together in a sample, regardless of the order. The pairing of a and b when we are not concerned with the order is called a *combination*. To determine the number of combinations, let us look again at the example of the first five letters of the alphabet. There were 20 permutations of two letters selected from five letters. But since we will now not be interested in the order of a particular sample, we will only have ten combinations. That is, instead of counting each of those pairings twice it will be counted only once. Therefore, to find the number of combinations we can divide the number of permutations (20) by 2. In general, the number of combinations can be calculated by the following formula:

$$\frac{n(n-1)\ldots(n-r+1)}{r!}$$

where n = size of population; r = size of sample; and $r!$ signifies r factorial which can also be written $r(r-1)(r-2)\ldots(1)$. In this example $r = 2$, $(r-1) = 1$ which is the last number used in the series. Therefore, $r(r-1) = 2(1) = 2$. The denominator, then, is 2. The numerator for this equation is the same as that for permutations discussed above. We found in our example that the numerator was 20. Thus, if we continue our example of estimating the mean income of a population of five on the basis of a sample of two we discover ten possible combinations.

$$\frac{5 \cdot 4}{2 \cdot 1} = \frac{20}{2} = 10.$$

These ten possible combinations follow:

$5,000 + \$ 7,000$ $7,000 + \$10,000$ $10,000 + \$15,000$ $15,000 + \$25,000$
$5,000 + \$10,000$ $7,000 + \$15,000$ $10,000 + \$25,000$
$5,000 + \$15,000$ $7,000 + \$25,000$
$5,000 + \$25,000$

Let us now calculate the means of each of these samples.

$$\frac{5,000 + 7,000}{2} = 6,000 \qquad \frac{7,000 + 15,000}{2} = 11,000$$

$$\frac{5,000 + 10,000}{2} = 7,500 \qquad \frac{7,000 + 25,000}{2} = 16,000$$

$$\frac{5,000 + 15,000}{2} = 10,000 \qquad \frac{10,000 + 15,000}{2} = 12,500$$

$$\frac{5,000 + 25,000}{2} = 15,000 \qquad \frac{10,000 + 25,000}{2} = 17,500$$

$$\frac{7,000 + 10,000}{2} = 8,500 \qquad \frac{15,000 + 25,000}{2} = 20,000$$

The first thing you should notice is that there is no way, if we chose a sample of only two, that we would know the precise mean of the population. But the important question is, how accurately can we estimate the population mean based on these samples. Let us say, for instance, that you are willing to allow your estimate to be within ± $2,000 of the actual mean of the five individuals. Let us see how many of the sample means vary by $2,000 or less from the population mean. Two out of ten of these means fall within a range of ± $2,000 from the actual population mean of $12,400: $11,000 and $12,500. This means that you have two chances out of ten of estimating the population mean within ± $2,000. The two chances out of ten are called the *confidence level*. This is how confident you are of making an estimate which is accurate within ± $2,000. The ± $2,000 interval is called the *confidence interval*. There are four more cases which deviate between approximately $2,000 and $4,000 from the actual population mean: $8,500, $16,000, $10,000, and $15,000. There are two more which deviate between $4,000 and $6,000 from the population mean: $7,500 and $17,500. And, finally, there are two which deviate more than ± $6,000 from the actual mean: $6,000 and $20,000.

Given this distribution, six of the ten estimates are within ± $4,000 of the actual population mean; eight of the ten estimates are within ± $6,000 of the actual mean; and two of ten are more than $6,000 away from the actual mean. This means that as you increase your confidence intervals, that is, as you agree to tolerate the possibility of a larger error, you also increase your confidence level. You can be very sure of estimating the population mean within $6,000 but less sure of being within $2,000.

Let us recapitulate. We know that we have a population of five individuals with a given distribution of income levels and a given mean income level. We know that when we take a sample of two from this population, there are ten possible combinations of two which are possible. When we compute the mean from each of the ten possible samples, we get a distribution of means. This distribution of sample means is called a *sampling distribution*, since it is a distribution of statistics derived from samples chosen from a population. By examining this sampling distribution we can say something about the probability that a mean derived from a sample will approximate the actual population mean.

This is the basic process involved in determining whether the results you have achieved in testing your hypothesis have been due to chance or not. First you phrase your hypothesis. Then you draw your sample and compute whatever statistics you desire. Next you compare your results to a sampling distribution to determine the chances of getting a result like that. You need not worry about calculating the sampling distribution each time you want to determine if your results are due to chance. Fortunately for us, others have already computed a variety of differing sampling distributions for use with differing statistics and differing levels of measurement. In this chapter we will discuss the use of three of these distributions in hypothesis testing: the *normal curve distribution*, the *chi square distribution*, and the *t distribution*. Let us examine the use of these in turn to illustrate more concretely the steps involved in calculating the effect of chance in testing hypotheses.

THE NORMAL CURVE SAMPLING DISTRIBUTION

So far we have been using a fairly unrealistic example for the sake of simplicity. It is hard to imagine a case in which you would take a sample from a population of only five. But it is easy to think of cases where you may want to test hypotheses concerning means. Therefore, we will continue with the example of mean income level in this section. Let us assume that you are doing an investigation of the effect of a social service program in your state. As part of this investigation you wish to know if the particular program has raised the income level in a certain low-income area. Let us assume that the average yearly income level before the program was $8,500 for a family of four. After the program had been in effect for four years, a sample was taken and the mean income level of that sample was $10,500.

Now the question is this: Is the change from $8,500 to $10,500 really the result of change in income in the area or is it actually due to the effect of chance operating on the particular combination of individuals chosen for the two samples? We can never answer this important question absolutely. But what we can do is determine the probability of getting a difference this large. If it appears that the odds for such a difference are slim, we have to decide if we are willing to risk concluding that a change has really occurred.

To determine the probability of getting a mean income level of $10,500 from a sample despite the fact the actual mean is still $8,500, you would have to examine a sampling distribution as we did in the previous section. If we are dealing, as we are in this example, with a variable which can assume a continuous number of values, that is, if the variable is measured at the interval level, it is possible to assume that the shape of the distribution will be a normal bell curve. But the distribution of sample means will be different for different distributions of income. Let us see why this is the case. In our example above, the income distribution was $5,000, $7,000, $10,000, $15,000 and $25,000. The sampling distribution of sample means was $6,000, $7,500, $8,500, $10,000, $11,000, $12,500, $15,000, $16,000, $17,500, and $20,000. The mean of this sampling distribution is $12,400, the same as the mean of the distribution itself. *The mean of the sampling distribution always equals the mean of the distribution.*

Let us assume you have another population of five people with the following income distribution: $4,000, $5,000, $6,000, $7,000, and $8,000. The actual mean of this distribution is $6,000. If we draw samples of two from this distribution and calculated the sample means, we would have the following sampling distribution: $4,500, $5,000, $5,500, $5,500, $6,000, $6,000, $6,500, $6,500, $7,000, and $7,500. The sampling distributions are different because the actual population distributions are different.

Because the sampling distributions are different, the probabilities associated with drawing a sample with a particular mean income are different. For instance, let us assume for some reason you want to know the probability of getting a sample mean between $4,500 and $6,500. In the first sampling distribution we computed, which we will refer to as distribution A, only one sample mean was in this range; so the probability is one in ten. In the second sampling distribution, which we will refer to as distribution B, eight of the sample means were in this range; so the probability is eight in ten. The probability associated with drawing a sample with a particular mean income is determined by the nature of the income distribution in the population.

It would obviously be very cumbersome to have to develop a different sampling distribution for each distribution of values for every separate variable. To avoid this, statisticians have developed ways to express scores so that the probability of their occurrence can be compared, even if the scores come from different sampling distributions. The way this is done is by standardizing the scores. Once scores are standardized, it is possible to compare all scores to one sampling distribution which is called the *standard normal distribution*.

Let us examine how we can standardize scores to use the standard normal distribution. We will use the two distributions above as a base for our discussion. The probability of getting a sample with a mean of $7,500 is different for each distribution. Somehow we want to express the score of $7,500 in a way that we can compare the probability of that score occurring in each separate distribution. The first thing we can do is to examine the relationship of the score to the means of sampling distributions. In the first place, we notice that on distribution A, $7,500 is below the mean, and on distribution B, it is above the mean. That is, if you had an income of $7,500 in distribution B, you would be richer than average, and in distribution A, you would be poorer than average. Notice that by relating the score of $7,500 to the mean score of each distribution, we can start to analyze the meaning of that score on each distribution.

We can be even more precise and determine by exactly how much $7,500 varies from the means of the distributions. We can do this by subtracting each mean score from $7,500. For instance, on distribution A, $7,500 is $4,900 below the mean ($7,500−$12,400 = −$4,900). On distribution B, $7,500 is $1,500 above the mean ($7,500−$6,000 = $1,500). Now we have expressed the score of $7,500 in terms of the precise amount by which it deviates from the means of the two distributions. We know that $7,500 deviates by a much larger amount on distribution A than on distribution B. Therefore, it might make sense intuitively to conclude that the probability of $7,500 occurring as a sample mean is much less if the sample is drawn from distribution A with an actual mean of $12,400 than if the sample is drawn from distribution B with a mean of $6,000, since the size of the deviation from the mean is greater ($4,900 compared to $1,500).

The problem with accepting this intuitive conclusion is the fact that the variation in distribution A is much greater than in distribution B. The variance in the values of a distribution will affect how much the sample means can deviate from the mean of the distribution. If scores varied between $4,000 and $8,000, we would expect much less possible deviation between sample means and the distribution mean than if scores varied between $5,000 and $25,000. Therefore, by expressing the score $7,500 as the amount by which it deviates from a mean of a distribution, we have only taken the first step in standardizing the score. The second step is to find some way to determine how likely it is that a deviation of that size might occur. We must compare that deviation to a measure of variation for the distribution. Remember a measure of variation is the amount by which the values of a distribution vary. The most commonly used measure of variation for interval data is the standard deviation. Therefore, we can compare the deviation of the sample mean from the distribution mean to the standard deviation. We can compare the two by seeing how large the deviation is, compared to the standard deviation. To compare the sizes we can express the deviation as a proportion of the standard deviation.

Let us see what results we get when we compare the deviations of $7,500 from the sampling distribution means to the standard deviations of the distributions. The standard deviation of distribution A is $7,172. The deviation of $7,500 from the mean of the sampling distribution is $4,900. Thus, it is $\frac{4,900}{7,172}$ or about 0.68 of a standard deviation from the mean. The standard deviation of distribution B is $1,414. The deviation of $7,500 from the mean distribution B is 1,500 . It is, therefore, $\frac{1,500}{1,414}$ or 1.06 standard deviations from the mean. Originally, because the score of $7,500 deviates by a larger amount from the mean of the sampling distribution A than from the mean of sampling distribution B, we assumed the probability of drawing a sample with a mean of $7,500 from distribution A was less than drawing a sample with that mean from distribution B. But when we compare the actual size of those deviations to the "average" or standard deviations, we find that the $4,900 deviation is smaller than the average deviation in distribution A, while the $1,500 deviation is larger than the average deviation in distribution B. So, the probability of getting $7,500 as a sample mean in distribution B is less than the probability of getting that as a sample mean in distribution A.

Let us summarize what we have done here. First we have determined by how much a sample mean deviates from the mean of a distribution by subtracting the two ($\bar{x}-\mu$). Then we have tried to determine how this deviation compares to the average deviation of the distribution by expressing the deviation as a proportion of the standard deviation. That is, we divide the deviation by the standard deviation. This form of a standardized score is called a *z score*. The formula for a z score then is:

$$z = \frac{\bar{x} - \mu}{\sigma}$$

where $\bar{x}$ = the score being standardized (in this case we are examining the mean of a sample); μ = the mean of the distribution; and σ = the standard deviation of the distribution. Using a z score transformation converts all scores into a proportion of the standard deviation of the distribution. Since all scores are expressed in identical terms—as a proportion of the standard deviation—it is possible to compare scores, even though they may have come from different distributions.

Let us now return to our example of the social service investigation and see how we can use the z-score transformation to determine the probability that the mean income level has actually changed. If we hypothesized that in fact it had changed, we would have to specify exactly how much it had changed and the direction in which it had changed. Then we would calculate the probability of getting a sample mean of $10,500 from a population with the mean score we had hypothesized. Obviously, specifying the direction and degree of the change would be very difficult. Instead of hypothesizing the degree and direction of change, researchers take an easier route. They hypothesize that there has been no change, even if they believe, or want to believe, there has been a change. This hypothesis of no change is called the *null hypothesis*.

In our example, then, we would hypothesize that the mean income level has not changed and is still $8,500. Then we compute the z score for the sample value of $10,500. To do this we need to know the standard deviation. Since we will be referring to the standard normal table to determine the probability of chance affecting our relationship, we must use the standard deviation of that distribution. This distribution, remember, is a sampling distribution and is composed of the means of various samples chosen from a population. These means are estimates of the population mean. The degree to which they vary from the population mean, the standard deviation of the sampling distribution, is the amount of error you would make if you used those sample means to estimate the population mean. Therefore, the standard deviation of a sampling distribution is called the *standard error*. The standard error is calculated by dividing the standard deviation of the distribution by the square root of the sample size:

$$\frac{\sigma}{\sqrt{N}}$$

Therefore, when we are calculating a z score in order to compare it to the standard normal sampling distribution, the formula is:

$$Z = \frac{\bar{x} - \mu}{\sigma/\sqrt{N}}$$

where $\bar{x}$ = mean of the sample; μ = hypothesized mean of the population distribution; σ = standard deviation of the population distribution; and N = sample size. In this case we will assume this value is 2,000. Then the z score is $\frac{10,500 - 8,500}{2,000} = \frac{2,000}{2,000} = 1$. This means that the change observed in the second sample is equal to one standard deviation. In order to determine the probability of getting a score by chance which deviates by one standard deviation, we must compare the score to a sampling distribution of the standard normal curve. Before considering how to compare your z score to the sampling distribution, let us describe this distribution. This sampling distribution is a normal bell-shaped curve. Such a distribution is symmetrical. This means that one side of the distribution is identical to the other side. One-half of all sample means will be larger than or equal to the distribution mean, and they will be graphed on the right side of the curve. Half of the sample means will be smaller than or equal to the distribution mean, and they will be graphed on the left side of the curve.

When we use a standard normal sampling distribution we are primarily concerned with the tails of the distribution. The word tail refers to the extreme end of the distribution, as shown in Figure 11-1. Remember, the size of the area under the curve indicates the probability that a sample mean will have a value in that range. The small area under the tails of the curve indicates there is only a small chance that a sample will be drawn with a

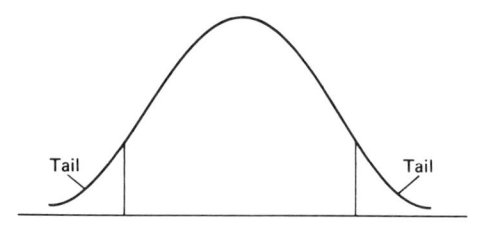

Figure 11-1 STANDARD NORMAL DISTRIBUTION.

sample mean that deviates by that amount from the distribution mean. What we want to know, basically, is how close to the tail our sample mean falls.

If we are interested in the probability of a mean deviating by that much in either direction, we would have to consider both tails of the curve. In our example, we are only interested in whether mean income had increased. That is, our hypothesis specifies the direction of the deviation in which we are interested. That means we only have to consider the one on the right, or positive side of the curve. When considering both tails of the curve in a test, it is called a *two-tailed test*. When considering only one tail, it is a *one-tailed test*.

Now let us get down to the nitty gritty of using the standard normal sampling distribution to test the null hypothesis that the social service program has not changed the income level among the target population. To use the sampling distribution we must first establish two things: what critical value we will use and whether we will use a one- or two-tailed test. The *critical value* is the probability level we will use to determine whether to accept or reject the null hypothesis. The critical value should be set before you examine your data or even before you gather your data. The most common level which is used by political and social scientists is 0.05. In other words, only if a particular result could have occurred by chance in 5% or less of the samples should the null hypothesis of no change be rejected. If the score does deviate by that much from the hypothesized mean, it is likely that the sample mean actually came from a different distribution. That is, in our example, it would be likely that the income distribution had changed.

The second thing we must decide is whether to use a one- or a two-tailed test. Remember, in a one-tailed test we assume that we have specified a direction to our hypothesis. In our example we hypothesized that the social program would increase income. Thus, if our sample mean was found under the last 5% of the distribution on the right side of the curve we would reject the null hypothesis and accept the hypothesis that social services has in fact increased income. If we did not hypothesize the direction of the relationship we would have to use a two-tailed test, and, therefore, divide 0.05 by 2. To reject the null hypothesis, then, the sample mean would have to fall under 0.025 of either end of the distribution, quite far from the assumed population mean. You would use a two-tailed test if you had framed a hypothesis

270 TESTING HYPOTHESES

such as "Government spending affects inflation." There would have to be a great increase or decrease in inflation with regard to government spending to assume that chance was not operating. This is because we were unable to predict the direction theoretically (see Figure 11-2).

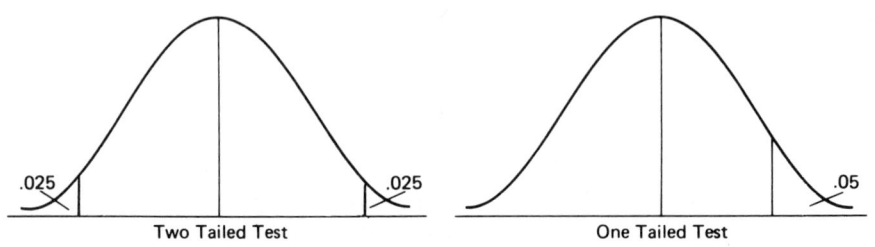

Figure 11-2 CRITICAL VALUES FOR NORMAL CURVES

Now let us return to our example and employ a one-tailed test with a critical value of 0.05. The first step is to examine the area of a normal curve where one standard deviation would fall. The Statistical Tables of this book include a table of the Areas for a Standard Normal Distribution. To find the probability of getting a z score of 1.00, look down the left-hand column until you find 1.0. Then look across the columns until you find .−0. In that space you will find the number .3413. Since the curve is symmetrical, the table includes probabilities for only one-half of the curve. What this .3413 tells you is that slightly more than 34% of samples drawn from the distribution whose mean is $8,500 would have means which deviate by as much as one standard deviation above the mean. Since the curve is symmetrical, the same number deviate by that much below the mean. Therefore, approximately 68% of all samples would have means which deviate by plus or minus one standard deviation from the mean.

Now we would want to know the probability of a sample mean differing by more than that amount. If we were using a two-tailed test we could determine this by subtracting the 68% from the total number of sample means, 100%. This means that 100% − 68% = 32% of the samples drawn from this distribution would have means which deviate by more than plus or minus one standard deviation. In our example, since we hypothesized the direction of the relation, we should use a one-tailed test. We are only interested in the sample means which deviate positively from the mean of the distribution. One-half of the sample means deviate positively from the distribution mean. Thus, 50% − 34%, or 16% of the samples from this distribution have means that deviate above the distribution mean by more than one standard deviation.

Now what decision should we make about our null hypothesis such that the mean of the distribution is $8,500, that is, the social service program has had no effect on the income level in the target population and that the sample mean of $10,500 is the result solely of sampling error? Our examination of the standard normal sampling distribution tells us that in 16% of the samples that could be drawn from a distribution with a mean of $8500, the sample mean would deviate above the mean by more than one standard deviation. So, if we conclude that there has actually been a change in income, we have a 16% chance of being wrong. We decided before our examination of the table that we would only tolerate a 5% chance of being wrong. That is, we decided we would conclude that there had been a change only if the mean of the sample deviated so far from the hypothesized mean ($8,500) that it could have happened by chance in only 5% of the samples. Therefore, we cannot reject the null hypothesis that the income level is still $8,500.

What would we have needed to enable us to reject the null hypothesis with only a 5% chance of error? Let us look again at the standard normal distribution. If, as in our example, we are using a one-tailed test, we would need a sample mean which deviates by so much that 45% of the samples will fall closer to the mean. Find in the table a score that is closest to 45%. This is .4505. Now see what z score corresponds to this number: 1.65. This means that you would need a sample mean which deviates by 1.65 standard deviations from the hypothesized mean before you could reject the null hypothesis using a one-tailed test. If you are using a two-tailed test, the 5% chance of error is divided between the two tails. That means that a sample mean would have deviated by so much that 95% of the cases fall closer to the mean; 47.5% of these would be above the mean, and 47.5% would be below the mean. Find .4750 in the table. The z score which corresponds to .4750 is 1.96. This means that a score must deviate by almost two standard deviations from the mean before you could reject the null hypothesis using a two-tailed test.

Of course, as we saw before, it is possible that a change has occurred and the mean actually is now $10,500. In that case we would be accepting a false hypothesis when we accept the null hypothesis. Accepting a false hypothesis is known as a Type II error. We have no way of knowing the probability that we are committing a Type II error. What we do know is that we run a certain risk of rejecting the null hypothesis when it is actually true. The critical value of .05 tells you that 5 out of 100 samples would produce differences that large, by chance. But by setting the critical value at that level we are saying that we are willing to tolerate that probability of error. The .05, therefore, tells you the probability you will be making a Type I error, or rejecting a true hypothesis. This critical value is also called the *level of significance* and tests to determine the probability of committing a Type I error are called *significance tests*. The term is unfortunately somewhat misleading because it does not necessarily mean the results are important. It just tells you the probability of getting your results by chance. You should notice that science is very skeptical and conservative. By setting the critical value at .05 we are making it very difficult to reject the null hypothesis. The method of hypothesis testing stacks the deck on the side of the null hypothesis—no change, no relation, no difference, and so forth. Scientists are explicitly saying that they would rather not accept evidence for change until that evidence is overwhelming.

As we said above, the standard normal distribution should only be used if you have a variable with a continuous distribution of values. That means that only if you have a variable which has been measured at the interval level should you use the standard normal distribution to test hypotheses. There are, however, numerous other significance tests. All such tests differ in the way they are calculated, but all rely upon the same logic as the z-score test. We will discuss two others here: t tests and the chi square.

THE t SAMPLING DISTRIBUTION

We will first look at t tests since they are closely related to the z-score test. To compute a z score, you have to know the standard deviation of the population. In most cases we simply have no way of knowing that measurement. One way of estimating the population standard deviation is to use the standard deviation of the sample you have drawn. Using the sample standard deviation provides a reasonably accurate estimate of the population standard deviation if you have a large sample. But the estimate can be misleading if the sample is small.

To avoid this problem W. S. Gosset developed an alternative test statistic to use in place of z when the population standard deviation is not known. He called the statistic t, and since he was writing under the pseudonym of "Student" the statistic is often referred to as "Student's t." The t statistic is calculated by using the following formula:

$$t = \frac{\bar{x} - \mu}{s/\sqrt{N - 1}}$$

where $\bar{x}$ = the sample mean; μ = the hypothesized population mean; s = the standard deviation of the sample; and N = the size of the sample. You will notice that the numerator of the statistic is the same as the numerator of the z score. The denominator, however, is different. We are using the standard deviation of the sample (indicated by s) in place of the unknown standard deviation of the population. Instead of the term $\sqrt{N}$, the term $\sqrt{N-1}$ is used.

As in the case of the z score, to use the t statistic you must have interval data and you must compare the score to a sampling distribution, in this case the t sampling distribution. The t distribution is symmetrical like the standard normal distribution, but it is slightly flatter than the standard normal distribution. This means that more of the cases fall within the tails of the distribution. There are actually different t sampling distributions for different sample sizes. This is so because each additional case in the sample is a factor which can increase the variation. A factor which produces variation is called a *degree of freedom*. If there is a single case, there is no source of variation. Since each case adds a degree of freedom, the total number of degrees of freedom in a sample is $N-1$, where N is the sample size.[1]

Let us examine how to use the t statistic and t sampling distribution to test a hypothesis. We will use the same example that we used to illustrate the z score: the impact of the social service program on mean income level. Therefore, the numerator will be the sample mean minus the hypothesized population mean: $10,500 − $8,500 = $2,000. Let us assume that we drew a sample of twenty-six and the standard deviation of that sample was $2,000. The denominator, then, would be $2,000/$\sqrt{26-1}$ = $2,000/$\sqrt{25}$ = $2,000/5 = $400. So, the t statistic would be 2,000/400 = 5.00.

Now turn to the t distribution in the Statistical Tables. You will notice that the column on the left is headed df. This refers to *degree of freedom*. In this example we have $N-1$ or $26-1 = 25$ degrees of freedom. So you look down that column until you find the number 25. Also notice that the rest of the columns in the table are headed by different levels of significance for both one-tail and two-tail tests. So, look across the row corresponding to 25 degrees of freedom until you find the level of significance you have specified as your critical value for either a one-tail or two-tail test. In our example we specified a critical value of .05 and a one-tail test. Therefore, we will go to the second column in the table. In that column is the number 1.316. To be significant at the .05 level, with a one-tail test and 25 degrees of freedom, the t statistic must be at least 1.316 or larger. Since we obtained a t of 5.00, we know that the finding is significant. That is, we know that in less than 5% of the samples could we have found a difference in means this large solely by chance. Therefore, we can reject the null hypothesis. The reason that this result was significant and the z-score was not is simply due to the fact that we altered the size of the standard deviation in this example to make computation easier. Normally, the larger the sample size, the more likely the results will be significant.

You will notice that the t table only provides exact values for samples up to 30 cases. For samples between 30 and 120, it would be necessary to interpolate the values. Beyond 120 there are no t scores calculated. This is so because, as we said before, the sample standard deviation provides an acceptable estimate for the population standard deviation in the case of large samples. This means that the standard normal table can be used for large sample sizes.

With both the z score and the t test you must have interval data. This is so because they test for differences between a sample mean and a hypothesized population mean. Means, of course, are interval level mea-

---

1. This intuitively pleasing explanation of degrees of freedom was suggested by Judith D. Handel, *Introductory Statistics for Sociology* (Englewood Cliffs, N.J.: Prentice-Hall, 1978), pp. 326–27.

surements. Now we will consider a significance test which can be used with both nominal and ordinal data: the chi square.

THE CHI SQUARE SAMPLING DISTRIBUTION

The chi square statistic is based on the same logic as all significance tests. It asks the question of whether the results obtained could be due solely to chance. If the probability that the results are due solely to chance is small, then the null hypothesis is rejected. In the case of chi square, we are concerned about the way the cases are distributed among the cells of a cross-tabulation table. To determine if there is some pattern in the way the cases are distributed in the table, we compare the actual frequencies in the cells with the frequencies we would expect if the relationship were completely random. If there is a large difference between the observed frequencies and the expected frequencies, then it is less risky to conclude that there is a nonrandom relationship between the variables in the table. What the chi square statistic does is measure the amount of difference between observed and expected frequencies, standardize the differences for the size of the sample, and relate this final figure to a sampling distribution which is called the chi square distribution.

Let us now look at the steps involved in computing and interpreting a chi square. The first step, of course, is to arrange the cases in a cross-tabulation table as we discussed in the last chapter. Let us take for an example a table which illustrates the relationship between party identification and voting:

	Democrat	Republican	Total
Vote	cell a 9	cell b 8	17
Didn't vote	cell c 10	cell d 6	16
Total	19	14	33

Once the table has been set up, the next step is to calculate the expected frequency for each cell. That is, we want to know the distribution of cases in this table if the relationship between party identification and voting were completely random. To do this we examine the marginals of the table. Remember, these are the row and column totals of the table. We notice that out of the thirty-three cases in this table, seventeen of them voted. That is, the proportion of voters in the table as a whole is $\frac{17}{33}$. Now, if there is no patterned relationship between party identification and voting, you would expect the proportion of voting Democrats and the proportion of voters in the total sample to be the same. That is, if $\frac{17}{33}$ of the sample vote, and the order is random, $\frac{17}{33}$ of the Democrats should also vote. Therefore, to find the expected frequency of Democrats who vote, you would multiply the total number of Democrats in the sample (19) by $\frac{17}{33}$. This will give you 9.8, which is the expected frequency for cell a of the table above. You can follow the same reasoning to calculate the expected frequency for cell b. If $\frac{17}{33}$ of the sample vote, then you would expect $\frac{17}{33}$ of the Republicans to vote if there is no relationship between party identification and voting. Therefore, you multiply the total number of Republicans in the sample (14) by $\frac{17}{33}$. That gives you an expected frequency of 7.2 for cell b.

The same reasoning is used to determine the expected frequencies of cells c and d. In these cells we are examining the proportion of nonvoters. We find that $\frac{16}{33}$ of the total sample did not vote. We would, therefore, expect that if the pattern is random, $\frac{16}{33}$ of the Democrats should be nonvoters and $\frac{16}{33}$ of the Republicans should also be nonvoters. So, we multiply the total number of Democrats (19) and the total number of Republicans (14) by $\frac{16}{33}$. The results are, respectively, 9.2 for cell c and 6.8 for cell d.

We now have computed the expected frequencies for each of the cells in the table. Next, we must determine the degree to which the actual frequencies differ from the expected frequencies. To do this, we simply subtract the expected frequencies (fe) from the actual frequencies (fo):

$$\begin{array}{l} \text{fo} - \text{fe} \\ 9 - 9.8 = -0.8 \\ 8 - 7.2 = 0.8 \\ 10 - 9.2 = 0.8 \\ 6 - 6.8 = -0.8 \end{array}$$

The next step would be to add these quantities to determine the overall magnitude of the difference between observed and expected frequencies in the table. However, if we add these differences, they will sum 0. Whereas only in a 2×2 table would the differences in each cell be the same, it is always the case that the sum of fo−fe will be 0. That is so because we are basing our calculations on the total number of cases in the table, and if some cells have fewer cases than one would expect, those cases have to occur in some other cells in the table which then have more cases than expected. Some way must be found to avoid this problem we so can get a measure of the size of the difference between observed and expected frequencies in the table. The solution which is used is the same as that used to get around the same problem in the calculation of the standard deviation: We square the size of the difference in each cell. Squaring the negative numbers produces a positive number and, therefore, does away with the problem of signs. In this example, we would have the following:

$$\begin{array}{rl} (\text{fo} - \text{fe})^2 = & -0.8^2 = 0.64 \\ & 0.8^2 = 0.64 \\ & 0.8^2 = 0.64 \\ & -0.8^2 = 0.64 \end{array}$$

276 TESTING HYPOTHESES

Now we have one final adjustment to make before we can finally find the sum of the differences between observed and expected frequencies. It is obviously the case that the size of the differences will be partially dependent on the number of cases in the table. A table with 1,000 cases will potentially have larger differences than a table with 10 cases, even if in both tables the variables had an equal degree of relationship. To get around this problem we must somehow try to standardize the differences for sample size. To do this we simply divide each squared difference (fo − fe)² by the expected frequency (fe) in order to compare the scores to those expected when no relationship exists. If all your scores were what you would expect by chance you would have no variance. The greater the variance, the less likely it is due to chance. In this case, therefore, we would have:

$$\frac{0.64}{9.8} = 0.065 \quad \frac{0.64}{7.2} = 0.089 \quad \frac{0.64}{9.2} = 0.069 \quad \frac{0.64}{6.8} = 0.094$$

Now we are finally ready to find the size of the difference between observed and expected frequencies in the table. To do this, we simply add the values above: 0.065 + 0.089 + 0.069 + 0.094 = 0.317. That is the value of the chi square. We can summarize all the steps we have taken so far by this formula:

$$\text{chi square} = \Sigma \frac{(fo - fe)^2}{fe}.$$

Remember, Σ means the sum of the quantities.

The final step is to look up the value we computed above in a chi square table (see Statistical Tables). This table, like the table of the standard normal distribution and the t distribution, is a sampling distribution. It tells us the probability of getting a chi square of various sizes. In the chi square table, as in the t distribution table, the probabilities are listed across the top, and the values of the chi square are listed in the body of the table.

Before you can determine the probability of getting a particular chi square you must know one more thing. You will notice that the left-hand column of the chi square is labeled df. The df again stands for degrees of freedom. In computing the chi square, degrees of freedom refers to the amount of values which one may freely assign before the other values are predetermined. To make that clearer, let us look at the situation with the cross-tabulation table above. Taking that table and its marginals as given, you may arbitrarily assign a value to one of the cells, as we have below:

	Democrat	Republican	Total
Vote	cell a 7	cell b	17
Didn't Vote	cell c	cell d	16
Total	19	14	

Once we have arbitrarily assigned the value of 7 to cell a, the number of cases in all of the other cells is automatically predetermined because of the size of the marginals. Cell b has to have 10 cases to add up to 17, and cell c has to have 12 cases to add up to 19. Since cell c has to have 12 cases, cell d has to have 4 cases to sum 16. In this case we say there is one degree of freedom. Only one cell can be allocated arbitrarily. In a larger table, more cells could be allocated arbitrarily before the other cells are predetermined. For instance, in the following table, there are two degrees of freedom:

	Democrat	Republican	Independent	Total
Vote				17
Didn't Vote				16
Total	13	12	8	

Test this for yourself by filling in two of the cells arbitrarily. The general formula for calculating the number of degrees of freedom is to multiply the number of rows minus 1 by the number of columns minus 1: degrees of freedom (df) = $(r-1)(c-1)$. In the case of the 2×2 table: $(2-1)(2-1) = (1)(1) = 1$. The number of degrees of freedom is important because, in actuality, the chi square distribution is a series of distributions. There are different chi square distributions for different degrees of freedom. Therefore, you must calculate the degrees of freedom before you can refer to the proper chi square distribution.

Let us now complete our interpretation of the chi square we obtained above. To determine the probability of getting a chi square of 0.317 with one degree of freedom, look in the chi square table in the row which corresponds to one degree of freedom. As you look across that row, you will find .148 in the column which is headed by a probability value of 70% and .455 in the column which is headed by a probability value of 50%. Since .317 falls between the values of .148 and .455, we know the probability of getting a chi square of that size is somewhere between 50% and 70%. Therefore, in this case we would not be able to reject the null hypothesis of no relationship. Looking again at the table, you can see that if you had specified a critical value of .05, you would have needed a chi square of 3.841 or larger before you could reject the null hypothesis.

The z-score test, the t test, and the chi-square test are used to determine the probability of chance in your data. As we have said before, there are many other significance tests. We do not have the space in this book to discuss them all. What we have tried to do is to give you a basic understanding of the logic which underlies all such tests. If these tests are inadequate for the data you are planning to analyze, we would recommend that you refer to a more advanced statistics text to determine if any of the other tests may suit your purposes better than either the z-score, t test, or chi-square test.

Before leaving this topic, we should emphasize an important point about the interpretation of tests of significance. As we said before, when we say a relationship is significant, all that we are saying is that the probability is low that the relationship is due solely to chance. It does not mean that the relationship is somehow important or meaningful. The terminology is unfortunate because in common usage we often use significance as a synonym for importance. You will simply have to keep in mind that significance, when used in the context of a statistical analysis, refers only to the probability of getting a particular finding by chance. It is quite possible for a relationship to be very small or inconsequential and still be statistically significant. In fact, if your sample is very large, you will almost always have results that are statistically significant. This should make sense intuitively since tests of significance tell you if you can generalize about the population based on the sample. If the sample is large, it is obviously safer to believe it is representative of the population. This means that you should ask two questions about every relationship: (1) How strong is the relationship? and (2) Is the relationship statistically significant? To determine how strong the relationship is we must use other statistics which are called *measures of association*. As with tests of significance, there are many different measures of association. In the next two chapters we will describe a few of these measures. Chapter Twelve will describe measures which can be used for nominal or ordinal levels of measurement. Chapter Thirteen will discuss measures for interval level data.

SUMMARY
TESTS OF SIGNIFICANCE

Level of Measurement	Statistic	Formula	Interpretation
Nominal Ordinal	Chi Sq. (χ^2)	$\chi^2 = \sum \frac{(fo - fe)^2}{fe}$	Probability the results are due to chance
Interval	z Score	$z = \frac{x - \mu}{\sigma/\sqrt{N}}$	Probability the results are due to chance
Interval	t test	$t = \frac{x - \mu}{s/\sqrt{N - 1}}$	Probability the results are due to chance

STUDY QUESTIONS

1. What is the meaning of "significance" with regard to the statistical test of hypotheses?
2. Discuss the process by which a researcher can decide if the results he obtains are due solely to chance (that is, discuss the process involved in using a test of significance).

3. What is a null hypothesis? Why do we seek to test a null hypothesis rather than the alternate or research hypothesis?
4. You have computed a raw chi square of 2.441. What steps must you go through and what additional information do you need to determine if your results are significant? Explain what a significance level of 0.01 means.
5. Compute and interpret a chi square for the following table:

Education Level

Prejudice	High	Low
High	5	20
Low	20	5

6. You have just completed a study of voter education and voter turnout. In your control group of ten cities the mean voter turnout was 31%. In your experimental group of ten cities where you conducted extensive voter education workshops the voting turnout was 37% with a standard deviation 0.04. Do a t test to determine if the results are significant. If your sample consisted of 100 cities in each group, you would want to test for significance using z scores and the area for a standard normal distribution. In that case would your results be significant?

Measuring Association: Nominal and Ordinal

Chapter Twelve

The statistical tests which measure the strength of the relationship between two variables produce single measures which are called correlation coefficients.[1] These coefficients are standardized so that they vary from 0 to 1 for nominal level data and from −1 to +1 for ordinal and interval level data. The closer the coefficient is to 1, the stronger the relationship between the two variables. With both the ordinal and interval level of measurement, the data are ordered in an ascending or descending pattern. Thus, the direction of relationship is important, and this is indicated by the sign (positive or negative) which precedes the coefficient. A positive relationship is one in which the values of both variables change simultaneously in the same direction. For example: as variable A increases, variable B also increases. (↑A→↑B) In other words, both increase or both decrease. A negative relationship is one in which the values of the variables change in opposite directions. For instance, an increase in variable A results in a decrease in variable B (↑A→↓B), or vice versa.

These correlation coefficients are not the only way we can examine the relationship between two variables. Much of the last two chapters discussed

---

[1] Most social scientists call these measures *correlation coefficients*. Some statisticians use the term only for linear measures or only for the measures for interval data which are discussed in Chapter Thirteen.

the use of cross-tabulation tables to determine relationships between variables. Correlation coefficients, however, have some definite advantages over tables as a means of expressing relationships.

In the first place, the correlation coefficient is much easier to communicate since it is a single measure. Secondly, the correlation coefficient is easier to interpret. Tables contain a large quantity of data. Presenting the data in a table helps to organize data, but determining whether there are relationships in the data is still a difficult process. The correlation coefficient summarizes the strength of the relationship and is, therefore, easier to grasp. This also means that more people will agree on an interpretation of a correlation coefficient than on an interpretation of a table. But this does not mean that interpreting correlation coefficients is an automatic process and that there is universal agreement as to what constitutes a "strong" as opposed to a "weak" relationship. We have often been intrigued by the fact that some researchers will claim a 0.25 correlation coefficient indicates a strong relationship while others will dismiss it as being too weak to be important. This is obviously a problem since it may mean that the conclusions of the two articles are contradictory when the results of the data analysis have actually been consistent.

There is also one disadvantage of using correlation coefficients rather than examining tables which you should keep in mind. As is the case with any summary measure, the correlation coefficient necessarily ignores some information.

Let us now turn to examining some correlation coefficients. We will first look at two coefficients which can be used with nominal level data: Goodman and Kruskal's tau and Guttman's lambda. In the nomenclature of statistics, the first name(s) refer to the "parent(s)" or inventor(s) of the statistic, and the last name (Greek letter) is simply the name given by the inventor to that particular procedure. This means, unfortunately, that different statistics may have the same "last names." For instance, there are lots of taus, which may obviously lead to some confusion. We will try to be careful about including the first names so that you will know precisely which statistic is meant.

NOMINAL LEVEL MEASURES OF ASSOCIATION

Goodman and Kruskal's Tau

The basic reasoning which underlies the tau correlation coefficient is quite simple. If two variables are perfectly related, the value of one variable would accurately predict the value of the other. On the other hand, if the variables are not related, knowing the value of one would not help you predict the value of the other. To calculate tau you subtract the number of errors you would make predicting the dependent variable when you know the value of the independent variable, from the number of errors you would make in predicting the value of the dependent variable when you do not know the value of the independent variable. This figure, then, is the extent to which knowledge of the value of the independent variable can increase your ability to predict the dependent variable.

Since this quantity is, of course, somewhat dependent on the sample size, some way must be found to standardize for the sample size. To do this, you divide by the number of errors you would make if you did not know the value of the independent variable. Tau, then, is the proportion by which you can reduce errors in predicting the dependent variable by considering the values of the independent variable when making the prediction. For this reason, tau is one of a group of statistics which are called *Proportionate-Reduction-in-Error Statistics,* for obvious reasons. The special advantage of this group of statistics is that the meaning is easily interpretable, which is not the case with some other measures of association.

Now let us look at how tau is computed. The first thing we have to figure is how many errors we would make in predicting the value of the dependent variable if we did not know the value of the independent variable. Let us look at an example (see Table 12-1). What we want to do is to predict which of the thirty-three people in this sample voted. Let us assume that all thirty-three people are lined up in a random order outside a door. It is our job as they walk through the door to guess whether they voted or not. The only guide we have for these guesses is the marginals of the table. We know from the marginals that seventeen of the group voted and sixteen did not. So, as each person walks through the door we will predict (guess, actually) that seventeen voted and that sixteen did not vote. But it should be obvious that a certain percentage of these guesses will be wrong. Of the seventeen people we guessed had voted, a certain proportion will not have voted. We have to estimate what proportion of those guesses would be wrong. We know that $\frac{16}{33}$ of the sample as a whole did not vote. So, we have every reason to believe that $\frac{16}{33}$ of the seventeen we guessed were actually nonvoters. Therefore, to determine the number of wrong guesses, we can simply multiply the number of guesses (seventeen) by the proportion of those guesses we expect to be wrong (17) ($\frac{16}{33}$). The result is 8.20. So we know that in guessing the number of voters we can expect to make eight mistakes.

Table 12-1 Hypothetical relationship between sex and voting—1

	Male	Female	Total
Vote	9	8	17
Didn't Vote	10	6	16
Total	19	14	33

Now let us look at the number of mistakes we would make in guessing the nonvoters. The logic is the same as that used in the case of voters. First we would guess that sixteen of the thirty-three were nonvoters. But we would expect a certain proportion of those guesses to be incorrect. We expect the proportion of incorrect guesses would be equal to the proportion of voters in the sample, which is $\frac{17}{33}$. So we multiply the number of guesses (16) by the proportion we expect to be wrong ($\frac{17}{33}$) and we get 8.20. The total number of mistakes we can expect to make in guessing which of the thirty-three vote and which do not, using only the marginals rather than the independent variable as a guide, is 8.2+8.2 or 16.4.

Now let us see the number of mistakes we could expect to make if we used the independent variable as a guide. We know there are nineteen males in the sample and that of those nineteen, nine voted and ten did not. So, we will only look at those nineteen and try to guess which voted and which did not vote. (Of course, if there were a perfect relationship, all males would either have voted or not voted, depending on what the relationship was. But in real life there are rarely such perfect relationships.) We would guess that nine of the nineteen voted. But we would expect a proportion of those guesses to be wrong. Once again we would expect the proportion of wrong guesses to be equal to the proportion of nonvoters in this subsample of males, $\frac{10}{19}$. So, we multiply the number of guesses by $\frac{10}{19}$ and we get 4.7. Similarly, we would guess that ten of the nineteen did not vote. We would expect that $\frac{9}{19}$ of those guesses would be wrong since that is the proportion of voters in the subsample. Therefore, we would multiply 10 by $\frac{9}{19}$ and the result is 4.7.

Finally, we predict the number of voters and nonvoters within the subsample of females. There are fourteen females. Of that number, eight voted and six did not. So, we guess that eight voted, knowing that $\frac{6}{14}$ of those guesses will be wrong. This means there will be 3.4 mistakes. By the same logic, there are 3.4 mistakes in our sample of female nonvoters.

The total number of mistakes we would make using the independent variable as a guide is 16.2. We can now transfer these values into the formula for tau.

$$\tau = \frac{\text{Number of errors made not knowing the independent variable} - \text{Number of errors made knowing the independent variable}}{\text{Number of errors made not knowing the independent variable}} =$$

$$\frac{16.4 - 16.2}{16.4} = \frac{0.2}{16.4} = 0.01$$

It is obvious that there virtually is no relationship between sex and voting—within this sample at least—since knowledge of the independent

284 MEASURING ASSOCIATION: NOMINAL AND ORDINAL

variable did not reduce the errors made in predicting the dependent variable. There was almost no difference in the number of errors made in predicting the dependent variable whether or not the value of the independent variable was considered. The situation can be simplified as follows:

$$\frac{1-1}{1} = \frac{0}{1} = 0.$$

If the relationship between sex and voting had been perfect, we would have made no mistakes in guessing the value of the dependent variable and the formula would have looked like this:

$$\frac{16.4 - 0}{16.4} = 1 \text{ or, as above, } \frac{1-0}{1} = 1$$

Tau, therefore, varies from 0 (for no relationship) to 1 (for a perfect relationship).

Guttman's Lambda

Guttman's lambda is in many ways very similar to Goodman and Kruskal's tau. Like tau, lambda is a proportionate reduction in error statistic. Therefore, the basic formula for lambda is identical to tau:

$$\lambda = \frac{\text{Errors made not knowing the independent variable} - \text{Errors made knowing independent variable}}{\text{Errors made not knowing the independent variable}}$$

The only difference between tau and lambda is the method used to calculate the number of errors made. In the first place, tau and lambda are based on different methods of guessing the value of the dependent variable. When calculating tau, we guessed on the basis of the marginals. If you use lambda, you guess on the basis of the most frequent category—the mode—of the dependent variable. We guess that all of the cases fall into the modal category. This means that it is easier for us to calculate the number of errors which will be made in those guesses. With tau, we estimated that a certain proportion of all guesses would be wrong, unless there was a perfect relationship between the independent and dependent variable. With lambda, we know the number of errors. Since we guess that every case has the modal value on the dependent variable, we will be correct in all those cases in which the case actually has the modal value. Of course, we are wrong for all those cases which do not have the modal value. The total number of errors, then, is the number of guesses minus the number of cases in the modal category.

Let us use lambda to measure the degree of relationship in our hypothetical data (see Table 12-2).

Table 12-2 Hypothetical relationship between sex and voting—II

	Male	Female	Total
Vote	9	8	17
Didn't Vote	10	6	16
Total	19	14	33

First we predict the value of the dependent variable without using the independent variable as a guide. Since the modal category is the seventeen people who voted, we will guess that all thirty-three people voted. In doing so, we will be wrong 33−17 cases, or 16 times. Now we will predict the value of the dependent variable using the independent variable as a guide. First we will examine the number of males in the sample. Of the nineteen males, ten did not vote, which is the modal category. In guessing all males did not vote, we would be wrong $19-10 = 9$ times. Next we will turn to the females, with eight of the fourteen females voting, making that the modal category. If we guessed that all females voted, we would be wrong $14-8 = 6$ times. So the total number of errors we would make using the independent variable as a guide is $9+6 = 15$. The general formula is:

$$\lambda = \frac{\text{Errors made not knowing the independent variable} - \text{Errors made knowing independent variable}}{\text{Errors made not knowing independent variable}} =$$

$$\frac{16-15}{16} = \frac{1}{16} = 0.06$$

The result is slightly higher than the result obtained by using tau, but we would still have to conclude that there is really no relationship in this sample between sex and voting.

As you may have noticed, lambda is somewhat easier to calculate than is tau. So you may wonder why tau is ever used, assuming one had to do the calculations by hand rather than using a computer. One reason is that in some circumstances lambda will always be zero, regardless of the degree of relationship between the independent and dependent variables. Lambda will always be zero if the modal frequencies of the independent variable are all concentrated in one category of the dependent variable. We will develop hypothetical data to illustrate this situation (see Table 12-3). For the value of males of the independent variable, the modal category for the dependent variable is Vote. For the value of female for the independent variable, the modal category for the dependent variable is also Vote. Now let us calculate lambda: The original number of mistakes would be 33−18 = 15. The number of mistakes made when the independent variable is used as a guide is: (19−10) = 9+(14−8) = 6, or 15. Therefore, we would have $\frac{15-15}{15} = 0$. If the distribution of cases in a table is such that the modal category is always the same category of the dependent variable, you should use tau as a measure of association rather than lambda.

Table 12-3 Hypothetical relationship between sex and voting—III

	Male	Female	Total
Vote	10	8	18
Didn't Vote	9	6	15
Total	19	14	33

MEASURES OF ASSOCIATION FOR ORDINAL LEVEL DATA

Gamma and Its Relatives

In the first part of this chapter we discussed measures of association which can be used for nominal data. We examined two measures which relied on the same basic logic. In our discussion of ordinal measures of association we will also discuss a "family" of measures which rely on the same logic in their calculations. We will discuss this group of statistics by first examining the statistic which is easiest to calculate and which forms the basis for the other statistics. This statistic is gamma.

With ordinal-level data, unlike nominal-level data, the position of a case in a table is significant. With the example we have been using, we could have rearranged the table in any way we desired. That is, it would make no difference if the table looked like Table 12-4 or 12-5. By definition, with ordinal level data the order of the values has meaning. For instance, let's examine two variables with ordered values: interest in politics and occupational status. We might set up the table as in Table 12-6. There are other ways to arrange this table, but we would always have to preserve the Low, Medium, High or High, Medium, Low order among the categories.

Table 12-4 Format for nominal variables—I

	Male	Female
Vote		
Didn't Vote		

Table 12-5 Format for nominal variables—II

	Female	Male
Didn't Vote		
Vote		

Table 12-6 Format for ordinal variables

		Occupational Status		
		Low	Medium	High
Interest in Politics	Low			
	Medium			
	High			

The computation of gamma makes use of the fact that with ordinal-level data, the order in the table is meaningful. The basic logic of gamma is that if two variables are positively related, pairs of cases in the table should be ordered on the independent variable in the same way that they are ordered on the dependent variable. That is, in our example above, if Sally Jones has a higher value on occupational status than does John Doe, then she should also have a higher value on interest in politics if the two variables are positively related. They should appear in the table in this way (see Table 12-7). If both the independent and dependent variables order pairs of cases in the same way, this is known as *agreement*.

Table 12-7 Agreement between variables

		Occupational Status		
		Low	Medium	High
Interest in Politics	Low	John Doe		
	Medium			
	High		Sally Jones	

If the two variables are negatively related, you would expect that pairs of cases would be ordered differently on the two variables. That is, Sally may be higher than John on occupational status, but lower than he on political interest. In that case, they would appear in the table as shown in Table 12-8. If the independent and dependent variables order pairs of cases differently, it is known as *disagreement*. If there is no pattern in the way pairs of cases are ordered, then we can conclude that the two variables are unrelated.

Table 12-8 Disagreement between variables

		Occupational Status		
		Low	Medium	High
Interest in Politics	Low		Sally	
	Medium	John		
	High			

To determine the value of gamma, consider all possible pairwise comparisons, counting the number of agreements and the number of disagreements in those pairs. The formula for computing gamma is

$$\gamma = \frac{\text{Agreements} - \text{Disagreements}}{\text{Agreements} + \text{Disagreements}}$$

If the relationship is positive, the number of agreements will be larger than the number of disagreements. If the relationship is negative, the number of disagreements will be larger than the number of agreements and the value of gamma will, therefore, be negative. To determine if the value obtained in the numerator is large enough to conclude there is a relationship between the two variables we have to standardize the value. For gamma, the value is standardized by expressing it as a proportion of all possible agreements, which is determined by adding the number of agreements and the number of disagreements. This means that in computing gamma, any time two cases have the same value on a variable, it is ignored. These cases are called ties.

Table 12-9 Example for calculating gamma

		Occupational Status		
		High	Medium	Low
Interest in Politics	High	a		d
	Medium		b	e
	Low		c	f

Let us look at a simple illustration of computing gamma (see Table 12-9). Remember, for there to be agreement, one case in a pairwise comparison must rank higher than the other on both the independent and the dependent variable. For there to be disagreement, one case must be higher than the other on one variable and lower than the other on the other variable. And, finally, a tie is a situation in which the two cases rank the same on either variable. Since there are six cases, there are fifteen possible pairwise comparisons: ab, ac, ad, ae, af, bc, bd, be, bf, cd, ce, cf, de, df, and ef. Case a may be compared with cases b, c, d, e, and f. Four of those five comparisons produce agreements. That is, a has higher values on both occupational status and interest in politics than do cases b, c, e, and f. Case d and case a have the same value on interest in politics and is, therefore, considered a tie. Case b may be compared with cases c, d, e, and f. One of these comparisons produces agreement: b and f. Two of the comparisons produces ties: b and e, and b and c. And one of the comparisons produces disagreement: b and d. Case c can be compared with cases d, e, and f. Two of these comparisons produce disagreement: c and d, and c and e. The comparison of c and f is a tie. Case d may be compared with e and f. Both of these comparisons are ties. And, finally, e may be compared with f, and that comparison is a tie. In all there are five agreements, three disagreements, and seven ties. We will now transfer these values into the formula for gamma:

$$\frac{\text{Agreements (5)} - \text{Disagreements (3)}}{\text{Agreements (5)} + \text{Disagreements (3)}} = \frac{2}{8} = 0.25$$

Before we discuss the interpretation of the value of gamma, let us examine how we can calculate gamma more quickly and easily than compariing every single pair in a table. If you examine what we found with Table 12-9, you will notice that all of the cases which were agreements with a occurred below and to the right of the cell in which a appears. Similarly, the agreement with b occurs with f, which is in a cell below and to the right of b. If the table is arranged in this way, with the high value for both variables in the upper left-hand corner of the table, agreements can always be found in the cells below and to the right of any given cell. Obviously, if the table with which you are dealing is not arranged like this, you will have to examine the table to determine in what direction the agreements occur. You should also notice that in this table, the disagreements occur when comparing two cases, one of which occurs in a cell below and to the left of the other. Again, the fact that these comparisons are disagreements is due to the way that the table is set up.

Once you have examined a table and determined along which diagonal agreements and disagreements appear, it becomes much easier to compute gamma. To determine the number of pairwise comparisons which are agreements, you multiply the number of cases in each cell by the total number of cases in those cells which are—in the case of this table—below and to the right. And to determine the number of cases which are disagreements in this case, you would multiply the number of cases in each cell by the number of cases which occur in cells below and to the left. To illustrate this procedure, let us look again at Table 12-9. We would first multiply the number of cases in cell a by the number of cases in all cells below and to the right of a: a(b+c+e+f). In this example, we are assuming that each of those cells contains only one case. Therefore, we would have 1(1+1+1+1) = 1(4) = 4.

Then we would go to the cell in which b occurs. There is only one cell below and to the right of cell b, and so we have b(f), or 1(1) = 1. None of the other cells in the table in which cases occur are positioned so that other occupied cells are below and to the right. Therefore, the total number of agreements equals: 1(1+1+1+1) + 1(1) = 4+1 = 5.

Now let us compute the number of disagreements. You will notice that both b and c occur in cells below and to the left of the cell in which d occurs. Therefore, the number of pairwise comparisons with d which are disagreements are d(b+c) or 1(1+1) = 2. The cell in which c occurs is also below and to the left of the cell in which e occurs. Therefore, the number of pairwise comparisons with e equals e(c) = 1(1) = 1. No other cells are positioned so that other occupied cells are below and to the left. The total number of disagreements equals 1(1+1) + 1(1) = 2+1 = 3. In a table with this few cases this procedure may not look any easier than examining each individual pairwise comparison. But consider how burdensome it would be to look at each individual pair if there were several hundred cases included in the table. Just remember that before you start multiplying, you first have to examine the table to determine in what direction agreements and disagreements will occur.

We are now ready to try an example with numbers in the cells (see Table 12-10).

Table 12-10 Hypothetical relationship between occupational status and interest in politics—I

		Occupational Status		
		High	Medium	Low
Interest in Politics	High	4	0	2
	Medium	0	3	1
	High	0	6	1

Agreements

4 × (3 + 6 + 1 + 1) = 44
3 × (1)   = 3
                 ──
                 47

Disagreements

2 × (3 + 6) = 18
1 × (6)   = 6
              ──
              24

$$\gamma = \frac{A - D}{A + D} = \frac{47 - 24}{47 + 24} = \frac{23}{71} = 0.32$$

Let us now consider the interpretation of gamma. There are two general points which should help you interpret gamma. In the first place, gamma tests for the existence of a linear relationship between two variables. That is, gamma measures the degree to which the dependent variable consistently increases or decreases when the value of the independent variable increases. As we indicated above, the diagonal of agreement is a straight line. It is also called a *monotonic* relationship because the variables are related in one consistent direction. If the relationship were plotted on graph paper, a perfect *linear* relationship would look like Figure 12-1. Some relationships,

Figure 12-1 LINEAR RELATIONSHIP

however, may be *curvilinear*. That is, as the value of the independent variable increases, the value of dependent variable may first increase and, beyond some point, then decrease. In other words, at some stage the direction of the relationship changes. For instance, the relationship between age and political participation is curvilinear. Young people have low rates of participation. As they grow older, they tend to participate with greater frequency. But this pattern does not continue. Beyond a certain point, as age increases the level of participation decreases. The curvilinear relationship between age and participation may be graphed in this way (see Figure 12-2).

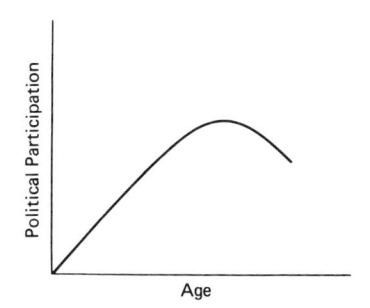

Figure 12-2 CURVILINEAR RELATIONSHIP

Since gamma measures the strength of linear relations, it may be low even though there really is a relationship between the independent and dependent variables—if that relationship is curvilinear. It is not as stringent as other measures, however, because it tolerates ties and does not require a one-to-one increase between the independent and dependent variables. For this reason we say it only measures a weak monotonic relationship.

A second point you should know about gamma is that, like the nominal measures we discussed, it can be interpreted in terms of the proportional reduction in error. That is, if two variables are perfectly related, then you could always predict the ranking of two cases on the dependent variable if you know their scores on the independent variable. If the two variables are not related, then knowing the value of two cases on the independent variable will not help you predict their ranking on the dependent variable. Thus, a large gamma will indicate that knowing the value of the independent variable will reduce the proportion of errors you will make in predicting the ranking of cases on the dependent variable.

How large is large enough? There is no universal agreement on this question. But one researcher has suggested the following guide for interpreting gamma:[2]

0.00	no association
±0.01 - 0.09	negligible association
±0.10 - 0.29	low association
±0.30 - 0.49	moderate association
±0.50 - 0.69	substantial association
±0.70 - 0.99	very strong association
±1	perfect association

These standards do not necessarily constitute "the word from on high inscribed on stone," but they might give you a rough guideline to use. Gamma is not a particularly stringent measure and, therefore, a lower correlation using another statistic must be evaluated in terms of its rigor.

In your research, you should not be surprised to find few, if any, correlation coefficients as large as 0.50. In most political science research the correlation coefficients will not be in the "substantial" or "very strong" range. This is so because the correlation coefficients measure the relation between two variables only. But with the complex political phenomena we are attempting to understand, there are many variables involved. This means that one variable can only account for part of the variation in the dependent variable.

When correlations are high, for example, 0.80 or more, you should be suspicious that you may be using the same measure for both independent and dependent variables. For instance, assume you wanted to predict the success a group might have in securing the passage of legislation it favors. Also assume that you decided to use power as the independent variable to aid in this prediction. If you measure the group's power in terms of its previous success in securing legislation, you might expect to find a very high correlation between power and success in securing desired legislation. Past and

---

2. J. A. David, *Elementary Survey Analysis* (Englewood Cliffs, N.J.: Prentice-Hall, 1971), p. 49.

future successes are not exactly the same thing. Still, the finding that the two are strongly related is not exactly startling and does not really tell you anything new about the effect of power. Of course, not all high correlations are flukes. We are only saying that you should be wary of results that seem too good to be true because they might be just that.

As we indicated, gamma forms the basis for two other measures of association for ordinal-level data. One of these other measures is Somers' d_{yx}. The only difference between gamma and Somers' d_{yx} is the treatment of cases which are tied. In the computation of Somers' d_{yx}, those scores which are tied on the dependent variable are included in the denominator. Therefore, the formula for Somers' d_{yx} is $\frac{A - D}{A + D + Ty}$, where Ty indicates the cases which are tied on y, or the dependent variable. The other measures which are related to gamma are various versions of Kendall's tau. To calculate Kendall's tau, the number of agreements minus disagreements (which is the numerator in all of these measures) is divided by all possible pairwise combinations. The formula for Kendall's tau$_a$ is $\frac{A - D}{N(N - 1)/2}$. If there are a large number of ties, however, there is a second version of Kendall's tau which should be used, namely tau$_b$. Again, the numerator remains the same. But in this case the denominator is the following:

$$\sqrt{(A + D + Tx)(A + D + Ty)}$$

The denominator in this case includes a correction for ties. If there are many ties, Kendall's tau$_b$ will be higher than Kendall's tau. The formula is:

$$\tau_b = \frac{A - D}{\sqrt{(A + D + Tx)(A + D + Ty)}}$$

A third version is Kendall's tau$_c$. This statistic is used when there are different numbers of rows and columns in your contingency tables. Again, the numerator remains the same. The denominator becomes

$$N^2[(m - 1)/m]/2$$

where N is the number of cases in the sample and m equals the number of rows or columns, depending on which is the smaller number. That is, if you were dealing with a table with two rows and three columns, m would equal two. The formula for Kendall's tau$_c$ is:

$$\tau_c = \frac{A - D}{N^2[(m - 1)/m]/2}$$

Now the question obviously is which measure to use where and what does each tell you. Since both Somers' d and Kendall's tau are calculated on the same principle as gamma, both are also linear measures and proportionate-reduction-in-error measures. But each will, in most cases, give you slightly different scores for the same set of data. Gamma is the least restrictive measure since its denominator only includes agreements plus disagreements. Somers' d, with the same numerator, has a denominator which includes one set of ties. If there are any ties on the dependent variable, they will increase the size of the denominator of Somers' d and the resulting score will be smaller than gamma. Kendall's tau includes all pairwise combinations in the denominator. Therefore, any ties in the data will increase the size of the denominator. If there are any ties on the independent variable, Kendall's tau will be smaller than either gamma or Somers' d.

Basically, we are saying that Kendall's tau is the most stringent measure of the three. Only if there are no ties on either the independent or the dependent variable will Kendall's tau reach a perfect 1.0. Thus, Kendall's tau measures the existence of a pure linear relationship. Kendall's tau$_b$, as we noted, is not as restrictive as tau$_a$ if there are ties. All of the Kendall's tau measures are symmetrical, meaning that we do not need to specify which is the independent and which is the dependent variable. Somers' d is less stringent than tau. It is an asymmetric measure, which means that we must specify the independent and the dependent variables. Somers' d will reach a score of 1.0 if there are no tied scores on the dependent variable, even if there are tied scores on the independent variable. Finally, gamma is the least stringent measure since it ignores all tied scores. Gamma thus measures the existence of a weak monotonic relationship, as noted above.

There are two other points we should make about interpreting gamma. In the first place, by ignoring all ties, the value of gamma may, in fact, be based on very few cases. For instance, look at Table 12-11.

Table 12-11 Hypothetical relationship between occupational status and interest in politics—II

		Occupational Status	
		High	Low
Interest in	High	10	0
Politics	Low	15	8

In this table there are 43 cases. That means that there are 903 possible pairwise comparisons. But in computing gamma, any comparison in which there is a tie is ignored. This means only 80 pairwise comparisons will be included in computing gamma (10×8).

The second point to make about gamma is that if one cell of the table is empty, as is the case in Table 12-11, gamma will always be 1.00. All of the 80 pairwise comparisons occur along the positive diagonal. You may be unwilling to consider the relationship in Table 12-11 as actually a perfect relationship. Therefore, you should be cautious in using gamma with tables with empty cells.

The measure to be used to a large extent depends upon what you initially hypothesize to be the relationship between the independent and dependent variables. Many social scientists would argue that the criteria of Kendall's tau are too stringent for the kinds of relationships which exist in social science data. But it might be instructive to compute all three measures to give you a more comprehensive picture of the relationships in your data.

Let us return to Table 12-10. Remember, we calculated gamma to be 0.32. Now let us see what the values of the other measures would be for the same set of data. First we will calculate Somers' d. The numerator is the same: $47-24 = 23$. The denominator is $47+24+Ty$. We are only concerned with ties on the dependent variable

$$\begin{aligned} Ty = 4 \times 2 &= 8 \\ 3 \times 1 &= 3 \\ 6 \times 1 &= \underline{6} \\ &17 \end{aligned}$$

$$\text{Somer's } d = \frac{47-24}{47+24+17} = \frac{23}{88} = 0.26$$

Next let us compute Kendall's tau_a. The numerator again is $47 - 24 = 23$. The denominator is based on the number of possible pairwise comparisons: $N(N-1)/2$. Since there are 17 cases, the denominator becomes $17(16)/2 = 136$.

$$\text{Kendall's Tau}_a = \frac{23}{136} = 0.17$$

The denominator in Kendall's tau_b includes a correction for ties $\sqrt{(A + D + Tx)(A + D + Ty)}$. To fill in this equation, we need to obtain the value of Tx.

$$\begin{aligned} Tx = 3 \times 6 &= 18 \\ 2 \times (1 + 1) &= 4 \\ 1 \times 1 &= \underline{1} \\ &23 \end{aligned}$$

$$\text{Kendall's Tau}_b = \frac{23}{\sqrt{(47 + 24 + 23)(47 + 24 + 17)}} = \frac{23}{\sqrt{(94)(88)}}$$

$$= \frac{23}{\sqrt{8272}} = \frac{23}{90.0} = 0.25$$

Since the number of columns and rows is equal in our example, Kendall's tau_c is inappropriate.

The divergence between gamma at 0.32 and Kendall's tau_a at 0.17 should make you well aware of the fact that you must understand a statistic before you use it. The values we calculated all came from the same table.

Therefore, in interpreting your data, you must not be too ecstatic with a gamma of 0.32 nor too depressed with a Kendall's tau$_a$ of 0.17. Rather, you should try to use the difference in those two scores to help you understand the nature of the relationship between the independent and dependent variables. Too many people just look at the raw numbers and do not know how to interpret them. In the era of computers, you may never be called upon to calculate a statistic by hand, but the numbers can only have meaning if you understand the significance of the computer's work.

Some people may consciously or unconsciously "lie with statistics" by reporting the highest values to make their findings look more impressive. You should watch for this in your reading. As we have said before, one of the most useful things about understanding the research process is being able to evaluate other research. Of course, you too should be honest and straightforward in reporting your findings.

In this chapter, we have considered several statistics that can help us measure the association between two nominal or two ordinal variables. You should realize that if you get a correlation coefficient which supports your hypothesis, you should also consider if the relationship could have been due to chance. In other words, you should use a test of significance as well as a measure of association. For nominal and ordinal data, you could use the chi square statistic we discussed in the last chapter. In addition, there are tests of significance designed specifically for Kendall's tau and gamma. We do not have space here to consider these separate tests, but you could find discussions of them in statistics texts we have listed in the Suggested Readings.

In the next chapter we will discuss how to measure the strength of association between two interval variables.

SUMMARY
MEASURES OF ASSOCIATION

Level of Measurement	Statistic	Formula	Interpretation
Nominal	Goodman's & Kruskal's tau	Tau = (number of errors made not knowing independent variable − number of errors made knowing independent variable) / number of errors made not knowing independent variable	Asymmetric
	Guttman's lambda	λ = (number of errors made not knowing independent variable − number of errors made knowing independent variable) / number of errors made not knowing independent variable	Asymmetric strict monotonic

Ordinal	Goodman's & Kruskal's gamma	$\gamma = \dfrac{A - D}{A + D}$	Symmetric, weak monotonic
	Somers' d	$d_{yx} = \dfrac{A - D}{A + D + T_y}$	Asymmetric, moderate monotonic
	Kendall's tau$_a$	$\tau_a = \dfrac{A - D}{N(N - 1)/2}$	Symmetric, strict monotonic relationship
	Kendall's tau$_b$	$\tau_b = \dfrac{A - D}{\sqrt{(A + D + T_x)(A + D + T_y)}}$	Symmetric, strict monotonic relationship; used in case of many ties
	Kendall's tau$_c$	$\tau_c = \dfrac{A - D}{N^2[(m - 1)(m)]/2}$	Symmetric, moderate monotonic relationship; used in tables with unequal number of columns and rows

STUDY QUESTIONS

1. Compute Guttman's lambda and Goodman and Kruskal's tau for the following:

	Race		
Party ID	Black	White	Total
Democrat	299	891	1190
Republican	151	759	910
Total	450	1650	2100

Interpret your results.

2. Calculate gamma, Somers' d, and Kendall's tau for the following table:

		Income		
		High	Medium	Low
Political Participation	High	30	15	5
	Medium	20	10	10
	Low	20	25	20

Interpret your findings.

3. Why do you get different values for gamma, Somers' d, and Kendall's tau?
4. What statistic would be most appropriate for calculating the degree of association in the following table? Calculate and interpret your results.

		Trust in Government	
		High	Low
Political Participation	High	20	7
	Medium	20	33
	Low	5	75

5. The measures of association we discussed are proportionate-reduction-in-error measures. Discuss the basic logic of these measures and how they are interpreted.

Measuring Association: Interval Data

Chapter Thirteen

Political scientists do not often have the luxury of dealing with data which can be measured at the interval level. It is often very tempting to cheat and claim the data is interval because the statistics available at the interval level are so much more powerful than ordinal- or nominal-level statistics (one temptation, obviously, which should be resisted).

The statistical results you would get would be meaningless. Interval measurement implies precise distances between numbers. Nominal and ordinal measurement does not have such precision. Like the statistics we discussed in the last chapter, the goal of the interval-level statistics we will be examining here is to determine the pattern among variables. With interval-level data we can go beyond just examining the positioning of cases in a table. Because the data are measured by a scale with known intervals we can determine the precise effect of one variable on another. To do this, we examine how many units the dependent variable changes with respect to each unit change in the independent variable.

There are two interrelated procedures which we will consider in this chapter. The first procedure is *regression*. Regression is aimed at predicting the value of one variable on the basis of the value of another variable or variables. Notice that regression is the first technique which we have discussed which is capable of examining relationships among many variables as well as the relationship between just two variables. Regression can be used in multivariate relationships, as opposed to the bivariate relationships we previously discussed. The second procedure is *Pearson's correlation (r)* which, like the statistics we covered in the last chapter, is a measure of association. Pearson's correlation is based on regression and can determine how accurate the predictions made from the regression procedure would be. Let us first explain the procedure of regression.[1]

REGRESSION ANALYSIS

The aim of regression analysis is to be able to predict the value of the dependent variable on the basis of the known value of the independent variable. The idea of predicting formed the basis of the proportionate-reduction-in-error measures of association we discussed in the last chapter. The difference with regression is that we are dealing with the interval level of measurement, and this means that we have a much more precise basis for predicting. Instead of using such techniques as predicting on the basis of the modal value or on the basis of positioning of cases in a table, in regression analysis we develop a mathematical equation which expresses the relationship between the dependent variable and the independent variables. We want this equation to tell us how many units the dependent variable will change for each unit change of the independent variables. As with the asymmetric measures discussed in the last chapter, you should notice that it is essential that you specify what you believe to be the direction of causation before you can use the regression procedure. That is, you must specify the dependent and independent variables. As usual, the theoretical structure, which is the conceptual foundation for your research, should be of help. Now let us consider how we can develop a mathematical statement which characterizes the relationship among variables. For simplicity's sake we will first examine the case in which we have only one independent variable.

The best thing to do when you wish to describe the relationship between two interval-level variables is to construct a graph of the values of the variables for each of several individual cases. Such a graph is called a *scattergram.*

For simplicity's sake let us look at a sample with ten cases. The two variables represent the number of memberships in political interest groups and the number of acts of political participation in a two-year period. We will assume that we have established a theoretical basis for believing that the level of political participation is the dependent variable (y) and the level of group membership is the independent variable (x). Let us assume that the ten cases had the following values for the two variables.

All we have to do to express these values graphically is place one point on a graph for each case. The position of the point is determined by the

---

1. Hubert M. Blalock, *Social Statistics,* 2nd ed. (New York: McGraw-Hill, 1972). Much of this chapter relies upon Blalock's discussion of correlation and regression.

Measuring Association: Interval Data 301

Person	Y	X
1	1	0
2	3	1
3	5	2
4	7	3
5	9	4
6	11	5
7	13	6
8	15	7
9	17	8
10	19	9

values the case has on both x and y. The perpendicular axis of a graph is the y axis. Therefore, the value a case has on y determines how high the point will be. The horizontal axis is the x axis. The value each case has on x will determine how far to the right on the x axis the point will be. In the case of the data above, we would have the following set of points on the graph as shown in Figure 13-1.

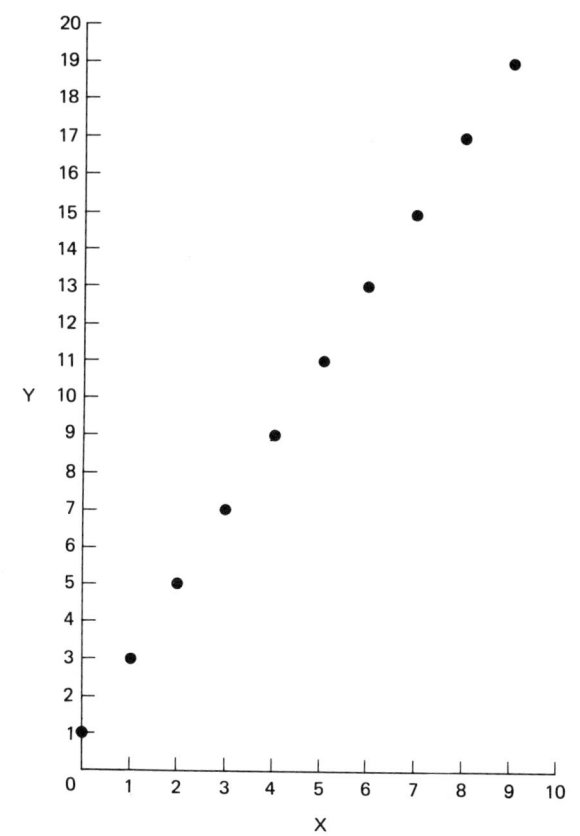

Figure 13-1 HYPOTHETICAL LINEAR RELATIONSHIP

By examining this graph it appears quite obvious that the data are monotonic and linear. That is, the data could easily be represented by a straight line which would pass through each of the ten points. This means that we could express the relationship between the two variables by the mathematical formula for a straight line. That formula, if you remember your high school math, is $y = a + bx$. In this formula, y is, of course, the dependent variable and x is the independent variable. The a value is a constant. It indicates the point at which the line will intercept or cross the y axis of the graph. It is equal to the value of the dependent variable when the independent variable is absent. In our hypothetical data above we had a person who belonged to no political interest groups. He had, however, taken part in one act of political participation. Therefore, with this set of data the constant a value is one.

The b is the value in which we are most interested. That value tells us the degree of unit change in y per unit change in x. By examining these data we can easily see that each time the number of interest group memberships increases by one, the number of acts of political participation increases by two. Therefore, the b value for these data is two (the slope of the line). It tells us how great an impact the independent variable has on the dependent variable. We know that for this set of data we can write a mathematical equation which will perfectly describe the relationship between the two variables. That formula is $y = 1 + 2x$. The line which is prescribed by this formula is called a regression line. Given this formula, you could easily predict the value of y. All you would need to do to predict the value of y is to multiply the value of x by two and add one.

This is all very well, but it is rare to have such a simple pattern in the values of two variables. So where would something like this be useful in actual research? We should point out that it is not always useful. So far, we have already uncovered several assumptions which we must be able to make before we can use the regression procedure: (1) in the first place, we must have interval level data; (2) we must be able to specify a dependent and an independent variable, and (3) we must also be able to assume that the relationship between the two variables can be characterized by a straight line. Some relationships, of course, are not perfectly linear. In our example, it is quite possible that there would be something besides a linear relationship. That is, it is possible interest group membership will result in higher levels of participation, but only up to a certain point. Beyond that point there may be no change in the levels of participation (see Figure 13-2).

Now there is obviously a relationship between these two variables, but it is not possible to characterize that relationship accurately by the formula for a straight line. There are procedures to enable you to express this relation-

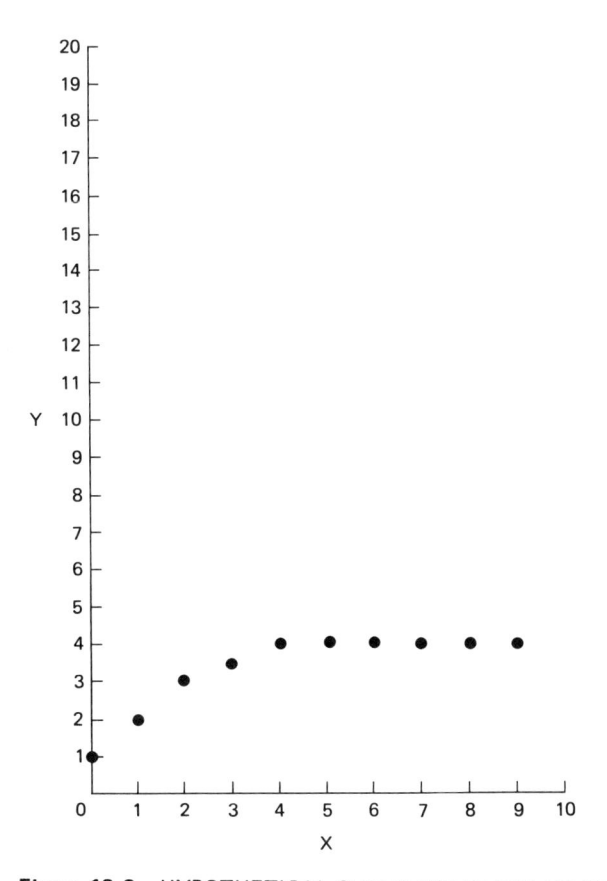

Figure 13-2 HYPOTHETICAL CURVILINEAR RELATIONSHIP

ship mathematically. These procedures are beyond the scope of this book,[2] but you must be aware that there may be perfect relationships which are not linear in form. These relationships cannot be accurately characterized by the linear regression procedure we will be discussing here. If you are dealing with only two variables, it is always a good idea to graph the data so that you can visually tell the shape of the relationship. If you are dealing with more than two variables you will have to rely upon your own judgment and your theory to determine if the assumption of a linear relationship is warranted.

---

2. The following books provide a good starting place for investigation of curvilinear regression techniques: Mordecai Ezekiel and Karl A. Fox, *Methods of Correlations and Regression Analysis*, 3rd ed. (New York: Wiley, 1969); George W. Snedecor, *Statistical Methods*, 6th ed. (Ames: Iowa State University Press, 1967); and Fred N. Kerlinger and E. Pedhazur, *Multiple Regression in Behavioral Research* (New York: Holt, Rinehart & Winston, 1973).

304 *MEASURING ASSOCIATION: INTERVAL DATA*

There are also other assumptions which have to be made to use regression analysis. We must assume the data have been gathered by random sampling and that the variables each have distributions the shape of a normal curve. We must also assume that all the causes of the dependent variable which have not been included in the regression equation have minor effects and will cancel each other out. We must also assume that any of these other causes are in no way related to the independent variable in the equation. The basic point is that regression, although a very powerful and useful technique, should not be used indiscriminately.

Even with that point in mind, you may still wonder how to use regression analysis without the simplified data of our first example. What if, for instance, we had the pattern of points shown in Figure 13-3 on a graph?

Now, by examining this graph, it is clear that the relationship is basically linear. It is also clear that this is not a simple linear relationship. It would not be possible to draw one straight line which would go through all of the ten points. What we could still do, though, is draw a line which fits these

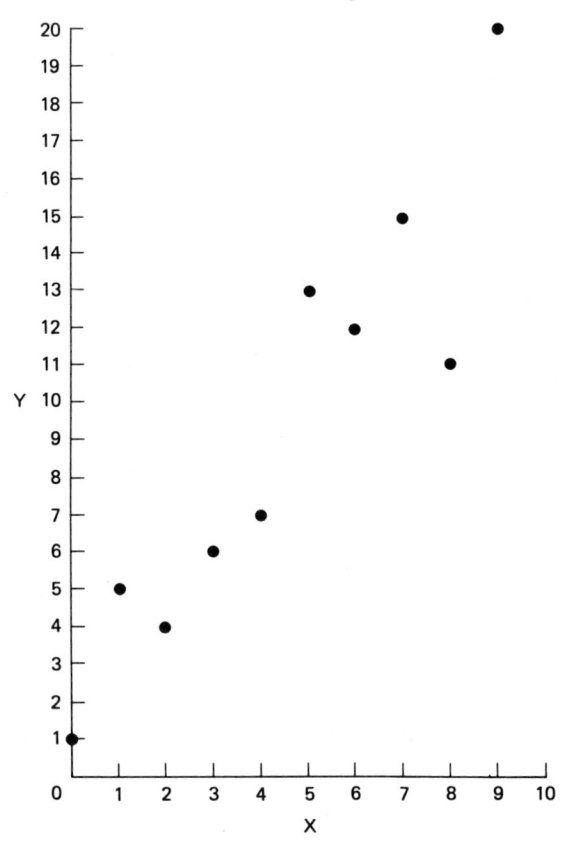

Figure 13-3 HYPOTHETICAL DISTRIBUTION OF DATA

points as closely as possible. We might do that by a trial and error method. For instance, we might try positioning a ruler over the points until we have a line which we think is the best approximation of all the points. But this, of course, would be a tedious and highly subjective process. Statisticians have, therefore, developed criteria to be used in place of this "free-hand" regression.

The first step in using these criteria is to examine the way the points are distributed around any regression line. Unless there is a perfect relationship, as in our first example, no matter where a line is drawn, some data points will not fall exactly on the line. In other words, the actual values which the cases have on y will not be the same as the values which would be predicted by the formula for any straight line. The deviations between the actual values and the values which would be predicted from the equation for any given line are called *residuals*. The basic idea of the criteria developed by statisticians is to draw a line which would minimize the size of these residuals. To do this, we would first have to determine how we would measure the deviations. For instance, let us look at the following regression line and two points which deviate from that line (Figure 13-4). It would be possible to measure the

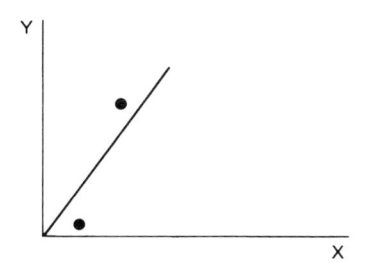

Figure 13-4 REGRESSION LINE WITH DEVIANT POINTS

amount by which these points deviate from the regression line by determining how large the perpendicular distance is from each point to the line. That is, we would draw a line from each point to the place where it intercepted the regression line at a 90° angle and then determine the size of that deviation. In that case, the deviations would look like Figure 13-5. Or we could simply

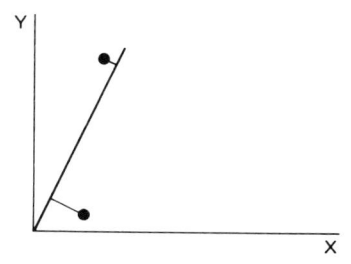

Figure 13-5 REGRESSION LINE WITH DEVIATIONS MEASURED FROM PERPENDICULAR

draw a vertical line from the data points to the regression line and then determine how large that deviation is. In that case, the deviations would look like Figure 13-6. It is this latter criterion which is most frequently used in

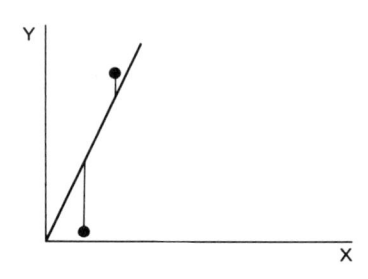

FIGURE 13-6 REGRESSION LINE WITH DEVIATIONS MEASURED VERTICALLY

regression analysis. We draw a line (or more accurately, we determine the formula for a line) which will minimize the total amount by which the data points deviate from the line. We measure the size of the deviation by measuring the vertical distance from the data point to the regression line.

One other problem has to be taken care of. Obviously, some data points will have higher or lower y values than the regression formula would predict. If we simply add two such deviations they might cancel each other out (for example, $(+2)+(-2) = 0$). Some way must be found to get around this problem of signs in summing the deviations. The solution is the same we used in calculating the standard deviation and the chi square. We square the actual vertical deviations before we add them. The actual criterion used to determine which regression line is drawn is that the line must minimize the size of the summed squares of the vertical deviations of the data points from the regression line. This criterion is called, appropriately enough, the *least-squares criterion*.

How do we determine which formula for a regression line will fit this criterion? Fortunately for us, the statisticians who gave us the criterion have also given us formulas to use to draw a line which satisfies the criterion. They have shown the criterion is satisfied when the following formulas are used to determine the constants in the regression equation:

$$b = \frac{\Sigma \ (x - \bar{x}) \ (y - \bar{y})}{\Sigma \ (x - \bar{x})^2}$$

$$a = \bar{y} - b\bar{x}$$

(Remember, $\bar{x}$ indicates the mean of the values of the independent variable, and $\bar{y}$ indicates the mean of the values of the dependent variable.) Let us examine these formulas in slightly greater depth. The formula for the *b* coefficient is the amount of the covariation of the independent and dependent variable expressed as a proportion of the amount of variation of the independent variable. We have mentioned covariation before. The basic idea of covariation is that as the value of one variable changes, the value of another variable changes. This means that particular values of two variables tend to be associated. This idea is the basis for the numerator of the formula for b. If two variables are positively related, you would expect to find high values of x associated with high values of y, and vice-versa. If two variables are negatively related, you would expect to find high values of x associated with low values of y, or vice-versa. To determine if one of these patterns exists, the first step is to determine the amount by which an individual case has scores on x and y which deviate from the mean scores of x and y. To do this we compute the following quantities: $(x - \bar{x})$ and $(y - \bar{y})$. If both scores are above the mean or if both are below it, multiplying the two deviations will produce a positive value. If one score is above and one is below the mean, multiplying the values will produce a negative value. If there is no systematic relationship between the two variables, the positive and negative numbers will cancel each other out and the covariation will equal zero. This measure of the covariation of x and y is expressed as a proportion of the total variation of the independent variable. The total variation of the independent variable is measured by the sum of the squared deviations of each x score from the mean: $\Sigma(x - \bar{x})^2$. This formula should look familiar to you since it is the numerator of the formula for the standard deviation.

The formula for the constant a in the regression equation is $a = \bar{y} - b\bar{x}$. This formula is nothing more than an algebraic transformation of the formula for a line: $y = a + bx$. Instead of solving the equation for the value of y, here we assume we know the value of y (or more precisely, the mean value of y) and we are solving for the value of a. As further proof of this formula, we present the following derivation:

$y = a + bx$
$-a = -y + bx$ (Solving for a; transfers from one side of an equation to the other results in a change of sign.)
$a = y - bx$ (Multiply the entire equation by -1.)

We use the mean values of x and y because we are not interested in only finding the line for any individual x and y values, but in finding a line which best fits all of the x and y values in the data set.

The formula for the a constant could be easily calculated by hand. The formula for the b constant, however, would lead to some rather long and complex calculations. To simplify the calculations of b by hand, statisticians have developed the following computational formula:

$$b = \frac{\Sigma xy - \frac{(\Sigma x)(\Sigma y)}{N}}{\Sigma x^2 - \frac{(\Sigma x)^2}{N}}$$

308 MEASURING ASSOCIATION: INTERVAL DATA

This formula looks imposing, but instead of having to determine the deviation of each x and y score from the mean and then multiplying, the only quantities one needs to know are Σxy, Σx, Σy, and Σx^2.

Let us take a simple example We are trying to determine the relationship between citizenship scores (our independent variable) and acts of political participation (our dependent variable). We will set up the following hypothetical situation with five people (for the sake of simplicity of calculations). Person one scores 5 on the citizenship test and participates in one political act. Person two scores 7 and participates in three political acts. Persons three and four each score 10 and participate in five and seven acts, respectively. Person five scores 12 and participates in nine political acts. The results can be seen graphically in Figure 13-7. Now let us array our data and make our computation:

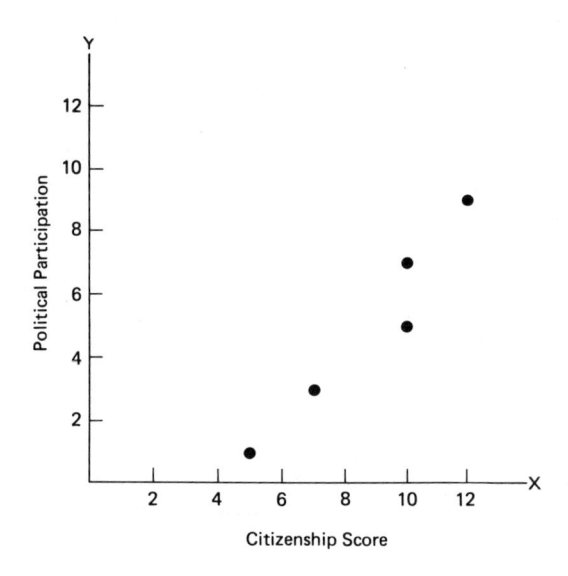

Figure 13-7 HYPOTHETICAL GRAPH OF CITIZENSHIP SCORE AND POLITICAL PARTICIPATION

x	y	xy	x^2	
5	1	5	25	$\overline{x} = 8.8$
7	3	21	49	$\overline{y} = 5$
10	5	50	100	
10	7	70	100	
12	9	108	144	
$\Sigma x = 44$	$\Sigma y = 25$	$\Sigma xy = 254$	$\Sigma x^2 = 418$	$N = 5$

$$b = \frac{\Sigma xy - \frac{(\Sigma x)(\Sigma y)}{N}}{\Sigma x^2 - \frac{(\Sigma x)^2}{N}}$$

$$b = \frac{254 - \frac{(44)(25)}{5}}{418 - \frac{(1936)}{5}} = \frac{254 - \frac{1100}{5}}{418 - \frac{1936}{5}} = \frac{254 - 220}{418 - 387.2} = \frac{34}{30.8} = 1.10$$

$a = \bar{y} - b\bar{x} = a = 5 - (1.10)(8.8) = 5 - 9.68 = -4.68$

$y = a + bx = y = -4.68 + 1.10(x)$

Looking at the scattergram in Figure 13-7, we are not surprised that we calculated a negative value for a or the y intercept, since the line would intercept the y axis below the level of the x axis. Using the equation $y = -4.68 - 1.10(x)$, we can now predict the level of participation of any individual if we know his score on the citizenship test. As of yet we do not know how good our prediction will be. That will be discussed below.

One word of warning is in order. Although you may be able to make predictions, you might not be able to explain them. This is where your theoretical formulation is important. While prediction is a first step in advancing knowledge, it is also necessary to try to understand why one variable affects another in a certain way. This is why this book presents a comprehensive overview of the research process. You must not get overwhelmed by numbers and lose sight of their underlying meanings.

In most cases, if you use a regression analysis, you will probably have a computer do the actual calculations for you. It is not really very important that you memorize the formulas for the constants in a regression equation. If you do calculate a regression analysis by hand, you could easily look up the equation in this or any other statistics book. What is important is that you understand what assumptions have to be made before you can use regression and that you understand exactly what you have after you have performed a regression analysis.

Remember, the goal of regression is to predict the values of a dependent variable on the basis of the values of an independent variable. You want to do this by creating a mathematical equation which states the relationship between the variables. The equation which is most frequently used is the equation for a straight line: $y = a + bx$. In most cases, the data points will be distributed in a way that no one line can accurately represent the distribution. What we want to do is to determine what would be the "best" line. To define what we mean by the best line, we establish the least-squares criterion. That is, we say that the best line is the one which minimizes the squared vertical deviations from the data points to the line. The equations above will create for any set of data a line which meets the least-squares criterion. Once the equations have been solved for the a and b values, we then can easily predict the value of the dependent variable based on the value of the independent variable.

Of course, these predicted y scores will not be the exact y scores from the data. The predicted scores indicate what the value of the dependent variable would be if there were a perfect linear relationship between the independent variable and the dependent variable. The actual y scores will probably deviate from these predicted scores (indicated by y') by some amount. That amount can be determined by subtracting the predicted scores from the actual scores $(y-y')$.

To have some idea of the average amount of deviation between the actual and predicted scores, we could compute a measure called the *standard error of estimate*. To do this we would compute all of the deviations $(y-y')$, square the deviations to eliminate the problem of positive and negative deviations canceling each other out $(y-y')^2$ and then add all of the squared deviations: $\Sigma(y-y')^2$. Finally, we could divide by the number of data points to provide an average deviation and then take the square root to compensate for squaring the deviations. These steps can be summarized in this equation:

$$\sqrt{\frac{\Sigma(y-y')^2}{N}}$$

Once again, this formula should look more than vaguely familiar to you. What we have done is calculated a standard deviation. In this case it is not a standard deviation of data from the mean of a distribution, but the deviation of data points from the regression line. This formula will tell you the average difference between the actual scores and the scores predicted from the regression equation, or the average error you would make in using the regression equation to predict the scores of the dependent variable. For that reason, this measure is called the standard error of estimate. Obviously the lower the error of estimate, the better you can predict from the independent to dependent variable.

So far we have only considered a regression analysis with one independent variable. As we noted before, it is also possible to include more than one independent variable in the analysis. The mathematical calculations involved are much too complex to present here. But the interpretation of a multiple regression is quite similar to the interpretation of a bivariate regression. We can no longer deal with the simple notion of drawing a line to fit data points since the addition of more variables has moved us beyond the two-dimensional world of graph paper. But we still want to determine the "best fit," and we still use a least-squares criterion to define the best fit.

The regression equation for more than one independent variable will look as follows: $y = a + b_1x_1 + b_2x_2 + \cdots b_kx_k$. In this formula the b_1 is the b coefficient for the independent variable x_1, and b_2 is the coefficient for the independent variable x_2. The dots and the notation b_kx_k indicate that additional independent variables could be added to the equation. The b coefficients, however, must be interpreted slightly differently in a multiple regression than in a bivariate regression. In a bivariate regression, the b coefficient told you the unit change in y given a unit change in x. But all variables other than x and y were ignored in calculating the coefficient. In a multiple regression, other variables have to be taken into consideration. The b coefficients in a multiple regression indicate how much change will occur in the dependent variable given a unit change in one independent variable, when all the other independent variables in the equation have been held constant. The b coefficients in multiple regression, therefore, do not indicate the total effect of the independent variable on the dependent variable because the independent variable may have some additional indirect effect through its impact on another independent variable in the regression analysis which is being held constant. But the coefficients do indicate the direct effect of the independent variable on the dependent variable.

A researcher may often use a multiple regression to compare the relative size of the direct effects of different independent variables on the dependent variable. But it should be obvious that such comparisons are not meaningful if the independent variables have been measured by different standards. It is necessary, therefore, to find some way to standardize the b coefficients so that they are comparable, regardless of the units in which the variables have originally been measured. The b coefficients are standardized by multiplying them by the fraction $\frac{sx}{sy}$, which stands for the standard deviation of the independent variable divided by the standard deviation of the dependent variable. The resulting number, called a *beta coefficient*, is, therefore, calculated by the formula $\beta = b\frac{sx}{sy}$. The beta coefficients are, therefore, comparable since they have been standardized for the unit of measurement. By examining the beta coefficients, it is possible to determine which of the independent variables have the largest direct effect on the dependent variable. To compare the impacts of the independent variables we compare beta coefficients. To predict the dependent variable we use b coefficients.

Remember, though, both the b coefficients and the beta coefficients are based on the regression equation. This equation determines the line which minimizes the squared deviations of the actual scores from the line. A regression equation can be determined for any set of data, whether there is any relationship among the variables or not. Before using the regression technique to predict y scores or to compare the effects of independent variables on the dependent variable, we would obviously want to know more about how closely related the independent variable and the dependent variable are. We can do this by calculating a measure of association between the independent and dependent variable. The measure which is commonly used is Pearson's r, which we will discuss in the next section.

PEARSON'S CORRELATION COEFFICIENT

The correlation coefficient was introduced by Karl Pearson and is referred to as Pearson's r or the *product–moment coefficient*. Since the Pearson correlation coefficient, or Pearson's r, is a measure of association, it varies from $+1.00$ to -1.00. The formula for r is:

$$r = \frac{\Sigma(x - \bar{x})(y - \bar{y})}{\sqrt{[\Sigma(x - \bar{x})^2][\Sigma(y - \bar{y})^2]}}$$

Let us examine this formula to see what is involved in r. The numerator, as you may notice, is the same as that for the formula for b coefficients. That is, it is a measure of the covariation of the two variables x and y. The denominator for the b coefficient was a measure of the variance in the independent variable. The b coefficient is an asymmetric measure since it assumes that you have specified an independent and a dependent variable. Pearson's r is a symmetric measure, which means that it measures the strength of association between two variables without identifying the independent or dependent variables. Therefore, in r, the covariation is compared to the amount of variation in both the x and the y variables. The covariation, then, is expressed as a proportion of the square root of the product of the variation in x and the variation in y. It can also be described as the ratio of the covariance to the product of the standard deviations of X and Y.

The covariance can attain a value larger than one. By dividing the covariance by the product of the standard deviations of the two variables, the covariance is standardized so that it varies between $+1.0$ and -1.0, as do the other measures of association we discussed. Also, like the other measures of association, ± 1.00 indicates a perfect relationship between the two variables. Let us consider how we can interpret the intermediate values of r. To do this let us return to the regression line which can be drawn using the values of x and y.

One way to determine how "good" a prediction we could make using the regression line would be to look at the standard error of estimate which we discussed above. The standard error of estimate, remember, is equivalent to the standard deviation of the actual data points around the predicted regression line. If there is a large standard error of estimate, the regression equation cannot provide very accurate estimates of the y values. The problem with relying on the standard error of estimate to determine the accuracy of predictions from the regression line is that the size of the standard error is dependent on how the units of the dependent variable are measured. If we were trying to predict the mean income level of the United States population, consider what would happen if we changed our unit of measure from dollars to cents. Obviously, no one is likely to use cents in this case. But the point is that different variables are likely to be measured using different standards of measurement. This means that the different standard errors of estimate are not comparable. What we need is to express the deviation of the points from the regression in a way which is comparable for all variables regardless of how they are measured.

To do this we use the following logic. The numerator of the standard error of estimate is the sum of the squared deviations of the data points from the regression line: $\Sigma(y-y')^2$. The regression line has been drawn to minimize the squared deviations, and we have presumably included in the regression equation the variables which we would expect to give us the most accurate prediction of the dependent variable. In other words, we have done everything we know to minimize the deviation between the actual and predicted data points for the dependent variable. We, therefore, cannot explain why the actual scores vary from the predicted scores. The amount of difference between actual and predicted scores is the *unexplained variance*.

This quantity, as we said, is dependent to a certain extent on the units used to measure the data. Therefore, we want to standardize this measure. We do this by expressing the unexplained variance as a proportion of *total variance*. The total variance can be measured by the degree to which the actual data points deviate from the mean of the data. This total variance can be measured by summing the squared deviation of the actual scores from the mean: $\Sigma(y-\bar{y})^2$. This, of course, is the numerator of the equation for the standard deviation of a distribution. What we have, then, is a measure which is a ratio of unexplained variance to total variance:

$$\frac{\Sigma(y-y')^2}{\Sigma(y-\bar{y})^2}$$

The numerator of this measure tells us how accurate we can be in predicting the value of the dependent variable when we use the value of the independent variable as a guide. The denominator tells us how accurately we can predict the value of the dependent variable using only the mean score of the distribution as a guide. If there is not much difference between the accuracy of those predictions based on the independent variable and those based solely on the mean, we would conclude that there is little relationship between the independent and the dependent variable. The logic of this measure is, thus, similar to the logic of the proportionate-reduction-in-error measures we discussed in the last chapter.

If there was little or no improvement in the accuracy of prediction based on the regression line, the ratio of unexplained total variance will be close to 1; and if there is a large improvement, the ratio will be close to 0. Therefore, 1.00 would indicate no relationship and 0 would indicate a perfect relationship. This is exactly opposite to all the other measures of association we have discussed in which 0 equals no relationship and 1.00 equals a perfect relationship. To prevent confusion, then, we want to reverse the measure to make it comparable to other measures of association. We can do this by subtracting the ratio from 1. Therefore, the smaller the ratio, the larger the score of the correlation coefficient will be. The original ratio was $\frac{\text{unexplained variance}}{\text{total variance}}$. By subtracting that ratio from 1 we have a measure of the proportion of *explained variance*. The resulting measure, which is indicated by r^2 (*coefficient of determination*), is, therefore, a measure of the proportion of total variance in the dependent variable which is explained by the independent variable(s):

$$r^2 = 1 - \frac{(y-y')^2}{(y-\bar{y})^2}$$

where y = actual scores on the dependent variable; y' = scores of the dependent variable predicted using the regression equation; and $\bar{y}$ = the mean value of the actual scores of the dependent variable.

The square root of this measure, r, is Pearson's correlation coefficient. It is the value of r which is usually listed in research reports. But the value of r has no simple interpretation. In fact, the r may be misleading. An r of 0.5 sounds rather hefty. To interpret this, though, we would have to square 0.5, giving us $r^2 = 0.25$, which does not sound so impressive. The 0.25 tells us that 25% of the total variance is explained by the independent variable(s).

There are other warnings which we should give you about Pearson's correlation. In the first place, since it is based on the variance around the regression line, it can accurately measure the strength of only linear relations. Secondly, since it is based on the variance of scores, it is affected by extreme scores which vary by a large amount. The extreme score will result in either an artificially high or an artificially low r in a process similar to the way a mean can be pulled in the direction of an extreme score in a distribution. If there are extreme scores, it may make sense to examine the value of r both with and without the extremes. It is also a good idea to examine the extreme scores to see if they may indicate the possibility of a curvilinear relationship.

Finally, the size of the correlation coefficient may be low simply because there is not enough variability in the values of the independent variable. Again, remember that we determine that there is a relationship between two variables by explaining the way the variables covary. Remember, the defining formula for r is the covariance of the independent and dependent variables which is standardized by dividing by the product of the standard deviations of both variables. This means that if there is a small variance in the values of the independent variable, there is no way that we can establish a relationship between the independent and dependent variables. The solution to this problem, obviously, is to find some way to increase the amount of variability. This may mean increasing the sample size or increasing the strength of the experimental treatments. Increasing the variability may also help clear up the problems of extreme scores because we would have a more accurate picture of the actual relationship between the variables. Of course, we realize that it may not always be possible to increase the variability because of limited resources or simple infeasibility.

All of these warnings about the Pearson correlation coefficient lead to one fundamental recommendation. It is always a good idea when you are computing a Pearson's r to examine a scattergram of the two variables. Only by examining the actual distribution of data points can you know if you have a low r due to a couple of extreme scores, a curvilinear relationship, or, at least within this range of data, simply no relationship at all between the two variables.

Now let us compute the Pearson's r for the data we previously graphed on the scattergram in Figure 13-7. To do this, we will use the computational formula which statisticians have developed to simplify the calculations.

The scattergram of the distribution noted in Figure 13-7 makes it visually apparent that there was a strong relationship between our independent variable (citizenship test score) and the dependent variable (acts of political participation). The Pearson's $r = 0.97$. The value would almost never

$$r = \frac{N\Sigma xy - (\Sigma x)(\Sigma y)}{\sqrt{[N\Sigma x^2 - (\Sigma x)^2][N\Sigma y^2 - (\Sigma y)^2]}}$$

x	y	xy	x^2	y^2
5	1	5	25	1
7	3	21	49	9
10	5	50	100	25
10	7	70	100	49
12	9	108	144	81
$x = 44$	$y = 25$	$xy = 254$	$x^2 = 418$	$y^2 = 165$

$$r = \frac{N\Sigma xy - (\Sigma x)(\Sigma y)}{\sqrt{[N\Sigma x^2 - (\Sigma x)^2][N\Sigma y^2 - (\Sigma y)^2]}} = \frac{5(254) - (44)(25)}{\sqrt{[5(418) - (44)^2][5(165) - (25)^2]}}$$

$$= \frac{1270 - 1100}{\sqrt{(2090 - 1936)(825 - 625)}} = \frac{170}{\sqrt{(154)(200)}} = \frac{170}{\sqrt{30800}} = \frac{170}{175.5} = 0.97$$

occur in actual research. When using Pearson's r we generally consider a correlation of 0.4 to be moderate since there are so many other factors confounding relationships in the real world. If we wanted to interpret Pearson's r to gauge our prediction of the dependent variable (if we knew the independent variable), we would use r^2 or the coefficient of determination. In our example $r^2 = (0.97) \times (0.97) = 0.94$. In other words we could reduce the error in guessing the value of the dependent variable by a whopping 94% by knowing the independent value. To predict the value of the dependent variable for any value of the independent variable we would use the regression equation we derived earlier.

MULTIVARIATE MEASURES

The Pearson coefficient measures the relationship between two variables, as did all the measures of association we discussed in the last chapter. But a regression analysis can be computed using more than one independent variable (but always with only a single dependent variable). It would obviously be useful to have measures of association which are also multivariate. We will discuss two such multivariate measures which are based on the Pearson correlation coefficient.

The first of these multivariate measures is partial correlation. A *partial correlation* coefficient measures the relationship between two variables when the effects of another variable or other variables have been controlled. If you remember, we talked about the idea of control before. When we control in cross-tabulation tables, we hold the value of a variable constant in order to cancel out any effect that variable may have on the relationship in which we are interested. In a partial correlation, however, the effects of other variables are controlled by mathematically removing the effects of those variables from the relationship on which we are focusing. Let us see how this is done by examining the formula for a partial correlation coefficient:

$$r_{ij \cdot k} = \frac{r_{ij} - (r_{ik})(r_{jk})}{\sqrt{1 - r_{ik}^2}\sqrt{1 - r_{jk}^2}}$$

The first thing we should do is to explain the notation of this rather awesome formula. The $r_{ij \cdot k}$ indicates the correlation of the two variables i and j with the effect of the third variable, k, controlled. In general, any variables listed after a dot are control variables in partial correlation. The r_{ij} indicates the correlation between variable i and variable j. And, obviously, r_{ik} indicates the correlation between variable i and k, the control variable, and r_{jk} is the correlation between variable j and the control variable (k).

The first value in the numerator of this formula, then, is the total relationship between the two variables in which we are interested, variables i and j. Then we subtract from this total relationship the combined relationship between the control variable and variable i and between the control variable and variable j. Thus, we are letting the control variable explain all it can in both variables i and j. Then we subtract that amount from the total relationship of i and j. What we have left is the amount of relationship between i and j with the effects of k controlled, since the effects of k have been mathematically removed.

The denominator is a measure of the total variance remaining in variables i and j after the control variable has been removed. If total variance equals 1, then $1-r_{ik}^2$ is the amount of variance left in variable i after the control variable has been removed. Similarly, $1-r_{jk}^2$ is the amount of variance left in j after the effects of k have been removed.

The partial correlation coefficient, then, is the amount of covariation between i and j after the effects of the control variable have been removed, expressed as a proportion of total variance left in i and j. Like the Pearson correlation coefficient, the partial correlation coefficient is the amount of explained variance expressed as a proportion of total variance. Also, the partial correlation coefficient must be squared to be interpreted meaningfully. Once squared, the partial correlation coefficient may be interpreted as the percentage of variation in the dependent variable which cannot be explained by the control variable but which is explained by the independent variable.

We have been talking about using a partial correlation to control for the effects of one variable. It is also possible to control for the effects of more than one variable using the same logic. When we control for one variable only, the partial correlation is called the first-order partial correlation. When we control for two variables, the partial correlation is called the second-order partial, and so on. Because of this, the original correlation between two variables when no variables have been controlled is often called the zero-order correlation.

Although the means of controlling for variables is different in partial correlation than it is in cross-tabulation, the interpretation of the results of controlling is the same. If the relationship after controlling is the same as it was before, then we know the control variable has no effect. If the relation disappears, then we know that the relationship is spurious, or that the control variable intervenes between the independent and dependent variable. If the relationship appears or is reversed as a result of controlling, then we know the control variable is related to both the independent and dependent variables and in a direction opposite to the original relationship with the dependent variable (see Chapter Eleven).

318 MEASURING ASSOCIATION: INTERVAL DATA

There are a couple of advantages of using a partial correlation to control rather than contingency tables. In the first place, to use partial correlation it is not necessary to break down our sample into subsamples. That means we do not have to worry about ending up with too few cases to permit generalization. This also means it is more feasible to control for more than one variable. Secondly, the partial correlation coefficient is a single summary measure. That means that it is easier to interpret than a series of separate tables, one for each category of the control variable or variables. Of course, you can only use partial correlation with interval data.

Let us consider an example of calculating and interpreting a partial correlation. Let us assume that you are interested in determining the effect of the mean income level of a community on the proportion of eligible voters who voted. Therefore, you have gathered data from several communities following the 1980 Presidential election. You have calculated a Pearson's r (r_{ij}) to measure the relationship between income level and proportion voting. You found the relationship was 0.61. You suspect, however, that it is possible that the effect of the mean educational level may be confounding the relationship between income and voting. Therefore, you decide to control for educational level.

To do this you first have to calculate the Pearson's r for the relationship between income and education (r_{ik}) and for the relationship between voting and education (r_{jk}). Let us assume these values are $r_{ik} = 0.80$ and $r_{jk} = 0.70$. Now we can substitute these values into the formula for partial correlation:

$$r_{ij \cdot k} = \frac{r_{ij} - (r_{ik})(r_{jk})}{\sqrt{1 - r_{ik}^2} \sqrt{1 - r_{jk}^2}}$$

$$= \frac{0.61 - (0.80)(0.70)}{\sqrt{1 - (0.80)^2} \sqrt{1 - (0.70)^2}}$$

$$= \frac{0.61 - 0.56}{\sqrt{1 - 0.64} \sqrt{1 - 0.49}}$$

$$= \frac{0.05}{\sqrt{0.36} \sqrt{0.51}}$$

$$= \frac{0.05}{(0.60)(0.71)}$$

$$= \frac{0.05}{0.43} = 0.12$$

In our hypothetical example our suspicion that the relationship between the mean income of a community and voting rate was being affected by a third variable, education, is confirmed. After removing the effects of education by controlling through the technique of partial correlation, we find that the relationship between income and voting drops from 0.61 to 0.12. It would seem to be that education affects both income and voting, and income alone has relatively little relationship to voting.

The second multivariate measure we will discuss is *multiple correlation*. A multiple correlation coefficient indicates the amount of variance in the dependent variable which can be explained by all the independent variables considered together. Let us look at the formula for a multiple correlation for a case in which there are only two independent variables:

$$R^2_{i \cdot jk} = r^2_{ij} + r^2_{ik \cdot j}(1 - r^2_{ij})$$

Once again, let us explain the notation of this formula. A capital R indicates a multiple correlation. The first subscript i indicates the dependent variable. The subscripts j and k which follow the dot are the independent variables. Note that this notation is different than that used in partial correlation. (The reason for the inconsistent notation is beyond us and a source of frustration to us and to you, we are sure.) The notation $R^2_{i \cdot jk}$ therefore, indicates the proportion of variance of the dependent variable i which is explained by the two independent variables, j and k, acting together.

The rest of the formula explains how we compute the quantity $R^2_{i \cdot jk}$. In the first place, we have the quantity r^2_{ij}. This indicates that we let the variable j explain all the variance it can in the dependent variable. The remaining variance then is $(1 - r^2_{ij})$. We then let the second independent variable explain all of this remaining variance. But since we are now only interested in the effect of the second variable, we must, therefore, control for the effects of the first variable. That means that we have $r^2_{ik \cdot j}$ which indicates the partial correlation of i and k, controlling for j. This is then multiplied by the variance unexplained by j: $r^2_{ik \cdot j}(1 - r^2_{ij})$. This amount is then added to r^2_{ij}. The multiple correlation coefficient $R^2_{i \cdot jk}$ is thus calculated by adding the following quantities:

$$R^2_{i \cdot jk} = r^2_{ij} + r^2_{ik \cdot j}(1 - r^2_{ij})$$

where r^2_{ij} = the proportion of variance of i explained by j; $r^2_{ik \cdot j}$ = the additional proportion explained by k; and $1 - r^2_{ij}$ = the proportion unexplained by j. Like partial correlation the multiple correlation, formula can be extended to include more than two independent variables.

Let us now consider how we could calculate a multiple correlation coefficient. We will use the same hypothetical data we used above in our illustration of partial correlation. In that example we were interested in the relationship between mean income in communities and the proportion of eligible voters who voted in the 1980 election. We examined the relationship between income and voting when the effect of education was controlled. Now let us consider the relationship between voting and both income and education considered together. To do this we need to know the following values: r_{ij}^2, or the relation between income and voting and $r_{ik \cdot j}^2$ or the relation between education and voting with the effect of income controlled. We know from the previous example that r_{ij} is 0.61. Therefore, $r_{ij}^2 = (0.61)^2 = 0.37$. We will have to calculate $r_{ik \cdot j}^2$ using the partial correlation formula above. (Now you know why computers are so handy!) That formula in this case is

$$r_{ik \cdot j} = \frac{r_{ik} - (r_{ij})(r_{kj})}{\left(\sqrt{1 - r_{ij}^2}\right)\left(\sqrt{1 - r_{kj}^2}\right)}$$

$$= \frac{0.80 - (0.61)(0.70)}{\left(\sqrt{1 - (0.61)^2}\right)\left(\sqrt{1 - (0.70)^2}\right)}$$

$$= \frac{0.80 - 0.43}{\left(\sqrt{1 - 0.37}\right)\left(\sqrt{1 - 0.49}\right)}$$

$$= \frac{0.37}{0.56} = 0.66$$

Now let us substitute these values into the formula for multiple correlation.

$$\begin{aligned}R_{i \cdot jk}^2 &= r_{ij}^2 + r_{ik \cdot j}^2 (1 - r_{ij}^2) \\ &= (0.61)^2 + (0.66)^2 [1 - (0.61)^2] \\ &= 0.37 + 0.43(1 - 0.37) \\ &= 0.37 + 0.43(0.63) \\ &= 0.37 + 0.27 \\ &= 0.64\end{aligned}$$

Therefore, by considering both income and education together, we could explain 64% of the variance in the dependent variable, voting.

In this chapter we have examined some of the most common statistical techniques which are used with interval-level data. Since interval-level data can be precisely measured, the statistics used with the data are much more sophisticated than are statistics for nominal- or ordinal-level data. This means they are somewhat more difficult to calculate, but it also means that they produce much more information. It is for this reason that political scientists continuously attempt to increase the precision with which variables can be measured.

TESTS OF SIGNIFICANCE

As we said in the last chapter, if you find a measure of association which supports your hypothesis, it is necessary for you to consider if the measure is significant. For each of the measures of association which we have discussed here, there are specific tests of significance. The logic of these tests is derived from a statistical procedure which we have not discussed: *analysis of variance*. An analysis of variance is a significance test for the difference among means of more than two samples. It produces a statistic called F which has a sampling distribution. The F is calculated by comparing the amount of explained variance to the amount of unexplained variance. The amount of explained and unexplained variance is estimated in different ways for different types of problems.

In the case of correlation coefficients, it is very easy to estimate the two types of variance. As we said above, the square of each of the three correlation coefficients can be interpreted as the amount of variance in the dependent variable which can be explained by the independent variable. To determine unexplained variance, we can simply subtract the amount of explained variance (the square of the correlation coefficient) from the total possible variance, which is 1: unexplained variance = 1 − explained variance. To compare the amount of explained and unexplained variance we express the explained variance as a proportion of the unexplained variance: $\frac{\text{explained variance}}{\text{unexplained variance}}$. As with both the t test and the chi square, we have to take into consideration the number of degrees of freedom. With the F statistic the number of degrees of freedom is included in the calculation. Now let us examine the formula for F for each of the correlation coefficients we discussed.

For Pearson's r, the F statistic can be calculated by using the following formula:

$$F = \frac{r^2(N-2)}{1-r^2}$$

The r^2 in the numerator is the amount of variance in the dependent variable explained by the independent variable. The $1-r^2$ in the denominator is the amount of unexplained variance. The N-2 is the number of degrees of freedom, where N equals the number of cases. The two degrees of freedom are lost by the calculation of the a and b constants in the regression line on which the correlation coefficient is based.

For both the partial and multiple correlation coefficients, more than one independent variable is being considered. Additional degrees of freedom are lost by the consideration of those variables. The formula for the F statistic for multiple correlation is:

$$F = \left(\frac{R^2}{1-R^2}\right)\left(\frac{N-k-1}{k}\right)$$

where R^2 = explained variance; $1-R^2$ = unexplained variance; N = number of cases; and k = number of variables. For the partial correlation, the formula for the F statistic is

$$F = \frac{(\text{partial } r)^2 \, (N-k-1)}{1-(\text{partial } r)^2}$$

where $(\text{partial } r)^2$ = amount of variance in the dependent variable explained by one independent variable with the other independent variable controlled; $1-(\text{partial } r)^2$ = unexplained variance; N = number of cases; and k = number of variables.

Once the F values are calculated, we must compare the values to a sampling distribution. As with the t test and the chi square, there are different sampling distributions for different degrees of freedom. The degrees of freedom of F are affected both by the number of cases and the number of independent variables. The degrees of freedom due to the number of cases are referred to as df_2. For the simple Pearson r, df_2 is equal to N-2. For multiple and partial r, the df_2 can be calculated by the following formula:

$$df_2 = N - k$$

where N = number of cases and k = number of variables. The degrees of freedom due to the number of variables are referred to as df_1. The formula for df_1 is

$$df_1 = k - 1$$

where k = number of variables. The tables for the F distribution, therefore, have three dimensions: the probability level, df_1 and df_2. Since three dimensions can not be graphed onto a single table, the F distribution is pictured in separate tables for various levels of significance. The tables for the F distribution are included in the Statistical Tables.

Now let us use these formulas to determine if the correlation coefficients we computed are significant. The Pearson r we computed was 0.97. There were five cases in the sample. Therefore, substituting into the equation we have

$$F = \frac{(0.97)^2 (5-2)}{1 - (0.97)^2}$$

$$= \frac{(0.94)(3)}{0.06}$$

$$= \frac{2.82}{0.06}$$

$$= 47$$

In this case with two variables, $df_1 = 2 - 1 = 1$. With five cases, $df_2 = 5 - 2 = 3$. Looking at an F distribution at a 0.05 probability level for df_1 of 1 and df_2 of 3, we find the 10.13. The F statistic would have to be equal to or larger than 10.13 for it to be significant at the 0.05 level. Our coefficient is obviously significant at that level.

The partial correlation we computed was 0.12, based on the same sample size and with one variable controlled. Therefore, substituting we have

$$F = \frac{(0.12)^2 (5 - 3 - 1)}{1 - (0.12)^2}$$

$$= \frac{(0.01)(1)}{1 - (0.01)}$$

$$= \frac{0.01}{0.99}$$

$$= 0.01$$
$$df_1 = 3 - 1 = 2$$
$$df_2 = 5 - 3 = 2$$

Checking the F distribution for df_1 of 2 and df_2 of 2 at the 0.05 level, we find 19.00. Our F statistic does not equal or exceed 19.00; therefore, the partial correlation is not significant at the 0.05 level.

324 MEASURING ASSOCIATION: INTERVAL DATA

Finally, let us look at the multiple correlation coefficient.

$$F = \frac{(0.64)^2}{1 - (0.64)^2} \left(\frac{5 - 3 - 1}{3}\right)$$

$$= \left(\frac{0.41}{1 - 0.41}\right)\left(\frac{1}{3}\right)$$

$$= \left(\frac{0.41}{0.59}\right)\left(\frac{1}{3}\right)$$

$$= 6.9 \times \frac{1}{3}$$

$$= 0.23$$

Looking in the F distribution table at a 0.05 level of significance, we see the value of F would have to equal or exceed 19.00 to be significant. The multiple correlation is, therefore, not significant.

We have now examined all of the stages involved in doing research. All that remains is to fit the pieces of the puzzle together and report what we have found. In the last chapter we will try to show you how we integrate these steps and give you some hints about writing a good research report.

SUMMARY
MEASURES OF ASSOCIATION
AND TESTS OF SIGNIFICANCE

Level of Measurement	Statistic	Formula	Interpretation
Interval	b coefficient	$b = \dfrac{\Sigma xy - \dfrac{(\Sigma x)(\Sigma y)}{N}}{\Sigma x^2 - \dfrac{(\Sigma x)^2}{N}}$	Impact of the independent variable on the dependent variable
Interval	Beta coefficient	$\beta = b \left(\dfrac{s_x}{s_y}\right)$	Standardized b coefficient
Interval	Pearson's r	$r = \dfrac{N\Sigma XY - (\Sigma X)(\Sigma Y)}{\sqrt{[N\Sigma X^2 - (\Sigma X)^2][N\Sigma Y^2 - (\Sigma Y)^2]}}$	Symmetric, strict monotonic
Interval	Coefficient of determination	$r^2 = 1 - \dfrac{(y - y')^2}{(y - \bar{y})^2}$	Interpretation of amount of variance in the dependent variable explained by the independent variable

Interval	Partial correlation	$r_{ij \cdot k} = \dfrac{r_{ij} - (r_{ik})(r_{jk})}{\sqrt{1 - r_{ik}^2} \sqrt{1 - r_{jk}^2}}$	Variance in dependent variable unexplained by the control variable and explained by the independent variable
Interval	Multiple correlation	$R_{i \cdot jk}^2 = r_{ij}^2 + r_{ik \cdot j}^2 (1 - r_{ij}^2)$	Variance in dependent variable explained by multiple independent variables
Interval	F	$F = \dfrac{r^2(N-2)}{1-r^2}$	Probability the results are due to chance
Interval	F	$F = \left(\dfrac{R^2}{1-R^2}\right)\left(\dfrac{N-k-1}{k}\right)$	Probability the results are due to chance
Interval	F	$F = \dfrac{(\text{partial } r)^2 (N-k-1)}{1 - (\text{partial } r)^2}$	Probability the results are due to chance

STUDY QUESTIONS

Answer the following questions using the following hypothetical information you might accumulate in a ten-nation study.

	% Literate	Mean Income (in thousands of dollars)	Voter Turnout (%)
United States	85	12.4	48
Great Britain	93	8.2	66
France	82	7.1	46
West Germany	97	10.5	46
Yugoslavia	71	3.9	71
U.S.S.R.	87	5.0	97
Iran	43	1.7	33
India	21	0.8	40
China	69	3.9	98
Brazil	56	2.7	62

1. Calculate and interpret the relationship between literacy and voter turnout using Pearson's r. What proportion of the variance is explained?
2. Calculate a simple regression between income and voter turnout. Interpret your results.
3. What is the difference between b and beta?
4. Calculate the relationship between literacy and voter turnout controlling for income. Compare your results to your finding in question 1 and interpret.
5. What is the R^2 between literacy, income, and voter turnout with voter turnout as the dependent variable? Interpret.

Epilogue

Part Five

Doing Political Analysis

Chapter Fourteen

It must seem to you that we have come a very long way from our discussion of science and theory building. What we want to do in this chapter is to try to show you that all of the various topics we discussed are really part of the integrated process of political research. We think it is important for you to see the research process as a series of related activities.

If you want to understand the political world, you must gather information about that world. But research involves much more than just gathering facts. The goal of the research process is to structure the facts and organize them to allow us to understand what the political world is like.

Research is born in the world of ideas and if research is to mean anything, it must never get too far removed from that world. To be more precise, research is born in the very elementary recognition that there are things we do not know that we want to know. Prior to understanding any research it is necessary to determine what it is we want to know and then decide how we can know it. These questions immediately embroil us in the search for a philosophy of knowledge. Science provides one way to answer these difficult questions. But we have tried to point out that science is not the only possible answer to the search for knowledge. To a large extent, whether you use science or some other method depends upon what makes the most sense to you. We do not mean to be flippant. It actually depends upon what questions interest you and what kinds of verification satisfies you.

A scientist wants knowledge about the empirical world and confirms or verifies it by observation. It is the empiricism of science which gives the research process its character. It is to fulfill the requirement of empiricism that we look for empirical indicators of our concepts. It is to conform to empiricism that we gather empirical data to verify our "hunches" about the world around us. But it is an *understanding* of that world for which the scientist searches. That means that he must go beyond simply collecting and storing random bits of information he picks up from his observations. Such random bits can not provide understanding. He must fit those bits together into meaningful patterns which explain the empirical world. Those meaningful patterns are theories. It is the search for such theories that puts the scientist once again right back in the world of ideas.

As we have stated, theory building is the process of interrelating generalizations into a logical structure. To some, the logical structure must be a deductive structure. To interrelate generalizations deductively it is necessary to have universal generalizations, which means generalizations which hold for 100% of the cases which have been observed. This is a very rigorous, perhaps too rigorous, standard for political scientists to achieve. Therefore, some political scientists argue that as long as generalizations can be interrelated by a common focus the structure can be considered theory. Such theories are known as concatenated theories.

The process of scientific research is circular. The first stage is to ask the research question: "Hey, what's going on here?" The next stage is to gather the empirical information that we will use to answer that question. The final stage is to interpret all the data and return to the question that started us off in the first place. Of course, this is a very simplistic statement of the research process. The information that we gather will almost always suggest new questions or fail to answer our initial questions as fully or as absolutely as we would wish. This process of building knowledge is no simple mechanical process. You cannot automatically use a set repertoire of techniques. It is a constant and cumulative process of adding bits and pieces of information and struggling in your mind to find the pattern, to see the order.

Sometimes it is difficult when you are drawing a sample, sitting in the library, struggling with the computer, or interpreting a chi square to keep the whole goal and purpose of research in mind. It is easy to lose your perspective—to miss the forest for the trees, as the old cliché says. If you allow that to happen, you are no longer a scientist, political or otherwise. You are a technician. No matter how technically proficient you may be, your research will not be meaningful unless it starts with a desire to understand and ends with an answer to the question, "What does it all mean?"

It is because of all of this that we say that research is not isolated from the rest of the discipline of political science nor from the "real world" politics of the newspapers and TV evening news. A science of politics is aimed at understanding the empirical political world which surrounds us. How much we know and the quality of what we know are the results of the research.

Even if you do not conduct that research yourself, your understanding of that process can make it possible for you to evaluate the research you consume. Before you accept the conclusions of research, you should understand the process by which the information was gathered. You should know how many observations were made. The more observations which are made, the more sure we can be that the patterns are representative of the population and not just a random occurrence. You should know if the way the observations were made could have caused biased findings. If the researcher read one thousand books by the PLO (Palestine Liberation Organization) or the John Birch Society, he or she would certainly have many observations, but the data would probably not provide a representative picture of the world. Once you start evaluating and analyzing research reports, you become an equal partner in the research process.

We have tried to introduce you to the separate stages of an empirical research project. However, we have not yet considered the very last stage in research: reporting your findings. We will devote the rest of this chapter to a discussion of what you should include in your research report.

THE RESEARCH REPORT

There are two general points we would like to make about the research report. In the first place, it is very important that you do not simply look for and report the data which support your hypothesis. You must be honest with both yourself and with those who read your research report; you should report the data which support your hypothesis as well as the data which do not. This is often very painful since you have devoted much time and effort to attempt to substantiate your hypothesis. But you must remember that you are engaged in a process which has broad implications. The ultimate goal is not to substantiate your hypothesis but to aid in building theories of politics. This is a cumulative process. What is substantiated in your research should provide the foundation for further research. If you distort your findings so that your hypothesis appears to be supported when it actually has not been, others may be misled into using that hypothesis as a basis for their research. For instance, you may report that your research has supported the hypothesis that socioeconomic status is related to political participation. Other researchers may accept that finding and then devote their research efforts to trying to discover why socioeconomic status is related to participation. Obviously, if you have misrepresented your data, these other researchers will be wasting their time.

Although we would all like to claim "victory" and be able to report that our data have supported our hypothesis, misrepresenting our findings benefits no one. On the other hand, honestly reporting that the data have not substantiated our hypothesis does advance our knowledge about the political phenomena in which we are interested. We would know at least that that particular hypothesis does not accurately portray the patterning among the political events which exists in this particular set of data. This does not necessarily mean that the hypothesis is totally wrong. You, or others, using different data, a different operational definition, different techniques, may want to retest the hypothesis. But in this case there has been no attempt to mislead others.

The second thing to keep in mind in reporting your research is to be as clear, precise, and thorough as possible about specifying the procedures you followed. Again, this is vital because the results of your research should be part of a cumulative process of gathering information to be used in theory building. Others probably will be—or should be—unwilling to accept your conclusions without evaluating the methods you used to reach those conclusions. If others believe your data base was inadequate or inappropriate or that the standards you set for establishing support for your hypothesis were not stringent enough, and so forth, they would probably be unwilling to accept your conclusions as a basis for their research. Clear reporting of the procedures used in research is also a way of counteracting any effect the researcher's values may have had on the project. By knowing exactly what procedures he or she followed, we can duplicate the research to see if we would draw the same conclusions despite possible differences in our values.

Writing The Research Report.

There are six different topics which should be discussed in the report. Although the order in which these topics are covered may vary, we will discuss them in the order we feel is most commonly used.

Stating the Question. The first step in a research project is deciding exactly what hypothesis you will be testing and phrasing the hypothesis clearly and precisely. That means identifying the concepts involved and specifying the relationship between the concepts. We have said that by stating the hypothesis clearly you can avoid many false starts and irrelevant tangents in the research process. We also think that stating the hypothesis clearly is an important first step in reporting the research. We feel that it is nice to let the reader in on what is going on as soon as possible. You should not make him dredge through several pages, or even the whole report, wondering what you are doing.

Reviewing the Literature. Research does not occur in a vacuum. As we have said, the impetus for a research project comes from the realization that there is something you want to know. The first thing you can do is to find out what others have to say about whatever it is that has caught your attention. There is no reason why you should spend time researching a question if others have already found the answer to it. On the other hand, you may find that others have performed research on some aspects of the problem in which you are interested. But the information they report may be only one piece in the puzzle on which you are working. Or you may actually find that others have researched the same question, but you may feel for a variety of reasons, that you want to proceed with your own research. For example, the other research may have produced unclear or contradictory results, or it may have used a measurement, or a sample, or a statistical technique which you thought was unsatisfactory. In other words, knowing what others have done will help you decide whether more research is necessary and, if so, in what areas the research should concentrate. The review of the literature can provide a direction for your research. In addition, the literature review can provide a justification for the research should it establish that no satisfactory answer has been provided for the question you are asking. By discussing the literature review in the research report you can explain to your reader why you have done research on this topic and how your research fits together with the rest of the literature to build our knowledge.

For this reason you must do library research even if you expect to gather your own data. You will not only be able to place your research in the context of other research, you can also learn from their successes and failures and get ideas as to which methods might be most appropriate. The literature review, therefore, provides a basis for the next component of a research project: establishing the importance of the research.

Establishing the Importance of Research. Presumably you would not take the time and effort necessary for research unless you thought the topic were important. It is a good idea, however, for you to analyze why you believe it is important. That, like the literature review, may help you decide on a direction or focus for your research. You should also point out the importance of your work to your readers. Chances are they may question this themselves.

There are two ways you can establish the importance of your research. In the first place, you may be able to point out the practical uses of your research. In other words, you can point out how the answer to your research question could be important information for people other than political scientists. For instance, if you are investigating the relationship between socioeconomic status and political activity, you may find that those low in socioeconomic status are prone to violent activity such as riots. This may be important information to people in political office who are considering various proposals to increase the income level of the poor. Of course, the fact that the political scientists can point out that their research is relevant to practical problems does not necessarily mean they should specify how the information should be used. As we have said before, this depends on what they believe to be the role of values in political science.

The second way to establish the importance of your research is to show how the information produced can help build or validate portions of a theory of politics. To do this, you would want to show if and how the generalization you are researching relates to other generalizations which have been previously developed. For instance, if you are investigating the relationship between socioeconomic status and political activity, you might discuss how this relationship relates to other knowledge you have on other determinants of political activity such as political trust or patriotism. Research does not take place in a vacuum. We are not interested in isolated bits and pieces of information. We want to fit those bits and pieces together into a whole which can help us better understand the world around us.

Of course, as we have argued many times before, we believe the practical and the theoretical aspects of research are not really two different things, but simply different sides of the same coin. Understanding the world around us, which is the goal of empirical theory, is a very practical goal. It is the understanding that theory provides that allows us to make statements about relationships in the world. This understanding may be all that some people may desire. Government officials or others active in politics may want to use that understanding as a guide to their behavior. By suggesting that you discuss both the practical importance and the theoretical importance of your research we do not mean these things are unrelated. We simply mean that you should make clear to your reader all ways that your research is useful and important.

Now that we have thoroughly discussed the environment from which our research question was derived, let us consider the actual research project. The next thing you should include in your research report is a thorough discussion of how you planned and set up your research project.

Describing the Research Project. Remember, the fundamental guideline here is to be thorough. To meet the requirement of intersubjectivity, we have to spell out all the procedures we used in enough depth to enable other researchers to duplicate our research project. So, all the procedures you used must be completely discussed. You must state exactly what hypothesis you will be using and be sure the hypothesis is clearly and precisely specified. That means identifying the concepts involved and specifying the relationship between the concepts. Next you should specify how you measured your variables. This means that if you are dealing with a concept which is not directly observable, you should specify how you operationalized the concept.

If you operationalized the concept, you should clarify how you attempted to establish the reliability and validity of the operationalization. If you have used an index, you should say why you included the various indicators and why they do belong together in measuring one underlying concept. Any assumptions you made about the importance or weight of the items in the index should also be spelled out. If you used a scale, you should point out that it met all of the assumptions of the scaling procedure. For instance, if you used a Guttman scale, you should list the coefficient of reproducibility and coefficient of scalability.

In your library research you should note the various operationalizations of the variables. If there is a more or less standard operationalization, you will probably want to use it in your research if at all possible. If you will be replicating some of these studies, you might want to use the same sources (perhaps updated), same questionnaire, same type of analysis, etc.

Next you should thoroughly discuss what data you needed to test the hypothesis. You should discuss the level of analysis as well as the unit of analysis with which you dealt. State very clearly the universe to which you want your hypothesis to apply. If you have sampled, explain what basic list of the universe you used and what sampling plan you used. This means covering how you chose the sample size and what sampling procedure you used.

If you collect your own data you should examine the research strategy you used to collect the data. How did you try to control the problems of internal and external validity? Did you have a control group? If so, could you randomize the assignment of cases to the control group and the experimental group? Did you give a pretest? If you did not do these things, you should explain to your reader why you did not and what other controls you might have used to reduce the effect of factors which threaten internal and external validity. The readers should be told if no controls were used to assure internal and external validity since that will obviously affect how much stock they can put in your research findings.

If you are using data gathered by others, it is obvious that many factors are beyond control. You should note any limitations imposed by your data sources.

Finally, you should explain what technique you used to gather data. If you used a questionnaire, it should be included in an appendix. You should explain how the questionnaire was administered, that is, by phone, mail, face-to-face, and so forth. You should spell out any possible problems of bias due to the types of people who did not respond. If you gathered data by observation, you should specify what was observed and how you structured the observations. With content analysis you should describe what documents you selected and how you categorized the content. If you used studies reported by others, you should report how they gathered their data.

The point is, obviously, that you must be thorough. It may seem tedious to put down all this information. It may also be tedious for the readers to plow through it all. But the point is there is no way they can decide how much they can rely upon your findings unless they know on what information you are basing your conclusions. You should honestly tell your readers all of the inevitable compromises you made to gather evidence in your research. That also means that if you are going to be an intelligent reader, you should always plow through all of the information. Let us now proceed to the next topic in our research report: data analysis.

Analyzing the Data. We emphasized the importance of thoroughness in describing the research project. Here we want to emphasize the importance of both thoroughness and honesty.

If you are using logic and qualitative information to derive your conclusions, you must construct your argument carefully. The standards for evidence should have been determined before the study began. If your data are limited, your conclusions must be speculative. If your findings differ from the existing body of literature, you must ascertain why. If you are reviewing the research of others or case studies done by others, you are attempting to isolate commonalities which account for similar results. Case studies are valuable as sources of in-depth information in specific cases. But you must be aware of the limitations of generalizing based on case studies. At the same time it may be possible to hypothesize that research on other cases may lead to similar conclusions because of some underlying relationships.

If you are using quantitative data, you may use statistics as a tool in summarizing your data. Statistics may make it easier to see relationships clearly and determine more precisely the meaning of those relationships. It is not always simple to interpret the statistics, and we wish to reiterate that numbers do not make the findings any more meaningful if those numbers are unrepresentative or analyzed incorrectly.

You must also pay attention to the level of measurement. You can be much more precise with interval measurement than with nominal measurement, which is essentially qualitative. The analysis stage is too late to lament the lack of interval-level data. This again points to the integrated nature of the research process. When planning research you must consider how you will want to analyze your data later. It is, as people say, possible to lie with statistics. You now know some ways you could do that. If you had a highly skewed distribution, you could use the mean as the measure of central tendency rather than the median, if that would make your findings more consistent with what you wanted. Or you could use gamma as a measure of association with ordinal data rather than a more restrictive measure such as

Kendall's tau. You could change the level of significance you would be willing to tolerate from 0.05 to 0.10.

But you should not play games with the data. You should decide which are the most appropriate statistics for your data. You should explain to your reader why you chose those statistics and report those values honestly. Of course, that does not mean you should not look at any other measures. There is always the possibility of an unexpected finding. For instance, you might have hypothesized that there was a linear relationship between two variables. The Kendall's tau, which measures a linear relationship for ordinal data, might be low. It would probably be a good idea to look at the values of gamma and Somers' *d,* which are also ordinal measures of association. By doing that you might get a better idea of the nature of the relationship. But you should not report your hypothesis as confirmed if the gamma is large, since gamma does not test for a strict linear relationship. Any time that you are talking about the strength of association between two variables, remember that you should report both the measure of association you used as well as a test of significance which indicates the probability that the results could have been obtained by chance.

Remember, even if you may be fortunate enough to have a computer to do the actual calculations for you, it is important to understand the logic in any statistical procedure you use. Only by understanding a statistic can you be sure that you are using the right statistic and interpreting it properly. Once we have thoroughly reported the results of our data analysis, we are ready for the last section of the research project: drawing conclusions.

Drawing Conclusions. The final step is to look at your findings and decide what it all means. The first thing you should do is to indicate whether or not your hypothesis appears to have been confirmed. There is a good possibility that your data will not present a perfectly clear, unambiguous conclusion. Of course, you should be honest about any conflicting evidence, but you also owe it to your reader to conclude what in general you believe the evidence indicates.

You should also briefly interpret the implications of the findings. To do this you should refer to the practical and theoretical significance of the research which you previously discussed. That is, you should indicate how the research findings could be used by decision-makers or by others active in politics. You should also indicate how these findings contribute to building theories in political science. Remember, if the hypothesis is confirmed, that is evidence to support the theory on which the hypothesis is based. If the hypothesis is not confirmed, you should attempt to explain why you think the findings were negative. Finally, you might also indicate what direction you think future research should take.

CONCLUSION

We hope that this review has clarified the process of fitting the stages of research together. Through all of the stages, from asking the question, to planning how to gather evidence, analyzing the evidence, and drawing the conclusions, the goal is always the same: to increase our knowledge about and understanding of the political world around us. Theory and research are not the concerns of intellectuals in ivory towers. They are the concerns of curious people like you who want to know more about the world around them.

We also hope that this summary has given you some idea of what to look for when you read a research report. It is no longer sufficient to merely look at the introduction and conclusion. The conclusion is only as valid as the process of getting there. Therefore, you should never be willing to accept researchers' conclusions unless you know how they gathered and analyzed the evidence on which those conclusions were based.

We have said before that science is skeptical. It requires constant questioning and verification to establish the validity of its findings. You should be equally skeptical. Before you accept the claims of others, whether it be an article in an academic journal, a newspaper story, or Joe from the corner bar, you should ask on what evidence the claim is based. Science provides standards that you can use to evaluate that evidence. We hope that by understanding the standards of scientific research you will become a much more critical evaluator of the claims and counterclaims which bombard us daily.

Appendix

SUGGESTED READINGS

Part I—Philosophy of Political Science

Overview of Discipline

CRICK, BERNARD, *In Defense of Politics*. London: Weidenfeld and Nicholson, 1962.

DAHL, ROBERT, *Modern Political Analysis* (3rd. ed.). Englewood Cliffs, N.J.: Prentice-Hall, 1976

EASTON, DAVID, *The Political System* (2nd ed.). New York: Knopf, 1971.

EULAU, HEINZ, *The Behavioral Persuasion in Politics*. New York: Random House, 1963.

GRAHAM, GEORGE, JR. and GEORGE W. CAREY, eds., *The Post Behavioral Era: Perspectives on Political Science*. New York: David McKay Co., 1972.

HYNEMAN, CHARLES, *The Study of Politics*. Urbana, Ill.: University of Illinois Press, 1959.

LASSWELL, HAROLD, *Politics: Who Gets What, When, How*. New York: Meridian Press 1958.

MCCOY, CHARLES A. and JOHN PLAYFORD, eds., *Apolitical Politics: A Critique of Behavioralism*. New York: Thomas Y. Crowell, 1967.

SOMIT, ALBERT and JOSEPH TANENHAUS, *The Development of Political Science*. Boston: Allyn & Bacon, 1967.

STORING, HERBERT, ed., *Essays on the Scientific Study of Politics*. New York: Holt, Rinehart & Winston, 1962.

Philosophy of Science

BRAITHWAITE, R.B., *Scientific Explanation*. New York: Harper Torchbook, 1953.

BROWN, ROBERT, *Explanation in Social Science*. Chicago: Aldine, 1963.

FEIGL, HERBERT and MAY BRODBECK, eds., *Readings in the Philosophy of Science*. New York: Appleton-Century-Crofts, 1953.

GRAHAM, GEORGE, JR., *Methodological Foundations for Political Analysis*. Waltham, Mass.: Xerox College Publishing, 1971.

GROSS, LLEWELLYN, ed., *Symposium on Sociological Theory*. Evanston: Row, Peterson, 1959.

HEMPEL, CARL, *Philosophy of Natural Science*. Englewood Cliffs, N.J.: Prentice-Hall, 1966.

KAPLAN, ABRAHAM, *The Conduct of Inquiry*. San Francisco: Chandler Publishing, 1964.

KUHN, THOMAS S., *The Structure of Scientific Revolution*. (2nd ed.). Chicago: University of Chicago Press, 1970.

MEEHAN, EUGENE, *The Theory and Method of Political Analysis*. Homewood, Ill.: Dorsey Press, 1965.

NAGEL, ERNEST, *The Structure of Science*. New York: Harcourt Brace Jovanovich, 1961.

REICHENBACH, HANS, *The Rise of Scientific Philosophy*. Berkeley: University of California Press, 1951.

RUDNER, RICHARD, *Philosophy of Social Science*. Englewood Cliffs, N.J.: Prentice-Hall, 1966.

VAN DYKE, VERNON, *Political Science: A Philosophical Analysis*. Stanford: Stanford University Press, 1960.

ZETTERBERG, HANS, *On Theory and Verification in Sociology*. Totowa, N.J.: Bedminister Press, 1963.

Ethics in Research

AMERICAN POLITICAL SCIENCE ASSOCIATION COMMITTEE on PROFESSIONAL STANDARDS and RESPONSIBILITIES. Ethical Problems of Academic Political Science," P.S., I, no. 3 (1968).

BLISSET, MARLAN, *Politics in Science*, Boston: Little Brown, 1972.

COOK, STUART W., "Ethical Issues in the Conduct of Research in Social Relations," in *Research Methods in Social Relations* (3rd ed.), ed. Claire Selltiz et al. New York: Holt, Rinehart & Winston, 1976

DEGRAZIA, ALFRED, et al., eds., *The Velikovsky Affair*. New Hyde Park, N.Y.: University Books, 1966.

FREUND, PAUL A., *Experimentation with Human Subjects*. New York: George Braziller, 1970

HOROWITZ, IRVING LOUIS, *The Rise and Fall of Project Camelot*. Cambridge, Mass: M.I.T. Press, 1967.
KELMAN, HERBERT, *A Time to Speak: On Human Values and Social Research*. San Francisco: Jossey-Boss, 1968.
MAC RAE, DUNCAN, JR., *The Social Function of Social Science*. New Haven: Yale University Press, 1976.
Office of Science and Technology, Executive Office of the President. *Privacy and Behavioral Research*. Washington, D.C.: U.S. Government Printing Office, 1967.
RITZER, GEORGE, ed., *Social Realities: Dynamic Perspectives*. Boston: Allyn & Bacon, 1974.
SJOBERG, GIDEON, ed., *Ethics, Politics and Social Research*. Cambridge, Mass.: Schenkman, 1967.
—— and ROGER NETT, *A Methodology for Social Research*. New York: Harper & Row, 1968.

Part II—Conceptual Analysis

General Scope
CHARLESWORTH, JAMES C., ed., *Contemporary Political Analysis*. New York: Free Press, 1967.
CONWAY, M. MARGARET and FRANK B. FEIGERT, *Political Analysis: An Introduction* (2nd. ed.). Boston: Allyn & Bacon, 1976.
EASTON, DAVID, ed., *Varieties of Political Theory*, Englewood Cliffs, N.J.: Prentice-Hall, 1966.
EVERSON, DAVID H. and JOANN POPARAD PAINE, *An Introduction to Systematic Political Science*. Homewood, Ill.: Dorsey Press, 1973.
ISAAK, ALAN C., *Scope and Methods of Political Science* (revised ed.). Homewood, Ill.: Dorsey Press, 1975.
JAROS, DEAN and LAWRENCE V. GRANT, *Political Behavior: Choices and Perspectives*. New York: St. Martin's Press, 1974.
MAYER, LAWRENCE C., *Comparative Political Inquiry*. Homewood, Ill.: Dorsey Press, 1972.
WELSH, WILLIAM A., *Studying Politics*. New York: Praeger, 1973.
YOUNG, ROLAND, ed., *Approaches to the Study of Politics*. Evanston, Ill.: Northwestern University Press, 1958.

Political Socialization
DAWSON, RICHARD E., KENNETH PREWITT, and KAREN S. DAWSON, *Political Socialization* (2nd ed.). Boston: Little, Brown, 1977.
DENNIS, JACK, ed., *Socialization to Politics*. New York: John Wiley, 1973.
EASTON, DAVID and JACK DENNIS, *Children in the Political System*. New York: McGraw-Hill, 1969.
GREENSTEIN, FRED, *Children and Politics*. New Haven: Yale University Press, 1965.
HESS, ROBERT and JUDITH V. TORNEY, *The Development of Political Attitudes in Children*. Chicago: Aldine, 1967.
HYMAN, HERBERT H., *Political Socialization*. New York: The Free Press, 1959.

JAROS, DEAN, *Socialization to Politics*. New York: Praeger, 1973.
LANGTON, KENNETH, *Political Socialization*. New York: Oxford University Press, 1969.
SIGEL, ROBERTA, ed., *Learning About Politics: Studies in Political Socialization*. New York: Random House, 1973.
WEISSBERG, ROBERT, *Political Learning, Political Choice & Democratic Citizenship*. Englewood Cliffs, N.J.: Prentice-Hall, 1974.

Political Culture

ALMOND, GABRIEL and SIDNEY VERBA, *The Civic Culture*. Boston: Little, Brown, 1965.
BANFIELD, EDWARD C., *The Moral Basis of a Backward Society*. Glencoe, Ill.: The Free Press, 1965.
BLUHM, WILLIAM T., *Ideologies and Attitudes: Modern Political Culture*. Englewood Cliffs, N.J.: Prentice-Hall, 1974.
DEVINE, DONALD J., *The Political Culture of the United States*. Boston: Little Brown, 1972.
ELAZAR, DANIEL J., *American Federalism: A View from the States*. (2nd ed.). New York: Thomas Y. Crowell, 1972.
FAGEN, RICHARD R., *The Transformation of Political Culture in Cuba*. Stanford: Stanford University Press, 1969.
PYE, LUCIAN and SIDNEY VERBA, eds., *Political Culture and Political Development*. Princeton, N.J.: Princeton University Press, 1965.
RICHARDSON, BRADLEY, *The Political Culture of Japan*. Berkeley: University of California Press, 1974.
ROSENBAUM, WALTER A., *Political Culture*. New York: Praeger, 1975.
WYLIE, LAWRENCE, *Village in the Vaucluse*. New York: Harper & Row, 1964.

Power

AGGER, ROBERT E., DANIEL GOLDRICH, and BERT SWANSON, *The Rulers and the Ruled*. New York: John Wiley, 1964.
BACHRACH, PETER and MORTON BARATZ, *Power and Poverty*. New York: Oxford University Press, 1970.
CLAUDE, INIS L., JR., *Power and International Relations*. New York: Random House, 1962.
CRENSON, MATTHEW A., *The Un-Politics of Air Pollution: A Study of Non-Decisionmaking in the Cities*. Baltimore: Johns Hopkins Press, 1971.
DAHL, ROBERT, *Who Governs? Democracy and Power in an American City*. New Haven: Yale University Press, 1961.
HAWLEY, WILLIS D. and FREDERICK M. WIRT, eds., *The Search for Community Power* (2nd ed.). Englewood Cliffs, N.J.: Prentice-Hall, 1974
HUNTER, FLOYD, *Community Power Structure*. Garden City, N.Y.: Anchor Books, 1963.
LASSWELL, HAROLD and ABRAHAM KAPLAN, *Power and Society: A Framework for Political Inquiry*. New Haven: Yale University Press, 1950.
MILLS, C. WRIGHT, *The Power Elite*. New York: Oxford University Press, 1956.
MORGANTHAU, HANS, *Politics Among Nations* (4th ed.). New York: Knopf, 1967.
POLSBY, NELSON, *Community Power and Political Theory*. New Haven: Yale University Press, 1963.

Rose, Arnold M., *The Power Structure*. New York: Oxford University Press, 1967.

Group
Bentley, Arthur F., *The Process of Government*. Chicago: University of Chicago Press, 1908.
Dahl, Robert, *A Preface to Democratic Theory*. Chicago: University of Chicago Press, 1956.
Herring, E. Pendleton, *Group Representation Before Congress*. Baltimore: Johns Hopkins Press, 1929.
Homans, George C., *The Human Group*. New York: Harcourt Brace Jovanovich, 1950.
Kornhauser, William, *The Politics of Mass Society*. Glencoe, Ill.: The Free Press, 1954.
La Palombara, Joseph, *Interest Groups in Italian Politics*. Princeton, N.J.: Princeton University Press, 1964.
Latham, Earl, *The Group Basis of Politics*. Ithaca, New York: Cornell University Press, 1952.
Olson, Mancur, Jr., *The Logic of Collective Action*. Cambridge, Mass.: Harvard University Press, 1965.
Truman, David B., *The Governmental Process: Political Interests and Public Opinion* (2nd. ed.). New York: Knopf, 1971.

Conflict
Boulding, Kenneth, *Conflict and Defense: A General Theory*. New York: Harper & Row, 1962.
Cobb, Roger and Charles D. Elder, *Participation in American Politics: The Dynamics of Agenda Building*. Boston: Allyn & Bacon, 1972.
Coleman, James S., *Community Conflict*. Glencoe, Ill.: The Free Press, 1957.
Coser, Lewis, *The Functions of Social Conflict*. New York: The Free Press, 1956.
Gamson, William, *Power and Discontent*. Homewood, Ill.: Dorsey Press, 1968.
Rapoport, Anatol, *Fights, Games and Debates*. Ann Arbor: University of Michigan Press, 1960.
Riker, William H., *A Theory of Political Coalitions*. New Haven: Yale University Press, 1962.
Schattschneider, E. E., *The Semi-Sovereign People*. New York: Holt, Rinehart & Winston, 1960.
Schelling, Thomas C., *The Strategy of Conflict*. New York: Oxford University Press, 1963.

Systems
Almond, Gabriel and James S. Coleman, eds., *The Politics of Developing Areas*. Princeton, N.J.: Princeton University Press, 1960.
────── and G. Bingham Powell, Jr., *Comparative Politics: A Developmental Approach*. Boston: Little, Brown, 1966.
Buckley, Walter, *Sociology and Modern Systems Theory*. Englewood Cliffs, N.J.: Prentice-Hall, 1967.
──────, ed., *Modern Systems Research for the Behavioral Scientist*. Chicago: Aldine, 1968.

EASTON, DAVID, *A Framework for Political Analysis*. Englewood Cliffs, N.J.: Prentice-Hall, 1965.

———, *A Systems Analysis of Political Life*. New York: John Wiley, 1965.

LEVY, MARION, *The Structure of Society*. Princeton, N.J.: Princeton University Press, 1952.

MERTON, ROBERT K., *Social Theory and Social Structure* (revised ed.). New York: The Free Press, 1957.

MITCHELL, WILLIAM C., *The American Polity*. New York: The Free Press, 1970.

PARSONS, TALCOTT, *The Social System*. New York: The Free Press, 1951.

VON BERTALANFFY, LUDWIG, *General Systems Theory: Foundations, Development, Applications*. New York: George Braziller, 1968.

YOUNG, ORAN R., *Systems of Political Science*. Englewood Cliffs, N.J.: Prentice-Hall, 1968.

Communications

ASHBY, W. ROSS, *An Introduction to Cybernetics* (3rd. ed.) New York: John Wiley, 1958.

DEUTSCH, KARL W., *Nationalism and Social Communication*. New York: John Wiley, 1953.

———, *The Nerves of Government*. New York: The Free Press, 1966.

FAGEN, RICHARD R., *Politics and Communication*. Boston: Little, Brown, 1966.

JACOB, PHILIP E. and JAMES V. TOSCANO, eds., *The Integration of Political Communities*. Philadelphia: Lippincott, 1964.

MEIER, RICHARD L., *A Communication Theory of Urban Growth*. Cambridge, Mass.: MIT Press, 1962.

PYE, LUCIAN W., ed., *Communications and Political Development*. Princeton, N.J.: Princeton University Press, 1963.

SCHRAMM, WILBUR, *Mass Media and National Development: The Role of Information in the Developing Countries*. Stanford: Stanford University Press, 1964.

SHANNON, CLAUDE E. and WARREN WEAVER, *The Mathematical Theory of Communication*. Urbana: University of Illinois Press, 1959.

STEINBRUNER, JOHN D., *The Cybernetic Theory of Decision*. Princeton, N.J.: Princeton University Press, 1974.

WEINER, NORBERT, *The Human Use of Human Beings*. Boston: Houghton Mifflin, 1950.

———, *Cybernetics* (2nd. ed.). Cambridge, Mass.: MIT Press, 1961.

Decision-Making

ALLISON, GRAHAM T., *Essence of Decision: Exploring the Cuban Missile Crisis*. Boston: Little, Brown, 1971.

BRAYBROOKE, DAVID and CHARLES LINDBLOM, *A Strategy of Decision*. New York: The Free Press, 1963.

BUCHANAN, JAMES M. and GORDON TULLOCK, *The Calculus of Consent: Logical Foundations of Constitutional Democracy*. Ann Arbor: University of Michigan Press, 1962.

DOWNS, ANTHONY, *An Economic Theory of Democracy*. New York: Harper & Row, 1957.

DROR, YEHEZKEL, *Public Policy Reexamined*. San Francisco: Chandler, 1968.

ETZIONI, AMITAI, *The Active Society: A Theory of Social and Political Processes*. New York: The Free Press, 1968.
JANIS, IRVING L., *Victims of Groupthink*. Boston: Houghton Mifflin, 1972.
LINDBLOM, CHARLES, *The Intelligence of Democracy*. New York: The Free Press, 1965.
MARCH, JAMES G. and HERBERT A. SIMON, *Organizations*. New York: John Wiley, 1958.
SHUBIK, MARTIN, ed., *Game Theory and Related Approaches*. New York: John Wiley, 1964.
SNYDER, RICHARD C., H. W. BRUCK, and BURTON SAPIN, *Decision-Making as an Approach to the Study of International Politics*. Princeton, N.J.: Foreign Policy Analysis Series, No. 3, 1954.
VON NEUMANN, JOHN and OSCAR MORGENSTERN, *Theory of Games and Economic Behavior*. Princeton, N.J.: Princeton University Press, 1944.

Policy

ANDERSON, JAMES E, *Public Policy Making* (2nd ed.). New York: Holt, Rinehart & Winston, 1979.
BAUER, RAYMOND, ITHIEL DE SOLA POOL, and LEWIS DEXTER, *American Business and Public Policy*. New York: Atherton, 1963.
────── and KENNETH GERGEN, eds., *The Study of Policy Formation*. New York: The Free Press, 1968.
DAHL, ROBERT A. and CHARLES E. LINDBLOM, *Politics, Economics and Welfare*. New York: Harper & Row, 1953.
DYE, THOMAS R., *Understanding Public Policy* (3rd ed.). Englewood Cliffs, N.J.: Prentice-Hall, 1978.
EDELMAN, MURRAY, *The Symbolic Uses of Politics*. Urbana: University of Illinois Press, 1964.
JONES, CHARLES O., *An Introduction to the Study of Public Policy* (2nd ed.). North Scituate, Mass.: Duxbury Press, 1977.
LINDBLOM, CHARLES E., *The Policy Making Process*. Englewood Cliffs, N.J.: Prentice-Hall, 1968.
LOWI, THEODORE J., *The End of Liberalism* (2nd ed.). New York: Norton, 1979.
MCCONNELL, GRANT, *Private Power and American Democracy*. New York: Knopf, 1966.
MACRAE, DUNCAN, JR. and JAMES A. WILDE, *Policy Analysis for Public Decisions*. North Scituate, Mass.: Duxbury, 1979.
PRESSMAN, JEFFREY and AARON B. WILDAVSKY, *Implementation*. Berkeley: University of California Press, 1973.
RIVLIN, ALICE M., *Systematic Thinking for Social Action*. Washington, D.C.: The Brookings Institute, 1971.
SUCHMAN, EDWARD, *Evaluative Research*. New York: Russell Sage, 1967.
WEISS, CAROL H., *Evaluation Research*. Englewood Cliffs, N.J.: Prentice-Hall, 1972.

Part III—Research Techniques

BABBIE, EARL R., *Survey Research Methods*. Belmont, Calif.: Wadsworth, 1973.
──────, *The Practice of Social Research*. Belmont, Calif.: Wadsworth, 1975.
BACKSTROM, CHARLES H. and GERALD D. HURSH, *Survey Research*. Evanston, Ill.: Northwestern University Press, 1963.

BENNETT, WILLIAM R., *Computer Applications for Non-Science Students (BASIC)*. Englewood Cliffs, N.J.: Prentice-Hall, 1976.
BERNSTEIN, ROBERT A. and JAMES A. DYER, *An Introduction to Political Science Methods*.
BLALOCK, HUBERT M., JR., *An Introduction to Social Research*. Englewood Cliffs, N.J.: Prentice-Hall, 1970.
——— and ANN BLALOCK, eds., *Methodology in Social Research*. New York: McGraw-Hill, 1968.
CAMPBELL, DONALD T. and JULIAN C. STANLEY, *Experimental and Quasi-Experimental Designs for Research*. Chicago: Rand McNally, 1963.
DEXTER, LEWIS A., *Elite and Specialized Interviewing*. Evanston, Ill.: Northwestern University Press, 1970.
DIXON, W. J., ed., *BMD Biomedical Computer Programs*. Los Angeles: University of California Press, 1970.
FIELDS, CRAIG, *About Computers*. Cambridge, Mass.: Winthrop, 1973.
GALTUNG, JOHAN, *Theory and Method of Social Research*. New York: Columbia University Press, 1967.
GARSON, G. DAVID, *Political Science Methods*. Boston: Holbrook, 1976.
GLASER, BARNEY and ANSELM L. STRAUSS, *The Discovery of Grounded Theory: Strategies for Qualitative Research*. Chicago: Aldine, 1967.
GURR, TED R., *Politimetrics: An Introduction to Qualitative Macropolitics*. Englewood Cliffs, N.J.: Prentice-Hall, 1972.
HARKINS, PETER B., THOMAS L. ISENHOUR, and PETER C. JURS, *Introduction to Computer Programming for the Social Sciences*. Boston: Allyn & Bacon, 1973.
HOLSTI, OLE R., *Content Analysis for the Social Sciences and Humanities*. Reading, Mass.: Addison-Wesley, 1969.
HY, RONN J., *Using the Computer in the Social Sciences: A Nontechnical Approach*. New York: Elsevier, 1977.
JANDA, KENNETH, *Data Processing* (2nd. ed.). Evanston, Ill.: Northwestern University Press, 1969.
JONES, E. TERRENCE, *Conducting Political Research*. New York: Harper & Row, 1971.
KERLINGER, FRED N., *Foundations of Behavioral Research* (2nd ed.). New York: Holt, Rinehart & Winston, 1973.
KISH, LESLIE, *Survey Sampling*. New York: John Wiley, 1965.
LAZARSFELD, PAUL and MORRIS ROSENBERG, eds., *The Language of Social Research*. Glencoe, Ill.: The Free Press, 1955.
LEEGE, DAVID C. and WAYNE L. FRANCIS, *Political Research Design, Measurement, and Analysis*. New York: Basic Books, 1974.
MCGAW, DICKINSON and GEORGE WATSON, *Political and Social Inquiry*, New York: John Wiley, 1976.
MILLER, DELBERT C. *Handbook of Research Design and Social Measurement* (3rd ed.). New York: David McKay, 1977.
MOORE, RICHARD, *Introduction to the Use of Computer Packages for Statistical Analysis*. Englewood Cliffs, N.J.: Prentice-Hall, 1978.
NIE, NORMAN, C. HADLAI HULL, JEAN G. JENKINS, KAREN STEINBRENNER, and DALE H. BENT. *SPSS: Statistical Package for the Social Sciences* (2nd ed.). New York: McGraw-Hill, 1975.

NORTH, ROBERT C., OLE R. HOLSTI, M. GEORGE ZANINOVICH, and DINA ZINNES. *Content Analysis: A Handbook With Applications for the Study of International Crisis.* Evanston, Ill.: Northwestern University Press, 1963.

OSIRIS III: An Integrated Collection of Computer Programs for the Management and Analysis of Social Science Data, Vols. 1–6, Ann Arbor, Mich.: Institute for Social Research, 1973.

PRZEWORSKI, ADAM and HENRY TEUNE, *The Logic of Comparative Social Inquiry.* New York: John Wiley, 1970.

RASER, JOHN R., *Simulation and Society.* Boston: Allyn & Bacon, 1969.

ROBINSON, JOHN P., JERROLD G. RUSK, and KENDRA B. HEAD, *Measures of Political Attitudes* (revised ed.). Ann Arbor, Mich.: Institute of Social Research, 1973.

ROSENBERG, MORRIS, *The Logic of Servey Analysis.* New York: Basic Books, 1968.

SAS76: Statistic Analysis System, Chapel Hill: University of North Carolina, 1976.

SIMON, JULIAN L., *Basic Research Methods in Social Science: The Art of Empirical Investigation* (2nd ed.). New York: Random House, 1978.

SUDMAN, SEYMOUR, *Applied Sampling.* New York: Academic Press, 1976.

VELDMAN, DONALD J., *Fortran Programming for the Behavioral Sciences.* New York: Holt, Rinehart & Winston, 1967.

WEBB, EUGENE J., D. T. CAMPBELL, R. D. SCHWARTZ, and L. SECHREST, *Unobtrusive Measures: Non-Reactive Research in Social Sciences.* Chicago: Rand McNally, 1966.

WEISBERG, HERBERT F. and BRUCE D. BOWEN, *An Introduction to Survey Research and Data Analysis.* San Francisco: Freeman, 1977.

Part IV—Statistical Analysis

BLALOCK, HUBERT M., JR., *Social Statistics* (2nd ed.). New York: McGraw-Hill, 1972.

———, *Causal Inferences in Nonexperimental Research.* Chapel Hill: University of North Carolina Press, 1961.

COOLEY, WILLIAM W. and PAUL R. LOHNES, *Multivariate Data Analysis.* New York: John Wiley, 1971.

EDWARDS, ALLEN L., *Statistical Methods* (3rd ed.). New York: Holt, Rinehart & Winston, 1973.

FREEMAN, LINTON C., *Elementary Applied Statistics for Students in Behavioral Science.* New York: John Wiley, 1965.

FREUND, JOHN E., *Modern Elementary Statistics.* (3rd ed.). Englewood Cliffs, N.J.: Prentice-Hall, 1967.

GARSON, G. DAVID, *Handbook of Political Science Methods* (2nd ed.). Boston: Holbrook, 1976.

HANDEL, JUDITH D., *Introductory Statistics for Sociology.* Englewood Cliffs, N.J.: Prentice-Hall, 1978.

HAUSER, PHILIP M., *Social Statistics in Use.* New York: Russell Sage Foundation, 1975.

HERZON, FREDERICK D. and MICHAEL HOOPER, *Introduction to Statistics for the Social Sciences.* New York: Crowell, 1976.

HOLLANDER, MYLES and DOUGLAS A. WOLFE, *Nonparametric Statistical Methods.* New York: John Wiley, 1973.

JOHNSON. ALLAN G., *Statistics Without Tears.* New York: McGraw-Hill, 1977.

KOHOUT, FRANK J., *Statistics for Social Scientists: A Coordinated Learning System.* New York: John Wiley, 1974.
NACHMIAS, DAVID and CLAVA NACHMIAS, *Research Methods in the Social Sciences.* New York: St. Martin's Press, 1976.
RAI, KUL B. and JOHN C. BLYDENBURGH, *Political Science Statistics.* Boston: Holbrook, 1973.
SHIVELY, W. PHILLIPS, *The Craft of Political Research: A Primer.* Englewood Cliffs, N.J.: Prentice-Hall, 1974.
SIEGEL, SIDNEY, *Nonparametric Statistics for the Behavioral Sciences.* New York: McGraw-Hill, 1956.
TUFTE, EDWARD R., *Data Analysis for Politics and Policy.* Englewood Cliffs, N.J.: Prentice-Hall, 1974.

GLOSSARY

Affect   Feeling or emotion.

Agreement   Examining pairs of cases in a cross-tabulation table to determine if one case is ranked higher than the other by both the independent and dependent variables.

Alphanumeric   The use of letters or other symbols to code data, rather than numbers.

Analysis of variance   A significance test which can test for the difference among means of more than two samples.

Approaches   Concepts which have broad, general applicability and which have generated much research in political science. These concepts provide a foundation for an entire framework for political analysis.

Assumption   A generalization which is taken to be true and will not be tested in the research.

Axiom   See assumption.

b Coefficient   The constant in a regression equation which indicates how much impact the independent variable has on the dependent variable. It indicates the amount of unit change in the dependent variable for every unit change in the independent variable.

Bar graph   A way of picturing a frequency distribution so that the height and/or the width of the bars indicate the number of cases assuming a particular value.

Batch mode   A form of computer processing in which jobs are read into the computer and stored until the computer can process the data.

Behavioralism   An orientation in political science which emphasizes the study of behavior by use of the scientific method.

Beta coefficient   The b coefficient in a regression equation in a standardized form. The beta coefficients can be used to compare the amount of impact various independent variables have on the dependent variable.

Bivariate   Having to do with two variables.

Byte The amount of computer space required to store one character.

Canned program A computer program written by others so that the researcher needs only to plug in information about his own data.

Case studies An in-depth study of certain phenomena with little effort to control variance.

Categoric group A collection of individuals who share some common characteristic, but the characteristic may not serve as a cue to behavior.

Cell A portion in a cross-tabulation table in which the number of cases are listed which share a particular combination of values on the variables being displayed.

Central processing unit The part of the computer which performs the actual manipulations.

Central tendency The central point in a frequency distribution.

Chi square A test of significance which is appropriate for nominal data. It involves comparing frequencies in the cells of a cross-tabulation table with the frequencies expected by chance.

Classification To sort out phenomena into different types or classes.

Cluster sample A sample drawn from certain geographical areas or clusters.

Coefficient of determination The square of Pearson's r It is interpreted as the amount of variance in the dependent variable which is statistically associated with variance in the independent variable.

Cognition The act of knowing or perceiving.

Cognitive development An explanation of how we learn based on the assumption that there are stages in our learning process. We first learn concrete things and later abstract ideas.

Cognitive dissonance The belief that the orientations to three components of an opinion situation must be brought into congruence. The three components are: (1) your own opinion, (2) your opinion of the other person, and (3) the other's opinion.

Combinations An arrangement of r objects from a set of n objects when the order of selection is not considered.

Comparison To classify phenomena so that they can be examined in terms of their possession of more or less of a given characteristic.

Computer A device which is programmed with a set of instructions to calculate arithmetical and logical functions.

Concatenated theory A series of generalizations which are related because of a common focus.

Concept A universal, descriptive word.

Conceptual scheme A listing of concepts which are believed to be related and a vague statement concerning the nature of the relationship.

Confidence interval How accurate we can be in making estimates about the population based on a sample.

Confidence level The level of probability associated with being able to make estimates about the population based on a sample.

Conflict A pattern of interaction which occurs when there are disagreements concerning the allocation of scarce resources.

Construct A concept which refers to something that cannot be directly observed.

Continuous variable A variable measured on a scale which can assume any value (for example, income).
Control To eliminate the effect of a variable either by holding the value constant or by removing its effect mathematically.
Control group A group with similar characteristics to another group. The other group, or experimental group, is exposed to some treatment while the control group is not. The comparison of the control group with the experimental group is the basis for determining the effect of the treatment.
Control Language A series of instructions to the computer necessary to run a program. It indicates such things as where data are stored, what language will be used, how much computer time is needed, etc.
Core A part of the computer which stores information for use in processing programs.
Correlation A procedure used to determine how closely related two variables are. Some statisticians use the term to refer only to Pearson's r, but most social scientists use the term to refer to procedures for all levels of data.
Counter-sorter A machine which sorts and counts computer cards into different piles based on the punches on specified columns.
Covering statement A universal generalization which is used to explain a particular phenomenon.
Critical value The probability level which must be achieved before the null hypothesis can be rejected.
Cross-sectional analysis A study based on data gathered at one point in time.
Cross-tabulation, or contingency tables A way to display the distributions of more than one variable simultaneously.
Curvilinear Being in the form of a curve.
Decisions A choice made between or among alternative courses of action.
Decision-making The process of choosing among alternative courses of action.
Decode To transform messages from a code to the original language or form.
Deduction To reason from the general to the specific.
Default option Programmed instructions which are followed automatically by the computer unless overridden by specifying other instructions.
Degrees of freedom The number of factors which can vary.
Demands Messages transmitted to the political system requesting some action from the system.
Dependent variable A variable which is believed to vary in response to changes in the independent variable.
Descriptive statistics Statistics which summarize a single variable's distribution or the relationship between or among variables.
Determinism The asumption that everything has a cause.
Disagreement Examining pairs of cases in a cross-tabulation table to determine if one case is ranked higher on one variable and lower on the other variable than the other case.
Discontinuity A disruption, or lack of continuity.
Discrete variable A variable which can assume a limited number of values (for example, party identification).
Disk pack A device similar to a stack of phonograph records which are used to store data in machine readable form.

Displacement To substitute one issue for another as the focus of concern.

Disproportionate stratified sample A sample drawn so that certain groups, or strata, are ensured of being included in sufficient numbers to permit generalization. The proportion of the strata in the sample is not equal to the proportion of the strata in the universe.

Distributive policy A policy which creates benefits for many groups with no obvious costs for any groups.

Ecological fallacy The mistake of assuming that since a group has a particular characteristic, all individuals in the group have that characteristic.

Elitist theory The belief that power is concentrated among a few, homogeneous groups in the population.

Empirical Having to do with the world which is perceived through the senses.

Encoding To transform messages from the original form into a format for ease of processing.

Essential definition A definition which is based on the core meaning, or essence, of a concept.

Experiment A design for conducting research aimed at maximizing experimental variance and controlling extraneous variance.

Experimental group That group in an experiment which is exposed to the stimulus, or the experimental variable.

Experimental mortality Observed changes between pretest and posttest due to a bias introduced by the kinds of people dropping out of the experiment.

Explained variance The amount of variance in the dependent variable which can be accounted for by covariance with the independent variable.

Explanation To show that something is a specific instance of a general pattern.

Ex post facto research Research which is based on examining the past to find causes for present conditions. In such research it is difficult to eliminate alternative explanations.

External validity Assuring we can safely generalize that relationships found in the research on a sample will also be found in the universe.

Face validity Establishing the degree to which a measurement is valid by subjectively determining that the measurement seems to measure what it is supposed to measure.

Fact Something that can be verified by observation of the empirical world and upon which there is, in principal, general agreement.

Feedback Information on the impact of the outputs of the political system which is communicated to the system to produce whatever corrective action may be needed.

Frequency distribution A listing of the possible values of a variable and the number of cases which have those values.

Function An activity which must be performed to assure the persistence of the political system.

Gamma (γ) A measure of association for ordinal data based on examining the distribution of cases in a cross-tabulation table. The formula is $\frac{A-D}{A+D}$ where A indicates agreement and D indicates disagreement. Ties are ignored in the computation.

Generalization A statement of the relationship between two concepts.

Goodman and Kruskal's tau (τ) A measure of association for nominal data, based on the principle of porportionate reduction in error. Differs from Guttman's lambda in the way errors are estimated.

Group Two or more individuals who share some common characteristic(s). Political scientists are concerned with these individuals when their common characteristic(s) affect political behavior.

Group concept A word which describes a characteristic of a collection of individuals.

Groupthink The tendency for a group to think alike due to desire of all to be alike and accepted.

Guttman's lambda (λ) A measure of association for nominal data based on the principle of proportionate reduction in error. It differs from Goodman's and Kruskal's tau in the way errors are estimated.

Hardware The actual physical equipment used in the mechanical processing of data.

Hawthorne effect Uncharacteristic behavior resulting from the realization that one is part of an experiment.

Histogram See Bar Graph.

History The impact of unrelated occurrences in the environment which can affect experimental outcomes.

Hypothesis A generalization which is derived from a theory. Alternatively, it is a generalization phrased in such a way that it can be tested.

Incrementalism A process of decision-making in which the primary guides to decision-making are what has been done previously and what can produce agreement.

Independent variable A variable which is believed to cause changes in a dependent variable.

Index A composite measure in which separate indicators are combined additively with no assumptions made about the underlying structure among the indicators.

Indicator An empirical "clue" we use to point to the existence of a non-observable concept.

Individual concept A word which describes a characteristic of a single person, rather than a group.

Induction To reason from the specific to the general.

Inferential statistics Statistics which measure the probability of being in error in inferring that characteristics of a sample can be used to estimate population characteristics.

Initial conditions Existing characteristics of the thing to be explained.

Inputs Messages (demands, supports) transmitted to a political system.

Institutional group A collection of individuals characterized by formality and structure.

Instrumentation Observed changes between the pretest and posttest due to measurement error.

Intensity of conflict The degree of the emotional orientations toward a conflict situation.

Interaction group A collection of individuals who get together because of a shared characteristic but do not have a formal organized structure.
Internal validity Assuring that changes in the dependent variable are due to the independent variable rather than the result of the way the research was designed.
Interpreter A machine which prints the meanings of punches on the computer card on the top of the card.
Interquartile range The two scores in a distribution which mark the points above and below which 25% of the cases fall.
Intersubjectivity Specifying the procedures used in a research project clearly enough that the research could be replicated. This is one way of attempting to control for the effect of values in the analysis of politics.
Interval A level of measurement in which there is a precise measuring standard. The numbers have meaning quantitatively and can be manipulated arithmetically.
Kendall's tau (τ) A measure of association for ordinal data based on examining the distribution of cases in a cross-tabulation table. The numerator is A−D, where A is agreement and D is disagreement. The denominator includes all pairs in tau_a, a correction for ties in tau_b, or a correction for tables with unequal numbers of rows and columns in Tau_c.
Keypunch machine A machine which punches holes in punch cards as a means of storing data for computer analysis.
Law A generalization which has been consistently verified in research.
Learning theory An explanation of how we learn based on the belief that we respond to stimuli because of imitation or because of selective application of reinforcement.
Least-squares criterion The most frequently used standard for drawing a regression line. The line is drawn to minimize the sum of the squared deviations of the data points from the line. This standard is used to determine the "best" line to approximate the distribution of the data.
Level of analysis Focusing on either the individual or the group in research.
Level of measurement The precision at which data are measured.
Level of significance The probability of error in inferring the sample characteristics can be used to estimate the population characteristics.
Linear Being in the form of a straight line.
Logical words Words which provide the structure of a language, for example, and, or.
Longitudinal data Data which have been gathered over time rather than at a single point in time.
Magnetic tape A means of storing data for computer analysis; similar to recording tape.
Marginal The totals of row or column frequencies in a cross-tabulation table.
Maturation The impact of unrelated changes in individuals which can affect experimental outcomes.
Mean A measure of central tendency for interval-level data; the average score.
Mean deviation A measure of variation of a distribution computed by summing the deviations of each score from the mean, ignoring the signs, and then dividing by the number of scores. The average deviation.

Measures of association   Tests which determine how closely variables are related.
Median   A measure of central tendency for ordinal data. It establishes the midpoint of a distribution such that 50% of the cases are above the median and 50% are below.
Memory   The capacity for storing messages or information.
Mixed-scanning   A process of decision-making which combines incremental and rational decision-making.
Mode   A measure of central tendency for nominal data. It is the most frequently occurring value.
Model   A theory whose logical structure is isomorphic to (identical to) another theory.
Monotonic   A relationship which involves one direction only.
Multiple correlation   A measurement of the relationship between a single dependent variable and more than one independent variable.
Multivariate   Having to do with more than two variables.
Nondecision making   Implicitly making a negative decision by refusing to consider a given issue or proposal.
Nominal   A level of measurement in which numbers are no more than numerical codes. The numbers themselves do not "mean" anything.
Nominal definition   A definition which is specified by a researcher to suit the requirements of his research.
Nomological model   The process of explanation based on deduction.
Nonequivalent control group design   Using a group not known to be equivalent to an experimental group as a point of comparison in a research setting.
Normal curve   A bell-shaped curve in which each side of the curve is symmetrical to the other side. The frequency distribution which is pictured by the curve is such that approximately 68% of the cases fall within one standard deviation of the mean, 95% fall within two standard deviations and 99% fall within three standard deviations.
Normative   Analysis based upon value premises.
Null hypothesis   A hypothesis formulated to provide a known standard against which to compare research results. It usually involves hypothesizing *no* relationship or no change.
Objectivity   Being free of bias or personal feelings.
Observational techniques   To gather data by watching the phenomena being studied.
One-tailed test   A test of significance which uses only one tail of the distribution as the critical region.
Operationalization   To specify empirical indicators of nonobservable concepts.
Optical scanner   A device which overviews coded forms and translates the data into machine readable form.
Ordinal   A level of measurement in which the numbers indicate greater or lesser possession of certain characteristics. The numbers are not based on a universal standard of measurement, but only rank cases.
Outputs   Actions (decisions, policies) produced by a political system.

Overload Messages intended for a communication channel which are in excess of what the channel can bear.
Paradigm The basic questions, concepts, and methods used as a foundation for research.
Partial correlation A measurement of the relationship between two variables when the effects of other variables have been controlled.
Pearson's correlation (r), or product-moment coefficient A measure of association for interval data based on determining how accurately a regression line approximates a set of data points.
Permutation Any particular arrangement of r objects from a set of n objects, regardless of their order.
Pie chart A way of picturing a frequency distribution in which the size of the slice or wedge indicates the number of cases assuming a particular value.
Pluralist theory The belief that power is widely distributed among various groups in the population.
Policies A series of decisions aimed at the accomplishment of an abstract goal.
Policy analysis An examination of policy aimed at developing policy types or at establishing criteria by which to evaluate policy.
Policy-making The process by which a series of decisions is produced which is aimed toward the accomplishment of an abstract goal.
Political culture The fundamental political orientations of a people.
Political socialization The way we learn about politics.
Politics Having to do with the exercise of legitimate power, or authority, in decisions for society.
Population The entire aggregate about which the research project intends to make conclusions.
Postbehavioralism An orientation in political science which combines the methods of science with normative judgment.
Posttest A measurement taken after a stimulus has been applied in an experiment.
Potential groups Those aggregates not currently organized which may conceivably organize and become active in the future.
Power The ability to make someone do something he would not have otherwise done.
Predictive validity Establishing the degree to which a measurement is valid by determining that the measure relates to a dependent variable in the same way the concept being measured relates to the variable.
Pre-experiments Research designs in which few attempts are made to control threats to internal validity. Examples include case studies and ex post facto research.
Pretest A measurement given before the application of the stimulus in an experiment.
Primary data Data gathered specifically for a given research project, as opposed to data gathered for another purpose and re-examined for the research project.
Primary group A collection of individuals characterized by frequent and constant interaction.
Printer The machine which prints the output from computer calculations on paper.

Privatization of conflict The attempt to limit the number of people involved in a conflict.

Probabilistic generalization A generalization which holds for only some known proportion of the cases.

Proportionate reduction in error A principle used in measures of association involving the degree to which knowledge of the independent variable reduces errors made in predicting the dependent variable.

Proportionate stratified sample A sample drawn so that certain groups, or strata, are represented in the sample in the same proportion as they exist in the universe.

Proposition A synonym for the term generalization.

Propositional inventory A series of generalizations in the area of a particular topic.

Punched card, or punch card A card on which data are stored in machine-readable form by punching holes in appropriate rows and columns.

Qualitative The ability to measure concepts on the basis of qualities or characteristics (sex, party identification, and so forth).

Quantitative The ability to measure concepts in numerical terms (income, age, and so forth).

Quasi-experiments Research designs which do not totally fulfill the requirements of an experimental design but do attempt to approximate that design by a variety of means.

Range The simplest measure of variation; the extreme scores of a distribution or the difference between those scores.

Ratio measurement The most precise level of measurment. It is based on a scale with precise intervals and an absolute zero (for example, age).

Rational decision-making The process of decision-making in which decisions are made to achieve specified goals with least cost and maximum benefits.

Redistributive policy A policy which distributes benefits for certain groups when other specific groups bear the cost of the benefits.

Reference group A collection of individuals to whom one refers for cues for opinions and behavior.

Regression A statistical technique involving expressing the relationship among variables by a formula. The formula which is used most frequently is that for a straight line $y = a + bx$

Regulatory policy Policy which establishes guidelines for behavior.

Reliability The degree to which a measure produces consistent results.

Research design The strategy, plan, and structure of conducting a research project.

Residuals The amount by which actual scores on the dependent variable differ from the scores predicted with a regression analysis.

Role Expected behavior in a given social location.

Sample A subgroup selected from a universe.

Sampling distribution A frequency distribution created by drawing repeated samples from a universe, calculating a given statistic for each sample, and then creating a frequency distribution of those statistics. In hypothesis testing the results are compared to a sampling distribution to determine the probability of getting those results by chance.

Scale A composite measure which assumes an underlying structure among the indicators.

Scattergram A graph in which cases are plotted based on how they scored on two variables.

Science A method of study characterized by four factors: empiricism, objectivity, determinism, and theory building.

Scope of conflict The numbers of people who are involved in a conflict situation.

Secondary data Data originally gathered for another purpose and re-examined in the process of a research project, as opposed to data gathered specifically for the project.

Secondary group A collection of individuals who interact with less frequency than primary groups.

Selection Observed changes between pretest and posttest due to the choice of atypical participants for the experiment.

Selective perception The tendency to see what one wants to see.

Separate sample pretest-posttest design Using data gathered on another group in place of a pretest in a research setting.

Significance tests Tests which determine the probability of error in inferring the sample characteristics can be used to estimate the population characteristics.

Simple random sampling A process of using a table of random numbers to select cases for a sample from a list of the universe.

Skewed curves A curve with extreme values on one end of the curve.

Socialization of conflict The attempt to increase the number of people involved in a conflict.

Software The instructions used in the mechanical processing of data.

Spurious An apparent relationship which is actually due to the effect of another factor.

Standard deviation The average amount by which values differ from the mean of a distribution.

Standard error The standard deviation of a sampling distribution.

Standard error of estimate The standard deviation of actual data points from a regression line.

Standard normal distribution A sampling distribution for z scores shaped as a normal curve.

Structural-functionalism The attempt to specify universal functions and to compare the structures which perform the functions in different systems.

Subsystem A part of a larger system viewed in and of itself as a system.

Supports Messages transmitted to the political system providing the system with resources necessary for the system to act.

System An interaction among identifiable units to achieve some purpose.

Systematic import How meaningful a concept is in the context of theory.

Systematic sampling Using some constant value to select a sample from a list of the universe.

***t* test** A test of significance used on interval data when the sample size is small.

Tautology A statement which involves circular reasoning.

Test-retest method A means to establish the reliability of measures. A measurement is given and later is given again. The degree of consistency between the two measurements is assessed.

Testing The effect of a pretest on the behavior of participants in an experiment.

Theory A series of logically related empirical generalizations.

Time series Using several measurements at various times to establish the existence of a pattern or trend before and after the application of an experimental stimulus.

Time sharing, or interactive input mode A form of computer processing in which one "talks" directly to the computer by means of a keyboard and receives immediate results.

Total variance The degree to which data points deviate from the mean of the distribution.

Traditionalism An orientation in political science which emphasizes history, institutions, and constitutions.

Two-tailed test A test of significance which uses both tails of the distribution as the critical region.

Type I error The error involved in rejecting a true hypothesis.

Type II error The error involved in accepting a false hypothesis.

Unexplained variance The amount of variance in the dependent variable which cannot be accounted for by the independent variable. In regression, it is the amount by which actual data points differ from the predicted points.

Unit of analysis The unit of data which is the focus of a research project, for example, behavior, attitudes, etc.

Universe The total group about which you wish to generalize as a result of your research. Also called a population.

Universal generalization A generalization which holds for *all* cases.

Universal words Words which refer to general classes of objects.

Validity The degree to which a measure actually measures what it is supposed to measure.

Value (normative) The relative worth or importance of something. This cannot be established by the method of science.

Variable A concept which can assume different values.

Variance The amount by which the values of a variable deviate from the mean. This can be measured by the following formula: $\frac{\Sigma(x - \bar{x})^2}{N}$

Visibility of conflict How aware people are of a conflict situation.

z score A score standardized by expressing it as a proportion of a standard deviation. Can be used as a test of significance for the difference between means.

Statistical Table 1 Random Numbers

94712	82297	29366	49973	98113	15174	66428	81181
64123	79480	40262	51940	29023	17360	31151	71044
6945	29077	39387	77262	23067	37989	80361	95964
89044	12659	97100	25395	9427	66295	72009	25988
29075	95240	31500	75155	73528	48157	66635	66241
73885	5441	35869	42202	97655	69928	14654	50982
94074	23252	75232	30223	80524	39830	26327	54645
87542	97143	52769	48948	83380	2398	60998	97710
25827	75494	24158	25066	61229	44131	31637	84920
76536	65130	47704	34743	39420	60903	71014	58487
53529	81274	62626	62126	89152	78752	85840	2187
55398	32359	59229	28800	6961	68707	55503	46961
82129	55810	89582	34134	28319	46226	78354	86730
89927	91800	23986	73404	2757	30059	60137	1569
9428	76454	70151	29813	85613	58668	89332	60910
80399	22163	61210	39808	93484	42756	40628	59489
23308	25782	14038	22099	51653	7915	37720	54980
69266	5123	40079	32930	49520	27940	95934	74178
64242	26133	58785	31686	93650	16702	76645	20286
19175	17201	63454	79313	63582	83010	40809	72245
99983	24311	93857	28567	39896	9623	77952	49337
56587	31308	1175	7556	30137	58796	23499	62650
43801	36247	14613	28875	98581	48709	34995	80758
59527	70237	66653	27204	39161	69520	31655	18173
42487	55480	9819	16951	22196	5053	94756	51079
94992	53199	33932	68372	70262	79190	82244	84798
56918	20448	68855	13915	58123	37780	82409	79836
31530	37741	58525	34443	34273	48243	91367	8054
53752	56199	48727	51036	23447	84770	29555	50116
21363	95272	2616	6552	9784	68706	19173	27352

91142	89926	11331	54420	52067	66704	57353	11690
39660	14758	86337	91992	31153	69095	67771	82302
4760	39484	13728	12142	23469	44598	11596	54361
4718	64391	67360	18830	18176	81559	18297	77994
57569	83480	85282	74058	60642	33144	82937	53257
24638	72128	25291	43897	36775	64188	67463	27570
3086	19941	83433	53217	24192	26723	8500	63105
1867	76808	48136	33402	34841	61963	96733	16541
39406	19867	9787	23411	40528	23019	54260	74497
32827	9	84170	29130	83287	23427	84712	9592
82071	1472	68675	79285	56531	83572	52925	53466
93294	3559	18152	28365	82683	59327	54329	67563
14428	61818	85590	78182	86218	45035	76274	25492
23765	50514	96145	85656	55182	76975	17785	32795
14371	84145	97471	41283	21744	94790	93290	1213
5363	64670	20880	2889	38132	39548	55225	2426
56924	48581	34814	32590	2463	41761	80234	55249
57148	77415	44659	3870	33001	6360	59946	95440
53516	71490	63121	5013	18132	77920	79392	85121
86835	75939	88536	31440	91783	16552	34385	8719
20660	6562	30603	10114	31906	39976	7785	46796
6504	5724	8215	34093	7109	34841	60790	541
17377	73434	94575	66576	52485	70030	6985	6876
47046	95922	41748	72403	93845	1605	83705	15910
54969	25501	11289	64341	37602	26297	13154	1859
63541	46234	85397	45624	71642	36665	86689	27007
59697	34931	80577	92601	99553	84163	12328	304
13026	32386	51492	29562	86073	84774	51823	4640
74445	95681	40796	93321	99672	43622	2791	6223
36520	11874	67653	62995	53664	96309	66241	87557
37778	39437	58974	68673	17174	9394	75479	63210
1625	57638	97641	89449	12556	32062	43936	49720
68458	73509	8300	30367	89914	1557	38928	51222

Generated by Al Lindem, University of North Dakota Computer Center

Statistical Table 2 F Distribution

5% (Roman Type) and 1% (Boldface Type) Points for the Distribution of F

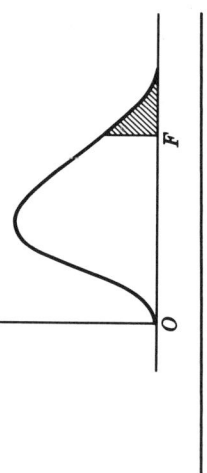

Degrees of freedom for denomina- tor (v_2)	1	2	3	4	5	6	7	8	9	10	11	12	14	16	20	24	30	40	50	75	100	200	500	∞
1	161 **4052**	200 **4999**	216 **5403**	225 **5625**	230 **5764**	234 **5859**	237 **5928**	239 **5981**	241 **6022**	242 **6056**	243 **6082**	244 **6106**	245 **6142**	246 **6169**	248 **6208**	249 **6234**	250 **6258**	251 **6286**	252 **6302**	253 **6323**	253 **6334**	254 **6352**	254 **6361**	254 **6366**
2	18.51 **98.49**	19.00 **99.01**	19.16 **99.17**	19.25 **99.25**	19.30 **99.30**	19.33 **99.33**	19.36 **99.34**	19.37 **99.36**	19.38 **99.38**	19.39 **99.40**	19.40 **99.41**	19.41 **99.42**	19.42 **99.43**	19.43 **99.44**	19.44 **99.45**	19.45 **99.46**	19.46 **99.47**	19.47 **99.48**	19.47 **99.48**	19.48 **99.49**	19.49 **99.49**	19.49 **99.49**	19.50 **99.50**	19.50 **99.50**
3	10.13 **34.12**	9.55 **30.81**	9.28 **29.46**	9.12 **28.71**	9.01 **28.24**	8.94 **27.91**	8.88 **27.67**	8.84 **27.49**	8.81 **27.34**	8.78 **27.23**	8.76 **27.13**	8.74 **27.05**	8.71 **26.92**	8.69 **26.83**	8.66 **26.69**	8.64 **26.60**	8.62 **26.50**	8.60 **26.41**	8.58 **26.30**	8.57 **26.27**	8.56 **26.23**	8.54 **26.18**	8.54 **26.14**	8.53 **26.12**
4	7.71 **21.20**	6.94 **18.00**	6.59 **16.69**	6.39 **15.98**	6.26 **15.52**	6.16 **15.21**	6.09 **14.98**	6.04 **14.80**	6.00 **14.66**	5.96 **14.54**	5.93 **14.45**	5.91 **14.37**	5.87 **14.24**	5.84 **14.15**	5.80 **14.02**	5.77 **13.93**	5.74 **13.83**	5.71 **13.74**	5.70 **13.69**	5.68 **13.61**	5.66 **13.57**	5.65 **13.52**	5.64 **13.48**	5.63 **13.46**
5	6.61 **16.26**	5.79 **13.27**	5.41 **12.06**	5.19 **11.39**	5.05 **10.97**	4.95 **10.67**	4.88 **10.45**	4.82 **10.27**	4.78 **10.15**	4.74 **10.05**	4.70 **9.96**	4.68 **9.89**	4.64 **9.77**	4.60 **9.68**	4.56 **9.55**	4.53 **9.47**	4.50 **9.38**	4.46 **9.29**	4.44 **9.24**	4.42 **9.17**	4.40 **9.13**	4.38 **9.07**	4.37 **9.04**	4.36 **9.02**
6	5.99 **13.74**	5.14 **10.92**	4.76 **9.78**	4.53 **9.15**	4.39 **8.75**	4.28 **8.47**	4.21 **8.26**	4.15 **8.10**	4.10 **7.98**	4.06 **7.87**	4.03 **7.79**	4.00 **7.72**	3.96 **7.60**	3.92 **7.52**	3.87 **7.39**	3.84 **7.31**	3.81 **7.23**	3.77 **7.14**	3.75 **7.09**	3.72 **7.02**	3.71 **6.99**	3.69 **6.94**	3.68 **6.90**	3.67 **6.88**
7	5.59 **12.25**	4.74 **9.55**	4.35 **8.45**	4.12 **7.85**	3.97 **7.46**	3.87 **7.19**	3.79 **7.00**	3.73 **6.84**	3.68 **6.71**	3.63 **6.62**	3.60 **6.54**	3.57 **6.47**	3.52 **6.35**	3.49 **6.27**	3.44 **6.15**	3.41 **6.07**	3.38 **5.98**	3.34 **5.90**	3.32 **5.85**	3.29 **5.78**	3.28 **5.75**	3.25 **5.70**	3.24 **5.67**	3.23 **5.65**
8	5.32 **11.26**	4.46 **8.65**	4.07 **7.59**	3.84 **7.01**	3.69 **6.63**	3.58 **6.37**	3.50 **6.19**	3.44 **6.03**	3.39 **5.91**	3.34 **5.82**	3.31 **5.74**	3.28 **5.67**	3.23 **5.56**	3.20 **5.48**	3.15 **5.36**	3.12 **5.28**	3.08 **5.20**	3.05 **5.11**	3.03 **5.06**	3.00 **5.00**	2.98 **4.96**	2.96 **4.91**	2.94 **4.88**	2.93 **4.86**
9	5.12 **10.56**	4.26 **8.02**	3.86 **6.99**	3.63 **6.42**	3.48 **6.06**	3.37 **5.80**	3.29 **5.62**	3.23 **5.47**	3.18 **5.35**	3.13 **5.26**	3.10 **5.18**	3.07 **5.11**	3.02 **5.00**	2.98 **4.92**	2.93 **4.80**	2.90 **4.73**	2.86 **4.64**	2.82 **4.56**	2.80 **4.51**	2.77 **4.45**	2.76 **4.41**	2.73 **4.36**	2.72 **4.33**	2.71 **4.31**

Degrees of freedom for numerator (v_1)

10	4.96 10.04	4.10 7.56	3.71 6.55	3.48 5.99	3.33 5.64	3.22 5.39	3.14 5.21	3.07 5.06	3.02 4.95	2.97 4.85	2.94 4.78	2.91 4.71	2.86 4.60	2.82 4.52	2.77 4.41	2.74 4.33	2.70 4.25	2.67 4.17	2.64 4.12	2.61 4.05	2.59 4.01	2.56 3.96	2.55 3.93	2.54 3.91
11	4.84 9.65	3.98 7.20	3.59 6.22	3.36 5.67	3.20 5.32	3.09 5.07	3.01 4.88	2.95 4.74	2.90 4.63	2.86 4.54	2.82 4.46	2.79 4.40	2.74 4.29	2.70 4.21	2.65 4.10	2.61 4.02	2.57 3.94	2.53 3.86	2.50 3.80	2.47 3.74	2.45 3.70	2.42 3.66	2.41 3.62	2.40 3.60
12	4.75 9.33	3.88 6.93	3.49 5.95	3.26 5.41	3.11 5.06	3.00 4.82	2.92 4.65	2.85 4.50	2.80 4.39	2.76 4.30	2.72 4.22	2.69 4.16	2.64 4.05	2.60 3.98	2.54 3.86	2.50 3.78	2.46 3.70	2.42 3.61	2.40 3.56	2.36 3.49	2.35 3.46	2.32 3.41	2.31 3.38	2.30 3.36
13	4.67 9.07	3.80 6.70	3.41 5.74	3.18 5.20	3.02 4.86	2.92 4.62	2.84 4.44	2.77 4.30	2.72 4.19	2.67 4.10	2.63 4.02	2.60 3.96	2.55 3.85	2.51 3.78	2.46 3.67	2.42 3.59	2.38 3.51	2.34 3.42	2.32 3.37	2.28 3.30	2.26 3.27	2.24 3.21	2.22 3.18	2.21 3.16
14	4.60 8.86	3.74 6.51	3.34 5.56	3.11 5.03	2.96 4.69	2.85 4.46	2.77 4.28	2.70 4.14	2.65 4.03	2.60 3.94	2.56 3.86	2.53 3.80	2.48 3.70	2.44 3.62	2.39 3.51	2.35 3.43	2.31 3.34	2.27 3.26	2.24 3.21	2.21 3.14	2.19 3.11	2.16 3.06	2.14 3.02	2.13 3.00
15	4.54 8.68	3.68 6.36	3.29 5.42	3.06 4.89	2.90 4.56	2.79 4.32	2.70 4.14	2.64 4.00	2.59 3.89	2.55 3.80	2.51 3.73	2.48 3.67	2.43 3.56	2.39 3.48	2.33 3.36	2.29 3.29	2.25 3.20	2.21 3.12	2.18 3.07	2.15 3.00	2.12 2.97	2.10 2.92	2.08 2.89	2.07 2.87
16	4.49 8.53	3.63 6.23	3.24 5.29	3.01 4.77	2.85 4.44	2.74 4.20	2.66 4.03	2.59 3.89	2.54 3.78	2.49 3.69	2.45 3.61	2.42 3.55	2.37 3.45	2.33 3.37	2.28 3.25	2.24 3.18	2.20 3.10	2.16 3.01	2.13 2.96	2.09 2.89	2.07 2.86	2.04 2.80	2.02 2.77	2.01 2.75
17	4.45 8.40	3.59 6.11	3.20 5.18	2.96 4.67	2.81 4.34	2.70 4.10	2.62 3.93	2.55 3.79	2.50 3.68	2.45 3.59	2.41 3.52	2.38 3.45	2.33 3.35	2.29 3.27	2.23 3.16	2.19 3.08	2.15 3.00	2.11 2.92	2.08 2.86	2.04 2.79	2.02 2.76	1.99 2.70	1.97 2.67	1.96 2.65
18	4.41 8.28	3.55 6.01	3.16 5.09	2.93 4.58	2.77 4.25	2.66 4.01	2.58 3.85	2.51 3.71	2.46 3.60	2.41 3.51	2.37 3.44	2.34 3.37	2.29 3.27	2.25 3.19	2.19 3.07	2.15 3.00	2.11 2.91	2.07 2.83	2.04 2.78	2.00 2.71	1.98 2.68	1.95 2.62	1.93 2.59	1.92 2.57
19	4.38 8.18	3.52 5.93	3.13 5.01	2.90 4.50	2.74 4.17	2.63 3.94	2.55 3.77	2.48 3.63	2.43 3.52	2.38 3.43	2.34 3.36	2.31 3.30	2.26 3.19	2.21 3.12	2.15 3.00	2.11 2.92	2.07 2.84	2.02 2.76	2.00 2.70	1.96 2.63	1.94 2.60	1.91 2.54	1.90 2.51	1.88 2.49
20	4.35 8.10	3.49 5.85	3.10 4.94	2.87 4.43	2.71 4.10	2.60 3.87	2.52 3.71	2.45 3.56	2.40 3.45	2.35 3.37	2.31 3.30	2.28 3.23	2.23 3.13	2.18 3.05	2.12 2.94	2.08 2.86	2.04 2.77	1.99 2.69	1.96 2.63	1.92 2.56	1.90 2.53	1.87 2.47	1.85 2.44	1.84 2.42
21	4.32 8.02	3.47 5.78	3.07 4.87	2.84 4.37	2.68 4.04	2.57 3.81	2.49 3.65	2.42 3.51	2.37 3.40	2.32 3.31	2.28 3.24	2.25 3.17	2.20 3.07	2.15 2.99	2.09 2.88	2.05 2.80	2.00 2.72	1.96 2.63	1.93 2.58	1.89 2.51	1.87 2.47	1.84 2.42	1.82 2.38	1.81 2.36
22	4.30 7.94	3.44 5.72	3.05 4.82	2.82 4.31	2.66 3.99	2.55 3.76	2.47 3.59	2.40 3.45	2.35 3.35	2.30 3.26	2.26 3.18	2.23 3.12	2.18 3.02	2.13 2.94	2.07 2.83	2.03 2.75	1.98 2.67	1.93 2.58	1.91 2.53	1.87 2.46	1.84 2.42	1.81 2.37	1.80 2.33	1.78 2.31
23	4.28 7.88	3.42 5.66	3.03 4.76	2.80 4.26	2.64 3.94	2.53 3.71	2.45 3.54	2.38 3.41	2.32 3.30	2.28 3.21	2.24 3.14	2.20 3.07	2.14 2.97	2.10 2.89	2.04 2.78	2.00 2.70	1.96 2.62	1.91 2.53	1.88 2.48	1.84 2.41	1.82 2.37	1.79 2.32	1.77 2.28	1.76 2.26
24	4.26 7.82	3.40 5.61	3.01 4.72	2.78 4.22	2.62 3.90	2.51 3.67	2.43 3.50	2.36 3.36	2.30 3.25	2.26 3.17	2.22 3.09	2.18 3.03	2.13 2.93	2.09 2.85	2.02 2.74	1.98 2.66	1.94 2.58	1.89 2.49	1.86 2.44	1.82 2.36	1.80 2.33	1.76 2.27	1.74 2.23	1.73 2.21
25	4.24 7.77	3.38 5.57	2.99 4.68	2.76 4.18	2.60 3.86	2.49 3.63	2.41 3.46	2.34 3.32	2.28 3.21	2.24 3.13	2.20 3.05	2.16 2.99	2.11 2.89	2.06 2.81	2.00 2.70	1.96 2.62	1.92 2.54	1.87 2.45	1.84 2.40	1.80 2.32	1.77 2.29	1.74 2.23	1.72 2.19	1.71 2.17

Statistical Table 2 (Continued)

Degrees of freedom for denominator (v_2)	\multicolumn{18}{c}{Degrees of freedom for numerator (v_1)}
	1	2	3	4	5	6	7	8	9	10	11	12	14	16	20	24	30	40	50	75	100	200	500	∞
26	4.22 / 7.72	3.37 / 5.53	2.89 / 4.64	2.74 / 4.14	2.59 / 3.82	2.47 / 3.59	2.39 / 3.42	2.32 / 3.29	2.27 / 3.17	2.22 / 3.09	2.18 / 3.02	2.15 / 2.96	2.10 / 2.86	2.05 / 2.77	1.99 / 2.66	1.95 / 2.58	1.90 / 2.50	1.85 / 2.41	1.82 / 2.36	1.78 / 2.28	1.76 / 2.25	1.72 / 2.19	1.70 / 2.15	1.69 / 2.13
27	4.21 / 7.68	3.35 / 5.49	2.96 / 4.60	2.73 / 4.11	2.57 / 3.79	2.46 / 3.56	2.37 / 3.39	2.30 / 3.26	2.25 / 3.14	2.20 / 3.06	2.16 / 2.98	2.13 / 2.93	2.08 / 2.83	2.03 / 2.74	1.97 / 2.63	1.93 / 2.55	1.88 / 2.47	1.84 / 2.38	1.80 / 2.33	1.76 / 2.25	1.74 / 2.21	1.71 / 2.16	1.68 / 2.12	1.67 / 2.10
28	4.20 / 7.64	3.34 / 5.45	2.95 / 4.57	2.71 / 4.07	2.56 / 3.76	2.44 / 3.53	2.36 / 3.36	2.29 / 3.23	3.24 / 3.11	2.19 / 3.03	2.15 / 2.95	2.12 / 2.90	2.06 / 2.80	2.02 / 2.71	1.96 / 2.60	1.91 / 2.52	1.87 / 2.44	1.81 / 2.35	1.78 / 2.30	1.75 / 2.22	1.72 / 2.18	1.69 / 2.13	1.67 / 2.09	1.65 / 2.06
29	4.18 / 7.60	3.33 / 5.52	2.93 / 4.54	2.70 / 4.04	2.54 / 3.73	2.43 / 3.50	2.35 / 3.33	2.28 / 3.20	2.22 / 3.08	2.18 / 3.00	2.14 / 2.92	2.10 / 2.87	2.05 / 2.77	2.00 / 2.68	1.94 / 2.57	1.90 / 2.49	1.85 / 2.41	1.80 / 2.32	1.77 / 2.27	1.73 / 2.19	1.71 / 2.15	1.68 / 2.10	1.65 / 2.06	1.64 / 2.03
30	4.17 / 7.56	3.32 / 5.39	2.92 / 4.51	2.69 / 4.02	2.53 / 3.70	2.42 / 3.47	2.34 / 3.30	2.27 / 3.17	2.21 / 3.06	2.16 / 2.98	2.12 / 2.00	2.09 / 2.84	2.04 / 2.74	1.99 / 2.66	1.93 / 2.55	1.89 / 2.47	1.84 / 2.38	1.79 / 2.29	1.76 / 2.24	1.72 / 2.16	1.69 / 2.13	1.66 / 2.07	1.64 / 2.03	1.62 / 2.01
32	4.15 / 7.50	3.30 / 5.34	2.90 / 4.46	2.67 / 3.97	2.51 / 3.66	2.40 / 3.42	2.32 / 3.25	2.25 / 3.12	2.19 / 3.01	2.14 / 2.94	2.10 / 2.86	2.07 / 2.80	2.02 / 2.70	1.97 / 2.62	1.91 / 2.51	1.86 / 2.42	1.82 / 2.34	1.76 / 2.25	1.74 / 2.20	1.69 / 2.12	1.67 / 2.08	1.64 / 2.02	1.61 / 1.98	1.59 / 1.96
34	4.13 / 7.44	3.28 / 5.29	2.88 / 4.42	2.65 / 3.93	2.49 / 3.61	2.38 / 3.38	2.30 / 3.21	2.23 / 3.08	2.17 / 2.97	2.12 / 2.89	2.08 / 2.82	2.05 / 2.76	2.00 / 2.66	1.95 / 2.58	1.89 / 2.47	1.84 / 2.38	1.80 / 2.30	1.74 / 2.21	1.71 / 2.15	1.67 / 2.08	1.64 / 2.04	1.61 / 1.98	1.59 / 1.94	1.57 / 1.91
36	4.11 / 7.39	3.26 / 5.25	2.86 / 4.38	2.63 / 3.89	2.48 / 3.58	2.36 / 3.35	2.28 / 3.18	2.21 / 3.04	2.15 / 2.94	2.10 / 2.86	2.06 / 2.78	2.03 / 2.72	1.89 / 2.62	1.93 / 2.54	1.87 / 2.43	1.82 / 2.35	1.78 / 2.26	1.72 / 2.17	1.69 / 2.12	1.65 / 2.04	1.62 / 2.00	1.59 / 1.94	1.56 / 1.90	1.55 / 1.87
38	4.10 / 7.35	3.25 / 5.21	2.85 / 4.34	2.62 / 3.86	2.46 / 3.54	2.35 / 3.32	2.26 / 3.15	2.19 / 3.02	2.14 / 2.91	2.09 / 2.82	2.05 / 2.75	2.02 / 2.69	1.96 / 2.59	1.92 / 2.51	1.85 / 2.40	1.80 / 2.32	1.76 / 2.22	1.71 / 2.14	1.67 / 2.08	1.63 / 2.00	1.60 / 1.97	1.57 / 1.90	1.54 / 1.86	1.53 / 1.84
40	4.08 / 7.31	3.23 / 5.18	2.84 / 4.31	2.61 / 3.83	2.45 / 3.51	2.34 / 3.29	2.25 / 3.12	2.18 / 2.99	2.12 / 2.88	2.07 / 2.80	2.04 / 2.73	2.00 / 2.66	1.95 / 2.56	1.90 / 2.49	1.84 / 2.37	1.79 / 2.29	1.74 / 2.20	1.69 / 2.11	1.66 / 2.05	1.61 / 1.97	1.59 / 1.94	1.55 / 1.88	1.53 / 1.84	1.51 / 1.81
42	4.07 / 7.27	3.22 / 5.15	2.83 / 4.29	2.59 / 3.80	2.44 / 3.49	2.32 / 3.26	2.24 / 3.10	2.17 / 2.96	2.11 / 2.86	2.06 / 2.77	2.02 / 2.70	1.99 / 2.64	1.94 / 2.54	1.89 / 2.46	1.82 / 2.35	1.78 / 2.26	1.73 / 2.17	1.68 / 2.08	1.64 / 2.02	1.60 / 1.94	1.57 / 1.91	1.54 / 1.85	1.51 / 1.80	1.49 / 1.78
44	4.06 / 7.24	3.21 / 5.12	2.82 / 4.26	2.58 / 3.78	2.43 / 3.46	2.31 / 3.24	2.23 / 3.07	2.16 / 2.94	2.10 / 2.84	2.05 / 2.75	2.01 / 2.68	1.98 / 2.62	1.92 / 2.52	1.88 / 2.44	1.81 / 2.32	1.76 / 2.24	1.72 / 2.15	1.66 / 2.06	1.63 / 2.00	1.58 / 1.92	1.56 / 1.88	1.52 / 1.82	1.50 / 1.78	1.48 / 1.75
46	4.05 / 7.21	3.20 / 5.10	2.81 / 4.24	2.57 / 3.76	2.42 / 3.44	2.30 / 3.22	2.22 / 3.05	2.14 / 2.92	2.09 / 2.82	2.04 / 2.73	2.00 / 2.66	1.97 / 2.60	1.91 / 2.50	1.87 / 2.42	1.80 / 2.30	1.75 / 2.22	1.71 / 2.13	1.65 / 2.04	1.62 / 1.98	1.57 / 1.90	1.54 / 1.86	1.51 / 1.80	1.48 / 1.76	1.46 / 1.72
48	4.04 / 7.19	3.19 / 5.08	2.80 / 4.22	2.56 / 3.74	2.41 / 3.42	2.30 / 3.20	2.21 / 3.04	2.14 / 2.90	2.08 / 2.80	2.03 / 2.71	1.99 / 2.64	1.96 / 2.58	1.90 / 2.48	1.86 / 2.40	1.79 / 2.28	1.74 / 2.20	1.70 / 2.11	1.64 / 2.02	1.61 / 1.96	1.56 / 1.88	1.53 / 1.84	1.50 / 1.78	1.47 / 1.73	1.45 / 1.70

50	4.03 7.17	3.18 5.06	2.79 4.20	2.56 3.72	2.40 3.41	2.29 3.18	2.20 3.02	2.13 2.88	2.07 2.78	2.02 2.70	1.98 2.62	1.95 2.56	1.90 2.46	1.85 2.39	1.78 2.26	1.74 2.18	1.69 2.10	1.63 2.00	1.60 1.94	1.55 1.86	1.52 1.82	1.48 1.76	1.46 1.71	1.44 1.68
55	4.02 7.12	3.17 5.01	2.78 4.16	2.54 3.68	2.38 3.37	2.27 3.15	2.18 2.98	2.11 2.85	2.05 2.75	2.00 2.66	1.97 2.59	1.93 2.53	1.88 2.43	1.83 2.35	1.76 2.23	1.72 2.15	1.67 2.06	1.61 1.96	1.58 1.90	1.52 1.82	1.50 1.78	1.46 1.71	1.43 1.66	1.41 1.64
60	4.00 7.08	3.15 4.98	2.76 4.13	2.52 3.65	2.37 3.34	2.25 3.12	2.17 2.95	2.10 2.82	2.04 2.72	1.99 2.63	1.95 2.56	1.92 2.50	1.86 2.40	1.81 2.32	1.75 2.20	1.70 2.12	1.65 2.03	1.59 1.93	1.56 1.87	1.50 1.79	1.48 1.74	1.44 1.68	1.41 1.63	1.39 1.60
65	3.99 7.04	3.14 4.95	2.75 4.10	2.51 3.62	2.36 3.31	2.24 3.09	2.15 2.93	2.08 2.79	2.02 2.70	1.98 2.61	1.94 2.54	1.90 2.47	1.85 2.37	1.80 2.30	1.73 2.18	1.68 2.09	1.63 2.00	1.57 1.90	1.54 1.84	1.49 1.76	1.46 1.71	1.42 1.64	1.39 1.60	1.37 1.56
70	3.98 7.01	3.13 4.92	2.74 4.08	2.50 3.60	2.35 3.29	2.32 3.07	2.14 2.91	2.07 2.77	2.01 2.67	1.97 2.59	1.93 2.51	1.89 2.45	1.84 2.35	1.79 2.28	1.72 2.15	1.67 2.07	1.62 1.98	1.56 1.88	1.53 1.82	1.47 1.74	1.45 1.69	1.40 1.63	1.37 1.56	1.35 1.53
80	3.96 6.96	3.11 4.88	2.72 4.04	2.48 3.56	2.33 3.25	2.21 3.04	2.12 2.87	2.05 2.74	1.99 2.64	1.95 2.55	1.91 2.48	1.88 2.41	1.82 2.32	1.77 2.24	1.70 2.11	1.65 2.03	1.60 1.94	1.54 1.84	1.51 1.78	1.45 1.70	1.42 1.65	1.38 1.57	1.35 1.52	1.32 1.49
100	3.94 6.90	3.09 4.82	2.70 3.98	2.46 3.51	2.30 3.20	2.19 2.99	2.10 2.82	2.03 2.69	1.97 2.59	1.92 2.51	1.88 2.43	1.85 2.36	1.79 2.26	1.75 2.19	1.68 2.06	1.63 1.98	1.57 1.89	1.51 1.79	1.48 1.73	1.42 1.64	1.39 1.59	1.34 1.51	1.30 1.46	1.28 1.43
125	3.92 6.84	3.07 4.78	2.68 3.94	2.44 3.47	2.29 3.17	2.17 2.95	2.08 2.79	2.01 2.65	1.95 2.56	1.90 2.47	1.86 2.40	1.83 2.33	1.78 2.23	1.72 2.15	1.65 2.03	1.60 1.94	1.55 1.85	1.49 1.75	1.45 1.68	1.39 1.59	1.36 1.54	1.31 1.46	1.27 1.40	1.25 1.37
150	3.91 6.81	3.06 4.75	2.67 3.91	2.43 3.44	2.27 3.13	2.16 2.92	2.07 2.76	2.00 2.62	1.94 2.53	1.89 2.44	1.85 2.37	1.82 2.30	1.76 2.20	1.71 2.12	1.64 2.00	1.59 1.91	1.54 1.83	1.47 1.72	1.44 1.66	1.37 1.56	1.34 1.51	1.29 1.43	1.25 1.37	1.22 1.33
200	3.89 6.76	3.04 4.71	2.65 3.88	2.41 3.41	2.26 3.11	2.14 2.90	2.05 2.73	1.98 2.60	1.92 2.50	1.87 2.41	1.83 2.34	1.80 2.28	1.74 1.17	1.69 2.09	1.62 1.97	1.57 1.88	1.52 1.79	1.45 1.69	1.42 1.62	1.35 1.53	1.32 1.48	1.26 1.39	1.22 1.33	1.19 1.28
400	3.86 6.70	3.02 4.66	2.62 3.83	2.39 3.36	2.23 3.06	2.12 2.85	2.03 2.69	1.96 2.55	1.90 2.46	1.85 2.37	1.81 2.29	1.78 2.23	1.72 2.12	1.67 2.04	1.60 1.92	1.54 1.84	1.49 1.74	1.42 1.64	1.38 1.57	1.32 1.47	1.28 1.42	1.22 1.32	1.16 1.24	1.13 1.19
1000	3.85 6.66	3.00 4.62	2.61 3.80	2.38 3.34	2.22 3.04	2.10 2.82	2.02 2.66	1.95 2.53	1.89 2.43	1.84 2.34	1.80 2.26	1.76 2.20	1.70 2.09	1.65 2.01	1.58 1.89	1.53 1.81	1.47 1.71	1.41 1.61	1.36 1.54	1.30 1.44	1.26 1.38	1.19 1.28	1.13 1.19	1.08 1.11
∞	3.84 6.64	2.99 4.60	2.60 3.78	2.37 3.32	2.21 3.02	2.09 2.80	2.01 2.64	1.94 2.51	1.88 2.41	1.83 2.32	1.79 2.24	1.75 2.18	1.69 2.07	1.64 1.99	1.57 1.87	1.52 1.79	1.46 1.69	1.40 1.59	1.35 1.52	1.28 1.41	1.24 1.36	1.17 1.25	1.11 1.15	1.00 1.00

Statistical Table 3 Areas for a Standard Normal Distribution

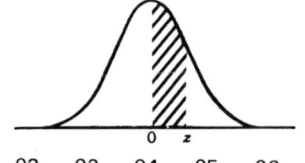

An entry in the table is the area under the curve, between $z = 0$ and a positive value of z. Areas for negative values of z are obtained by symmetry.

z   .00   .01   .02   .03   .04   .05   .06   .07   .08   .09

Second Decimal Place of z

z	.−0	.−1	.−2	.−3	.−4	.−5	.−6	.−7	.−8	.−9
0.0	.0000	.0040	.0080	.0120	.0160	.0199	.0239	.0279	.0319	.0359
0.1	.0398	.0438	.0478	.0517	.0557	.0596	.0636	.0675	.0714	.0753
0.2	.0793	.0832	.0871	.0910	.0948	.0987	.1026	.1064	.1103	.1141
0.3	.1179	.1217	.1255	.1293	.1331	.1368	.1406	.1443	.1480	.1517
0.4	.1554	.1591	.1628	.1664	.1700	.1736	.1772	.1808	.1844	.1879
0.5	.1915	.1950	.1985	.2019	.2054	.2088	.2123	.2157	.2190	.2224
0.6	.2257	.2291	.2324	.2357	.2389	.2422	.2454	.2486	.2517	.2549
0.7	.2580	.2611	.2642	.2673	.2703	.2734	.2764	.2794	.2823	.2852
0.8	.2881	.2910	.2939	.2967	.2995	.3023	.3051	.3078	.3106	.3133
0.9	.3159	.3186	.3212	.3238	.3264	.3289	.3315	.3340	.3365	.3389
1.0	.3413	.3438	.3461	.3485	.3508	.3531	.3554	.3577	.3599	.3621
1.1	.3643	.3665	.3686	.3708	.3729	.3749	.3770	.3790	.3810	.3830
1.2	.3849	.3869	.3888	.3907	.3925	.3944	.3962	.3980	.3997	.4015
1.3	.4032	.4049	.4066	.4082	.4099	.4115	.4131	.4147	.4162	.4177
1.4	.4192	.4207	.4222	.4236	.4251	.4265	.4279	.4292	.4306	.4319
1.5	.4332	.4345	.4357	.4370	.4382	.4394	.4406	.4418	.4429	.4441
1.6	.4452	.4463	.4474	.4484	.4495	.4505	.4515	.4525	.4535	.4545
1.7	.4554	.4564	.4573	.4582	.4591	.4599	.4608	.4616	.4625	.4633
1.8	.4641	.4649	.4656	.4664	.4671	.4678	.4686	.4693	.4699	.4706
1.9	.4713	.4719	.4726	.4732	.4738	.4744	.4750	.4756	.4761	.4767
2.0	.4772	.4778	.4783	.4788	.4793	.4798	.4803	.4808	.4812	.4817
2.1	.4821	.4826	.4830	.4834	.4838	.4842	.4846	.4850	.4854	.4857
2.2	.4861	.4864	.4868	.4871	.4875	.4878	.4881	.4884	.4887	.4890
2.3	.4893	.4896	.4898	.4901	.4904	.4906	.4909	.4911	.4913	.4916
2.4	.4918	.4920	.4922	.4925	.4927	.4929	.4931	.4932	.4934	.4936
2.5	.4938	.4940	.4941	.4943	.4945	.4946	.4948	.4949	.4951	.4952
2.6	.4953	.4955	.4956	.4957	.4959	.4960	.4961	.4962	.4963	.4964
2.7	.4965	.4966	.4967	.4968	.4969	.4970	.4971	.4972	.4973	.4974
2.8	.4974	.4975	.4976	.4977	.4977	.4978	.4979	.4979	.4980	.4981
2.9	.4981	.4982	.4982	.4983	.4984	.4984	.4985	.4985	.4986	.4986
3.0	.4987	.4987	.4987	.4988	.4988	.4989	.4989	.4989	.4990	.4990

P. G. Hoel, *Elementary Statistics,* 2nd edition © 1966. Reprinted by permission of John Wiley & Sons, Inc., N.Y.

Statistical Table 4 Critical values of χ^2

Levels of Significance

The first column contains the number of degrees of freedom. The values in the body of the table are the values of χ^2 required for the listed probability levels. For example, a χ^2 of 4.22 with 1 df exceeds the tabled value of 3.84 for 1 df at the .05 level and would be judged significant at that level.

df	P = .99	.98	.95	.90	.80	.70	.50
1	.00016	.00063	.0039	.016	.064	.15	.46
2	.02	.04	.10	.21	.45	.71	1.39
3	.12	.18	.35	.58	1.00	1.42	2.37
4	.30	.43	.71	1.06	1.65	2.20	3.36
5	.55	.75	1.14	1.61	2.34	3.00	4.35
6	.87	1.13	1.64	2.20	3.07	3.83	5.35
7	1.24	1.56	2.17	2.83	3.82	4.67	6.35
8	1.65	2.03	2.73	3.49	4.59	5.53	7.34
9	2.09	2.53	3.32	4.17	5.38	6.39	8.34
10	2.56	3.06	3.94	4.86	6.18	7.27	9.34
11	3.05	3.61	4.58	5.58	6.99	8.15	10.34
12	3.57	4.18	5.23	6.30	7.81	9.03	11.34
13	4.11	4.76	5.89	7.04	8.63	9.93	12.34
14	4.66	5.37	6.57	7.79	9.47	10.82	13.34
15	5.23	5.98	7.26	8.55	10.31	11.72	14.34
16	5.81	6.61	7.96	9.31	11.15	12.62	15.34
17	6.41	7.26	8.67	10.08	12.00	13.53	16.34
18	7.02	7.91	9.39	10.86	12.86	14.44	17.34
19	7.63	8.57	10.12	11.65	13.72	15.35	18.34
20	8.26	9.24	10.85	12.44	14.58	16.27	19.34
21	8.90	9.92	11.59	13.24	15.44	17.18	20.34
22	9.54	10.60	12.34	14.04	16.31	18.10	21.34
23	10.20	11.29	13.09	14.85	17.19	19.02	22.34
24	10.86	11.99	13.85	15.66	18.06	19.94	23.34
25	11.52	12.70	14.61	16.47	18.94	20.87	24.34
26	12.20	13.41	15.38	17.29	19.82	21.79	25.34
27	12.88	14.12	16.15	18.11	20.70	22.72	26.34
28	13.56	14.85	16.93	18.94	21.59	23.65	27.34
29	14.26	15.57	17.71	19.77	22.48	24.58	28.34
30	14.95	16.31	18.49	20.60	23.36	25.51	29.34

Q. McNemar, *Psychological Statistics,* 3rd Ed. Reprinted by permission of John Wiley & Sons, Inc., N.Y.

Statistical Table 5 Critical Values of t

For any given df, the table shows the values of t corresponding to various levels of probability. Obtained f is significant at a given level if its absolute value is equal to *or greater than* the value shown in the table.

	\multicolumn{6}{c}{Level of significance for one-tailed test}
	.10	.05	.025	.01	.005	.0005
	\multicolumn{6}{c}{Level of significance for two-tailed test}
df	.20	.10	.05	.02	.01	.001
1	3.078	6.314	12.706	31.821	63.657	636.619
2	1.886	2.920	4.303	6.965	9.925	31.598
3	1.638	2.353	3.182	4.541	5.841	12.941
4	1.533	2.132	2.776	3.747	4.604	8.610
5	1.476	2.015	2.571	3.365	4.032	6.859
6	1.440	1.943	2.447	3.143	3.707	5.959
7	1.415	1.895	2.365	2.998	3.499	5.405
8	1.397	1.860	2.306	2.896	3.355	5.041
9	1.383	1.833	2.262	2.821	3.250	4.781
10	1.372	1.812	2.228	2.764	3.169	4.587
11	1.363	1.796	2.201	2.718	3.106	4.437
12	1.356	1.782	2.179	2.681	3.055	4.318
13	1.350	1.771	2.160	2.650	3.012	4.221
14	1.345	1.761	2.145	2.624	2.977	4.140
15	1.341	1.753	2.131	2.602	2.947	4.073
16	1.337	1.746	2.120	2.583	2.921	4.015
17	1.333	1.740	2.110	2.567	2.898	3.965
18	1.330	1.734	2.101	2.552	2.878	3.922
19	1.328	1.729	2.093	2.539	2.861	3.883
20	1.325	1.725	2.086	2.528	2.845	3.850
21	1.323	1.721	2.080	2.518	2.831	3.819
22	1.321	1.717	2.074	2.508	2.819	3.792
23	1.319	1.714	2.069	2.500	2.807	3.767
24	1.318	1.711	2.064	2.492	2.797	3.745
25	1.316	1.708	2.060	2.485	2.787	3.725
26	1.315	1.706	2.056	2.479	2.779	3.707
27	1.314	1.703	2.052	2.473	2.771	3.690
28	1.313	1.701	2.048	2.467	2.763	3.674
29	1.311	1.699	2.045	2.462	2.756	3.659
30	1.310	1.697	2.042	2.457	2.750	3.646
40	1.303	1.684	2.021	2.423	2.704	3.551
60	1.296	1.671	2.000	2.390	2.660	3.460
120	1.289	1.658	1.980	2.358	2.617	3.373
∞	1.282	1.645	1.960	2.326	2.576	3.291

Judith D. Handel, *Introductory Statistics for Sociology*, © 1978, p. 370. Reprinted by permission of Prentice-Hall, Inc Englewood Cliffs, New Jersey.

INDEX

Agger, Robert E., 342
Allison, Graham, 126, 128, 129, 132, 345
Allport, Gordon, 126
Almond, Gabriel, 72, 77–78, 80–81, 83, 107, 110–12, 115, 120, 139–41, 342, 344
American Political Science Association, 10
  Committee on Professional Standards and Responsibilities, 341
American Political Science Review, 10, 157
Analysis of variance, 321, 349
Anderson, James E., 131, 138, 142, 346
Anticipated reaction, 90
Arrow, Kenneth, 133
Arrow Paradox, 133
Ashby, W. Ross, 345

Babbie, Earl, 346
Bachrach, Peter, 90, 105, 115, 131, 343
Backstrom, Charles H., 346
Banfield, Edward C., 343
Baratz, Morton S., 90, 105, 115, 131, 343
Barber, James David, 127
Bauer, Raymond, 346
Bay, Christian, 36
b coefficient, 306–9, 311, 349
Behavioralism, 12–15, 349
Bennett, William R., 347
Bent, Dale H., 348
Bentley, Arthur F., 87, 93–94, 96, 118, 344
Berelson, Bernard R., 96
Bernstein, Robert A., 175, 347
Beta coefficient, 311, 349
Biomedical Computer Programs (BMD), 224–25, 347
Blalock, Ann, 347
Blalock, Hubert M., Jr., 300, 347, 348
Blisset, Marlan, 341
Bluhm, William T., 343
Bluntchli, J. K., 10
Blydenburgh, John C., 349
Bogdan, Robert, 37
Boulding, Kenneth, 344
Bowen, Bruce, 348
Braithwaite, R. B., 341
Braybrooke, David, 134, 345
Brinton, Crane, 102
Brodbeck, May, 341
Brown, Robert, 341
Browning, Rufus, 127
Bruck, H. W., 346
Buchanan, James M., 345
Buckley, Walter, 344

Campbell, Angus, 97
Campbell, Donald T., 187–88, 193, 347, 348

Carey, George W., 340
Case study, 193, 196, 350
Causation, 24, 91, 144
  criteria for, 25–26
Charlesworth, James C., 34, 342
Chi square. *See* Significance tests
Civic culture. *See* Political culture
Claude, Inis L., Jr., 92, 343
Coalition formation, 132
  size principle, 132–33
Cobb, Roger W., 100–105, 131, 344
Codebooks, 216–17
Coding, 213–15
Coefficient of determination, 314, 348
Coefficient of reproducibility, 172, 335
Coefficient of scalability, 172–73, 335
Cognitive development, 70, 350
Cognitive dissonance, 115–16, 350
Coleman, James S., 52–53, 102–3, 106, 110, 344
Communication, 87, 114–17, 120–21
  defined, 114, 120
  generalizations, 115, 120
  operationalization, 120
Computers, 217–26, 350
  hardware, 219–23
  software, 223–26, 358
Concept, 18–22, 164–74, 350
  defined, 18
  essential definition, 19, 352
  evaluating, 21–22
  group level, 79, 353
  individual level, 79, 353
  nominal definition, 19–20, 355
  role in theory, 17
  systematic import, 22
Confidence interval, 263, 350
Confidence level, 263, 350
Conflict, 87, 100–106, 119, 350
  defined, 100–101, 119
  generalizations, 103, 119
  operationalization, 119
Construct, 21, 350
Contingency tables. *See* Cross-tabulation tables
Converse, Philip E., 67
Conway, M. Margaret, 72–73, 342
Cook, Stuart W., 54, 341
Cooley, William W., 348
Correlation. *See* Measures of association
Coser, Lewis, 100, 344
Covariation, 306–7, 312
Covering statement. *See* Generalization
Crenson, Matthew A., 90, 343
Crick, Bernard, 340
Critical value, 269–71, 351

Cross-tabulation tables, 248–53, 351
  cell, 248
  marginals, 248
Curry, R. L., Jr., 138, 143

Dahl, Robert A., 12, 88–89, 91–93, 99, 125, 340, 343, 346
Dahlgren, Harold, 70, 72, 128
Data:
  cross-sectional, 351
  longitudinal, 67, 354
David, J. A., 292
Davies, James C., 102
Dawson, Karen S., 342
Dawson, Richard E., 72, 342
Decision-making, 122, 123–37, 145–46, 351
  decision unit, 125
  defined, 124, 145
  generalizations, 137, 146
  incremental, 136, 353
  individual influences on, 126–28
  operationalization, 145
  organizational influences on, 129–30
  rational, 131–36, 357
  system influences on, 130–31
Deduction, 27–28, 351
DeGrazia, Alfred, 51, 341
Degree of freedom, 273, 276–77, 351
Dennis, Jack, 64, 66, 342
Descriptive statistics, 230, 233–53, 351. *See also*, Frequency distribution; Measures of association; Measures of central tendency; Measures of variation
Determinism, 17, 351
Deutsch, Karl W., 87, 114, 345
Devine, Donald J., 81–82, 343
Dewey, John, 11
Dexter, Lewis, 346, 347
Dickson, William, 46
Dixon, W. J., 224, 347
Downs, Anthony, 132–34, 159–60, 345
Dror, Yehezkel, 345
Dupeux, Georges, 67
Dye, Thomas R., 138, 346
Dyer, James A., 175, 347

Easton, David, 14, 74, 86–87, 94, 100, 107–12, 340, 342, 345
Eckstein, Harry, 94
Ecological fallacy, 209, 352
Edelman, Murray, 104, 346
Edinger, Lewis G., 80
Edwards, Allen L., 348
Edwards, George C., III, 138
Elazar, Daniel J., 343
Elder, Charles D., 100–105, 131, 344

Elitism, 92–93, 98–99, 352
Ethics, 42–54
  anonymity, 48–49
  harm, 44–45, 47–48, 54
  honesty, 46–47
  objectivity, 49–51
  right of privacy, 44–46, 54
  social responsibility, 52–54
  voluntary participation, 44–47
Etzioni, Amitai, 136, 346
Eulau, Heinz, 340
Evans, Frederick J., 191
Everson, David H., 18, 342
Experimental design, 186–91. *See also* Pre-experimental design; Quasi-experimental design
  control group, 189, 335, 351
  experimental group, 189, 335, 352
  Solomon four group design, 190
Experiments, 35, 48, 144, 187, 352
Explanation, 26–27, 28, 31, 32, 352
  nomological model, 27, 355
Ezekiel, Mordecai, 303

Fact, 12–13, 30–31, 36–37, 352
Fagen, Richard R., 343, 345
Feigert, Frank B., 72–73, 342
Feigl, Herbert, 341
Fenno, Richard J., Jr., 112
Festinger, Leon, 115
Fields, Craig, 347
Fisk, Donald M., 144
Fleron, Frederic J., Jr., 68
Fox, Karl A., 303
Francis, Wayne L., 155, 160, 347
Freeman, Linton C., 348
Free will, 35–36
Frequency distribution, 235, 242–48, 352
Freund, John F., 348
Freund, Paul A., 341
Friedrich, Carl J., 90
Frohock, Fred M., 30
F Statistic. *See* Significance tests

Galtung, Johan, 347
Game theory, 134
Gamma. *See* Measures of association
Gamson, William, 104–5, 344
Garson, G. David, 347, 348
Generalization, 22–27, 174–76, 352
  covering statement, 27, 351
  defined, 22
  probabalistic, 26, 32–33, 357
  role in explanation, 26–27
  role in theory, 17
  universal, 26–27
Glaser, Barney, 347
Goldrich, Daniel, 343

Goodman and Kruskal's Tau. *See* Measures of association
Graham, George, Jr., 341
Graham, Hugh Douglas, 102
Grant, Lawrence V., 342
Graph:
 bar, 244, 246
 histogram, 244
 line, 246–48
Greenberg, Edward S., 75
Greenstein, Fred, 71, 75, 342
Gross, Llewellyn, 341
Group, 87, 93–100, 118–19, 353
 defined, 94–95, 118
 effects on government, 98–99
 effects on individuals, 97–98
 generalizations, 97–98, 118
 operationalization, 118
 primary, 97, 356
 secondary, 97, 358
 types, 95–96, 350, 353, 356
Groupthink, 130, 353
Gurr, Ted Robert, 102, 347
Guttman, Louis, 171
Guttman's lambda. *See* Measures of association

Hagan, Charles B., 94
Handel, Judith D., 273, 348
Harkins, Peter B., 347
Hatry, Harry P., 144
Hauser, Philip M., 348
Hawley, Willis D., 343
Hawthorne effect, 46, 190, 353
Head, Kendra B., 348
Hempel, Carl G., 18, 22, 341
Herring, E. Pendleton, 96, 344
Herzon, Frederick D., 348
Hess, Robert, 65, 66, 69, 70, 73, 74, 342
Hirsch, Herbert, 68
Hofferbert, Richard I., 138
Hollender, Myles, 349
Holsti, Ole R., 347, 348
Homans, George C., 344
Hopper, Michael, 348
Horowitz, Irving Louis, 54, 342
Hull, Hadlai, 348
Hume, David, 12–13, 17, 25, 30, 36, 37
Humphreys, Laud, 45–46
Hunter, Floyd, 91–92, 343
Hursch, Gerald D., 346
Hy, Ronn J., 347
Hyman, Herbert H., 70, 342
Hyneman, Charles, 340
Hypothesis:
 construction, 174–76, 332
 defined, 23, 353
Hypothesis testing:

chi square distribution, 274–77
 normal curve distribution, 268–72
 t distribution, 272–74

Incrementalism. *See* Decision-making
Index, 167–69, 335, 353
 item analysis, 170
Induction, 23, 353
Inferential statistics, 230, 261–78, 353.
Inhelder, Barbel, 70
Interest group, 96. *See also* Group
Intersubjectivity, 20, 165, 334
Inter-University Consortium for Political and Social Research (ICPSR), 209, 225
Interview techniques, 199–207
 face to face, 200–201
 self-administered, 199–200
 telephone, 200
Isaak, Alan C., 18, 22, 89, 98, 342
Isenhour, Thomas L., 347

Jacob, Phillip E., 345
Janda, Kenneth, 347
Janis, Irving, 130, 346
Jaros, Dean, 67–68, 70, 75, 342, 343
Jenkins, Jean G., 348
Jennings, M. Kent, 71, 73
Johnson, Allen G., 349
Jones, Charles O., 131, 346
Jones, E. Terrence, 180, 347
Jurs, Peter C., 347

Kaplan, Abraham, 33–34, 341, 343
Kelman, Herbert, 342
Kendall's tau. *See* Measures of association
Kerlinger, Fred N., 161, 163, 303, 347
Kingdon, John W., 98
Kish, Leslie, 347
Klapper, Joseph T., 73
Kohout, Frank J., 349
Kornhauser, William, 99, 344
Kuhn, Thomas, 11–12, 14, 29–30, 32, 50, 341

Langton, Kenneth, 343
La Palombara, Joseph, 344
Larsen, Edwin D., 66
Lasswell, Harold, 13–14, 127, 340, 343
Latham, Earl, 344
Law, 23, 352
Lazarsfeld, Paul, 347
Leaning theory, 69–70, 352
Leege, David C., 155, 160, 347
Level of analysis, 79, 179, 335, 336, 354
Levels of measurement. *See* Measurement, levels of
Levin, Martin, 72, 73

Levy, Marion, 345
Likert, Rensis, 169
Lindblom, Charles E., 132, 134, 136, 346
Lineberry, Robert L., 92
Lohnes, Paul R., 348
Lowi, Theodore J., 99, 123, 140–41, 346

Mc Closkey, Herbert, 70, 72, 128
Mc Connell, Grant, 346
Mc Coy, Charles A., 340
Mc Gaw, Dickinson, 18, 161–62, 347
Mac Rae, Duncan, Jr., 342, 346
Madison, James, 87
March, James G., 346
Mayer, Lawrence C., 22, 342
Measurement, levels of, 235–37, 336, 353
  interval, 236, 354
  nominal, 235, 355
  ordinal, 235, 355
  ratio, 236, 357
Measures of association, 278, 280–81, 354, 355
  gamma, 286–92, 294, 336, 352
  Goodman and Kruskal's tau, 281–84, 353
  Kendall's tau, 293–95, 337, 354
  multiple correlation, 319–20, 324, 355
  partial correlation, 316–19, 322–23, 356
  Pearson's correlation, 312–15, 356
  Somers' d, 293–95, 337
Measures of central tendency, 234, 237–39
  mean, 237–38, 354
  median, 238–39, 355
  mode, 239, 355
Measures of variation, 234, 239–42
  interquartile range, 240, 354
  mean deviation, 241–42, 354
  range, 240, 357
  standard deviation, 242, 358
  variance, 186–87, 242, 313–14, 321, 359
Meehan, Eugene, 22, 341
Meier, Richard L., 345
Merelman, Richard, 73
Merriam, Charles E., 16
Merton, Robert K., 345
Michels, Roberto, 11
Milbrath, Lester, 116
Milgram, Stanley, 46–47, 191
Miller, Delbert C., 347
Mills, C. Wright, 93, 99, 343
Mitchell, William C., 345
Mixed scanning, 136, 355
Moore, Richard, 347
Morganthau, Hans, 343
Morgenstern, Oscar, 346
Multiple correlation. *See* Measures of association

Nachmias, Clava, 349
Nachmias, David, 349
Nagel, Ernest, 25, 32–33, 341
Nett, Roger, 342
Nie, Norman C., 62, 224, 348
Niemi, Richard, 71, 73
Nomological model. *See* Explanation
Nondecision making, 90, 105, 355
Normal curve, 247, 268, 355
Normative, 159, 176, 355
North, Robert C., 348
Null hypothesis, 267, 355

Odegard, Peter H., 96
Olson, Mancur, Jr., 344
Operationalization, 21, 164–74, 335
  indicators, 167–68
Opportunity costs, 143
Organized Set of Integrated Routines for Investigation with Statistics (OSIRIS), 224–25, 348
Orne, Martin T., 191

Paige, Glenn D., 133
Paine, Joann Poparad, 18, 342
Paradigm, 11–12, 30, 356
Parsons, Malcolm, 12
Parsons, Talcott, 345
Partial correlation. *See* Measures of association
Pavlov, Ivan Petrovich, 38–39
Pearson's correlation coefficient (r). *See* Measures of association
Pedhazur, E., 303
Piaget, Jean, 70
Playford, John, 340
Pluralism, 11–12, 93, 99, 356
Policy, 137–46
  defined, 138, 146, 356
  generalizations, 140, 141, 146
  implementation, 141
  operationalization, 146
  types, 139–41
Policy analysis, 139, 142–45, 356
  evaluation, 143–45
Policy-making, 139–41, 356
Political culture, 63, 76–85
  civic culture, 80
  definition, 76–77, 84, 356
  generalizations, 81–82, 85
  operationalization, 78–79, 84
Political science:
  scope, 8–15 *See also* Communication; Conflict; Decision-making; Group; Policy; Political culture; Political socialization; Power; Systems
Political socialization, 63–76, 83–84, 356
  agents, 65, 71–73, 84
  defined, 63–65, 83

discontinuities, 66, 84
generalizations, 73, 84
operationalization, 65, 83–84
Polsby, Nelson, 343
Pool, Ithiel, 346
Popper, Karl, 158–59
Population. *See* Universe
Postbehavioralists, 13–14, 53, 356
Powell, G. Bingham, Jr., 111, 116, 139–141, 344
Power, 86–93, 117–18
  balance of, 92
  definition, 88–89, 117, 356
  generalizations, 92, 117–18
  operationalization, 92, 117
  resources, 89, 92
Pragmatism, 11–12
Pre-experimental design, 192–93, 356. *See also* Experimental design; Quasi-experimental design
  ex post facto, 192–93, 352
Pressman, Jeffrey L., 141, 346
Prewitt, Kenneth, 70, 72, 342
Price, Don K., 128
Primary data gathering, 194–207, 335, 356
  content analysis, 196–98
  observation, 194–96, 355
  simulation, 207–8
  survey research, 198–207
Probability distribution, 247
Project Camelot, 54
Proportionate-reduction-in-error, 282, 292, 294, 313, 357
Przeworski, Adam, 348
Pye, Lucian, 343, 345

Quasi-experimental design, 191–92, 357. *See also* Experimental design; Pre-experimental design
  multiple time series, 192
  nonequivalent control group designs, 191, 355
  separate sample pretest-posttest, 192, 358
  time series, 191–92, 359
Questionnaire construction, 201–6

Rai, Kul B., 349
Rapoport, Anatol, 344
Raser, John R., 348
Rationality, 134, 159–60, 207
Regression, 299, 300–312, 357
  least squares criterion, 306, 354
Reichenbach, Hans, 341
Reliability, 165–66, 335, 357
  test-retest, 166, 359
Research, types of:
  causal, 160
  descriptive, 160
  relational, 160
Research design, 163–64, 357
Response set, 170, 205–6
Rice, Berkeley, 53
Richardson, Bradley, 343
Rieselbach, Leroy, 106
Riker, William H., 132–33, 344
Ritzer, George, 342
Rivlin, Alice M., 143–44, 346
Robinson, John P., 73, 348
Roethlisberger, F. J., 46
Roles, 108, 111
Rose, Arnold M., 344
Rose, Richard, 80
Rosenau, James S., 126, 137
Rosenbaum, Walter A., 76–77, 343
Rosenberg, Morris, 348
Rudner, Richard, 341
Rusk, Jerrold G., 348

Sample size, 180–81
Sampling, 44, 180–86, 335, 357
  cluster, 185, 350
  disproportionate stratified, 184–85, 352
  proportionate stratified, 184, 357
  simple random, 182–83, 358
  systematic, 183–84, 358
Sampling distribution, 264, 357
Sampling error, 261
Sapin, Burton, 346
Scaling, 167–74
  Guttman, 170–74
  Likert, 169–70
Scattergram, 300–302
Schattschneider, E. E., 87, 96, 99–105, 344
Scheffler, Israel, 17
Schelling, Thomas, 344
Schramm, Wilbur, 345
Schwartz, R. D., 348
Scientific method, 17–29
Searle, John, 11, 30
Sechrest, L., 348
Secondary data gathering, 208–10, 335, 358
  data archives, 209–10
  library research, 208–9
Selective perception, 114–16, 358
Shannon, Claude E., 345
Sharkansky, Ira, 92, 138
Shively, W. Phillips, 349
Shockley, William, 53
Shubik, Martin, 134, 346
Siegel, Sidney, 349
Sigel, Roberta, 64, 343
Significance level, 271, 337, 354
Significance tests, 271, 278, 337, 358. *See also* Hypothesis testing
  chi square, 274–77

373

F statistic, 321–25
  one-tailed test, 269–71, 355
  t test, 272–74
  two-tailed test, 269–71
  z score, 265–72, 359
Simon, Herbert A., 346
Simon, Julian, 348
Sjoberg, Gideon, 342
Smith, Barbara Leigh, 10, 31
Snedecor, George W., 303
Snyder, Richard C., 124, 125, 126, 131, 133, 137, 346
Somers' d. *See* Measures of association
Somit, Albert, 9–10, 16, 341
Spurious relationship, 258–59, 358
Standard error, 268, 358
Standard error of estimate, 310, 358
Stanley, Julian C., 187–88, 193, 347
Statistical Analysis System (SAS), 224–25, 348
Statistical Package for the Social Sciences (SPSS), 224–25, 348
Steinbrenner, Karen, 348
Steinbruner, John D., 345
Steiner, Gary A., 96
Storing, Herbert, 34, 341
Strauss, Anselm L., 347
Structural-functionalism, 110–11, 358
Suchman, Edward A., 144, 346
Sudman, Seymour, 182, 348
Swanson, Bert, 343
Symbols, political, 104
System, 87, 106–13, 119–20
  boundary setting, 107–8
  components, 108–10
  defined, 106–7, 110, 119, 358
  operationalization, 112–13, 119

Tanenhaus, Joseph, 9–10, 16, 341
Tautology, 93, 165, 175, 358
Taylor, Charles, 30–31
Taylor, Steven J., 37
Tedin, Kent, 71
Tests of significance. *See* Significance tests
Teune, Henry, 348
Theory, 17, 27–29, 329–30
  concatenated, 34, 176–77, 330, 350
  defined, 28, 359
Torney, Judith V., 65, 66, 69, 70, 71, 73, 342
Toscano, James V., 345
Traditionalism, 13, 34–37, 359
Truman, David B., 87, 94–96, 98–99, 125, 344
t test. *See* Significance tests

Tufte, Edward R., 349
Tullock, Gordon, 345
Type I error, 257, 359
Type II error, 257, 359

Unit of analysis, 179, 335, 359
Universe, 179, 359

Valentine, Charles A., 76
Validity, 166–67, 335, 359
  external, 189, 335, 352
  face, 167, 168, 352
  internal, 188–89, 335, 354
  predictive, 167, 356
Value, 12–13, 30–31, 36–37, 159, 359
Van Dyke, Vernon, 341
Variable, 24, 359
  continuous, 246, 351
  dependent, 24, 186, 249, 351
  discrete, 246, 351
  independent, 24, 186, 249, 353
Variance. *See* Measures of variation
Veldman, Donald J., 219, 348
Velikovsky, Immanuel, 51
Verba, Sidney, 62, 72, 77–78, 80–81, 83, 343
Verification, 7
Von Bertalanffy, Ludwig, 345
Von Neumann, John, 346

Wade, Larry L., 138, 143
Walton, John, 91
Watson, George, 18, 161–62, 347
Weaver, Warren, 345
Webb, Eugene J., 195, 348
Weiner, Norbert, 345
Weisberg, Herbert F., 348
Weiss, Carol H., 346
Weissberg, Robert, 65, 343
Welsh, William A., 342
Wildavsky, Aaron, 136, 141, 346
Wilde, James A., 346
Winnie, Richard E., 144
Wirt, Frederick, 343
Wolfe, Douglas A., 349
Wylie, Lawrence, 343

Young, Oran R., 345
Young, Roland, 342

Zaninovich, George, 348
Zavoina, William J., 132
Zetterberg, Hans L., 25–26, 341
Zinnes, Dina, 348
z score. *See* Significance tests